MODERN
AIR COMBAT

The aircraft, tactics and weapons employed in aerial warfare today

The Saab JA37 Viggen was the first really modern fighter in non-Communist Europe.

Hardware is no good without humans, such as Capt Eric Coloney, 527th TFT (Aggressor) Sqn, USAF.

MODERN
AIR COMBAT

The aircraft, tactics and weapons employed in aerial warfare today

Bill Gunston ● Mike Spick

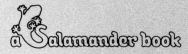
a Salamander book

Published by Salamander Books Limited
LONDON

A Salamander Book   Credits

Published by
Salamander Books Ltd.,
Salamander House,
27 Old Gloucester Street,
London WC1N 3AF,
United Kingdom.

© Salamander Books Ltd., 1983

ISBN 0 86101 1627

Distributed in the United Kingdom by
Hodder & Stoughton Services,
P.O. Box 6, Mill Road,
Dunton Green, Sevenoaks,
Kent TN13 2XX.

All correspondence concerning the content of this volume should be
addressed to the publisher.

Editor: Ray Bonds

Designer: Mark Holt

Colour artwork (aircraft section): Kai Choi, Terry Hadler,
Stephen Seymour, Mike Trim, and Tudor Art Studios Ltd.

Diagrams and aircraft three-views: TIGA.

Filmset by SX Composing Ltd.

Colour reproduction by Bantam Litho Ltd., and Rodney Howe Ltd.

Printed in Belgium by Henri Proost et Cie.

The publishers wish to thank wholeheartedly the many organisations
and individuals in the aerospace industry and the armed forces of
various nations, in particular the US Air Force, who have all been of
considerable help in the preparation of this book.

The Authors

Bill Gunston is a former RAF pilot and flying instructor, and he has spent most of his working life accumulating a wealth of information on aerospace technology and history. Since leaving the Service, he has acted as an advisor to several aviation companies and become one of the most internationally respected authors and broadcasters on aviation and scientific subjects. His numerous books include the Salamander titles "The Illustrated Encyclopedia of the World's Modern Military Aircraft", "The Encyclopedia of the World's Combat Aircraft", "The Illustrated Encyclopedia of the World's Rockets and Missiles", "Soviet Air Power" (with Bill Sweetman), and many of Salamander's successful illustrated guides to aviation subjects. He has also contributed to the authoritative "The Soviet War Machine" and "The US War Machine", by the same company, and carries out regular assignments for technical aviation periodicals. Mr. Gunston is also an assistant compiler of "Jane's All the World's Aircraft" and was formerly technical editor of "Flight International" and technology editor of "Science Journal".

Mike Spick was born in London less than three weeks before the Spitfire made its maiden flight. Educated at Churchers College, Petersfield (a school with a strong naval interest!), he later entered the construction industry and carried out considerable work on RAF airfields. An occasional broadcaster on aviation topics, Mr. Spick's interests include wargaming, which led him to a close study of air warfare, followed by a highly successful first book, "Air Battles in Miniature" (Patrick Stephens, 1978). He has another book to his credit, "Fighter Pilot Tactics" (Patrick Stephens, 1983), which is a historical study of the evolution of tactics, and he is currently working on a study of success in air combat.

Below: There is no "best fighter". Tornado ADV cannot match the F-16 in a dogfight, but the F-16 cannot fly the Tornado's 4½-hour patrols with stand-off kill power.

Contents

Foreword   8

The Technology of Air Combat Bill Gunston   10
Aircraft Design   14
Aerodynamics   18
Structure   26
Propulsion   30
Weapons   36
Electronic Warfare   48
Displays   66

The Aircraft and Their Weapons Bill Gunston   76
Aeritalia AM-X   80
BAe Buccaneer   82
BAe Harrier   84
BAe Hawk   86
BAe Lightning   88
BAe Sea Harrier   90
Dassault Breguet/Dornier Alpha Jet   92
Dassault Breguet Mirage III, 50   94

Dassault Breguet Mirage F1   96
Dassault Breguet Mirage 2000   98
Dassault Breguet Super Etendard   100
Fairchild A-10 Thunderbolt II   102
FMA IA Pucara   104
General Dynamics F-16 Fighting Falcon   106
General Dynamics F-111   108
Grumman A-6 Intruder   110
Grumman F-14 Tomcat   112
IAI Kfir C2   114
Lockheed F-104 Starfighter   116
McDonnell Douglas A-4 Skyhawk   118
McDonnell Douglas AV-8B/Harrier II   120
McDonnell Douglas F-4 Phantom II   122
McDonnell Douglas F-15 Eagle   124
McDonnell Douglas F/A-18 Hornet   126
Mikoyan/Gurevich MiG-21   128
Mikoyan/Gurevich MiG-23   130
Mikoyan/Gurevich MiG-25   132
Mikoyan/Gurevich MiG-27   134

Mitsubishi F-1   136
Nanzhang Q5   138
Northrop F-5   140
Panavia Tornado ADV   142
Panavia Tornado IDS   144
Saab Scania Draken   146
Saab Scania Viggen   148
Sepecat Jaguar   150
SOKO/CNIAR Orao/IAR-93   152
Sukhoi Su-7   154
Sukhoi Su-11   156
Sukhoi Su-15   158
Sukhoi Su-17/-22   160
Sukhoi Su-24   162
Tupolev Tu-128   164

Vought A-7 Crusader   166
Yakovlev Yak-28P   168
Yakovlev Yak-36MP   170

Air Combat Tactics Mike Spick   **172**
Basic Aerodynamics   176
Threats and Tasks   182
Fighting Effectiveness   186
Air Combat Methods   194
Manoeuvres   200
Training   214

Glossary   **220**

Index   **222**

Below: A swarm of F/A-18A Hornets from China Lake and Point Mugu over Nevada typify modern multirole airpower, with capability in attack and defence.

Foreword

This book is about fighting aircraft, but unlike most of the numerous books already written on this subject it is concerned with the true nitty-gritty of modern air warfare – the weapons, the systems and the tactics – while also including such familiar details as the wingspan and type of engine fitted. Many people have been brought up to believe that all fighter pilots have large moustaches and wear polka-dot scarves. There are those who feel that the subject of modern air combat is just too complicated for comprehension because they do not possess a PhD in electronics, nor major in infra-red technology. But we believe this book can open up the amazing world of modern air warfare to the ordinary reader. No PhD is needed.

That there is a problem in communication is evident from just skimming the pages of any modern defence magazine. One advertisement tells us: "High LCC is the enemy; but our VOR/ILS integrates multiplex data bus interfacing". Facing it is another ad which proclaims "The good news is that TRW has the necessary digital and RF VLSI . . . we're using VHSIC to build a compact brassboard NTWS for tomorrow's pilots". And modern fighters, it appears, just don't have a chance unless they have RSS, FBW, Hotas and a holographic HUD!

We have tried in this book to cut through the gobbledegook and explain some of the fundamentals of how modern warplanes are designed, how they fly their missions and how the jock who sits in the hot seat does his job. Nearly all these jocks are pilots. A few are called navigators, observers, radar intercept officers, naval flight officers or weapon-system operators; more commonly they are called the backseater, or even the GIB (guy in back). There is still some difference of opinion on just when a second crew-member is needed. Indeed, a decade ago it was fashionable to question whether even the man in the front was needed; the

Above: The front cockpit of Tornado A.02 shows the working environment of a modern fighter pilot. This aircraft retains a mix of TV-type computerized displays and dial-type instruments.

Below: Nellis AFB, Nevada, with Las Vegas in the background, does at least have the advantage of needing an ICBM to destroy it. But the Soviets have 1,398 ICBMs and over 602 SLBMs. What price Nellis?

initials RPV (remotely piloted vehicle) were then all the rage, and many experts sought to prove that fighter and attack aircraft, and certainly reconnaissance platforms, could do a better job if they were flown by a pilot who stayed out of harm's way, either on the ground or in another aircraft, controlling an RPV.

But then there's nothing new under the Sun. A quarter of a century ago the official British view was that manned combat aircraft as a class were obsolete. The actual wording was "Having regard to . . . the likely progress of ballistic rockets and missile defence, the Government have decided not to go on with the development of a supersonic manned bomber. . . . Work will proceed on a ground-to-air missile defence system which will in due course replace the manned aircraft of Fighter Command. . . The RAF are unlikely to have a requirement for fighter aircraft more advanced than the P.1 and work on such projects will stop."

Today's massed squadrons continue to exist not because people like to preserve obsolete concepts for sentimental reasons. One of the things this book perhaps cannot do is fully explain why we do continue to build so many combat aircraft. There are plenty of reasons why, for the defence of one's own territory, it is far more sensible to use nothing but SAM launchers, each with sufficent quickly available missiles to guarantee that they could never run out of firepower. And in a world populated (at least on the Soviet side) by thousands of nuclear warheads all waiting to be used atop missiles of proven pinpoint accuracy, it is difficult to understand why we go on building aircraft that cannot fly without runways. An airbase is the most inviting target a long-range nuclear missile could have. Some of the Soviet missiles may be targeted on ports, special military centres or cities, but we can take it for granted that *every* NATO airfield is covered by several missiles. Yet when I pointed this out ten years ago, and sent the manuscript to the Pentagon for comment, it was returned with this part described (without justification) as "a thinly disguised sales pitch for the Harrier".

The man who wrote that was a senior officer in the US Air Force. Occasionally, some of his light-blue buddies try to score off the dark blues of the Navy by saying "your carriers can be sunk, but nobody can sink our airfields". Fortunately we have not had a full-scale war for nearly 40 years, and nobody should draw too many conclusions from the way the runway at Port Stanley in the Falklands emerged almost unscathed from British attempts to render it unusable. We have come a very long way beyond the

500-pound bombs dropped manually on that runway, and the one point that must be rammed home is that modern airpower is virtually useless if it is based on concrete runways. Just 20 years ago this fact was recognised: USAF's SAC used to keep a proportion of its bombers in the air, on a gruelling "airborne alert" with live bombs on board, while RAF Strike Command shuttled its Vulcans and Victors from one base to another – including many not normally used – so that they should not be caught on the ground and sent up in fireballs. Today we in the West no longer bother. Incredibly, even our Harriers are at known airfield locations. Meanwhile, the number of Soviet ICBMs, IRBMs, LRBMs and SLBMs – not just initials but terrifying megatonnage – targeted on those airfields has grown day by day.

Any fighter pilot will tell you that the notion of aerial chivalry is a nice bit of fiction. When your life and mission are at stake, you play to win. But the warfare whose tools and techniques are laid bare in this book does at least rest on such basic assumptions as a first-order similarity between opposing types of aircraft, and a battle between aerial attackers and ground or ship defenders that is in no sense one-sided. But the 750-kiloton warhead landing at the intersection of the runways as the base sleeps at night makes it all seem rather pointless.

We hope this kind of war will never come. If nobody presses that kind of button, war with wings, bullets and electrons – however regrettable – will remain a valid topic. Now read how far it has come.

Below: "Today's massed squadrons continue to exist . . .", suggesting that the British Government erred when in 1957 it announced that manned fighters would be replaced by RPVs.

Right: The classic air combat is "one on one". Here an F-14A of US Navy squadron VF-143 tries to bag an Aggressor AT-38 of VF-43 over the Air Combat Maneuvering Range near Yuma, Arizona.

The Technology of Air

Combat

Below: The USAF's Arnold Engineering Development Center in Tennessee is trying to prepare for the next century. One of its many ideas is this parasol-winged fighter to fly at Mach 4.5. At first glance the idea seems ludicrous: unable to manoeuvre, vulnerable in the extreme, astronomically costly. But dare one ignore it?

Introduction

From the earliest days of aerial warfare technology – as an alternative to skilled pilots – had to come into it somewhere. This was especially the case with the start in 1915 of combat between aeroplanes. Such basics as flight speed, turn radius (associated with which has always been rate of roll) and maximum rate of climb have gone hand-in-hand with armament, armour, engine reliability and the ease with which a crippled aircraft could be flown by a wounded pilot, to determine the likely outcome of any particular engagement.

In World War I, however, all these matters were utterly secondary in comparison with the pilot. To a far greater degree the outcome of an air combat depended on piloting skill, experience, selection of tactics, eyesight, muscular strength, alertness, correct taking of quick decisions, and the ability to do accurate deflection shooting. Of course the pilot's mount was important, but the differences between one fighting scout and another were far less than between one pilot and another.

In World War II much the same variables were cranked into the equations of each combat, though the aircraft and their equipment began to play a crucial role, so that in the Pacific in 1944 many skilled and courageous Japanese fell before the firepower of highly inexperienced US pilots flying superior aircraft, such as the F6F and F4U. These same aircraft, incidentally, were among the first small fighters to carry radar for making interceptions at night. In such a role even a pilot on his first combat mission might well pull off a perfect interception, while if the radar failed a pilot

Above: While British Aerospace gets cracking on the ACA, MBB in West Germany wants to build the same aeroplane but call it by a German name. This is an impression of the proposed TKF 90 project.

Below: The three MFDs (multifunction displays) are reflected in bright electronic green in the vizor of an F/A-18A Hornet pilot. Today's combat aircraft is the ultimate example of man/machine symbiosis.

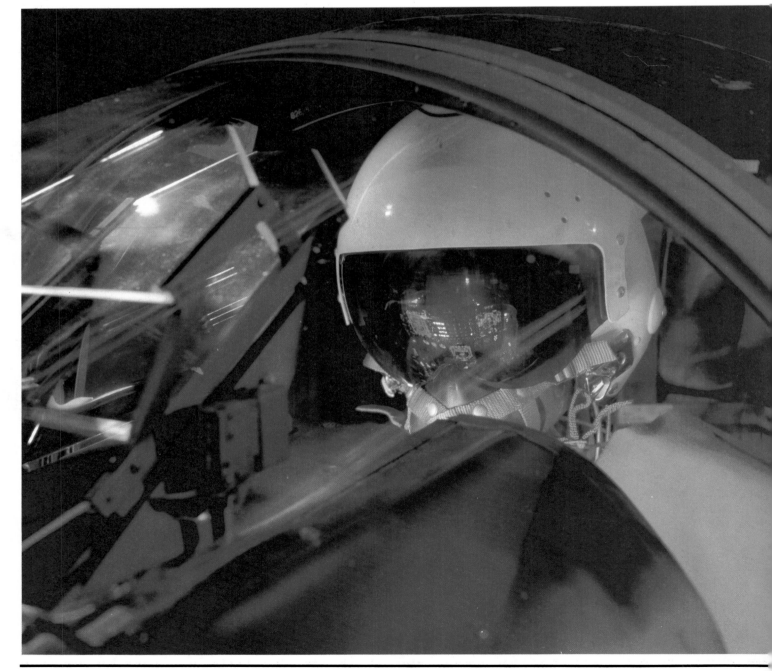

with 200 combat missions behind him would have no option but to return to base.

Today, for better or worse, the technology is dominant. There are very few active pilots today who are experienced in actual combat, and not even the best efforts of the Aggressors and their Warsaw Pact counterparts can quite equal the real thing (though it can come remarkably near to it). This certainly does not mean that all pilots are equal – very, very far from it! – but the results of air combat are increasingly likely to be dictated by the hardware.

This leads to the obvious question: will there ever come a day when the pilot is merely a passive supervisor, taken along for the ride in case anything happens that a human can cope with but for which the hardware had not been programmed? This leads back to the late 1950s when half the experts thought fighters were being replaced by SAMs and the other half thought they were being replaced by RPVs. Neither of these things has happened, but it is not difficult to argue the case for either. Certainly, in the situation which exists over NATO's Central European front, it seems foolish in the extreme to trade fighters one-for-one against a vastly superior number of enemy aircraft. Far better to use no fighters but large numbers of SAMs, which can unfailingly knock down the enemy on a 1-nil basis without any chance of scoring an unfortunate "own goal".

NATO is at present increasingly forced into the cleft stick of pretending it can overcome numerical inferiority by technical superiority. Wherever direct measurement is not possible the West makes cosy estimates which seek to prove that Soviet designers are nothing like as clever as those in the West. Their radars may be big, the argument goes, but they are said to be crude, low-powered and short-ranged, and the bigness is explained away as evidence of backwardness. Precisely the same goes for AAMs; for example the AA-6 Acrid is estimated by supposed Western experts to have a range of 23 miles (37km), though it is over 20ft long and weighs 1,650lb, while the US Navy's AIM-54 Phoenix flies more than 124 miles (it is 13ft long and weighs 1,000lb). But whenever direct measures are possible, as in the case of aircraft guns and numerous army weapons, the notion of inbuilt qualitative superiority vanishes.

Obviously this book cannot pretend to provide answers to the questions regarding the myth of Soviet technical inferiority, but at least it can provide a basic grounding in what the factors are, how they affect the design of present and future fighters, and what the fighters of the 1990s might be expected to be like.

If we study the outpourings of the publicity machines of the US manufacturing industry we might conclude that tomorrow's fighters will be souped-up versions of the SR-71, with fuselages about 90ft (27m) long, gross weights in the 100,000lb (45,000kg) class and speeds nudging Mach 3.5. One has only to think for a very few seconds to see that the real future will be very different.

First, inflation is already making it extremely hard to build any fighter aircraft at all. Unless we are extremely quick and very clever, as in the case of the F-16, even our small, cheap fighters are going to end up more expensive than the big, capable ones they were intended to replace (the F/A-18A Hornet is an obvious case in point). Second, stealth technology likes small combat aircraft rather than larger ones. Third, anyone who flies at Mach 3.5 needs his head examined; even Mach 2 is almost always nonsense, because it burns fuel quickly, takes time to achieve and eliminates any possibility of inflight manoeuvring.

Fourth, and certainly not the least important, the strange assumption that future wars will be marked by dropping a few bombs on runways, leaving "at least 800 metres for all our takeoffs and landings", is as nonsensical as mathematically precise calculations of the percentage of NATO aircraft that would still be operating on Day 3 of an all-out war. Leader of such calculations has for 20 years been the USAF, which because of its power and prestige exerts a major influence on military thought. But some of the minor air forces have already begun to realize that, should a major war ever break out, anything based on an airfield will be dead – probably before the war begins.

As the technology described in the following pages is very expensive indeed, Western air staffs owe it to their taxpayers not to waste it by placing it on an airfield. Dispersal to thousands of remote operating locations, on land or afloat, is the only apparent way to survive.

Below: Even more than the US Navy, the US Marine Corps will need all the multirole capability of the F/A-18A Hornet. This Sidewinder was fired in June 1983 from a Hornet from MCAS El Toro.

Above: In the author's view, we simply have to abandon, conventional takeoff and landing. This is a McDonnell proposal for the next generation beyond the AV-8B Harrier II.

Aircraft Design

Trying to define what we mean by "combat aircraft" is as difficult as trying to define the word "fighter". Indeed, though this chapter is concerned mainly with what are loosely called fighters, inevitably one has to look at air/ground missions which form an important part of most fighters' repertoire.

The design of combat aircraft has changed so much over the past 50 years that there is little to be learned by going back into history prior to about 1960, though a few trends are worth a brief glance. One of the obvious discontinuities in the generalized curves that normally thrust ever upwards is aircraft speed. Until the mid-1950s fighters naturally became ever-faster. Only two years after Artem Mikoyan and "Dutch" Kindelberger oversaw the basic design of the first production fighters able to accelerate to beyond Mach 1 on the level, in 1951, "Kelly" Johnson drew performance curves for what became the Lockheed 83 (F-104) and found that with the new J79 engine and properly schemed variable inlets and nozzle the thrust stayed ahead of the drag to beyond Mach 2 (at which point the aircraft was "redlined" to prevent structural overheating). A mere one year later Mikoyan's team studied the problems of flight at close to 1,553mph (2,500km/h or Mach 2.35), while Republic Aviation was deep in the challenging design of the monster XF-103 fighter to fly at Mach 3.7, or 2,446mph (3,936km/h).

There is no particular technical problem in building a 2,446mph fighter, but such an exercise would not be very useful. Speed is much less important than some people, notably the Dassault company, appear to believe. The faster an aircraft flies, the greater its radius of turn, because accelerative loading goes up not in proportion to speed but in proportion to the

Above: Two Sidewinders and the brand-new Vulcan six-barrel gun was a good combination for dogfighting in the 1950s, but the F-104 was not optimised for manoeuvrability. Later its speed and small radar signature were used in attack missions.

square of the speed. A fighter flying at 2,446mph flies in a very straight line indeed. If it were to encounter a hostile aircraft it would have to fly right on past it, and take some time to slow down sufficiently to make a reasonable turn. Having allowed the speed to bleed off, it is worse off than the slower aircraft, because the latter (other things being equal) can be smaller, shorter, lighter, cheaper and much more agile.

Prolonged study of the ten years of varied air combat in Southeast Asia in 1963-73 showed that, though afterburners were often used and supersonic speed occasionally reached, every air combat took place at subsonic speed which was usually between 280 and 450 knots. The slower it is possible to fly, the better the rate of

Above: To some extent today's counterpart of the F-104 is the Mirage 2000, which is the only modern fighter known to have been designed to have the highest possible flight performance. Low-level "ride" and fuel consumption suffer badly.

Below: What will Sweden's JAS39 Gripen do that cannot be done by today's JA37 Viggen? The answer is that it will be slightly better in a dogfight and will be much more economical to operate, besides being a generation newer in concept (first flight due 1986-7).

Above: Widely regarded as today's best fighter, in the broadest meaning of the word, the F-16 has already been dramatically developed beyond the standard of this early example. We can only dimly discern what will replace the F-16 in the year 2000.

turn, to such a degree that missiles able to pull a seemingly impossible 30g at Mach 3 can easily be avoided by a forewarned fighter pulling a mere 3g at 450 knots. When all the variables have been cranked into the fighter design process the answer that emerges is that Mach 2.5 is much faster than the ideal, and a good figure for a rarely attained maximum Mach number is 1.8. This is despite the fact that thanks to superior engines today's fighter has more than twice the thrust that could be packed into the preceding generation.

Even more important than the diminished importance of flight speed is the influence of inflation on cost. In World War II a team of 50 draughtsmen each earning £5 a week could turn out hundreds of actual production drawings every

week, and complete the design of a fighter in about two months. Today the design of a new fighter needs a team of thousands of engineers, each earning at least £150 a week and doing all sorts of vital things except producing actual drawings of parts.

Eventually hardware does get made, in some cases as the end product of computer graphics and magnetic tape which can steer the machine-tool cutting heads without any ordinary drawing having been created. We have been so busy sitting at our EDP graphics terminals in order to save time and work faster that today a new fighter design takes about six years and costs not hundreds of times more but thousands of times more. In a country such as Britain the Air Staff hardly need to bother writing ORs (Operational Requirements) any more. There is no money to have anything actually built, and if a decision were to be taken to go ahead the OR on which the design was based would be totally outdated years before the first flight of a prototype. Can this truly be regarded as "progress"?

Above: Big, heavy and in most respects typically Russian in its tough simplicity, the MiG-25 has always been a very inflexible aircraft. The last thing it wants to do is to slow down, turn corners or get into any kind of air combat with a manoeuvrable opponent.

Below: In contrast, air combat is just what the British Aerospace (or, one hopes, Panavia) Agile Combat Aircraft is built for. It represents a class of aircraft which, with the demise of the Lightning, is totally missing from Britain's RAF.

Above: Since 1969 the McDonnell Douglas Phantom has served the RAF well (here an FGR.2 is refuelled by a Victor K.2). But it kept the RAF tied to long-runway vulnerable airbases.

Below: Today the Panavia Tornado F.2 is in production as the RAF's next generation interceptor. But this too can at any time be knocked out by a nuclear missile on its immobile airbase.

These are two of the fundamental factors which affect the design of aircraft to defeat other aircraft, hit small targets on the ground in the face of winter storms and intense modern defence systems, keep flying around the clock without needing any attention, and keep on flying after the enemy's nuclear rockets have obliterated the West's airfields. Obviously, aircraft that can operate only from major airbases are worse than useless, because not only do they tie up large numbers of skilled personnel who would go up in the fireball just prior to the declaration of war but they also consume vast amounts of money that could otherwise be used for survivable defence systems.

So long as major war is avoided, the West can just about get away with the present situation in which enormous sums are spent on fighters whose price averages £1,000 per kg of empty weight. These are put into service in such small numbers that they could be eliminated by wiping out a mere 31 airbases, a task which the Soviet RVSN (strategic rocket troops) could accomplish at any moment while leaving 49 out of every 50 missiles still in their silos or on their mobile launchers.

Such costly aircraft are affordable in peacetime only because, whereas earlier fighters had an active lifetime which varied from a few weeks in World War II up to as long as four years in the 1950s, today's fighters have to last more than 20 years. Lest anyone might think such aircraft as the F-86 and Hunter lasted much longer than four years, the point must be made that each of these types kept on being replaced by a new version. The USAF 4th Fighter Wing in 1950-55 had each F-86 replaced on average eight times, in five successively improved models. But today the USAF 49th Wing is, in general, still flying the same F-15s it received in 1974.

It therefore follows inevitably that future air forces are going to rely on a very small number of aircraft, of a very small number of different types, and they are going to live with the same actual aircraft for maybe 20 years at a time. The design takes so long and costs so much it has to be as right as humanly possible, but to take years over each stage of planning and design is a recipe for disaster. The RAF, for example, was all set to receive a V/STOL aircraft with considerable flexibility and mission capability which had been conceived quite quickly in 1962-64 but which was cancelled in 1965 and replaced by a CTOL (long-runway) aircraft, the Phantom, itself designed in 1955-56 to

operate from US Navy carriers. The RAF still uses the Phantom, but will soon introduce the Tornado F.2 to meet its need for a long-endurance stand-off interceptor. As far as air-combat fighters are concerned the RAF has virtually nothing (the most passionate member of Lightning Training Flight at Binbrook could hardly argue) and has nothing in prospect. The three partners in Panavia have been talking about a new fighter for eight years, and in 1982 achieved the priceless initial goal of agreement on basic ideas for a common design. But inability at government level to demonstrate the slightest conviction or courage will probably so delay the ACA (Agile Combat Aircraft) programme that ultimate success will be impossible.

In the following analysis little account is taken of actual existing or projected programmes, nor such matters as programme management, funding or political affairs generally. It is offered merely as a plain man's overall guide to what is not only a gigantic subject but one in which experience and possibly luck play a not inconsiderable role. Expenditure of several years and a billion dollars is no guarantee of a good fighter, as witness the F-111B and XFV-12A. Today's wealth of additional design tools, such as computer graphics and precise simulation of future air combats, enables the designer to create a much better design quicker. But these aids are available also to the Bad Guys, and one has just as much chance today as in former years of ending up with a new fighter which comes a close second!

Above: Rockwell's HiMAT can reach only Mach 1.5, but this is more than enough for tomorrow's air combats which, like today's, are likely to be subsonic. Agility counts more than speed.

Below: Rockwell's predecessor, North American Aviation, was often No. 1 US defence contractor in the 1950s, and the company is striving to get back in the "big league" with projects such as this

Advanced Fighter Concept for the 1990s. It will have a wing of over 48ft (14.6m) span, and vectoring two-dimensional nozzles behind its 60ft (18.2m) fuselage. It is one of many proposals for USAF.

Above: The sole major example of a US attempt to build a vertical-rising fighter not tied to giant airbases was this XFV-12A, yet another Rockwell programme. Sadly, it is unsuccessful so far.

Aerodynamics

In the early 1960s some fighter studies, notably by Bristol Siddeley, eliminated wings and relied totally upon the thrust vector from engines such as the Pegasus and BS.100. A wingless fighter avoids many problems, but poses others, and we have yet to see one emerge. Today, over 80 years after the Wright Brothers, we still rely chiefly on wings in order both to fly and to manoeuvre. Compared with the birds our wings are amazingly primitive, but they continue to get better.

Around 30 years ago the chief arguments raged over whether the straight wing should be replaced by the swept wing or the delta. Today we know how to make wings so thin that the plan shape is much less important, using advanced structures to avoid the perils of aeroelastic distortion which 30 years ago terrified stressmen and, for example, made the designers of the F-100 put the ailerons inboard (which meant the wing could have no flaps).

Today we are so clever we are even using so-called supercritical profiles to make wings thicker. Some accompanying curves show the gains achieved by such a wing on an Alpha Jet (though the improved manoeuvrability of this wing was gained largely by adding powerful slats and all-speed flaps which would also have improved the original wing). Why make a wing thicker? A thicker wing is structurally much easier, and as its skins can be thinner the weight is dramatically reduced. Moreover its volume is obviously greater; the new Alpha Jet wing holds almost as much fuel as the original wing plus external drop tanks.

It is only common sense that any wing is ideal at only one particular condition of flight. Early fighters had fixed-geometry wings which were far from ideal in every part of a flight except the one for which the wing was designed. By 1935 movable flaps, and sometimes

Left: The US Navy Grumman F-14 Tomcat is aerodynamically one of the most efficient fighters ever built. Here its long wings are pivoted back at 68° for flight at speeds up to over Mach 2.

Right: Dassault followed the delta (triangular) Mirage III with this conventional tailed swept-wing fighter, the excellent Mirage F1. It has high-lift slats and flaps.

Below: Tornado can carry a heavier bombload under its fuselage than any other aircraft except the far bigger B-1B. Here eight 1,000lb (454kg) bombs are on board, leaving the wing for tanks and ECM.

slats, enabled the wing to change its behaviour so that it could be close to ideal in several different situations.

A much more powerful form of VG (variable geometry) arrived with the idea of variable sweepback in 1943, but it took another 17 years before this was made to work satisfactorily with widely spaced outboard pivots. In the first production application, the F-111, the upper surface of the fuselage is only gently curved and

extremely broad, downstream of leading edges swept at the acute angle of 72.5°. Outboard pivots enable the main outer wings to be swept at this same angle for high-speed flight at Mach numbers up to more than 2. For subsonic loiter, and takeoff and landing, the wings can be swung forward to only 16° and their lift greatly increased by extending full-span slats and double-slotted flaps.

With the wings spread it is possible to fly relatively slowly yet

carry heavy loads, and a major spinoff from this is that, if the landing gear is up to it, the aircraft can be flown from short strips with rough surfaces. Variable sweep is obviously good for carrier-based aircraft.

In the high-speed regime the fully swept wing has low wave drag and is close to the ideal for supersonic flight. Its very small span has a further advantage in that a wing of very low aspect ratio, with area distributed mainly from

front to rear rather than across a wide span, has what is called a flat lift curve. With ordinary wings the lift varies very sharply indeed with the angle of attack (the angle at which the wing meets the oncoming air), but the ultra-low aspect ratio "slender wing" shows only small changes in lift over quite large changes in angle of attack. This means a fighter can fly at full throttle through turbulent air close to the ground and hardly respond to the local upcurrents

F-111 With Supercritical Wing

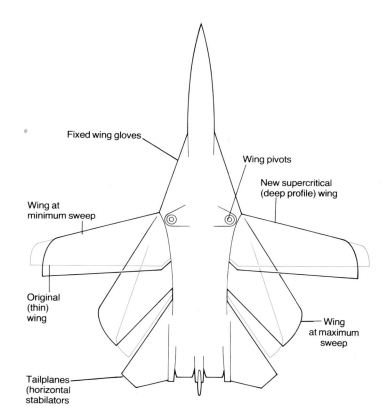

Above: The USAF, together with the US National Aeronautics and Space Administration, is testing a deep supercritical wing on an F-111, which has the advantage of being able to fly with the new wing at different angles of sweep. The new wing is the broad, short-span shape superimposed on the original wing.

Right: These four F-111C bombers of the Royal Australian Air Force demonstrate that it is possible to fly a formation with the wings at any angle from 72.5° (the lead aircraft) to only 16° (the rear aircraft). Normally the different angles would be for flight at markedly different speeds, 72.5° being supersonic only.

and downcurrents called gusts.

Gust response has been one of the chief factors to consider in designing modern fighter wings, because for 30 years it has been considered that the safest way to penetrate hostile airspace is to fly as low as possible. This gives defenders minimum time to get ready to fire, and in most existing air-defence radars there are technical difficulties in detecting targets very close to the ground. Of course there are problems in flying very low at high speed. As well as

the basic need to avoid hitting the ground, the mission range is greatly reduced because gas-turbine engines burn fuel several times faster at low level than in the very cold thin air at high altitude, and the density of the air greatly increases the stresses imposed on the aircraft structure. A very real difficulty in most regions is birdstrikes; no matter how well aircraft are designed to withstand impacts with birds, severe birdstrikes can kill the pilot, damage a tailplane enough to cause

an immediate dive into the ground, or simply wreck the engine or block up the air inlet(s).

Apart from this, the problem of gust response is a limiting factor in what a human crew can stand, especially in the crucial case of maximum speed at the lowest level. People who are not combat aircrew may not appreciate that the plot of gust response shown in the diagram translates into bone-crushing, eyeball-jerking movements in the vertical plane which also have the effect of eating

Above: Seen from behind, an F-16A Fighting Falcon of the USAF 8th Tactical Fighter Wing taking off. The flaps can be seen at 20° (see top wing profile on the facing page). When the wheels lift off, the leading edge will droop 15°.

into airframe fatigue life. The smooth ride of the VG aircraft is not just a matter of comfort but of being able to fly the mission properly. It is curious that several recent Western aircraft have been designed with fixed-geometry

Low-level Ride Comfort

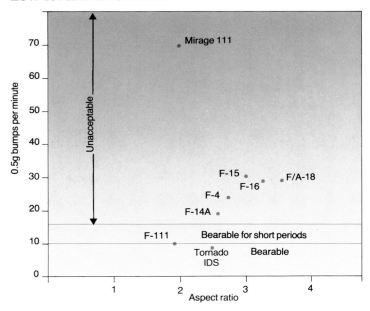

The Cambered Fixed Wing

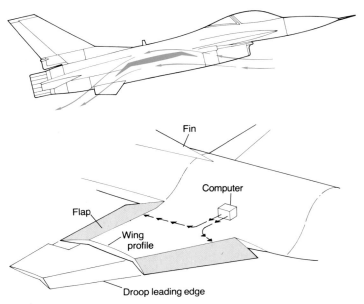

Above: In general, the shorter and stubbier a wing (ie, the lower its aspect ratio), the better the ride at high speed in the dense air at low level. Best of all are the VG swing-wing aircraft, all of which can fly at Mach 0.9 at sea level in good crew comfort. Other aircraft are too rough, and the large-area Mirage III is hopeless.

Above: Having built the VG F-111, General Dynamics then built the F-16 with a wing fixed in plan shape but variable in section profile. Both the leading and trailing edges are pivoted and can hinge up or down (see six profiles on facing page). The top drawing shows the F-16 with the wing set up for the approach to a landing.

wings because of a belief that VG adds too much weight or complexity, while in the Soviet Union every aircraft that flies a high-speed attack mission has a VG wing.

Nothing is as simple as it seems. While the oft-repeated suggestion that a VG wing makes it difficult to carry heavy loads of weapons and tuck the landing gear away is clearly nonsense (look at Tornado), the variable-sweep wing is just one way of doing it. In designing the F-16, and to a lesser extent the F/A-

18, the wing was given some VG capability by fitting full-span leading-edge droops and large trailing edge flaps. Computer-controlled, these adjust the profile of the wing to suit takeoff, cruise, high-g manoeuvres, supersonic flight and landing.

The ideal, of course, is a wing made of flexible material whose section profile and planform shape can all be varied continuously, and this is certainly beyond the present state of the art. The best that is practicable is to make the wing what the Americans call "mission adaptive" by changing its profile and, if possible, planform shape, in easy stages by providing it with various kinds of hinges and pivots. The best answer for each aircraft is a compromise between performance, complexity, cost and reliability, like most things in aviation.

There are many other aspects of fighter aerodynamics. Slender wings in which root chord exceeds the span can fly at angles of attack far beyond those at which ordinary wings stall. Fly an F-14 with the wings outspread and you have a conventional aeroplane with a wing that stalls at around 16° AOA (angle of attack), despite help from slats and flaps. Sweep the wing to 68° and in extreme conditions you can fly at AOA from 60° to beyond 90° (at least you could before the troubles with the TF30 engine brought AOA restrictions). It is doubtful that today's designers are working on a single fighter that cannot routinely fly at AOA greater than 60° in air-combat manoeuvres.

At high AOA it usually helps to have two vertical tails, though whether these are canted outwards

for greater effectiveness, or fixed vertical, or slope inwards to reduce roll due to rudder movement depends on the particular design. Like the fighting scouts of 1916 today's supersonic fighter often flies with no fixed fin, the slab rudder being just as good as the slab horizontal tail, "slab" meaning that the whole surface moves instead of being hinged to a fixed surface upstream.

Since 1958 slab rudders have only gradually become the favoured choice, but in modern

Above: Though it has become fashionable in the West to "knock" the VG swing wing, it happens to make possible vastly superior multirole aircraft. Here F-14A Tomcats are catapulted from a US Navy carrier.

fighters a fixed tailplane is rare indeed. Usually there are left and right surfaces called tailerons (tailplane/ailerons) which control the aircraft in roll as well as in pitch. Conventional ailerons may be used as well, either at low or

F-16 Wing Profiles

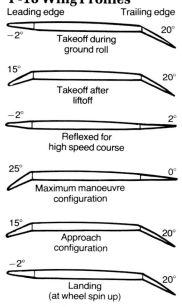

Leading edge   Trailing edge

−2°   20°
Takeoff during ground roll

15°   20°
Takeoff after liftoff

−2°   2°
Reflexed for high speed course

25°   0°
Maximum manoeuvre configuration

15°   20°
Approach configuration

−2°   20°
Landing (at wheel spin up)

Above: The six main flight regimes of the F-16A are characterized by a particular wing profile. The numbers show the angular setting of the hinged portions.

Why the VG "Swing Wing" is Superior

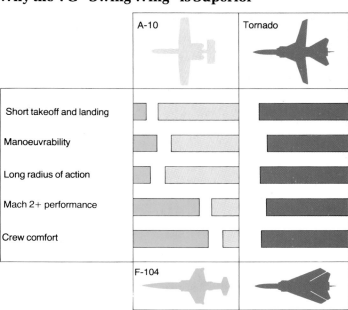

	A-10		Tornado	
Short takeoff and landing				
Manoeuvrability				
Long radius of action				
Mach 2+ performance				
Crew comfort				
F-104				

Above: A fixed-shape wing is good only in one condition of flight. Here the length of horizontal bar shows "marks out of ten" for each of five important variables for two

fixed-geometry aircraft, the F-104 (red) and A-10 (blue), and one VG aircraft (Tornado, mauve). The latter is good across the board, because it can redesign itself.

Contrasting Tail Geometries

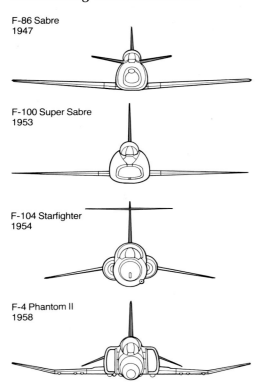

F-86 Sabre
1947

F-100 Super Sabre
1953

F-104 Starfighter
1954

F-4 Phantom II
1958

A-5 Vigilante
1958

MiG-25
1964

SR-71
1964

HiMAT
1979

Above: Eight high-speed jets (except for the first, all supersonic) showing different arrangements of tail surfaces. From the F-100 all have slab tailplanes, the A-5 being the first to use tailerons (tailplanes used for roll). All have fixed vertical fins except for the A-5 and SR-71 which have unusual slab vertical surfaces. There is no doubt the canard, as on HiMAT, will become much more common.

high speeds, or the wing may be fitted with spoilers. In the Jaguar spoilers are the primary roll control, the tailerons being brought in only at low airspeeds. In the Tornado the tailerons are the primary control, the spoilers being unlocked only as the wing is rotated into a reduced-sweep position.

A self-evident drawback to tailless aircraft, such as the Mirage III, is that on takeoff and landing the powerful elevons, which take the place of the usual powered tailplane, have to operate with a relatively small effective moment-arm, and so their downthrust has to be very large. This can add several tonnes to the effective aircraft weight, just at the worst possible time when the fixed-geometry thin delta wing is clawing at the air to try to get enough lift. The Mirage 2000 avoids this problem by having a wing of variable profile, with hinged leading as well as trailing surfaces, and it also has a small canard (forward tailplane, if that is not a contradiction in terms). More than a decade earlier Saab in Sweden had gone one better in giving the Viggen a large canard with trailing-edge flaps or elevators. Thus in the takeoff or landing regime the Viggen has lift from the main wing, plus lift from the flapped canard plus lift from the downward-depressed main-wing elevons.

In most regimes, but particularly

Above: A Tornado F.2 interceptor in combat air patrol configuration shows clearly how each tailplane is pivoted near mid-chord to move as one surface, in this case to control in both pitch and roll.

Below: The tailplanes of the F-4 were angled sharply down at 23° to maintain effectiveness at all AOA without excessive dihedral effect (accentuated by the upswept outer wings). Note Pave Tack pod.

Below: This Mirage 5 of the French Armée de l'Air is unwittingly demonstrating that conventional tailless deltas take off and land faster than necessary because of heavy elevon download.

Upthrust is Better than Downthrust

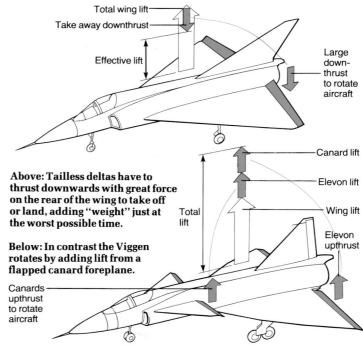

Total wing lift

Take away downthrust

Effective lift

Large down-thrust to rotate aircraft

Above: Tailless deltas have to thrust downwards with great force on the rear of the wing to take off or land, adding "weight" just at the worst possible time.

Below: In contrast the Viggen rotates by adding lift from a flapped canard foreplane.

Canard lift

Elevon lift

Wing lift

Elevon upthrust

Total lift

Canards upthrust to rotate aircraft

at high AOA, the Viggen's canards generate powerful vortices of rapidly spinning air, which writhe back behind the tips and scrub the upper surfaces of the outer wings. Vortices can be advantageous in such conditions in putting energy into the boundary layer of air in contact with the wing upper surface and, by preventing this layer from becoming sluggish, avoid flow breakaway.

The rows of small blades called turbulators or vortex generators, frequently seen along wings or on tails, are added for precisely this purpose. The jagged discontinuities on fighter leading edges known as dogteeth create powerful vortices, and so do the strakes or leading-edge root extensions on such aircraft as the F-16 and F/A-18. The sharp chines along the SR-71 Blackbird can also generate large vortices but in fact are for maintaining adequate weathercock (directional or yaw) stability at high AOA.

In the 1950s basic stability of supersonic fighters was often a problem, especially aircraft with long and heavy fuselages and relatively small wings. Yaw/roll coupling led to many mysterious crashes, and later to larger tails, ventral fins and even extended wingtips. In the maximum-sweep configuration the MiG-23 needs so much rear fin area it has an underfin which has to be folded sideways prior to landing.

Such a feature is unlikely to be seen in the new and exciting world of CCV (control-configured vehicle) technology. Here the fighter is deliberately designed without natural flight stability, the buzzword being RSS (relaxed static stability). As soon as it tries to fly, such an aircraft will attempt to swap ends, but such a motion would be instantly sensed by the flight control system and countered by split-second deflection of the control surfaces to keep the aircraft flying point-first.

CCV fighters rely totally upon the instantaneous reaction of their computerized flight control sensors and the only slightly slower deflections of their powered control surfaces. They are in principle like a dart whose flights have been taken from the tail and mounted on the point, and then put under the control of a fast-acting control system to keep the dart flying the right way round.

A CCV engineer in British Aerospace said that the task of the control system is exactly that of a man sitting on the bonnet of a 60mph car and pushing a bicycle back-to-front, steering it by the handlebars. Ordinary humans would lose control of such a bicycle at speeds greater than

Another Advantage of Canard Foreplanes

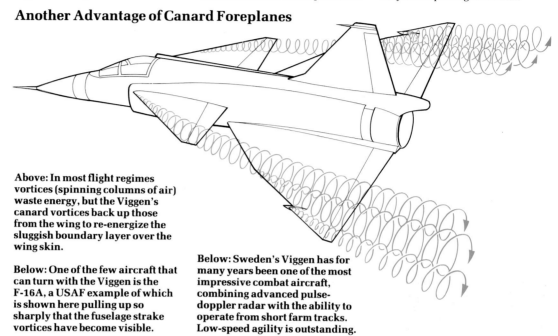

Above: In most flight regimes vortices (spinning columns of air) waste energy, but the Viggen's canard vortices back up those from the wing to re-energize the sluggish boundary layer over the wing skin.

Below: One of the few aircraft that can turn with the Viggen is the F-16A, a USAF example of which is shown here pulling up so sharply that the fuselage strake vortices have become visible.

Below: Sweden's Viggen has for many years been one of the most impressive combat aircraft, combining advanced pulse-doppler radar with the ability to operate from short farm tracks. Low-speed agility is outstanding.

Balancing the Conventional Fighter

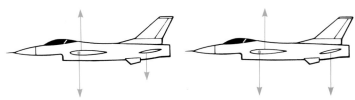

Balancing the CCV (RSS) Fighter

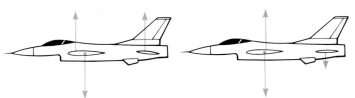

about 3mph (almost 5km/h), but the CCV flight controls react fast enough to keep it running accurately at 60mph (96.56km/h). There might be 100 control movements each second, each too small to be noticed.

CCV aircraft may not look unusual, but they have their CG (centre of gravity) far to the rear. Two aircraft which have penetrated well into the CCV domain are the F-16 and Mirage 2000. Such aircraft need FBW (fly by wire) electrically signalled flight controls, fast-acting surface

Right: CCV fighter's advantages over a traditional fighter. 1,2,3: the vertical translation mode, in which symmetric wing flaperon/tail deflection makes the aircraft rise or fall without altering the fuselage axis inclination. With body level the flight path can suddenly be inclined 5° or even 10°. 4,5,6: control of normal (vertical-axis) acceleration by direct lift flaperon control at a constant angle of attack A. This gives precision flight-path control, quicker dive recovery and increased manoeuvre load factor at constant AOA. 7,8,9: AOA pitching pointing, showing how it is possible to alter fuselage pitch attitude without changing V or flight-path.

Right: These plan views show the benefits – which to any fighter pilot seem amazing, and basically impossible – of direct side-force control. Like pitch force control, these demand instantaneous FBW flight control in a CCV-type fighter. 1,2,3: lateral translation provides instant control of aircraft lateral velocity at constant heading (maintained by constant-heading computer circuits in this mode). This mode instantly takes out drift on landing or errors in air-to-ground firing runs. 4,5,6: direct sideforce, using canards and rudder with roll control to maintain zero sideslip. This is for quick heading changes or for tracking laterally moving targets. 7,8,9: yaw pointing, using canards, rudder and roll control to change yaw angle (heading) whilst holding flight path constant. This gives near-instant aiming control.

Above: The first true attempt at a CCV fighter was this rebuild of the first YF-16 prototype with oblique canard control surfaces. Though very much an interim test vehicle it was sufficiently promising to lead to the much more advanced F-16 AFTI opposite.

power units, highly reliable and multi-redundant flight-control systems (typically with two pairs of hydraulic power systems and electric signalling so that any fault is countered by a 3-over-1 or 2-0 majority) and a new order of on-

AFTI Pitch Modes

Above: At subsonic speeds the conventional fighter needs tail downthrust to balance lift and weight forces, but the CCV (or Relaxed Static Stability) fighter gains from tail upthrust. At over Mach 1 both need downthrust at the tail, but the CCV force is small.

board EDP (electronic data processing) able to use much more flight information at much higher speed. The CCV fighter not only has potentially more rapid power of manoeuvre but can be made smaller, lighter and more

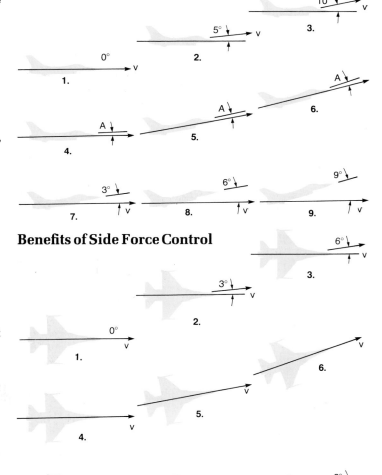

Benefits of Side Force Control

efficient in many other ways.

We have now got to the stage at which some manufacturers are putting the magic initials CCV into their brochures even when their aircraft are wholly conventional, and fitted with flight-control systems incapable of managing a CCV design. It is not practical to modify an existing fighter into a CCV machine, such test beds as MBB's F-104CCV being pure research tools incapable of flying valid military missions.

But one thing that can be done to existing fighters is to equip them with additional flight control surfaces which because of their location and thrust axis can impart direct forces normal to the flight path. At present this is impossible. Ailerons, spoilers or tailerons roll the aircraft, but the rudder or elevators (or tailplanes used in unison) cannot do more than rotate the aircraft about one of its axes. It is the rotation which, over a period, brings about the change in trajectory, and this is an imperfect way to manoeuvre – compared with a humming-bird, for instance.

Shortcomings of conventional fighters are clearly seen in an air-to-ground firing run. The pilot lines up on the target and, either because of inaccuracy or crosswind, finds he is off to left/right or above/below. He has to use his very imperfect control system to get on the correct alignment. To rise a few metres he pulls back on the stick and then has to push forward again, knowing from experience how much force or displacement to apply. Left/right motion is even more difficult. He has first to roll in the desired direction and then, after travelling what he thinks from experience ought to be about the right lateral displacement, he has to roll back again to get on the right trajectory.

Today the penny has at last dropped. Some of the first aircraft with DLC (direct lift control) were civil airliners, such as TriStars, which can get on the glidepath by opening or closing their slightly opened spoilers in unison to rise or fall just the required amount, without moving the elevators or altering the attitude of the fuselage. Fighters now have both DLC and

FBW Flight-control System

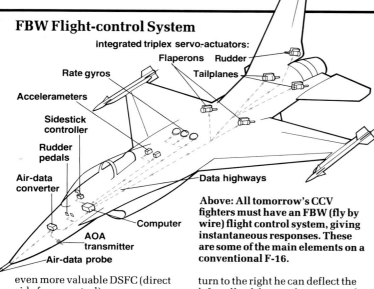

integrated triplex servo-actuators:
Flaperons   Rudder
Rate gyros   Tailplanes
Accelerameters
Sidestick
controller
Rudder
pedals
Air-data
converter
                    Data highways
                Computer
        AOA
        transmitter
    Air-data probe

Above: All tomorrow's CCV fighters must have an FBW (fly by wire) flight control system, giving instantaneous responses. These are some of the main elements on a conventional F-16.

Above: Another important and very challenging CCV programme is being run by the German MBB company. It uses an F-104G Starfighter which has been progressively modified and is now

flying with almost a complete duplicate tail to cause gross destabilization, assisted by 1,654lb (750kg) of ballast in the tail. This work will assist TKF.90/ACA fighter studies.

even more valuable DSFC (direct side force control).

Several research aircraft are testing various ideas, but a modified Alpha Jet shows one method. It has four large wing stores pylons which are more than they seem. If the pilot wishes to

turn to the right he can deflect the left walls of these pylons outwards, like small airbrakes, while moving the rudder to the right; this swings the aircraft on a new heading while keeping the wings level.

More useful is DSFC, also called direct translational maneouvre

capability. By opening the four left sides of the pylons as well as putting on left rudder the aircraft experiences a sudden and sustained sideways thrust to the right, moving it bodily sideways (actually diagonally, as it retains its forward motion), again without

the need to bank. In the F-16AFTI the effect is gained by combining rudder with the diagonal ventral canards under the inlet. In either case the pilot can start the aircraft moving any desired distance sideways instantly, without any need to bank or make a normal turn.

A VG Swing-wing Flight Control System

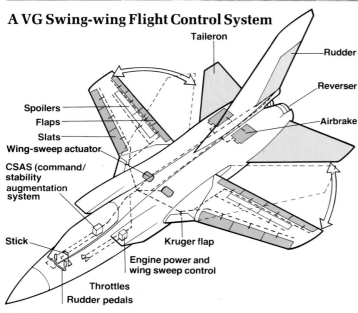

                    Taileron
                            Rudder
                            Reverser
Spoilers   Airbrake
Flaps
Slats
Wing-sweep actuator
CSAS (command/
stability
augmentation
system
Stick
        Kruger flap
    Engine power and
    wing sweep control
    Throttles
    Rudder pedals

Left: Elements of the flight control system of the Tornado. The system is of the triplex FBW type. Primary surfaces (blue) are rudder and tailerons, with roll assist by spoilers at small sweep angles.

Above and below: The AFTI F-16 has already demonstrated it can do things other aircraft find impossible. It raises the question of whether 1,000 F-16s could be thus modified.

Structure

Until the 1960s aluminium and its alloys was used for virtually 100 per cent of the airframe of all fighters. A few aberrations outside the mainstream of fighter development used mainly steel (MiG-25) or titanium (SR-71), while the development of very strong and stiff yet lightweight fibres of carbon/graphite or boron has increasingly led to the use of FRC (fibre-reinforced composites) in components where GRP (glass-reinforced plastics) might be equally strong but insufficiently stiff. Unlike typical metals in practical polycrystalline bulk, the new composite materials exhibit unidirectional stiffness. In other words a sheet, for example, can be made flexible in one direction and extremely rigid in another. By choosing the directions of the stiff reinforcing fibres it is possible to

create structures unlike any that were previously possible, able to bend in exactly the way the designer wishes.

Nobody is benefiting more from this than the designers of fighter aircraft. Previously a wing had to be made stiff, because if in a tight turn or dive pull-out it bent excessively the changed angle of incidence of the outer sections could cause what is called aeroelastic divergence. The bending would turn the wing to a greater angle to the airflow, and the suddenly increased air load could then bend the wing still further, and so on until the wing ripped off, the whole process occupying a small fraction of a second. It was for this reason that the FSW (forward-swept wing) could never be used, even though it was recognised as early as 1944 as better than the swept-back wing in

Above: Europe's most important combat aircraft programme is Tornado, nearly 1,000 of which are being built with assembly lines in three countries. This is the MBB line in Germany.

Below: Though it is a smaller and simpler aircraft the F-16 is being built in even greater numbers, again with assembly lines in three countries. This is General Dynamics in Texas.

Sustained Rate of Turn

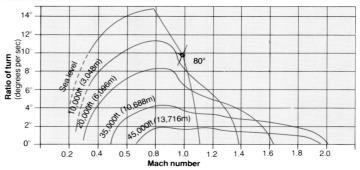

Sustained Load Factor

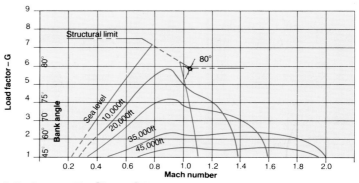

Minimum Radius of Turn

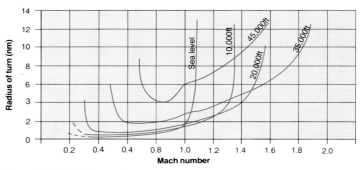

Level Flight Envelope

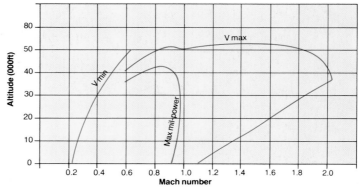

Above: These are four of the basic sets of curves that can be drawn for all aeroplanes, including Tiger Moths and 747s. These curves are for the McDonnell Douglas F-4E Phantom, and they show its level-flight sustained turn capability with the two J79-17 engines at maximum afterburning thrust. All these curves have been plotted for a flying weight of 42,777lb (19,404kg) which is for the clean aircraft with full internal fuel and just the four AIM-7 Sparrow missiles. Such curves ram home the basic facts about air combat. For example, it is possible to open the throttles and let speed build up to about Mach 0.8 and still make

tight turns. But if the speed is allowed to build up beyond Mach 1 the turn capability falls away dramatically. At anything like Mach 2 – which is attained only at high altitudes – even the Phantom has to fly in straight lines. The flight envelope emphasizes how narrow is the height band over which such high speeds can be reached. The curves of turn radius show that, at low level, turning ability vanishes completely at Mach numbers only just above 1. The plot of load factor is cut off at the low-speed end by inadequate wing lift (broken lines) and at the top by the limiting strength of the structure.

Payload/Combat Radius

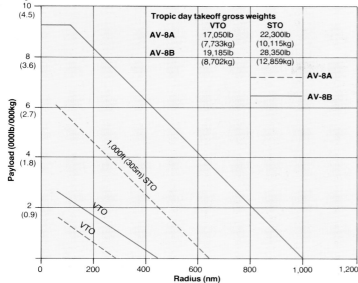

Tropic day takeoff gross weights		
	VTO	STO
AV-8A	17,050lb (7,733kg)	22,300lb (10,115kg)
AV-8B	19,185lb (8,702kg)	28,350lb (12,859kg)

- - - AV-8A
——— AV-8B

1,000ft (305m) STO

VTO

VTO

Level Flight Envelope

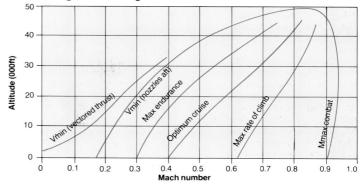

Vmin (vectored thrust) · Vmin (nozzles aft) · Max endurance · Optimum cruise · Max rate of climb · Mmax combat

Left: Plots of payload (weapon load) against range are similar for all aircraft. These apply to the AV-8B Harrier II, and show both the great gains achieved by taking a short run, instead of lifting vertically, and the advance made over Harrier I.

Above: The operational flight envelope here is plotted for the AV-8B Harrier II, flying without external stores at a weight of 17,345lb (7,868kg). The unique feature here is that the Vmin curve goes to zero. Thus, no airfield is needed.

almost every respect.

The FSW offers lower drag at almost all Mach numbers; therefore a fighter can have a smaller engine burning less fuel, which in turn reduces gross weight, so the wing can be smaller, and so on in a favorable circle of interacting effects. The FSW offers greater manoeuvrability at all speeds, better handling at low speeds, and lower stalling speed under good control, and thus reduced runway requirements. The FSW fighter can be made virtually spinproof, and certainly can be smaller and cheaper than any alternative shape.

This is really an aerodynamic argument, but it is covered here because the realization of the FSW has been entirely due to new

composite structures. These can be made so stiff, using skins reinforced with graphite fibres laid in appropriate directions, that the previously impossible FSW can be flown up to supersonic speeds and pulled into tight turns without the spectre of sudden divergence pulling the wings off.

Grumman has designed the first FSW aircraft, the X-29A, to fly in February 1984. It has a powered hinged trailing edge to give variable camber and a close-coupled foreplane for use as a primary flight control and to provide the necessary nose-up trim in the supersonic regime by an upward force, instead of by a downward force as is required by aircraft with trimming surfaces at the rear.

Above: One of the first of the modern (as distinct from German-1944) FSW proposals was this suggestion for an even more agile F-16 (FSW here rendered as SFW). It was not built.

Below: Powered by an F404 more powerful than the version used in the much bigger twin-engined F-18, the Grumman X-29A is expected to outmanoeuvre all other fighters.

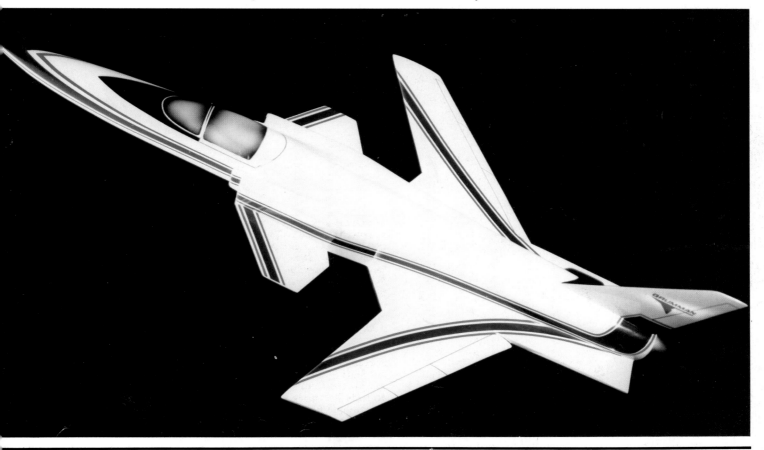

Structure

Another American research aircraft for future fighters is the Rockwell HiMAT (highly manoeuvrable aircraft technology). This is a pilotless RPV, powered by the same J85 afterburning turbojet as used in the twin-engined F-5E. Its wing and large canards are aeroelastically tailored so that, as they deflect upwards in tight manoeuvres, the angle of incidence does not increase but decrease. This is done by making the main structural parts of these surfaces out of graphite composite sheets with the plies oriented at carefully chosen angles, mainly diagonal, to control the change of the airfoil shape under severe loads. Again, HiMAT has mechanical camber change along leading and trailing edges.

For structural as well as aerodynamic reasons previous fighter canards have been used only as a trimming device or to enhance takeoff and landing and low-speed handling. Many, such as those of the Kfir and Mirage 2000, are mere fixed surfaces. On the HiMAT, two of which are flying, the canards have elevators and are used in conjunction with

HiMAT variations

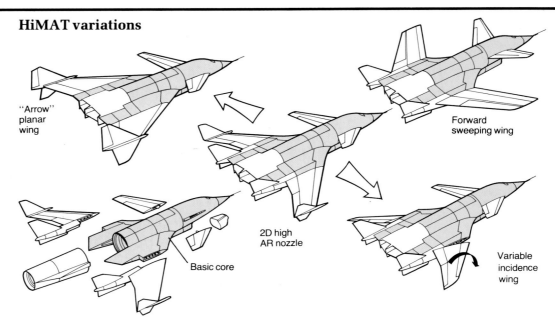

"Arrow" planar wing

Forward sweeping wing

2D high AR nozzle

Basic core

Variable incidence wing

Below: Yet another of Rockwell's bids to get back in the fighter business is this FSW mock-up, which also has swept canard surfaces. This could prove even more agile than HiMAT.

Above: HiMAT shown with some of the planned variations around it. These alternative forms can be produced by quick-change component changes.

Below: More than 90 per cent of the surface of the HiMAT was originally black, the colour of graphite epoxy composite material. This will become more common than shiny metal.

HiMAT Materials

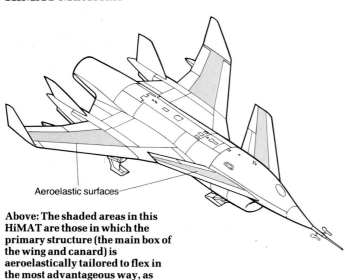

Aeroelastic surfaces

Above: The shaded areas in this HiMAT are those in which the primary structure (the main box of the wing and canard) is aeroelastically tailored to flex in the most advantageous way, as explained in the diagram on the right. Only 25 per cent of the HiMAT airframe is made of aluminium and its alloys; another 25 per cent is graphite/epoxy composite; 19 per cent is titanium

and its alloys; 9 per cent steel and 4 per cent glassfibre; a mix of materials accounting for the remaining 18 per cent. This kind of materials breakdown will become more common.

Aeroelastic Tailoring

Mechanical camber change on leading and trailing edges

Bend/twist coupling control

Cruise Manoevring 0.9M/8G/ 30,000ft

Cruise

Theoretical maximum

Wave and thickness effects

HiMAT design achievement

HiMAT goal

Aerodynamic efficiency M=0.90

Current technology

Percentage (0, 20, 40, 60, 80, 100)

Mach (0.2, 0.4, 0.6, 0.8, 1.0, 1.2)

Above: HiMAT is the first aircraft in which the unidirectional stiffness properties of advanced fibre-reinforced composite materials has been put to direct use to make the structure bend in

controlled ways. The wing has variable camber (a concept taken furthest in test wings added to a NASAF-111A) and its graphite/ epoxy plies reduce incidence as the wing flexes upward under g.

HiMAT Turn Radius

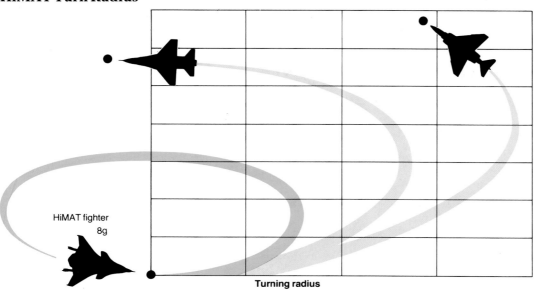

HiMAT fighter
8g

Turning radius

the variable-camber main wing to enhance agility throughout the entire flight envelope which extends to Mach 1.6. HiMAT has no fragile pilot and its positive g-limit is a bonecrushing +12, though the normal manoeuvring limit is a sustained turn at 8g at Mach 0.9 at 30,000ft (9,144m). Only 25 per cent of the present structure is light alloy, other percentages being: graphite composite 25, titanium 19, steel 9, glass-fibre 4, all other materials 18.

Another feature common to many modern fighters is a mix of aerodynamic and structural advantages called the blended root. It has long been known that, in some circumstances, drag is reduced if surfaces such as a wing and a fuselage are merged together around a radius rather than a sharp corner, and this curved junction often extends behind the trailing edge root to form a large fillet. By 1966 research had shown that, by blending a thin wing into the fuselage by progressively making it thicker, drag could be reduced, structure weight could be dramatically reduced by the much greater depth of the wing at the most highly stressed point, and considerable extra internal volume could be provided.

Saab went some way in this direction 30 years ago with the thick super-long-chord inboard wing of the Draken. McDonnell went the whole hog with their original FX design before finally building the F-15 with an almost flat upper surface which effectively removed one half of the blending. The process is seen well in the F-16, and to a lesser degree in the Mirage 2000. Of course the designer has to be careful not to let the structural need for more wing depth overcome the aerodynamicist's wish for less depth in order to keep down supersonic wave drag.

Above: Simplified sketch showing comparative turn radii of an F-4E with slatted wing, a regular F-16A and the initial form of HiMAT, in each case at a height of 30,000ft (9,144m) at Mach 0.9.

Below: As long ago as 1950 Saab in Sweden had roughed out the shape of the Model 35 Draken, with a fore-aft distribution of masses and a thickened inboard wing (virtually a blended form).

AAM Carriage

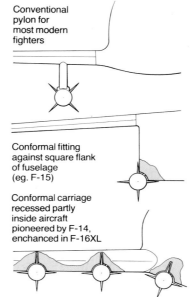

Conventional pylon for most modern fighters

Conformal fitting against square flank of fuselage (eg. F-15)

Conformal carriage recessed partly inside aircraft pioneered by F-14, enchanced in F-16XL

Above: Three ways to hang a large AAM for minimal aerodynamic drag: top, conventional high-drag pylon; centre, F-15 Eagle (part cutaway); bottom, conformal carriage (part cutaway) as on the F-16XL.

Below: In many ways potentially the most formidable fighter yet built, the F-16XL can carry colossal loads of weapons (roughly double the eight tons of earlier models). Here the first carries AIM-120 Amraams.

Propulsion

Almost all modern fighters are powered by augmented turbofans, the term augmented meaning that they have additional fuel burned in the air from the fan and in the hot gas from the core in the same way that an afterburner boosts the thrust of a turbojet. Some aircraft still use turbojets, though these tend to have relatively high fuel consumption except at high supersonic Mach numbers.

The turbojet is still competitive in the very few aircraft for which subsonic performance is relatively unimportant (such as the SR-71 and MiG-25). This is because at around Mach 3 the propulsion system depends to a large extent on the behaviour of the giant white-hot con/di (convergent and then divergent) nozzle, considerably larger in diameter than the rest of the engine, and on the large fully variable inlet system which in fact provides about 70 per cent of the thrust. The fact that the inlet and nozzle happen to have an engine somewhere between them is

almost a drawback; it would be far better if this encumbrance could be removed, leaving a highly efficient ramjet!

For most fighters Mach 3 is a dream world, and even aircraft such as the Mirage 2000 spend approximately 99.9 per cent of their flying life at Mach numbers much less than the maximum of which they are capable. It is strange therefore to note that the M53 engine of the Mirage 2000 is designed chiefly for the Mach 2-plus regime, where it performs well, rather than for the other 99.9 per cent of the aircraft's life.

Most engine designers are more realistic and aim for a good overall result, which means a turbofan with a much higher pressure ratio than the maximum of 9.3 achieved by the M53, and also a much higher bypass ratio (bypass ratio is the ratio of the cool airflow discharged from the fan through the surrounding bypass duct to the airflow which passes through the core, comprising the high-pressure compressor, combustor and turbine).

Above: Largest and most powerful powerplants in current use on fighter aircraft, the Tumanskii engines of the latest service version of MiG-25 (so-called Foxbat-E) have a maximum thrust of 30,864lb (14 tonnes). This Foxbat-E is seen with the engines at maximum power, accelerating from takeoff. At Mach 3 almost all the thrust is generated by variable inlets and nozzles.

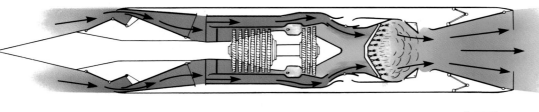

Left: A representation, based on an original drawing by Rolls-Royce, of a propulsion system for a combat aircraft capable of Mach 3 or more. It has variable geometry, with powered valves in the inlet, ahead of the compressor and upstream of the large afterburner, which is here shown in operation.

Above: This is a more conventional afterburning turbojet similar to that used to power Mach 2-plus fighters designed in the 1950s. Air is drawn in at the left, compressed and passed through the combustion chamber to the three-stage turbine driving the compressor. The hot gas then passes through the large afterburner and variable nozzle.

Below: Takeoff by an early Panavia Tornado, using full afterburner to demonstrate a short takeoff with an external load exceeding 20,000lb (9072kg). The unusual features of the RB199 engines of this aircraft are the use of three separate rotating spools, the amazingly compact overall size, and the incorporation of a thrust reverser upstream of the variable nozzle.

Figures published at the time of the 1974 USAF lightweight fighter competition underlined the importance of getting the engine right. When the General Dynamics 401, the predecessor of the F-16, was being designed calculations showed that with two of the neat little YJ101 afterburning turbojets the mission weight would be 21,470lb (9,739kg), whereas with one of the large F100 augmented turbofans (already in production for the twin-engined F-15) the weight would be an exciting 17,050lb (7,734kg)! If the two aircraft were adjusted to have equal weight, for example by putting more fuel into the F100-powered fighter, the latter would have a mission radius no less than 71 per cent greater! Of this, 45 per cent was due to the lighter propulsion installation, 40 per cent to reduced fuel flow, 11 per cent to lower airframe weight and 4 per cent to lower drag.

Later, General Electric turned the YJ101 turbojet into the F404 turbofan for the F/A-18A Hornet,

F-15 Propulsion System

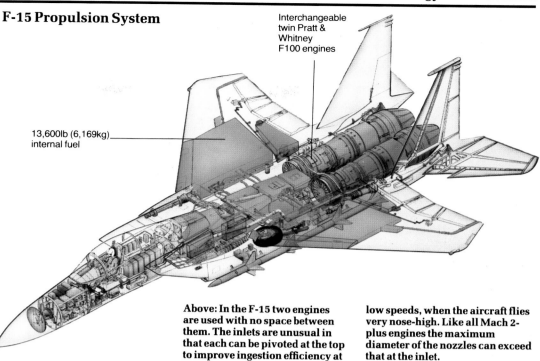

Interchangeable twin Pratt & Whitney F100 engines

13,600lb (6,169kg) internal fuel

Above: In the F-15 two engines are used with no space between them. The inlets are unusual in that each can be pivoted at the top to improve ingestion efficiency at low speeds, when the aircraft flies very nose-high. Like all Mach 2-plus engines the maximum diameter of the nozzles can exceed that at the inlet.

Above: As the powerplant of the F-15 and F-16 the Pratt & Whitney F100 augmented turbofan bears a crushing burden of responsibility. Unfortunately, as in the case of its predecessor, the TF30, its early years have been marked by problems which have resisted extremely prolonged and costly redesign efforts, but by 1983 the F100 had a great background of experience, most of it good.

Below: An F100 running at full power, which means maximum afterburner, on a P&WA test stand at West Palm Beach. No engine in history has ever been subject to more gruelling test programmes.

Note that, as it is at rest, the engine is running with the variable nozzle partly closed. At maximum flight Mach number of "more than 2.5" the nozzle would be opened and divergent.

Above: With minimum government funding Rolls-Royce has developed the Pegasus, the world's first successful jet-lift STOVL engine, to a very high degree of maturity, to the extent that in the world's worst weather off the Falklands in 1982 these Sea Harriers were ready around the clock and missed only 0.2 per cent of their planned sorties.

Below: Much slimmer than the Pegasus (one of which is seen at extreme left) the Turbo-Union RB199 is the most compact engine of its power in the world, despite incorporating a thrust reverser (the swinging-link doors of which can be seen on the second engine at the extreme top of the picture). Vertical assembly of engines is common today.

Fighter Engine Development

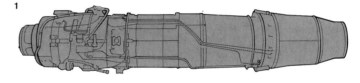

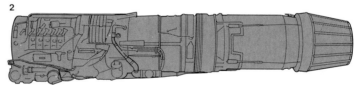

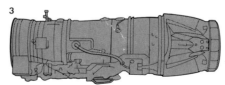

Above: Fighter jet engines in scale: 1, Allison J35-35 of 1951 (afterburning thrust 7,500lb with specific fuel consumption 2.0; length 195.5in, dry weight 2,850lb); 2, General Electric J79-17 of 1965 (afterburning thrust 17,820lb with sfc of 1.97; length 208.7in, dry weight 3,847lb); 3, Turbo-Union RB199 of 1975 (max thrust 16,000lb with sfc of 1.5; length 127in, dry weight 1,980lb).

but even this still has the modest bypass ratio of 0.34 compared with 0.7 for the big F100, and for this reason there is not the slightest doubt that the F-16 can do a bigger mission job on, say, 5,000lb (2,268kg) of fuel than can the F/A-18A. With an even higher bypass ratio the fuel economy is better still; some particularly fuel-efficient engines include the Adour (BPR about 0.8). RB.199 (1) and Pegasus (1.4). The drawback tends to be that the fan becomes

large, but the Harrier could hardly be any smaller in diameter and still accommodate the pilot, avionics and fuel. Later we shall see augmented Pegasus engines with PCB (plenum-chamber burning) to boost thrust for supersonic STOVL (short takeoff, vertical landing) successors to the Harrier which will be the only future combat aircraft (other than helicopters) able to fly after nuclear attack has wiped out all the fixed airbases.

Today's Harrier family are

unique in that their engine is of the so-called four-poster type. The fan and jetpipe each discharge through left/right pairs of nozzles, all four nozzles being rotatable in unison to provide lift, thrust or a combination of lift and reverse thrust for rapid inflight deceleration. The tremendous effectiveness of this arrangement is perhaps best appreciated by the pilots and ground troops of Argentina, but it is not ideal for future supersonic STOVLs.

The fan air inevitably has to come out from two lateral nozzles, which will incorporate PCB to give greatly increased thrust in just the same way that an afterburner boosts a turbojet. But it is possible to discharge the core jet through a single pipe and still provide for afterburning and for vectoring for STOVL aircraft. The simplest way to do this is to incorporate a short length of rotating pipe with slanted ends (typically with the mating faces inclined at 22½°). If this

Above: What the human eye usually cannot see is that, though the four jets from the Rolls-Royce Pegasus are angled slightly outwards in the vertical-lift mode, they give rise to a rapidly rising vertical gas column directly under the belly of the aircraft which, if trapped by suitable strakes and dams (as on the AV-8B Harrier II) can enhance lift.

Three- Versus Four-Poster Engines

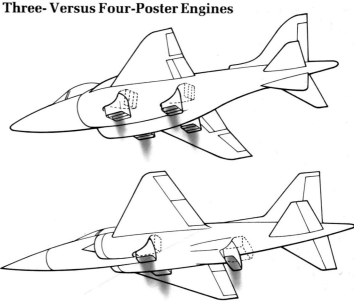

Above and below: The demands of greater cycle efficiency and higher propulsive efficiency have replaced the slim afterburning turbojet of the 1950s by today's augmented turbofan, which is shorter but handles vastly greater airflow. At General Electric the famed J79 (below), used in the F-104, F-4 and Kfir, has been overtaken by newer engines such as the F101 (above).

Above: All members of the Harrier family, the only true STOVL combat aircraft in the world, use a four-poster propulsion system. This can be boosted by PCB (plenum-chamber burning) in the front nozzles, but for tomorrow's supersonic STOVL aircraft a three-poster arrangement is more likely to be used. This makes it easy to use a rear afterburner.

inserted section is rotated through 180° the jet nozzle is vectored down through 90°, for vertical lift. The advantages of this arrangement, which is called the three-poster or tripod, are that aircraft drag can be reduced and, more importantly, the core afterburner is much more efficient at supersonic speeds with its unobstructed straight-through flow.

Since jet engines have been around for almost 50 years it is remarkable that most fighters have such primitive installations with so little variable geometry. Variable-area and variable-profile inlets came in with the second generation of supersonic aircraft in the mid-1950s, but the discovery that supersonic flight was in practice very rare led to the decision to use plain fixed inlets in most modern fighters including the F-16, F/A-18, Saab-39 Gripen (JAS) and IAI Lavi. In the B-1 supersonic bomber the variable inlets of the

Propulsion

Current and Possible Future Inlets

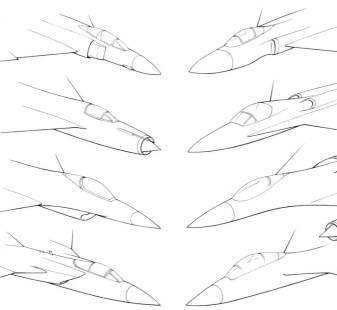

Above: Today it is rare for an aircraft design team to make a mess of the inlet design, but there is plenty of scope for variation. On the left are four familiar fighters: F-4 (top), MiG-21, F-16 and Tornado. On the right are four possible inlet arrangements which would reduce the signature on enemy radars. The best stealth inlets are often marred by poor aerodynamic efficiency, especially in flight at high AOA as in combat.

prototypes are to be replaced by plain fixed inlets on B-1B production aircraft. So clever inlets like those on the F-15 are in general being priced out of existence by inflation. The F-15's inlets not only have variable area and profile internally but also can be bodily tilted downwards to gulp air efficiently at low airspeeds with the aircraft at about 18° AOA (angle of attack).

Things are even worse at the other end. More than 99.99 per cent of all jet fighters have had plain nozzles which give thrust along a fixed axis. At least the Harrier can vector its thrust, but in this aircraft the four-poster thrust is carefully disposed evenly around the centre of gravity so that the aircraft is acted upon bodily but not rotated. There is no reason why vectoring should not be a normal feature of conventionally located rear nozzles. In this case the deflected thrust would not only give lift or drag but also a very

powerful turning moment.

Consider a fighter whose single tail nozzle was built like the sting of a wasp, able to tilt in any direction. We could at once remove the tail from this aircraft, and replace the forces previously imparted by the rudder and elevators by those provided by the suitably deflected jet. If we installed two engines side-by-side, preferably with a large lateral spacing as in the F-14, we could then vector the nozzles differentially and use the up/down jet thrust for roll control also. There is no evident advantage in trying to eliminate conventional control surfaces, but there is every reason for using the vectored main engine thrust for control as well as for mere propulsion.

One of the first aircraft to explore the possibilities may be the HiMAT, which because of its modular construction can readily test different wings, tails and engines. Even its engine is

Below: The two-dimensional wedge inlet of the F-15 Eagle is very unusual in that the whole forward inlet structure is pivoted at the bottom and can be rotated through an angle of 14°. In the fully depressed position, as shown

here, the inlet swallows the correct amount of air at high AOA and, among other advantages, avoids the high drag and possible flight-control difficulties caused by the need to spill large airflows overboard.

modular, with the afterburner housed in the tail of the fuselage which is removable. It is planned to fit a 2D (two-dimensional) nozzle, 2D meaning that its cross-section is the same all the way across the aircraft. General Electric and NASA have already tested a 2D nozzle with remote afterburning,

and in the form planned for HiMAT the jets on the left and right of the centreline could be vectored up or down independently. This is to be used both for basic lift enhancement and for increased longitudinal control power. In theory differential vectoring on HiMAT could impart roll.

When we consider that in almost all the newest fighters the total sea level installed thrust is greater than the clean gross weight it seems ridiculous not to make this great force lift the aircraft at takeoff or on landing. Cleverer nozzles will bring this possibility nearer, though simple geometry shows

that you cannot use vectored thrust at the tail for lift unless it is balanced by upthrust at the nose. For STOVL aircraft, which in a nuclear age seem the only kind that is survivable, the best answer still seems to be the three-poster or four-poster with nozzles arranged around the CG.

The Two-dimensional Nozzle

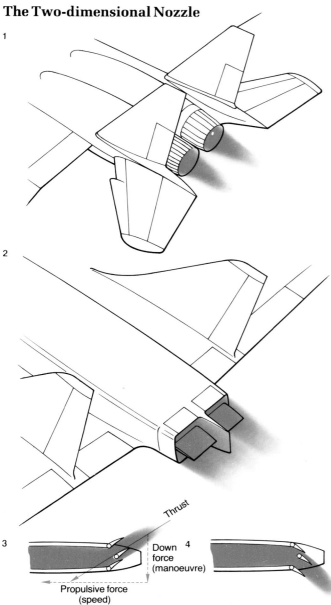

1

2

3

4

Thrust

Down force (manoeuvre)

Propulsive force (speed)

Above: Virtually every jet nozzle used on a production fighter has been circular and operated on an axis fixed with respect to the aircraft (eg, F-15, 1). In future we may see the two-dimensional vectorable nozzle (2). This can generate downthrust (3) or upthrust (4), and left/right differential vectoring gives roll.

Above: This Pratt & Whitney drawing shows the main features of a typical fighter engine of the 1960s, the TF30-414A, which is at last getting over the prolonged problems of the TF30 in the F-14 Tomcat. One of the features of the Dash-414A is a very strong fan case (extreme left) to contain an exploding fan. This is an engine which would benefit greatly from two-dimensional vectoring nozzles, because the left and right engines are far apart.

Above: Preflight inspection of a USAF F-16A, showing the simple fixed-geometry inlet. With a fully variable inlet this aircraft would be as fast as a Mirage 2000, but this would be pointless extra cost.

Below: Rear end of the F-16, showing large afterburner nozzle which forms the actual tail end of the fuselage. In combat the nozzle may be ceaselessly opening (with afterburner) and closing.

Weapons

Just as the advent of the turbojet made many people jump to the conclusion that propellers were obsolete, so did the advent of the SAM (surface-to-air missile) lead some important people in Britain to the conclusion that all manned fighters were obsolete. Another of these crassly simplistic beliefs stemmed from the invention of the AAM (air-to-air missile), which by the late 1950s had convinced many experts that fighter guns were obsolete. There are plenty of fat treatises on fighter armament dating from that period which ignore the gun completely, the only alternative to the AAM considered being the spin-stabilized rocket. The authors of those documents did not have the slightest indication that by 1965 the CO of the USAF 8th Tactical Fighter Wing in Vietnam would say publicly, "A fighter without a gun is like a bird without a wing."

Britain's RAF gradually recovered from the belief that it would need no more fighters, but even today it does not have a single true fighter in service with an internal gun. The trusty old 30mm Aden is fitted in the front of the ventral pack of a few surviving Lightnings, and it is also carried in external packs clipped under the fuselage of Harriers; the only aircraft with internal guns are the Jaguars which are dedicated attack and reconnaissance aircraft. No internal gun was asked for in the P.1154 Mach-2 V/STOL nor in the Phantom which replaced it, and as the RAF's mainstay (virtually only) fighter today the Phantom often has to carry a 20mm SUU-23A gun pod on the centreline pylon. Many USAF and Navy/Marines F-4 Phantoms carried the same pod in Vietnam, and on occasion blasted the enemy with three. Fundmentally, the use of an external gun pod is undesirable unless it is known that a gun will

seldom be needed. It sterilizes a pylon, invariably upsets aircraft trim when firing and makes accuracy unattainable.

Almost all modern Soviet combat aircraft have at least one internal gun, and the big Su-24 long-range interdictor has two which many analysts think are of different calibres (probably one 23mm and the other 30mm). An exception is the Yak-36MP shipboard VTOL aircraft, which has no internal armament: guns, along with everything else, have to be hung on the four pylons under the short inboard section of wing.

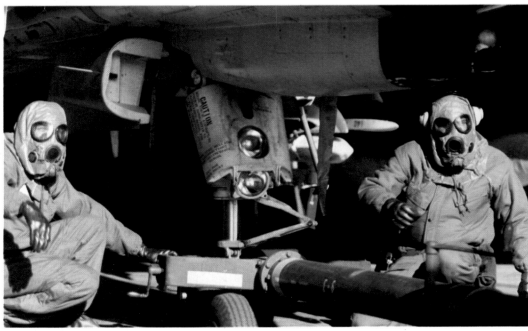

Top: In its day the Nudelmann-Richter NR-30 was the most powerful aircraft gun, firing projectiles with a typical weight of 0.4kg at high muzzle velocity. Here an NR-30 is in action aboard an Su-7B.

Below: The GAU-8/A is by far the most powerful gun ever flown (outside the Soviet Union, at least). Without the magazine drum at the rear this gun is 21ft (6.4m) long, half as long again as European family cars.

Above: A CBW-suited ground crew uncouple the towbar from an F-4E of the 86th TFW, USAF. The M61 gun pod is opened up ready for reloading the gun from the ammunition drum inside the forward fuselage.

Gun pods have also recently been seen on the various MiG-23/27 dedicated attack versions, despite the fact these have a multi-barrel internal gun with great hitting power on the ventral centreline. The reason for the external pods appears to be that in these the guns can be tilted down to about −20° for firing at ground targets without diving. Clearly, such fire cannot be sustained on one target and would normally sweep past at the groundspeed of the aircraft; and accuracy could never be high no matter what sight system was used.

One particular type of internal gun installation is powerful enough to defeat main battle tanks. These became important in World War II when guns up to 75 or even 105mm calibre were used, beside which today's weapons of 30mm size seem puny.

But in fact the US General Electric GAU-8/A Avenger around which was designed the A-10A Thunderbolt II is the most powerful gun, in terms of muzzle horsepower, ever flown. The ammunition is roughly milk-bottle sized; propellant charge is far greater than in other 30mm

weapons to achieve a muzzle velocity of 3,500ft (1,067m) per second with heavy armour-piercing projectiles which have cores of depleted uranium, one of the densest materials known. It takes 77hp just to drive the gun, and the recoil is such that the gun is installed 2° nose-down to eliminate pitching moments when firing, and offset in the left side of the nose so that the barrels fire exactly on the aircraft centreline. A similar gun is fitted to the Soviet Frogfoot (Su-25?).

There was great activity among Allied gun designers when they

discovered the progress made in the technology by Germany during World War II. In 1946-49 the West suddenly leaped ahead of 1917, which was the technology of the guns used by the Western Allies in World War II, and a dramatic breakthrough came in 1951-3 with the extremely successful development of the six-barrel Vulcan, produced by GE mainly as the 20mm M61 and T-171, the former for fighters and the latter for the tail of the B-58 and B-52H bombers. It is as if six wartime 20mm cannon had been combined in one gun and fed with vast

Bottom: Second only to the GAU-8/A in the non-Soviet lineup of aircraft guns, the Oerlikon KCA 30mm is fitted to the JA37 Viggen. It has a high rate of fire and much higher muzzle velocity than the Aden or DEFA 30mm weapons.

Below: Compared with the superb guns (for all purposes) in the Soviet Union, the General Electric multi-barrel cannon stand out as excellent Western counterparts, led by the giant GAU-8/A fitted to the A-10A tank killer.

Above: A firing run by a Fairchild A-10A can be devastating, though the gun's recoil is enormous and quickly slows the aircraft. The gun is mounted 2° nose-down, and the barrels come on to the aircraft centreline as they fire.

Below: Reloading the magazine of the KCA 30mm gun in a JA37 Viggen. One armourer feeds the rounds in while the other pulls them into the magazine (on the right side of the flat gun pod) using a hand crank.

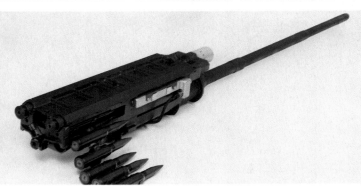

amounts of ammunition from a giant drum, in recent installations with a linkless feed system. The gun proved so effective it has been virtually standard on US fighters for over 25 years. In many installations (F-104, F-105, F-14, F-15, F-16) it has been well to one side of the centreline, where it at first kicked the aim off-target, though in today's fighters it automatically calls up rudder deflection via the computerized flight-control system.

A few modern US fighters, including the F-5E and F-20A, still use the even earlier M39 cannon, and a puzzling feature of these and of the F/A-18A (which has an M61) is that at night the blinding muzzle flash is directly in front of the pilot's windshield. More serious is the failure of the 25mm gun which was planned originally for the F-15, and was to have had self-consuming cases; storing or ejecting spent cases are both undesirable and fraught with problems, and a "caseless" round has been sought for some 60 years.

In the Soviet Union there has been unbroken continuity of aircraft gun development since 1931, but in the USA this important aspect of weaponry has given rise to many ulcers and disappointments. There is no evidence of any success in trying to achieve some commonality of ammunition among NATO air forces, and while Tornado and Alpha Jet squadrons use 27mm the

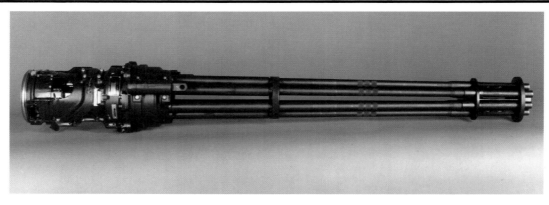

Above: Virtually the standard gun of all US fighters except the F-5 and the new AV-8B, the General Electric M61A1 has six barrels and fires high-velocity (1,036m/s) rounds at up to 100 per second.

new US calibre seems to be 25mm, initially in the AV-8B Harrier II, though this five-barrel gun is just a "son of Vulcan". RAF Harrier GR.5s will have the old 30mm Aden.

Having regard to the amount spent over the past 20 years by expensive NATO experts attending distant meetings on weapons policy, the taxpayer has a right eventually to see some kind of policy on aircraft guns that makes sense. When John Browning perfected his "fifty calibre" in 1918 he may well have thought it would see service in a World War more than 20 years later, but continued

production in 1984 (for example, for gun pods for Aermacchi MB.339s) appears ludicrous.

MISSILES

It is difficult to avoid being equally concerned at the failure of the NATO alliance to come up with any kind of plan for AAMs (air-to-air missiles). The ability of US industry, notably Ford Aerospace, to keep improving the Sidewinder has at least put progressively better close-range dogfight weapons in the hands of the troops, but Sidewinder itself is now over 30 years old. All that has been done over this period is to bolt on better nose guidance sections and control canards, and fit an improved smokeless motor in the tube at the rear, and in the all-aspect AIM-9L and 9M to incorporate a much better ABF (annular blast

fragmentation) warhead. Basic aerodynamics have hardly altered, and in any case the need to provide IR (infra-red, or heat) homing guidance or semi-active radar homing as a direct alternative has been consistently abandoned.

A semi-active radar missile flies towards the reflections from the target of radar signals transmitted by the fighter. The target, as seen by the missile, tends to be rather diffuse and variable, because the centroid (the apparent geometrical centre) keeps changing according to the target's attitude and other factors.

Below: BAe Dynamics has great experience with advanced AAMs which, have a vectoring rocket nozzle and can outmanoeuvre AAMs with nothing but aerodynamic control surfaces. This is a SRAAM firing.

Above: GE's GPU-5/A pod houses a GAU-13/A gun, a lighter version of the GAU-8/A, together with drives and ammunition. Some fighters can have three pods.

Below: The FFV Uni-Pod is ideal for light attack aircraft. It houses a 0.5in (12.7mm) Browning, usually with a 150-round box of ammunition.

Infra-red Wavelengths

Right: IR homing missiles can "see" only those parts of a target that emit radiation within a selected wavelength band. A Sidewinder's view of an F-16XL can be thought of as two diffuse red blobs.

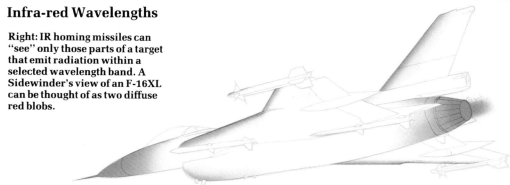

Radar Wavelengths

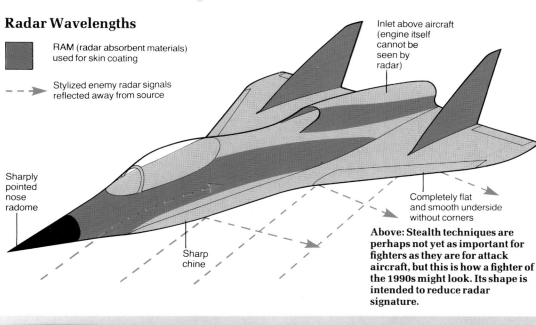

RAM (radar absorbent materials) used for skin coating

Stylized enemy radar signals reflected away from source

Inlet above aircraft (engine itself cannot be seen by radar)

Sharply pointed nose radome

Sharp chine

Completely flat and smooth underside without corners

Above: Stealth techniques are perhaps not yet as important for fighters as they are for attack aircraft, but this is how a fighter of the 1990s might look. Its shape is intended to reduce radar signature.

In contrast an IR missile sees only the hottest parts of the target, in particular the hot metal of the jetpipe or, better still, the final turbine stage as seen up the jetpipe (best of all, by far, is an operative afterburner). All-aspect IR missiles have particularly sensitive seeker heads which can unfailingly lock-on to the target aircraft regions which are only slightly hotter than the ambient background. Cunning filters and electronics are needed to prevent the missile from ever locking-on to either the Sun or ground reflections.

In general the only difference between radar and IR is one of wavelength, IR having a very much shorter wavelength close to that of visible light. Short wavelength can mean a more precise picture (for example, if we ourselves saw at radio/radar wavelengths we should have a very poor view indeed, compared with the fantastically rich picture we actually enjoy), but it also means rapid attenuation due to scattering of the energy by rain, atmospheric moisture, dust, fog, cloud and similar phenomena. In a tropical rainstorm the effective range of a Sidewinder would be measured in

Below: Puffy cumulus and blue sky is fine for the IR-homing Sidewinder, but in blizzard conditions its guidance reliability would be degraded even without use by the enemy of flares and other IRCM.

R550 Magic

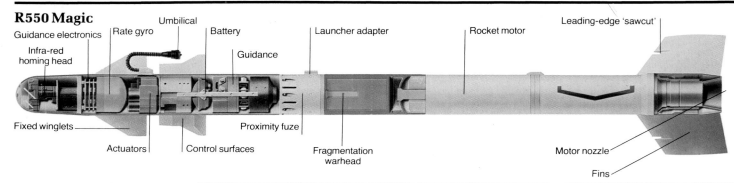

Guidance electronics · Rate gyro · Umbilical · Battery · Guidance · Launcher adapter · Rocket motor · Leading-edge 'sawcut'

Infra-red homing head

Fixed winglets · Actuators · Control surfaces · Proximity fuze · Fragmentation warhead · Motor nozzle · Fins

Above: Typical of today's IR-homing dogfight AAMs, the Matra 550 Magic is unusual in that it does not copy the Sidewinder's Rollerons (air-driven flywheel gyros on the tail fins). The umbilical feeds liquid nitrogen from the pylon to cool the sensitive IR seeker cell in the nose.

feet rather than miles.

It is extraordinary that, though there have been several studies for radar Sidewinders, and the AIM-9C was put into production (chiefly for the F-8 Crusader), every Sidewinder in service has IR guidance only. So do the French Magic, and Israel's Shafrir and Python 3.

In contrast, every known Soviet AAM is in service with a choice of radar or IR homing, and the usual load is pairs of missiles, one of each. This gives the greatest lethality according to the weather and other conditions, and also doubles the spread of wavelengths over which the enemy must provide countermeasures, as explained in the Electronic Warfare section (beginning on page 48)

The situation in the West is especially odd when it is realized that the main design effort is devoted to the basic aerodynamic shape of the missile. Getting the wings, tails, canards and other surfaces absolutely right can take several years. Indeed, following the philosophy adopted many years ago on combat aircraft, the Soviet Union first perfects a missile configuration, then scales it up or down for different ranges and warhead sizes, and then fits a choice of guidance to each size. In the West vast effort has been spent perfecting such totally different AAM shapes as Firestreak, Red Top, Shafrir, Python and Magic, and yet not one of them has any alternative to IR guidance.

In the same way, the West's medium-range missiles, such as Sparrow, Sky Flash, Aspide and Super 530, all have semi-active radar homing guidance. The longer wavelengths are certainly better suited to operations over long ranges, in the order of tens of miles, but the fact remains that even the largest and most powerful Soviet AAMs, such as AA-5 Ash and AA-6 Acrid, are invariably deployed in matched IR/radar pairs. Certainly the Soviet view, is that this gives each interceptor the highest possible chance of a successful kill.

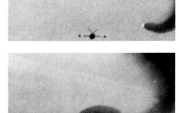

Above: This ciné film record of the overwing firing of a Magic AAM from a Jaguar shows the large and bright flame at the launch of a dogfight AAM of this type. The missile's SNPE Richard motor confers extremely high launch acceleration and then burns out, leaving the weapon to coast at rapidly diminishing speed. A ramjet or ramrocket would give sustained speed .

Above: Another Magic firing sequence, in this case showing a firing at close range behind a CT.20 target flying straight and level. The missile enters the jet pipe and destroys the target.

Shafrir 2

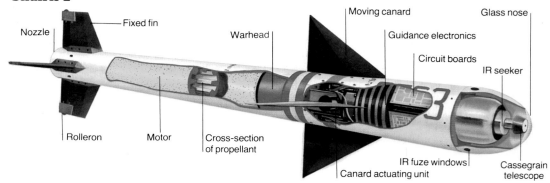

Fixed fin · Nozzle · Warhead · Moving canard · Glass nose · Guidance electronics · Circuit boards · IR seeker

Rolleron · Motor · Cross-section of propellant · Canard actuating unit · IR fuze windows · Cassegrain telescope

Above: One of the close-range AAMs which does copy the Sidewinder in using tailfin-mounted rollerons, the Israeli Rafael Shafrir 2 makes life easier for its designers in having a body diameter of 6.3in (160mm) compared with only 5in (127mm) for the pioneer US weapon. It weighs about 205lb (93kg), compared with 170lb (77kg) for AIM-9J Sidewinder and 196lb (89kg) for Magic. The four canard fins pivot in opposite pairs.

Right: In sharp contrast to the AAMs on the left-hand page, AIM-54 Phoenix can kill from ranges exceeding 100 miles (161km). It is carried only by the US Navy F-14 Tomcat, from which this example is being launched.

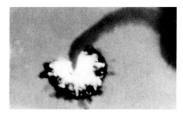

IR Homing Guidance

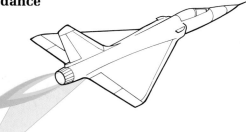

Above: Here being fired from a prototype Mirage 2000, the Matra Super 530 is a vast improvement on the same maker's R530 of the 1960s. Unlike the earlier AAM it comes with radar guidance only. Later Mirage 2000s will have the Super 530D compatible with pulse-doppler radar.

Below: The Soviet air defence forces believe in large missiles for large interceptors, mainly to kill over very large distances. Here AA-5 Ash AAMs are brought out to arm Tu-128 long-range interceptors. NATO has long given the range of this giant missile as 18 miles (30km), ludicrously low.

Above: This highly stylized drawing shows how the sensitive seeker cell in the nose of a heat-homing AAM scans over a limited arc and finally locks on to the best source of heat (at the correct kind of wavelength) it can find, here the jet nozzle of an enemy fighter. It could be fooled by IRCM flares.

Semi-active Radar Guidance

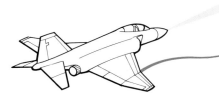

Some AAMs cannot find their targets unless the latter are "illuminated" by the radar of the fighter that carries the missile — no great handicap in a stern chase,

apart from broadcasting the whole operation to the enemy's radar warning system. Where it is a grave handicap is in a head-on attack from a distance.

For the very longest range of all there is no practical alternative to active homing, usually using radar wavelengths (though the missile could use IR or laser wavelengths). In active homing the missile itself emits the radiation that is reflected from the target, and the reason for adopting this method will be appreciated when it is remembered that emitted energy, such as radio or heat waves, falls away not in proportion to the distance but in proportion to the square of the distance.

An F-14 Tomcat can pick out an enemy aircraft at a typical distance of 125 miles (200km), even if the target is seen almost nose-on. To do this the radar waves have to travel 250 miles (400km), because they have to go to the target and then be reflected back to the F-14. Compared with the situation at 1¼ miles (2km) range, this means the received signals are 10,000 times weaker! This would be asking rather a lot of the miniaturized guidance in an F-14's Phoenix missile, so to begin with the missile is merely fired in the direction of the target, flying on

autopilot (which in the new AIM-54C version is a strapdown inertial unit). When it gets near the target the missile's own radar is switched on, the planar-array scanner searches and locks-on, and thereafter the missile homes on the reflections of its own radar.

Until the 1960s it was very difficult for fighters to intercept aircraft flying close to the ground. The land or sea tends to act as a giant reflector of radar waves, so that searching from above for an intruder at treetop height is pointless; the small reflection is

lost against the overall reflection from the ground. It took prolonged research, by no means all in the United States despite a common American belief, to produce "overland downlook" radars. Cunning computers and software in modern radars can process and manage the signals in such a way that all reflections from the Earth's surface, or all reflections from stationary objects, are eliminated. Thus the display in the cockpit looks blank except for items that are moving or which are well above ground level.

Even then there are problems. There has to be a lower speed limit at which the radar with MTI (moving-target indication) cuts out reflections. A fighter might well have to intercept attacking helicopters, and, though it would be helpless against a helicopter in the hover, it would certainly see one travelling above the lower limit, one level of which is commonly 93mph (150km/h).

Pilots of the F-15s of the USAFE's 36th Tactical Fighter Wing at Bitburg in West Germany have been frustrated by constantly locking-on to a Mercedes or BMW on the autobahn, where over 90mph (150km/h) is by no means uncommon. At the moment this is proving a thorny problem, and if the WarPac hordes actually crossed the frontier the private cars speeding west at over 90mph (150km/h) might render low-level interceptions dependent entirely on the "Mk 1 eyeball".

There are many other severe difficulties, which might not be immediately apparent. In a gale the billions of leaves on trees can behave as radar moving targets, and so can the waves on the sea surface, as well as the spume blown from the wave crests. It is for this reason that maritime aircraft need special circuitry in their radars which can, as far as possible, eliminate motions of the ocean itself while locking-on to a possible slow-moving submarine mast.

In general, over land, the problem of the low-level attacker has been solved, and the problems of firing up at a MiG-25 at 82,000ft (25,000m) are by comparison trivial, the chief challenge being the high energy needed from the AAM rocket motor in order quickly to climb to the enemy flight level while at the same time reaching his geographical position.

Most pilots of modern radar-equipped interceptors would agree

HUD Symbology: Air/Air Search

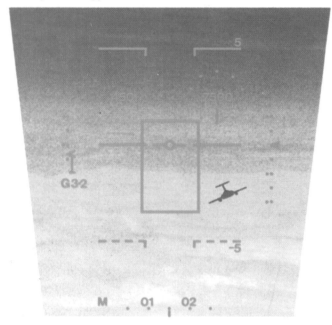

Above: The USAF F-15 Eagle fighter carries its AIM-7 Sparrow AAMs nestled under the chine of the fuselage. Each missile is first fired obliquely out and down, well away from the fighter, before its rocket motor ignites.

Left: In most modern air combats the pilots spend nearly all their time looking ahead through their HUD (head-up display) on which are bright computer-generated graphics giving all the information needed for a successful engagement. The display is varied automatically depending on the weapon(s) selected.
On the left is a typical HUD picture (it is that for the Ferranti Type 4500) in the AAM mode. A rectangle is first generated to help the pilot during the missile/target acquisition phase. Missile lock-on is indicated by a boxed ACQ appearing. When the firing conditions are correct the rectangle becomes a circle of probability containing letter M.

Search Mode	Acquisition Achieved	Firing Cue

 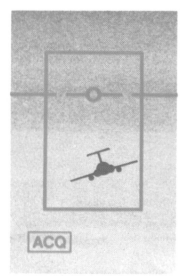 

Above: AAMs are often carried in the self-defence role. Here an AIM-9J Sidewinder, with preflight nosecap, is slid on to the tip rail of an F-16 about to fly a bombing mission. the extra weight and drag are small.

Below: Another example of self-defence missiles is this prototype Mirage 2000, carrying eight 551lb (250kg) bombs and two drop tanks, with a pair of Magics outboard. Obviously, such an aircraft would avoid combat.

Below: An AIM-9 Sidewinder being fired from an F-16 Fighting Falcon. Note how the turning fighter has already pulled clear of the AAM's smoke trail, which at the moment of launch started at the F-16 wingtip.

Bottom: The Soviet Su-15 interceptor, dedicated to killing from a distance, acknowledges the handicap of having to keep illuminating the target by having three separate radar/IR warning systems for its own protection.

that the chief remaining shortcomings of their kit are, first that the radar can lock on to a target at ranges far beyond those at which it can be positively identified, and, secondly, that the need to keep illuminating the target while an AAM is in flight is a very grave handicap indeed.

AVOIDING "OWN GOALS"

The problem of avoiding shooting at the wrong aircraft was solved in principle by the RAF in 1939 by the gradual introduction of IFF (identification friend or foe). An IFF is a small box which acts as a radio transmitter/receiver, or interrogator/responsor. In effect, it continuously sends out radio signals made up of repeated "trains" of complex coded pulses. These are electronic questions which ask "If there is anyone there,

are you a friend?" If there is a friend out there his compatible transponder (transmitter responder) will automatically be triggered by the questions and will send out different codes saying "Yes, this particular target is friendly."

IFF is fraught with difficulties. Clearly the codes have to be changed frequently, but the basic form of the interrogation has to be suited to the target. For several years NATO has been trying to construct a NIS (NATO Identification System) which will knit together all forces on land, sea and in the air. Such a system has to identify autonomously every friendly target the instant it is detected, in order to achieve the maximum capability of every weapon platform in which the NIS is fitted. To do this it has been found necessary to provide three

different types of interrogator: a low-band interrogator for user systems employing long-range radars, such as air-defence systems, ships and AEW aircraft; a radar interrogator for systems employing modern medium/short-range radars, such as fighter aircraft and mobile army radars; and a laser interrogator for systems employing high-resolution short-range optical and EO (electro-optical) sensors such as armoured vehicles and anti-tank helicopters. Each NIS interrogator will operate on a designated frequency, which in the case of radars will often be the same frequency (or, in today's radars, same rapidly varying spread of frequencies) as the host radar in the weapon platform.

It is planned to fit two types of transponder: a low-band/radar unit for aircraft and ships, and a laser/radar unit for battlefield

operations. But this still leaves problems. The orbiting Nimrod or Sentry cannot challenge a formation of anti-tank helicopters and get a satisfactory reply, and if the same aircraft happened to fly over a friendly armoured column it could not reply to the latter's challenge and could well be shot down.

In World War II it was commonly supposed that surface forces, and especially warships, used to fire at any aircraft first and ask questions afterwards. In the past 40 years we have tried with advanced IFF systems to avoid the foolish tragedy of shooting down friendly aircraft, yet it appears we still have some way to go. At the start of the shooting air war in the South Atlantic on 1 May 1982 an FAA Mirage which attempted to make an emergency landing at Porto Argentino (Port Stanley), one of the forward airbases, accidentally fired its two Magic AAMs (it is thought, as the result of an electrical fault). It was promptly shot down by Argentine flak, the pilot being killed. This kind of thing was commonplace in World War II, but modern IFF in theory could make it almost impossible. Argentina went on to score several further "own goals".

It goes without saying that the skill at aircraft recognition of many air and ground personnel whose fingers are on triggers is often worse than that of the average schoolboy. Thus the provision of long-range "visual identification" systems is seldom cost/effective, though such equipment has long been judged essential to the effective use of aircraft such as the F-14, which have the priceless capability of being able to kill at far BVR (beyond visual range). Many fighters have either no radar, other than a simple ranging unit for the gunsight such as fitted to most Mirage 5s, Kfirs and Daggers, or a radar of such limited capability that engagements are for practical purposes visual, or limited to ranges within about five miles (8km). With the powerful all-weather interceptor it is a different story.

Probably the first aircraft to be equipped with long-range "eyes" is the F-14, which for three years has usually been fitted with a Northrop TVSU (TV sighting unit), which is basically a high-quality TV camera whose sightline is slaved to that of the main AWG-9 radar. When the latter locks on to a target the TVSU can furnish the backseater with a greatly magnified TV picture of it. As early as 1977 F-14 crews were finding they could always identify the actual type of a fighter target at 10 to 15 miles (16 to 24km), and a 747 at 70 miles

AIM-54A Phoenix

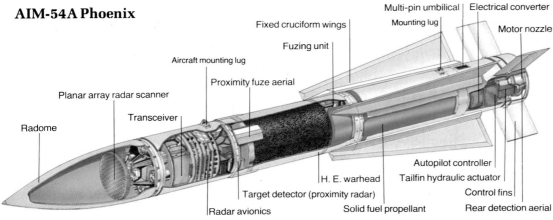

Radome
Planar array radar scanner
Transceiver
Aircraft mounting lug
Proximity fuze aerial
Fuzing unit
Fixed cruciform wings
Multi-pin umbilical
Mounting lug
Electrical converter
Motor nozzle
Autopilot controller
Tailfin hydraulic actuator
Control fins
Rear detection aerial
Solid fuel propellant
Target detector (proximity radar)
H. E. warhead
Radar avionics

Left: Much larger than other Western AAMs, but smaller than the longest-ranged Soviet types, Phoenix has active radar homing from a small radar in its nose.

Below: Part of the F-14 Tomcat's AWG-9 update (which includes better Phoenix AAMs) is this totally new backseat digital display. The bright radar picture is surrounded by touch switches forming a computer keyboard with instantly programmable software to handle changes in threats, radar modes and everything else affecting the way the fighter is operated.

(112km), without too much degradation from cloud, smoke or other interference (though this was not then a low light-level TV for night use). Today it is possible to obtain a sharper picture which can normally enable positive identification to be obtained at more than 20 miles (32km), which begins to approach the effective range limits of radar-guided missiles.

One of the very few aircraft in the same class is the RAF's forthcoming Tornado F.2, which likewise has to achieve positive identification of aerial targets at the greatest possible distance. In an unclassified outline of how the aircraft operates, Wg Cdr Mike Elsam, RAF, said in 1978, "Next comes the VAS (visual augmentation system), which is an EO device displaying a TV picture of the target giving positive identification by day in time for a front-hemisphere firing, and in starlight-only night conditions at ranges well in excess of what we need for safe shadowing and missile release." Mention of the VAS has been conspicuously absent from recent literature concerning this otherwise superb aircraft, but to axe it on typical British grounds of "economy" would be too ludicrous even to contemplate.

A VAS-type device is the essential complement to the ideal aim of all fighters of being able to see targets at a distance, say 100 miles, (160km), effect positive identification and then fire simultaneously on several (in the case of the F-14, six) which may well be flying in different directions at different heights. Almost every analyst who has actually studied air combat has come to the conclusion that, to quote Maj-Gen "Boots" Blesse, USAF ret, "The long-range kill is the way to go." But we still have to get our AAMs to the target.

In the case of the F-14 and its Phoenix there is no problem. This large and costly weapon is a "fire and forget" system, and as soon as it has been launched towards the enemy the F-14 can head for home and the ground crewman with a paint brush to add six more kill symbols. With semi-active radar

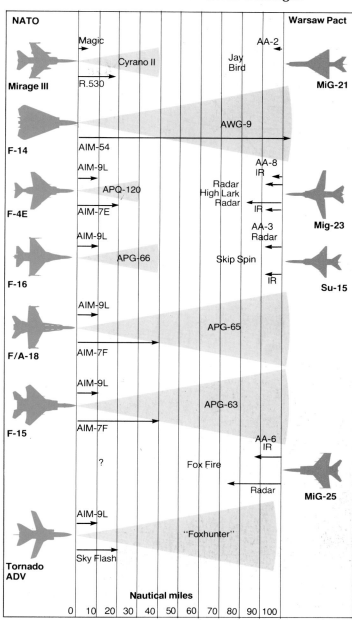

NATO/Warsaw Pact Radar and AAM Ranges

Above: The AAM carried by this F-14A is an AIM-120A Amraam, which will replace Sparrow. Smaller but more lethal than its predecessor, AIM-120 has the colossal advantage of being a "fire and forget" weapon.

Below: No other combat aircraft can equal the stand-off kill capability of the F-14A Tomcat with six AIM-54 Phoenix. Incidentally, it is unusual to have nozzles fully closed while the wings are fully swept back.

Above: The ranges indicated for the radars and AAMs of fighters of the NATO air forces (left) and WP air forces (right) are believed to be reasonably accurate, though they are much more even than the NATO official estimates. The latter are based on a totally unjustified assumption that Soviet technology is markedly inferior to that of NATO. This is then used to support a belief that NATO could shomehow win against numerically superior aircraft.

AIM-7 Sparrow

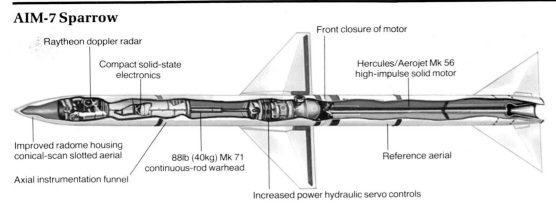

Raytheon doppler radar

Compact solid-state electronics

Improved radome housing conical-scan slotted aerial

Axial instrumentation funnel

Front closure of motor

Hercules/Aerojet Mk 56 high-impulse solid motor

88lb (40kg) Mk 71 continuous-rod warhead

Reference aerial

Increased power hydraulic servo controls

Above: No AAM has ever been developed so well as Sparrow. This AIM-7F/M, the final model in which more compact guidance resulted in a much bigger warhead being carried twice as far.

Below: Taken at 17,600ft (5,364m) at Mach 1.05, this sequence shows the first launch of an AIM-7F Sparrow from an F-16 prototype in November 1977. The photographs were taken 0.6

second apart. The USAF has never announced a plan to equip the F-16 with radar-guided medium-range AAMs, though its capable APG-66 radar could easily be made compatible.

homing AAMs such as Sparrow, the launch of the weapon is merely the start of the firing process. The enemy aircraft must be illuminated by the fighter's radar all the time the AAM is flying towards it, otherwise the missile will have no reflected radiation on which to home. Fighter radars are mounted in the nose, and like the weapons they point forwards. The only way to go on pumping out CW (continuous-wave) illuminating signals is to fly straight for the enemy, or at least to keep him within a 65° cone ahead.

Of course, this is the very last thing a fighter pilot normally wishes to do, unless he has a yearning to indulge in close combat. For a fighter armed with Sparrows, which in the case of the new AIM-7F and -7M have a range of 62 miles (100km), it seems foolish in the extreme to have to keep closing on the enemy all the time the missile is in flight, just to provide an essential guidance function.

The penalties have been self-evident for several years, as a result of carefully analysed evaluations by the USAF and US Navy. Time after time F-14s or F-15s would launch AIM-7 Sparrows at ranges of around 10 miles (16km) — today the range could be greater — and continue to fly towards the Aggressor F-5E while guiding the missile (of course the evaluations were scored electronically, not by using real missiles). Invariably, the austerely equipped F-5E pilot would see the big fighter in the far distance and smartly loose off a close-range Sidewinder, which needs no help once launched. A second or two later the F-5E would be figuratively destroyed by the Sparrow AAM, but a few seconds later still down would go the F-14 or F-15 as well.

There are two answers. One is to put the radar somewhere at the back of the fighter instead of at the front. The CW illuminating capability is usually separate from the main radar, though it often passes the signals through the same mechanically scanned flat-plate or Cassegrain aerial system. It would certainly add a small weight penalty to have a rear-facing CW guidance radar, but since fighters need rearward-facing warning systems the two tasks might be combined in one installation, using different aerial systems. It is not the sort of installation that would degrade performance significantly, and it might look rather like the aft-facing radars on such bombers as the B-52 and Backfire.

As it is problematical that a Sparrow or Sky Flash could be fired rearwards from a fighter, as suggested in a diagram, the answer is to fit a small stable platform, with low-quality parts to keep down cost, to hold the AAM on course while the fighter turns away through some 180°. Thereafter it can fly away from the enemy while providing the essential guidance for its missile(s).

Left: In its first guided launch, in October 1981, AIM-120A Amraam was fired from an F-16. It was a simple tail-on shot against a PQM-102 target, and the second frame shows the AAM's low-smoke motor burning.

Above: Amraam (again shown launched from an F-16A) is a fire-and-forget missile which will make a tremendous difference to the West's air-combat capability, because it does not need the fighter to illuminate the target.

Rearward-facing Radar

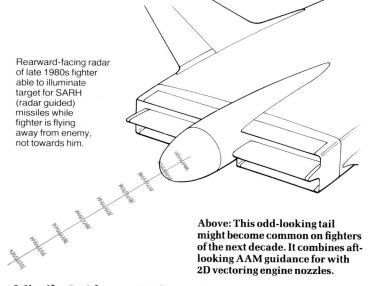

Rearward-facing radar of late 1980s fighter able to illuminate target for SARH (radar guided) missiles while fighter is flying away from enemy, not towards him.

Above: This odd-looking tail might become common on fighters of the next decade. It combines aft-looking AAM guidance for with 2D vectoring engine nozzles.

A far better answer is to replace our radar-guided semi-active missile by one with self-contained guidance, to give a LAL (launch and leave) capability. This is what the USAF is trying to do with Amraam (advanced medium-range AAM), which is to replace Sparrow. Compared with Sparrow the new missile is the same length (146in/3.7m) but has a body diameter of 7in (178mm) compared with 8in (203mm). Weight is thus reduced from some 503lb (228kg) to only 326lb (148kg). Despite this Amraam flies faster, has a useful range of more than 30 miles (48km) and incorporates a totally new guidance system. Once fired it flies

Below: The first firing of BAe Dynamics Sky Flash from a Tornado F.2 prototype, showing the swinging crutch which holds the missile well below the fuselage

by itself, and our F-15, Tornado F.2 or other fighters can at once beat a retreat and live to fight another day. Amraam maintains its course towards the enemy on a strapdown inertial system until, near its target, it activates the small active seeker in its nose. Details of this have not been disclosed but it could be a small radar operating on millimetric wavelengths at some 94GHz (94,000,000,000 cycles per second). Laser scanning could be needed to provide for positive target identification, and of course very clever fuzes will be needed to detonate the ABF warhead as the missile flies at Mach 4 in one direction and the target at Mach 2 in another.

before motor ignition. Sky Flash is much better than Sparrow but is still SARH-guided needing target-illumination until final closure, and detonation of the warhead.

Missile Guidance: Today and Tomorrow(?)

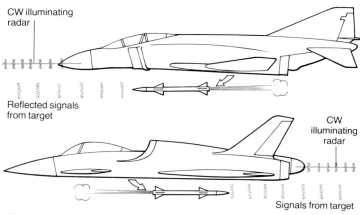

CW illuminating radar

Reflected signals from target

CW illuminating radar

Signals from target

Above: Today's fighter, such as the F-4 Phantom (upper drawing) has to keep flying towards the enemy in order to illuminate it with its nose radar to provide guidance for its SARH-type AAM. The lower drawing shows a better scheme.

With a tail-mounted radar the fighter could fly away from the enemy whilst still guiding its SARH missile. The latter is shown being fired to the rear, though there are severe problems in doing this.

Electronic warfare

The science – some would say black art – of EW today pervades almost every aspect of warfare. It exerts a powerful influence on the design, construction and use of weapons platforms, and this is especially the case with combat aircraft. We have now reached the point where EW governs the whole design of the aircraft, in what are called "stealth techniques". Today it is abundantly clear that an aircraft's EW performance is far more important to its survival in hostile airspace than its speed, height, firepower or even manoeuvrability.

Though this outline is necessarily general, it is of historical interest to recall that in 1944 Britain's RAF was far out in front as world leader in this subject. Backed by research in the TRE (Telecommunications Research Establishment, a cover name) at Malvern, and in industry, a wealth of operative devices reached the squadrons, chiefly of Bomber Command, to confuse and dilute enemy defences, make large bombers inconspicuous while making small aircraft look like large bombers or (by flying carefully prearranged patterns) an invasion fleet moving at 15 knots, warn crews of enemy night fighters, broadcast false messages

or spurious beacon or IFF responses, and generally harness the tame electron to much better effect than the enemy.

It is easy to be too clever. More than 4,500 RAF "heavies" were fitted with the small Monica radar under the tail turret to scan the sky behind and give a warning of approaching night fighters. In the crowded streams of bombers, in which the rules for separation were merely that one should try to avoid collisions, there were so many amber and red warning lights triggered by the Monica reacting to friendly bombers that crews often switched it off. In doing so they probably saved their lives, because the Luftwaffe did the obvious thing and fitted its night fighters with a Flensburg receiver tuned to the exact wavelength of Monica.

On July 13, 1944, the RAF was presented with one of the latest Ju 88G night fighters which landed in England by mistake. On test its Flensburg proved itself able to give brilliantly clear guidance to any selected one of 71 Lancasters orbiting in a tight ring between Cambridge and Gloucester with Monica switched on. Immediately the order went out to leave Monica switched off.

This story is told to emphasize that it is fatally easy to equip a mid-1980s warplane with such clever

Above: When designed (1957-60) the Westinghouse radar of early F-4s was the world's best fighter radar. It uses many vacuum tubes and has a mechanically scanned parabolic dish aerial to reflect the radiation.

Below: Designed over ten years later than the F-4C radar, the F-15's Hughes APG-63 is almost wholly solid-state and contained in modular packages. It has far more diverse operating modes, and a flat-plate aerial.

Fundamental Types of Radar Signal

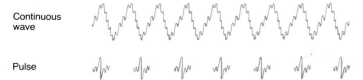

Continuous wave

Pulse

Above: To be useful, radar signals have to be coded, though they need not be modulated like broadcast signals which convey messages. The CW (continuous-wave) signal **is useful in missile guidance because it illuminates the target all the time. Nearly all fighters use pulsed radars, some dopplers which sense target motion.**

Discernible Emissions

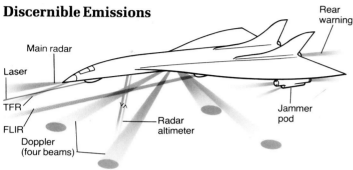

Rear warning

Main radar

Laser

TFR

FLIR

Doppler (four beams)

Radar altimeter

Jammer pod

Above: The height of absurdity would be a carefully designed stealth aircraft which was then outfitted with powerful emitters. Obviously, a stealth aircraft has to be electronically silent throughout each combat mission.

Below: An oblique photograph taken of a US airport, and (bottom of page) a real time vertical image from the F-15's APG-63 radar taken a few moments later, from overhead. Note the scale of tonal values.

radars that it acts as an aerial lighthouse, broadcasting its presence and location to the enemy. There is a true story of a Luftwaffe night-fighter pilot who was sent home from the Eastern Front to fly against the lavishly equipped Lancasters and Halifaxes, and found his task simple by comparison. "The trouble was," he said, "the Russians are so backward they have no radar, and that made our task very difficult."

True to other developments in warfare, every radar is soon followed by an appropriate ECM (electronic countermeasure). In its turn, every ECM is soon followed by the appropriate ECCM (electronic counter-counter-measure). Today it should be possible to modify an existing ECM device to counter a new threat in a matter of hours, unless the new threat incorporates some kind of fundamental advance in technology.

The fact that Israeli aircraft had no ECM effective against the

Soviet-supplied SA-6 SAMs in October 1973 rested on the fact that neither Israel nor its suppliers, chiefly American, had produced ECM for use against CW (continuous-wave) radars. It is difficult to comprehend how this could happen, especially as the USA had for years been exporting the CW Hawk SAM. Had it been merely a matter of changing the wavelength the Israeli squadrons might have done this "in house" on the bases, but to fit ECM with CW jamming is a back-to-the-factory job.

Thus we have already seen that EW is a ding/dong battle which shows no intrinsic favours to either attack or defence. We have also seen that anything which is "active", in other words anything that emits any kind of detectable radiation, automatically signals its presence and possibly its location, speed, course and height. There is little point in building a "stealth" aircraft and then packing it with forward looking radars, doppler radar, terrain-following radar, a radar altimeter, mapping and navigational radar, rear-warning radar and a mass of high-power jammers.

On the other hand there is every reason to equip modern combat aircraft with passive (non-emitting) receivers and analysers

Below: The aircraft is an F-4 Phantom, but the radar is the neat Westinghouse APG-66 developed for the F-16. It weighs only 236lb (107kg) and is aircooled. Larger and more powerful radars require the complexity of liquid cooling.

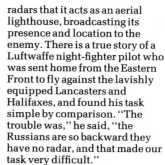

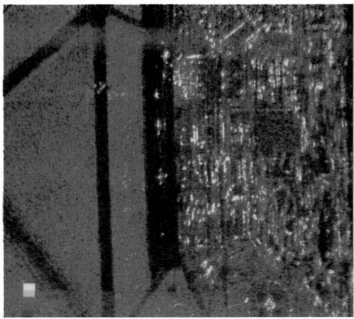

which will unfailingly detect all hostile emissions, record them and subject them to lightning-fast computer processing in order to determine their geographical source and signal characteristics. The characteristics are in effect the unique fingerprint of each emission. Features which would be measured include the basic frequency, operating mode, PRF (pulse repetition frequency), amplitude (the signal strength or height of each pulse above the baseline) and probably the TOA (time of arrival) of each pulse and the DOA (direction of arrival).

With good modern analysis systems it is possible to identify the actual type of radar, radio or other emitter, and possibly to distinguish between one particular radar and another of the same type. The task of finding out all the enemy's emissions is called Elint (electronic intelligence), and it is on this that most of EW is based.

Of course EW is concerned with all emissions, not only with radars but also lasers, IR (infrared) and EO (electro-optical). What has become known as C³ or C-cubed, from the initial letters of command, control and communications, is now just as vital to every military force; another popular acronym is CNI, for communications, navigation and identification. Every fighter has to be subject to C-cubed and properly equipped with CNI. But here we are concerned mainly with what might be called the ECM equipments that fit a fighter for electronic combat. These are of

three basic types: the RWR (radar warning receiver), jammers and expendables.

The RWR is the standard form of Elint device carried by small combat aircraft and able to do the things listed previously. As a passive device it has the priceless advantage of not betraying the presence of the platform which carries it, and though RWRs can vary tremendously in sophistication and price they usually impose only small burdens in weight, drag or electrical power

consumption.

In almost all combat aircraft it is desirable to have all-round cover. The RWR must therefore be supplied with signals sensed by aerials (antennae) which can "see" ahead and behind, to each side, and above and below. Usually there is incomplete coverage, either because of reception being blanked off by parts of the aircraft or because there are insufficient aerials.

There are invariably at least two aerials, frequently four and

Above: All versions of Tornado have neat and accessible radars. This is the attack radar, by TI, with an oval main forward-looking scanner housed inside the radome with the smaller terrain-following radar below.

Below: The Hughes APG-65 radar of the McDonnell Douglas F/A-18A Hornet is pulled out forwards on rails after its radome has been swung open through 180°. No TFR is fitted to this aircraft, which will probably do little terrain following.

Above: Taken during an air-to-ground rocket attack, this photograph shows the Harrier GR.3 RWR mounted at the tail.

Below: Details of the EW receivers pictured on this page. 1, the RWR of the RAF Harrier is served by two similar aerials facing to front and rear. 2, a typical pod-type EW receiver, such as is seen on the MiG-23 or Viggen. 3, inside such a pod will usually be found a helical spiral aerial wound on a cone of insulating material.

EW Receivers

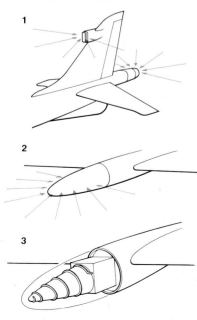

occasionally more. One of the commonest aerial forms, especially for looking sideways, is the flat spiral, a metal foil spiral element being mounted on a dielectric (insulating) disc backed by a cavity and bolted in place flush with the skin of the aircraft, typically in the fin but occasionally in a tip pod or, in helicopters, in the fuselage. The usual alternative form is the Archimedean spiral, in which a spiral element is coiled and pressed and angled into the surface of a dielectric cone, which is mounted in the aircraft to face to the front or rear – typically near the top of the fin or on the wings – and faired inside a streamlined radome.

Each RWR aerial is linked via its own pre-amplifier and interface unit to a central receiver and processor. Until the late 1970s analog systems were common, but today digital technology is universal for RWRs, just as it is for almost all other avionic systems. Early analog RWRs gave a warning red flashing light in the cockpit, an audible alarm, and usually some indication of where the threat was located. For example the ARI.18223 used in the RAF Harrier and Jaguar merely illuminates a 90° segment of a circular display to show the quadrant containing the greatest threat. The generally similar 18228 used in the Buccaneer and RAF Phantom has a small CRT (cathode ray tube) display for the backseater who can see radial lines giving the accurate directions of several threats.

Modern digital RWRs have much greater capability. Their crystal video or superheterodyne receivers are tuned to operate in groups covering all usable frequency bands. The Itek ALR-45, for example, fitted to many US Navy aircraft, provides complete coverage from 2 to 14GHz, while the USAF's new ALR-46 goes up to 18GHz. Crystal video receivers are still the preferred type, despite their rather low sensitivity, because they are basically simple and compact.

Above: All modern Soviet combat aircraft are fully equipped with passive and active EW systems. The MiG-23 family usually (but not always) have two RWR receiver pods on the wing leading edge to give coverage of the forward hemisphere.

Below: An AJ37 Viggen of Swedish attack wing F15 showing the RWR receiver pod on the wing leading edge. Such an installation has a spin-off advantage in that it generates an enhanced vortex.

Whereas old analog RWRs were "hardwired", modern installations are highly variable and controlled by a digital processor with a quickly reprogrammable threat library (stored details of all known enemy emitters likely to be encountered). As well as accurate DF (direction finding) the display includes alphanumeric readout showing the class and even specific type of emitter, and further information showing when there are several overlapping threats.

When any aircraft flies over a populated country it is bound to fly through what used to be called the radio "ether", which is densely populated with electromagnetic emissions of all kinds. In an attack mission our fighter is bound to pass through numerous kinds of radar emissions, and it would be a pointless distraction to warn the pilot every time this happened, because he could not take any useful action. The RWR has to ignore all non-threat emissions,

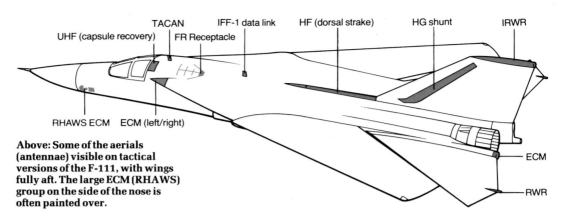

Above: Some of the aerials (antennae) visible on tactical versions of the F-111, with wings fully aft. The large ECM (RHAWS) group on the side of the nose is often painted over.

and react instantly to one that poses a perceived threat.

Such an emission would be a hostile radar locked-on to the fighter in the tracking mode. Typically an RWR is arranged to warn that a track has been established whenever a high PRF (pulse repetition frequence) (say,

1,000 per second) is sustained for a preselected period, which may be from 0.5 seconds up to several seconds. This demonstrates the unpalatable fact that the enemy not only knows we are coming but has locked-on to our own aircraft. From then on our own EW systems work at full power.

One factor that greatly complicates both attack and defence is that in the real world neither the atmosphere nor the man-made sensors behave exactly according to the textbook. At any time the only way to find out exactly how a given radar or other emitter actually radiates through a large volume of sky is to take precise measurements. The results will be found to vary slightly from one radar and another of the same type. More important, they will vary from day to day, and hour to hour, and occasionally the emission is so grossly distorted that anaprop (anomlous propagation) is said to be taking place. A diagram shows how anaprop can result in excellent coverage by ground radars at extremely low levels close to the Earth's surface, while an upper layer (around 450ft/137m is shown, but it could be at over 1,000ft/304m) becomes almost impervious to the signals and thus provides a kind of corridor for attacking aircraft. Ferranti is one company busy with IMP (indication of microwave propagation) devices which could help pilots select the best height at which to remain undetected.

Not many warning receivers are in use at near-optical wavelengths, but the Soviet FA and the USAF use several types of IRWR (infrared warning receiver), principally to warn of missile launches. The USAF F-111 force have long used the ALR-23 or -34, and these are now being replaced by the AAR-44, the specification for which demanded the ability to keep searching the entire hemisphere below the aircraft while simultaneously verifying any SAM launch and tracking the missile subsequently. The system has to handle threats from massed SAM firings, and also discriminate missiles against such possible false sources as reflected sunlight or IRCM (IR countermeasures) launched by the F-111 itself or accompanying friendly aircraft.

An accompanying illustration shows a typical RWR installation for a large and highly priced fighter, the F-15. The Loral ALR-56 has two circularly polarized spiral aerials facing aft behind the tips of the fins and two larger ones facing forward from the wingtips, to provide 360° coverage of high-band signals, as well as a blade

Attacking "Under the Radar" (Ideal)

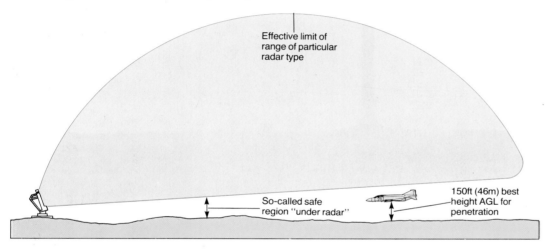

Above: In an ideal world a hostile surveillance radar used for air-defence purposes would be unable to obtain clear returns from hostile aircraft below an angle of several degrees above the horizon (ignoring the curvature of the Earth). This is because of interference between the main beam and its side lobes and the **Earth's surface (which reflects radar signals). Thus our F-4 is safe at 500ft (152m), but would be visible to the radar at all heights above this.**

Attacking "Under the Radar" (Real)

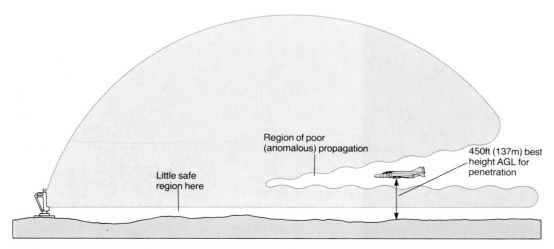

Above: The assumptions of the defence planners are often invalidated because real phenomena are very complex. Any actual radar will give a more complicated pattern of coverage than the ideal one, and it will vary from hour to hour because of changes in the atmosphere. Anomalous propagation (anaprop) **can result in important gaps in the coverage. Sensors able to give warning of anaprop conditions would make it possible for our F-4 to be safe at higher level.**

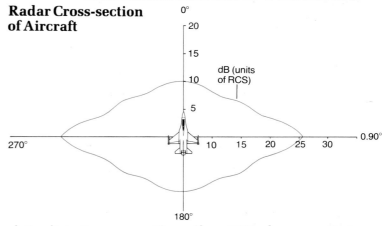

Radar Cross-section of Aircraft

Above: Complementing the diagram on the facing page, this photograph shows the IRWR (in this case an ALE-23) fitted at the top of the fin of an F-111A, as well as the RHAWS and ECM aft-facing aerials each side of the jet nozzles.

Below: The F-15 was particularly well equipped from the start, one of the more visible installations being the Loral ALR-56 RWR system with aft-facing aerials (1), forward-facing aerials (2) and a blade (3) covering the underside.

aerial under the forward fuselage for coverage of low-band signals in the hemisphere below the aircraft. Use of YIG (yttrium indium garnet) RF tuning gives extreme accuracy, and the fast processor has a reprogrammable threat store and carries out self-calibration, tuning, threat analysis and classification. Thus the pilot can almost instantly be presented with a threat's characteristics (and identify it if it is a known type), as well as bearing and distance, readable in bright sunlight and with pilot-selectable

clutter-elimination programs. The whole aircraft installation weighs 138lb (63kg).

Software control is especially necessary for fighters which, like the F-15, have considerable ECM capability. The RWR has to function correctly in the presence of the fighter's own jamming; it would be ludicrous, for example, if it were to warn the pilot of very powerful radar signals which were coming from the aircraft itself. If possible an RWR should be able to go on studying the threat to see

Above: RCS (radar cross-section) obviously varies depending on the aspect, just as a fighter looks bigger from directly below than from astern. This is a plot of RCS variation in the horizontal plane; it looks biggest from the sides.

how it reacts to attempts at jamming.

The second part of the fighter EW capability is its jammer(s). The simplest type of jammer is chaff, but this is an expendable and discussed later. Next comes the

barrage jammer which in a "brute force and ignorance" technique simply tries to fill the sky with RF power and thus blanket the hostile radar screen(s) so that they cannot indicate discrete targets such as our own aircraft.

But though this was a practicable goal in 1944 it is hardly possible today. For one thing a fighter cannot hope to match the radiated power of a giant ground-based radar. For another, the sheer diversity of frequencies usable by modern high-power radars is astronomic, the number of pulses per second easily exceeding 250,000 at carrier frequencies of perhaps 20GHz (20 thousand million cycles per second).

In any practical fighter the jamming has to be carefully organized to have maximum effect for minimum consumption of power. The USAF, and to a lesser degree the Soviet Air Force, has favoured high-power jammers contained in external pods which consume large amounts of power and need a great deal of cooling. Early jammers relied upon cavity magnetrons to generate the microwave power needed.

By far the most important source of microwave power in modern jammers is the TWT (travelling-wave tube), which unlike the magnetron is an axial (linear) device in which energy is passed to a beam of microwaves from a beam

of electrons travelling with it. This can send out energy at extremely high power – hundreds of times higher than from a domestic microwave cooker, and extremely dangerous to humans if they let the beam fall on them.

We have used the word beam, but in fact most jammers are crude devices which radiate to many points of the compass, all the time they are switched on. Thus perhaps 99.9 per cent of the power is wasted. We need a good RWR and computer to provide what is called power management. Ideally we want to concentrate all our jamming effort on the right frequencies, sent out in just the right direction, and only at the right times.

In every case the microwave energy is ducted along waveguides to one or more aerials which are usually of the tapered or exponential horn type rather like an old-fashioned gramophone. Most airborne jammers radiate from front and rear, or ahead only, but some can emit in any other desired pattern. Electrical power can be drawn from the basic aircraft system, but really high-power jamming is best done with a self-contained pod with a windmill turbogenerator. Cooling may be by ram air, but usually

involves a refrigeration circuit, typically filled with Freon like most domestic refrigerators.

Barrage jamming may be the crudest kind but it still needs careful management if effective radiated power (ERP) is to be more than a very small fraction of the electric power input. The problems are that the thing we are trying to jam is a particular hostile device, at a particular location, emitting over a discrete spread of frequencies and in all probability hopping thousands of times a second from one frequency to another. We cannot expect to have high efficiency if we pump out barrage jamming to all points of the compass and covering the entire

The EW Suite for a Modern Fighter

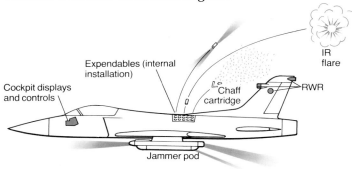

Above: Aircraft that operate in the presence of enemies must either be of stealth design, and stay silent, or try to protect themselves with active jammers and dispensed "expendables", as suggested here.

Below: Northrop packages the ALQ-171(V) into a pod which can be hung below any aircraft instead of being tailored to just one type. Here the first mock-up pod is being fitted to an F-4 at Eglin AFB.

A Typical ECM Pod

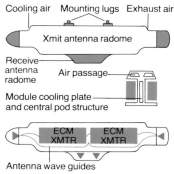

Above: Basic arrangement of an ECM pod such as the ALQ-131. It is air-cooled with heat drawn off by a central aluminium plate. (XMTR means transmitter). Waveguides are precision-made metal ducts.

Below: Northrop's ALQ-171(V) is a CCS (conformal counter-measures system) installations fitting snugly against the outer skin of the aircraft. This F-5E also carries a drop tank below it.

spread of frequencies over which the threat is known to operate.

The deeper one goes into jamming the more one becomes immersed in advanced technology, and with scores of acronyms and abbreviations, but the important fact is that we have to be clever and make every bit of radiated energy count.

Virtually all modern jammers can operate in different modes, such as pulse, CW, noise, transponder and repeater. Noise is the least efficient mode, also called barrage jamming. Transponder and repeater modes trigger the hammer by the incoming hostile signal, and though it is never quite possible to match the hostile frequency pulse

for pulse, it is possible to be quite clever in degrading the value of the equipment to the enemy.

Every time a pulse, or wave, of RF energy reaches our aircraft it will send back some of its energy to the enemy in what is called a "skin paint" or "skin return", and we can do nothing about this, unless stealth technology succeeds in making us invisible at microwave wavelengths. So what we have to do is either send back a lot of closely related signals that will smother our skin return, or send back something that looks like a skin return but is not quite accurate.

Without going too far into the techniques, the most common is

probably RGPO (range-gate pull-off), or range-gate stealing. Like all other forms of DECM (deception ECM) it is an attempt to take over the AGC (automatic gain control) of the enemy radar, and it does so by using a transponder (transmitter responder) which, each time it is triggered by a pulse from the enemy radar, sends back a "reflected" pulse much larger in amplitude than the natural skin return from our aircraft. The transponder is programmed to inject a very small time delay every time it sends back a pulse, so instead of seeing a small skin return the enemy sees a large pulse which moves slowly away from our true position. Usually the false

position is astern of our aircraft, though this is not always the case.

Thus, even though we may have been unable to break the lock of the radar tracking our aircraft, we have injected a range deception or miss-distance. This suffices to render radar-predicted AAA (triple A, anti-aircraft artillery) or radar guided SAMs or AAMs inaccurate enough to be harmless.

Another DECM technique is repeater jamming, usually of the inverse-gain type. The fighter's jammer re-transmits hostile pulses with power inversely proportional to the received pulse. Strong incoming signals are sent back as very weak ones, and vice versa. This causes angular inaccuracies

A European ECM Jammer Pod

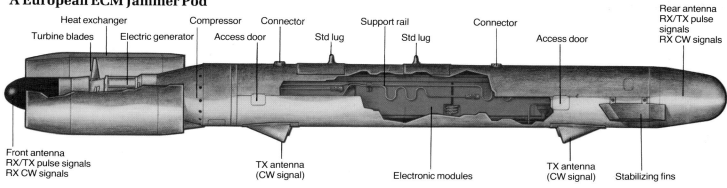

Heat exchanger · Turbine blades · Electric generator · Compressor · Access door · Connector · Std lug · Support rail · Std lug · Connector · Access door · Rear antenna RX/TX pulse signals RX CW signals

Front antenna RX/TX pulse signals RX CW signals · TX antenna (CW signal) · Electronic modules · TX antenna (CW signal) · Stabilizing fins

Above: Pods by the Italian firm of Elettronica SpA are energized by a front windmill in a duct (like a turbofan in reverse). RX means receive, TX transmit. Standard lugs (STD LUG) fit the pylon.

Below: A simpler-looking pod is the French Thomson-CSF DB3163 (hung next to gun pod on Mirage F1). It has aerials at front and rear, bootstrap cooling from a ram inlet in the pylon and no windmill.

Below: Another Italian pod, the ALQ-234 by Selenia SpA, is for self-defence of supersonic aircraft (though here it is hung on a subsonic Alpha Jet). It needs no air inlet because it has liquid cooling.

Bottom: Among the very first active jammer pods were a series of QRC-335 (this is a 335-3, hung on an F-4) by Westinghouse in 1966-68. From these were derived the ALQ-101 and -119.

in the azimuth (direction) and elevation (apparent height) of the target as seen by the enemy radar.

There are several other kinds of DECM, some extremely clever and most of them highly classified. ECCM in the enemy radars aims to defeat such techniques, but in turn the ECCM features can sometimes be turned to the attacker's advantage. There is no apparent end to the see-saw battle of the electrons.

The third kind of EW payload comes under the general heading of "expendables". The very first type of ECM to be used was the first of this category, and it is still more widely used than all other expendables and all the jammer pods put together. It was invented by Dr Downing of TRE in late 1940, but the RAF did not dare use it for fear that the Luftwaffe would follow suit! In May 1943 the Japanese suddenly invented it and put it to use at once, but the Americans did not inform Britain, so the RAF held off until July 24, 1943, at the start of the great Battle of Hamburg. They called it "Window", the Japanese "Giman-shi", and the Germans "Düppel", but the name that stuck was the American one, "chaff".

As metal reflects radar energy, it is possible to fill the sky with the most diffuse and dispersed metal that can be constructed and produce such a cloud that anything inside or beyond it will be invisible to enemy radars. Early chaff was made of aluminium foil, often

Above: Elettronica EL/73 (ECM jammer pod) on left wingtip and Philips BOZ 100 (dispenser) on right, of a Tornado with four Kormoran and two Sidewinder missiles.

backed by paper, but today it is usually extremely thin Mylar film or fine glass fibres metallized on the surface with aluminium or zinc.

For maximum effectiveness chaff is made in the form of extremely small hair-like strips with a length equal to the wavelength of the hostile emitter, or to an exact multiple of it. Each strip, which may be no longer than one of the words on this page but is usually rather longer, acts as a miniature dipole (two-ended rod) aerial, efficiently reflecting radiation of a particular wavelength.

Early chaff was packed in bundles which a bomber crew had to unwrap and then drop through a chute. Modern chaff for fighters is prepackaged into neat drums of standardized size. Bomber chaff, and that from some top-rank interdictors, is stored in the form of hundreds of miles of continuous strip called roving which, upon crew command or when triggered by the RWR, is automatically chopped into lengths matched to the wavelength of the perceived threat, immediately before being fed overboard. A typical bulk dispenser for a large attack aircraft can chop up chaff at the rate of 10,000,000 dipole-inches per second, which clearly can form a large cloud very quickly.

Above: The Swedish Viggen is well equipped with all-Swedish defensive electronics including an SATT AQ-31 deception jammer (right wing) and a Philips BOX 9 (Swedish AF version of BOZ 100) dispenser (left wing).

Below: The BOC cockpit control unit for another Philips airborne ECM system, the BO 300. It provides a digital computer interface, and also indicates the number remaining of each kind of dispensed expendable.

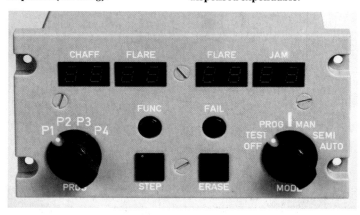

Rapid-bloom Chaff (RBC)

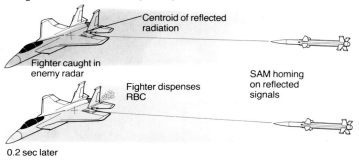

Centroid of reflected radiation

Fighter caught in enemy radar

SAM homing on reflected signals

Fighter dispenses RBC

0.2 sec later

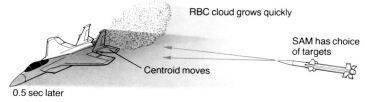

RBC cloud grows quickly

SAM has choice of targets

Centroid moves

0.5 sec later

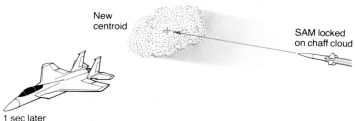

New centroid

SAM locked on chaff cloud

1 sec later

Above: Highly stylized and greatly simplified, this indicates the way in which a combat aircraft can put a radar homing missile off the scent by using rapid-bloom chaff. The missile has no real inbuilt intelligence and merely homes on the centroid of the biggest and best radar reflective target within its range of vision. A sudden cloud of RBC can make it "break lock" and home on what looks a better target.

Various chaff installations were investigated for the RAF Harriers as early as 1967, but, as nothing was actually done about it, Harriers in the South Atlantic in 1982 went to war with bundles of unwrapped chaff either jammed between the bombs and their pylon ejector-racks or pinched between the airbrake and the fuselage, from where they were released by a brief selection of airbrake!

Other air forces have properly designed installations, and by far the commonest for small combat aircraft are the dispensers. Each drum forms a cartridge, typically of 40mm diameter but variously of 74mm, 55, 42, 30 or 25mm, or square and measuring 23mm along each side – about the size of a large Crunchie bar. A small charge can pop the dispensed payload out whilst automatically opening it or breaking up the case. Usually we do not want a small dense blob of chaff but a large cloud, because what we are trying to do is to create a reflective cloud that has an RCS (radar cross-section) larger than that of our own aircraft. So RBC (rapid-bloom chaff) is selling around the world like hot cakes, all guaranteed to exceed an attack-aircraft RCS within two seconds, and sometimes within one second.

Chaff can be dispensed on command by the pilot or another crewman, or automatically by the EW suite, the dispenser being programmed to give any chosen arrangement. For example, the common Lundy ALE-44 supersonic-compatible dispenser can release 1 or 2 payloads per burst, either 1, 2, 4, 8 or continuous bursts per programme and at the rate of ½, 1, 2 or 4 bursts per second.

Of course, having designed a standardized dispenser, the payloads need not be just chaff. They could be IRCM (IR countermeasures), aerosols, smoke or even active jammers. IRCM take the form of expendable flares, or alternatively large pods resembling oddly shaped drop

Above: The Goodyear ALE-39 dispenser system is used by all combat aircraft of the US Navy and Marine Corps. The two dispensers can fire up to 60 of various payloads, a chaff, flare and jammer cartridge being shown separately in front of the cockpit control unit. The white chaff cartridge is sized to E/G/I bands.

Below: A French Alkan (countermeasures dispenser with two magazines of 40mm chaff cartridges and two filled with large 74mm flare cartridges (IRCM).

Above: SEPECAT Jaguars of France's Armée de l'Air are fitted with this Alkan type 5020 conformal dispenser under each wing root. It fires up to 56 payloads each of the 40mm calibre, most usually being chaff cartridges.

Below: One of Britain's few products in this field is the new Wallop Industries Masquerade system, which neatly packages chaff and IR flare cartridges into a standard CBLS (container bomb light store) type 200.

tanks, which remain with the aircraft.

In either case the objective is to create an IR (heat) source stronger than that of the aircraft. Typical 40mm flares have an output of 15kW in the 3.5 micron wavelength range, burning for about three seconds. Such expendables were on the world's TV screens during the Israeli bombing of West Beirut in the summer of 1982.

The short effective life of such flares can be overcome by using a non-expendable IRCM, such as the ALQ-147 which burns JP fuel in a blast of ram air to heat a ceramic IR source whose radiation is then mechanically modulated so that, while it cannot be seen visually, even at night, it will transfer the IR seeker head of an AAM or a SAM from the aircraft to the flare.

Clearly the spurious or decoy IR source must have stronger radiation than the aircraft. If dispensed it must be fired in such a direction that, when the flare burns out or has been struck by the missile, the latter is no longer in a position to re-acquire the aircraft. Typically flare payloads are fired downwards at about 90ft (27m) per second. Most dispensed flares have one or more pellets of magnesium metal plus tetrafluoroethylene, which give a bright flame at 2,200K.

The third common expendable payload is the jammer. As these are obviously much more complex

index and a size resonant to the threat wavelength. Relatively diffuse clouds of such materials as smoke from white phosphorus or the proprietary aerosol produced by MB Associates can produce virtually total obscuration of otherwise clearly visible targets.

Methods depend on whether we are trying to protect aircraft in flight or parked on the airfield. In the former case the need is for precursor EW aircraft flying ahead of the main attacking force to "seed" the sky with trails which obscure the attackers. While doing so they would also dispense chaff.

One subject not yet touched on is the use of dedicated EW aircraft. Loosely the word dedicated means that the hardware item is assigned to that purpose only; for example, if we are talking about a radar and say that it has a dedicated computer, we mean that the computer controls that particular radar and nothing else. Likewise, some RAF Jaguars are dedicated

and expensive than chaff or flare payloads they are used in smaller numbers, but they can fit the same dispensers. The jammer is not a chaff pod but a compact active transmitter, usually pretuned and preprogrammed. Its role is to jam the hostile emitters with high power during the brief period, typically less than 30 seconds, that it takes for the payload to fall to the ground. In some aircraft installations the operating time is extended by initially firing all dispensed payloads upwards. The F-14, for example, fires upwards from above the extreme tail between the engine afterburners.

Though they are not yet widely used, aerosols are also of great interest to fighter designers, because they are the most effective countermeasures to systems operating at visual or near-visual wavelengths, which are rapidly growing in importance as defence systems. A carbon dioxide superpower laser was used as far back as November 1976 as a weapon in its own right to bring down a high-speed RPV at White Sands Missile Range, New Mexico. Lasers will also be increasingly important in warfare outside the atmosphere, but already they play a major role in SAM guidance and numerous precision designation and ranging devices.

TV is at least as important in identification and tracking of surface-to-air systems, and there are other wavelengths which are becoming of interest. All are extremely important in attacking airfields. Defeating these calls for anything that will effectively scatter and break up EM radiation near visual wavelengths, even an intense collimated (parallel) beam of coherent light from a megawatt-range laser.

We are almost back to the era of the searchlight, because the threat is not dissimilar. A plain smokescreen is one answer, and the cheapest way of generating smoke is to inject main-engine fuel into the jetpipe (not in afterburner, because then it would merely burn). This is crude, but simple and operationally attractive.

More effective are tailored aerosols selected because their particles have high refractive

Above: Wearing the tail stripe of the USAF Aeronautical Systems Division, this NKC-135A was rebuilt three times as a high-energy laser laboratory for the AF Weapons Lab at Kirtland AFB.

Below: Picture of EA-6B taken by the ECMO (ECM Officer) in right front seat of another EA-6B. He is responsible for communications, navigation, defensive ECM and chaff dispensing.

reconnaissance aircraft (No II Sqn), though in this case they could be used for attack missions if the need arose. But a dedicated EW aircraft is usually so completely given over to electronics that it could not carry any weapons.

As noted earlier, in 1944 the RAF led the world in airborne EW, and deployed more than 250 dedicated EW platforms of such diverse types as the Halifax, Fortress, Liberator, Wellington, Anson, Mosquito and Defiant. Today it does not have a single aircraft in this category, though the USAF and US Navy have regarded such platforms as important since 1952 and today use such specially designed aircraft as the Navy EA-6B Prowler and Air Force EF-111A "Electric Fox". Both contain the large ALQ-99, which was the first really capable computer-controlled SNJ (smart noise jammer) able to match its emissions accurately to the particular perceived threats. Both aircraft sense threat emissions

EF-111A Fin Pod

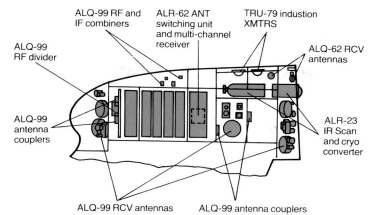

to all points of the compass and feed information on hostile RF threats into the ALQ-99E system. In addition the ALR-23 has a cryogenic (refrigerated) seeker cell which detects IR threats.

Above: The fin pod carried by the USAF EF-111A is the most capable EW receiver group ever devised. It weighs 953lb (432kg) and contains 583lb (264.4kg) of electronics. The spiral disc RF receiver aerials face

with a battery of passive receiver aerials at the top of the fin, and these have to be clever enough to ignore the far more powerful (because much closer) radiations from the aircraft itself, even though these try to match the hostile signals as closely as possible.

There are significant differences between these two vitally important aircraft which extend to the missions. Dedicated EW aircraft are needed to defeat the enemy's anti-aircraft electronic and related emissions, and one basic role is the SOJ (stand-off jammer), which pumps out ECM power from a range of around 62 miles (100km). Thus, while it keeps as far as possible out of harm's way, it can still monitor the enemy threats and do its best to nullify them, especially during an attack by friendly aircraft that must penetrate hostile airspace or during operations by enemy radar-equipped aircraft. This is called the EW support mission, and it is

Left: At one time 66-049, one of the EF-111A development aircraft, was painted in this non-standard colour scheme. This view shows the ALQ-99E canoe radar under the belly, serving the large ECM jammer group installed in the former weapons bay.

Below: Serving with the 388th EWS (Electronic Warfare Squadron), USAF, this EF-111A is pictured from an angle that emphasizes the fin pod, and especially the ALR-23 IR scanner.

one that only a dedicated platform can perform. Another is the EW escort mission, and here the EW aircraft flies with, or usually just ahead of, the attackers. Thus it needs self-protection ECM as well as chaff, jamming, flares and other activities designed to protect the attackers. To fly the escort mission demands the same kind of speed and terrain-following capability as the attack aircraft.

While the EA-6B has no difficulty escorting bomb-laden A-6E Intruders, the escort of supersonic aircraft following the terrain to a land target would be quite beyond it. The EF-111A, however, is roughly as fast as any other F-111 at low level, and as it has no external payload may be a good deal faster. It has the same APQ-110 TFR (terrain-following

radar), and so can fly escort with no fundamental difficulties. As it is several years newer in concept it requires less manual ECM management than does the EA-6B, and thus has a crew of only two, the pilot on the left and the EWO (electronic-warfare officer) on the right. All known threat emissions likely to be important on any mission are preprogrammed into the ALQ-99 software, leaving the electronic-warfare officer only with the task of general supervision and occasional response to a previously unknown or unexpected threat.

In the Soviet Union various types of Yak-28 have been the most favoured aircraft for use as dedicated EW platforms since 1969, though several later FA (Frontal Aviation) types have been

The AI Radar Jamming Role

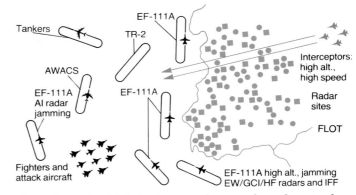

Above: One of the chief roles for which the EF-111A has been designed is the standoff jamming of the AI radars in hostile interceptors. The EF-111A would play a preplanned racetrack pattern at a height where it would have a perfect view of all oncoming enemy aircraft. But it could still be shot down by SAMs.

The EF-111A Close-in Role

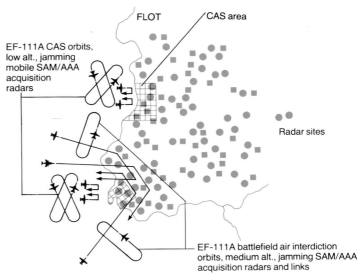

Above: One of the most important types of mission for the EF-111A would be flying orbits only just behind the FLOT (forward line of troops, ie front line). CAS (close air support) orbits are flown at low level to jam mobile SAM and AAA radars. BAI (battlefield air interdiction) orbits are at medium altitude and jam all air defence.

Above: The R/H half of the EF-111A cockpit, almost entirely different from that of ordinary F-111s providing a large digital display and full jamming controls.

Below: A jammed radar display is so covered with bright spots that even a skilled radar operator finds it virtually impossible to extract any information from it.

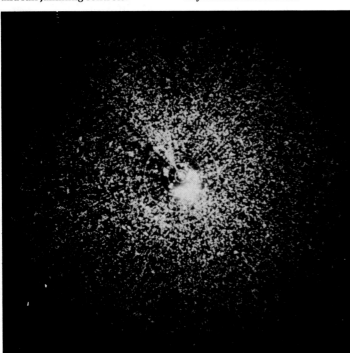

The Penetration Escort Role

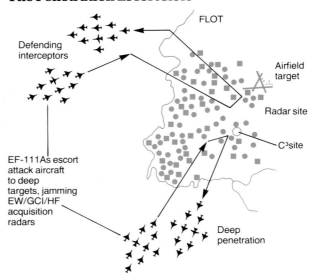

Above: The EF-111A could accompany low-level high-speed attack aircraft on missions deep into hostile territory. A single "Electric Fox" could protect a large friendly force by jamming enemy acquisition and surveillance radars, heightfinders, GCI stations and communications.

Above: Known as Coot-A to NATO, this rebuilt Ilyushin Il-18 transport is one of the world's largest dedicated EW aircraft. Some of these serve a jamming function but most are believed to be equipped for the Elint (electronic intelligence) role, with the ability to record and analyse all kinds of signals.

at least evaluated, and the big Tu-16 Badger serves in several different forms for EW support in the strategic and maritime roles. Other dedicated EW platforms include versions of the An-12 and Il-18, used for Elint and stand-off jamming.

Most of the world's air forces have no EW aircraft, and the fact that the RAF is in this situation can hardly be due solely to financial stringency. A few Canberras have been used to train aircrew in ECM techniques, and others have served as "silent targets" with a block of concrete replacing the radar, but this is not quite as useful as an ALQ-99. It is to be hoped no Buccaneer replaced by a Tornado will be scrapped, when it could probably fly at least a further 2,000 hours without fatigue problems,

because it could be turned into an excellent EW platform and fill a dangerous gap in the RAF's order of battle.

We have left until last one of the easier areas of EW to understand; this is the debate over whether EW installations should be built inside the aircraft or hung externally. At first glance it seems obvious that they should be internal. This reduces drag and probably reduces the likelihood of these rather delicate devices from suffering damage. Moreover, external installation probably means that a stores pylon has to be removed from the list of those available for weapons, and as some aircraft only have two pylons this could knock 50 per cent off the mission load. Yet the world's first really well designed EW platform, the EA-6B, carries all its enormous jamming installations on up to five external pylons, so clearly there are two sides to this particular coin.

Previously we noted that the ideal protection for a fighter or attack aircraft would not be limited in angular coverage. Both the RWR or RHAWS and the active ECM should be able to "look" through 360° in azimuth and also as far as possible above and below. Though the area of most interest to an attacking aircraft is the segment ahead, within perhaps 20° to left and right of the future track, and looking slightly downwards, it is unwise to dismiss any direction as being unworthy of interest. In practice, of course, all-round spherical coverage is not capable of being attained except at unreasonable cost.

Indeed, straightforward problems with money are at the back of most of the world's air forces' poor showing in the matter of EW. The usual situation is that the air force has heard about EW, but finds it quite difficult enough to buy fuel and spare parts without worrying about items which,

A Jamming "Corridor"

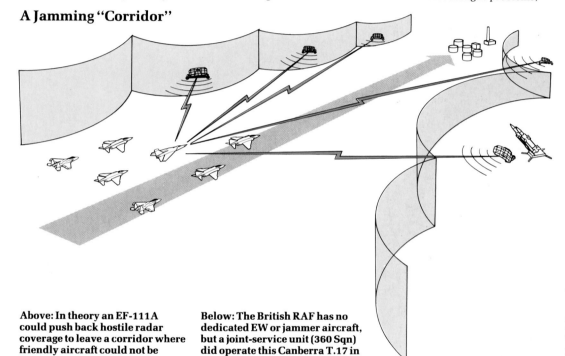

Above: In theory an EF-111A could push back hostile radar coverage to leave a corridor where friendly aircraft could not be detected.

Below: The British RAF has no dedicated EW or jammer aircraft, but a joint-service unit (360 Sqn) did operate this Canberra T.17 in the EW/ECM crew training role.

rightly or wrongly, come lower down the list of priorities. EW training and procurement has been discussed by air staffs all over the world, but the best that can be done in most countries is to send one or two officers on a course and possibly buy one or two secondhand ECM pods.

Thus sheer price to a large extent determines the answers to such questions as where the EW capability is installed. Most of today's fighters and attack aircraft were not designed with any internal EW kit, so they will stay that way. The simplest answer is to buy what seems to be the least-expensive RWR, and if possible get it installed by one's own air force, and an off-the-shelf type of jammer pod which, increasingly, is the type of hardware coming on to the secondhand market.

There are in fact three ways of installing jammers: internal, conformal and pod. Conformal is half-way between the others, in that it is essentially a pod configured to fit flush against the skin, usually of the fuselage. The

advantages are that it is much easier to instal as a modification than an internal jammer, yet does not occupy a pylon and offers less aerodynamic drag than a pod. A possible drawback is that a conformal item may be so tailored to one type of aircraft that it cannot be fitted on a different type, and in any case it demands internal modification in installing electric supplies, probably a cooling system and attachment lugs, which, together with the

installation design, may be quite expensive.

Obviously some fighters are so crowded internally that there is no room for an internal installation unless, as in Soviet aircraft, provision was designed in at the outset. The RAF and USAF have been trying to arrive at meaningful figures for the available internal volume in many of their fighter and attack aircraft, and it is a very difficult task. Many small compartments cannot

conveniently be used, others are too hot or suffer vibration, while other spaces may be competed for by additional sensors, interface units, a GPS Navstar receiver and controlled-direction aerial, a data-link to a Sentry or Nimrod AEW 3, and many other items which the service hopes to introduce. Usually the overall answer is that there is insufficient room for an internal ECM suite – the word suite usually means the whole shooting-match, including the RWR and

ECM Pod Installations

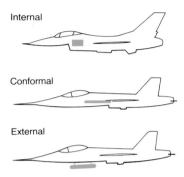

Internal

Conformal

External

Conformal Pallet ECM

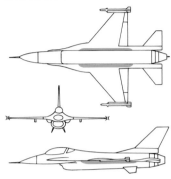

Internal Installation

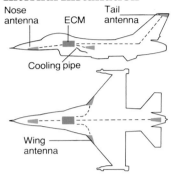

Nose antenna   ECM   Tail antenna

Cooling pipe

Wing antenna

Below: Pending the availability of the ALQ-165 (ASPJ) the most important jammer pod in the USAF is the Westinghouse ALQ-131(V), seen here hung on a Phantom. It is a modular dual-mode (noise/deception) pod with its own internal digital computer. See drawings on page 54.

Above: ECM jammer pods, and similar EW installations, can be mounted internally if the aircraft is thus designed. Conformal installations are outside, but tailored to fit closely on the aircraft skin. The ordinary external pod is simple but takes up a pylon and adds drag.

Above: Aircraft not designed to house internal countermeasures are increasingly appearing with conformal pallets. An example is the French Jaguar (page 57). The F-16 shown here has been studied with various conformal systems, but may eventually find room for the ALQ-165 internally.

Above: A typical internal ECM installation might have the liquid-cooled jammer connected by long waveguides (which lose power and add system delays) to aerials (antennae) facing in all directions. Internal installations are costly, but they do not use pylons and cause virtually no drag.

Internal ECM Spatial Coverage

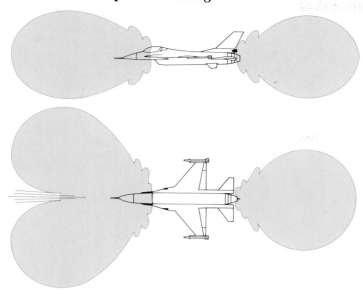

Conformal Pallet Spatial Coverage

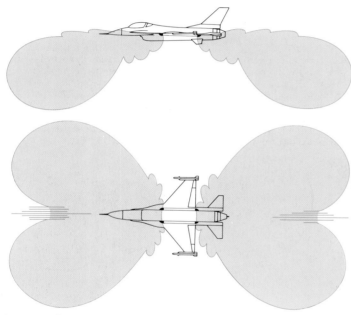

External Pod Spatial Coverage

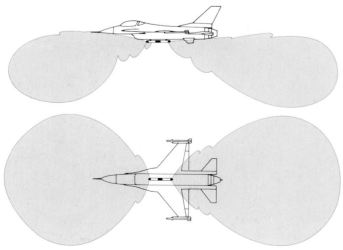

Above: The protection given by an ECM jammer system depends to some extent on the kind of installation. Though an F-16 is shown, the results are not specifically meant to refer to that aircraft. Note that the internal installation (top) has wing-root strake aerials facing forward and a rear-facing aerial just above the jet nozzle. In the examples shown, this is the only installation giving protection above the horizontal plane through the aircraft.

cockpit displays – though on more than one occasion this belief has been overturned by industry succeeding in miniaturizing the size of its ECM.

In general it is possible to miniaturize electronics, but not high-power equipment. If you are dealing in megawatts you need lots of electric power, large cables and high-capacity cooling systems. To generate the power you can uprate the main alternators or DC generators driven by the engine(s); on the EF-111A, for example, each engine drives a 90-kVA alternator compared with a 60-kVA on regular attack F-111s. The Freon cooling circuits have roughly the same capacity as the glycol radiators on a wartime Spitfire. This kind of hardware is hard to miniaturize.

In any case internal installation demands a lot of wiring, usually to the outlying parts of the aircraft where the devices can "see" clearly without masking or reflections from other parts of the aircraft or externally carried stores. In some installations, not so far put into production, different parts of jammers were quite widely distributed around the aircraft, though this is extremely undesirable because it means extra weight and losses in the microwave waveguides and cooling systems.

Most air forces are quite happy with the old-fashioned pod. This can be made what is called a stand-alone device, in that it can work without backup or any significant aircraft modification other than a 12-volt supply and a switch in the cockpit.

Pods are today of modular design; a few can be repackaged internally to cater for different or additional threats, and some are even constructed on the building-block principle so that they can be added to by the user squadron to become physically larger and offer extra capabilities. Some of the most powerful jammers have their own windmill turbogenerator, which runs throughout each mission without significant drag.

The EA-6B can carry up to five pods, each with its own 40-kVA turbogenerator on the nose, the current being delivered to two impressive smart noise generators emitting through high-gain aerials which are electronically steerable towards the particular threat. The number of pods carried depends on the expected threats to be encountered on the mission. Hanging all five jammers on the EA-6B reduces full-throttle speed at sea level from 623 to 651mph (1,002 to 1,047km/h; 716 to 748 knots).

In contrast, the USAF has gone for a completely internal suite in the EF-111A, but for its combat aircraft it has until recently been convinced the right way to go in fighters has been to deploy large

Above: More trials programmes have been flown with the F-4 Phantom than with any other fighter. This was one of the first with a Pave Tack target acquisition laser designator pod, on the centre line.

Below: At present the standard ECM pod carried by the F-16 Fighting Falcon is the ALQ-131, one of the most modern examples of an external installation. This F-16 comes from Hahn's 10th TFS, 50th TFW.

numbers of modular and reliable pods. Westinghouse has supplied the numerous ALQ-101 family, some of which were bought secondhand from the USAF to equip RAF Buccaneers, as well as the more sophisticated ALQ-119 used on F-111s and the later ALQ-131 which is still the standard kit aboard F-16s.

But for the planned next-generation ASPJ (advanced self-protection jammer) the goals were so challenging, and the rewards so great, that a team effort was necessary and the winner was the team of Westinghouse/ITT. The resulting ALQ-165 will be the first-ever standardized internal system, with great power, digital software control and many new features. Its only evident shortcoming is that the present upper frequency limit of 18GHz is already well below that of many known Soviet threats. ALQ-165 is to be built into the F/A-18A Hornet eventually, and into whatever Enhanced Tactical Fighter the USAF selects, as well as (it is hoped) the AV-8B, later F-16s and probably existing F-111s and EA-6Bs.

Expendables likewise can be tucked away inside if the designer has left room, or stuck on the outside. Though not quite as embarrassing as the Harrier chaff bundles jammed between bombs and pylons, the installations in most Western aircraft leave much to be desired. Four out of five aircraft have the dispenser on the side of a deep pylon, where drag could hardly be higher.

Several dispensers, notably the Lundy ALE-44, fit fairly snugly in the belly Sparrow AAM recesses on the F-4, but when Sparrows must be carried the F-4 often sticks Tracor ALE-40s on a pylon. In contrast the same ALE-40 is carried above the rear fuselage of KLu (Royal Netherlands AF) NF-5 fighters, with a streamlined fairing upstream, without severe penalties in drag or tail airflow qualities, while in the F-16 and A-10 the same dispenser are mounted

Above: So far as is known the only ECM pods that have reached RAF combat units have been Westinghouse first-generation jammers bought secondhand from the USAF in Germany. This Buccaneer has an ALQ-101(V)8, the first model in the series to have a full-length gondola beneath the original tube. This gives increased frequence coverage and makes the (V)8 almost equal to the ALQ-119.

Right: Here seen carried by an A-10A, the ALQ-119 was the next generation that followed the 101 (and preceded the 131 on page 63). Many 119s now have computerized power management.

Below: Unusually, this trials Buccaneer is carrying two different sub-types of ALQ-101 pod, as well as a tank and a Paveway II (Mk 13/18) laser-guided smart bomb.

Grumman EA-6B EW Systems

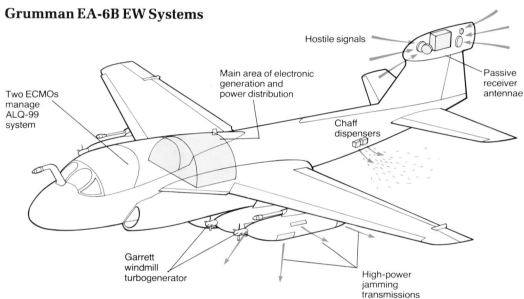

Hostile signals

Main area of electronic
generation and
power distribution

Two ECMOs
manage
ALQ-99
system

Passive
receiver
antennae

Chaff
dispensers

Garrett
windmill
turbogenerator

High-power
jamming
transmissions

Above: A Navy EA-6B Prowler on a low-level overland mission with three jammer pods and two tanks. The pod turbogenerators spin throughout the flight, but when no current is being drawn the aerodynamic drag is quite small.

Left: Main features of the Grumman EA-6B Prowler, whose ALQ-99 jammer system requires a separate pair of backseat crew, assisted by the ECMO in the right front seat.

Below: Close-up of the left side of an F/A-18A Hornet showing the FLIR (Forward-looking Infra-red) pod on the air intake duct, providing night acquisition and identification of targets. In the same position on the other side is a Laser Spot Tracker (LST) which allows acquisition of laser-illuminated targets. Under the belly is a Rockeye CBU.

internally. In the A-10 there is a massive installation, with four dispensers in each wheel well and four in each wingtip for a maximum of 480 chaff cartridges or IR flares!

Thus modern air combat is likely to see the sky absolutely plastered with high-power radiations at all sorts of wavelengths, billions of slivers of chaff, and enough IR sources to rival the Milky Way (if we had eyes sensitive to IR). One must not forget that, despite all this, our own navigation systems, doppler, terrain-following radar, Tacan and other helpful systems must continue to work in the manner intended without batting an eyelid at what we are trying to do to the somewhat similar systems operated by the Bad Guys.

Of course in the real world a few things will go wrong, and while the enemy radars may either burn through our jamming or even find out from its location where we are, the same jamming may incapacitate vital electronics in the friendly aircraft in front or behind in the formation.

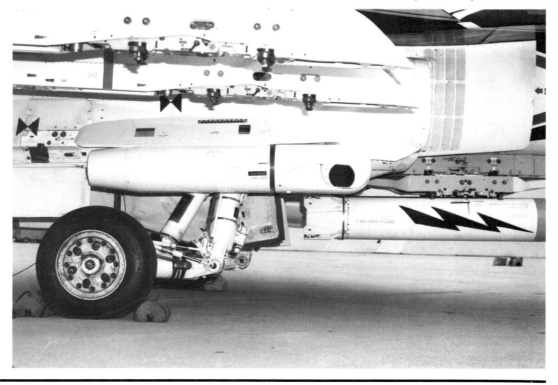

Displays

The last topic covered in this brief outline concerns the gradual change from the dial-instrument cockpit of World War II to the electronic display which faces the pilot of today's combat aircraft. A related subject is the need to provide for the best possible view all round, with especial attention to the view behind for fighter pilots and the view ahead for attack pilots – or, some would say, vice versa.

One cannot help noticing the surprising degradation in forward view between the early MiG-21, which had a frameless forward canopy (albeit with imperfect optical qualities) and the amazing array of massive windshield frames, HUD-sight, four indicator instruments, two large mirrors and four pitot heads which obstruct the forward vision of the pilot of today's MiG-23BN. On a recent social call a Soviet Frontal

Aviation regimental commander was asked about this, his reply being, "We are used to it, we can do our job". This is a remarkable viewpoint, not shared by, for example, the RAF pilot ("Bee" Beaumont) who successfully fought for better forward vision in attack aircraft such as the Typhoon/Tempest 40 years ago.

Of course the entire spectrum of electromagnetic sensors – radars, lasers, TV and IR, for example – can "see" without being bothered by windscreen frames and other obstructions. Some 25 years ago it was becoming fashionable to regard the fighter pilot as an obsolescent animal that in a few years would be extinct. The experts of that era might have been surprised to learn that the main debate going on today in the Pentagon, and probably in the Kremlin, over the manning of future fighters for the 1990s, is

Above: Many attack pilots would be highly critical of the restricted forward view from the cockpit of the MiG-23BN and MiG-27 series, though in many other respects these tough aircraft are outstandingly good.

Left: The second (F110-engined) F-16XL prototype has two seats, because the USAF doubts the ability of a single pilot to fly all-weather missions.

Below: The Tornado IDS has two men in tandem. In the left picture the TV tabs are set up for mission planning. Below is the trainer, whose rear cockpit has throttles and a real control column.

whether one man alone can do the job. The consensus of opinion in the USAF is that he cannot. It will be recalled that the single-seat Tornado was abandoned, and all four of the initial customers agreed on a tandem two-seater.

But there are a few contrary voices. General Dynamics has made the F-16 so capable that, with major avionic updates, it is convinced it can meet the USAF's need for an ETF (enhanced tactical fighter) with one man, and it used a two-seater as the basis for the second "arrow wing" F-16XL only because it was told to.

Going back 20 years the same company not only designed the USAF's F-111 as a two-seater but it put the crew side-by-side. There are a few side-by-side combat aircraft, but the F-111 is the only one that was originally planned (at least in theory) as a fighter. The fact that the same arrangement is seen in the Su-24 shows the colossal influence that the F-111 exerted over Soviet procurement officials, and it certainly led them to a rare case of mistaken emulation. Not only does side-by-side seating increase drag but it prevents the pilot from seeing outside except over a rather limited arc around the left side.

Navigators, in the right seat, are no more enamoured of the idea. According to one F-111 right-seater, "The nice thing about flying side-by-side (and there are *very* few nice things about flying side-by-side) is that the pilots are so totally in awe of what's going on in

Above: Few One-Eleven crew-members like the rather cramped matiness of their side-by-side seats. This is an FB-111A of SAC, whose crews are more geared to such seating than people who call themselves fighter jocks.

Below: The US Navy/Marines Grumman A-6 Intruder was never called a "fighter" so there was less overt resistance to side-by-side seating. Note that in addition to a Kaiser head-up display (HUD) the pilot also has his own radar

display, which in a two-seater is unusual. The right-seater (WSO or navigator) spends much time punching buttons but also has a small joystick (bottom right) for directing the main radar antenna.

Above: Taken by the WSO (right-seat crew-member) of a USAF F-111F, this dramatic photograph shows terrain-following flight at low level in mountainous country. The wings were level; it was the terrain that was not!

Above: When the F-5 was designed there was no such thing as Hotas, and traditional dial instruments reigned supreme. This is the cockpit of an F-5E from USAF 527th TFW ("Aggressors"); an F-16 pilot would think it ancient.

Below: Typical of the previous generation, the IAI Kfir is at least much more modern than the Mirage III from which it was derived. Note the restricted view ahead, and the absence of multifunction displays.

Above: Sweden has no reason to be ashamed of the splendid cockpit of the JA37 Viggen, which has two multifunction displays as well as a modern HUD. There is nothing wrong in extensive written notes.

Below: Backseater's view in a 54 Sqn RAF Jaguar formation. The HUD is in PLF (precise local fix) track mode, with alphanumeric readout of speed and range and a central flight director.

the right seat that they give us no static at all".

There's a story that civil airline pilots have to keep having their pay increased because of the extra workload caused by all the labour-saving devices. Something of the sort, apart from the increased pay, is true inside military cockpits. The factors which make life difficult for the modern pilot include the high speed of the aircraft (which dramatically reduces the time available for both decisions and actions), the high risk of destruction if height above ground is allowed to exceed about 200ft (60m), the need to handle both air-to-air and air-to-ground operations in typical missions, the virtual impossibility of orbiting to "have a second look" or make a more accurate second attack on a surface target, and the sustained stress of having to keep at least three eyes in his head to look for targets, hostile aircraft, ground

obstructions, enemy SAMs and other defences, friendly aircraft, and sudden changes in visibility caused, for example, by snow squalls. The mental, not to say physical, workload probably exceeds that in any other human activity.

The earliest fighters were simple, flown visually by pilots whose eyes were of necessity outside the cockpit, looking urgently in all directions. Today the pilot is confronted with as many as 190 separate instruments or controls. Because there is so much more to go wrong, and because of the pilot's absolute reliance on "systems" for navigation, intercepting the enemy, aiming all kinds of weapons and finally landing back at base, he has to spend far more of his time "head down", looking inside the cockpit.

There is no way we can cut down on the complexity of the on-board

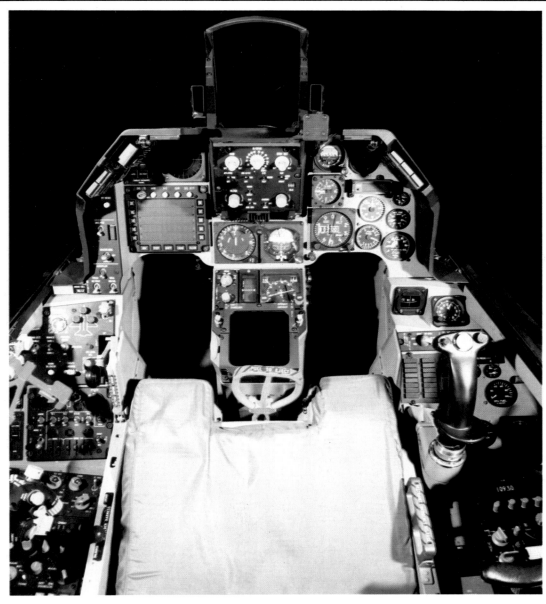

systems, but designers have gradually been revolutionizing the interface with the human pilot. Like their colleagues working on civil airliners, the fighter cockpit engineers have realized that the 50 years of simply adding complexity ought to be arrested, and the whole purpose of the cockpit rethought.

Despite a 1957 obsession with missiles, and a 1970-73 fixation on RPVs, we accept now that there has to be a human pilot, in a posture suitable for violent manoeuvres. Even this posture is now having to be re-thought because, with the advent of direct force control, the cockpit is liable to be suddenly accelerated up, down, left, right or in any other direction, as well as rotated, and seat designers have not previously had to contend with aircraft capable of such agility. There has to be a streamlined canopy that will provide an essentially undistorted view through 360° and yet withstand supersonic impact with birds and hailstones. The wide-angle holographic HUD has come to stay, but even this superb device cannot present all the information the pilot might ever need. We therefore need some kind of HDD (head-down display), but we must forget about dial instruments and traditional one-function switches. Instead we can call up the interfaces we want on a screen.

First, we have to equip the entire aircraft with one or more extremely comprehensive digital electronic systems, comprising sensors to measure or notice things, data highways to carry the signals and microprocessors to operate on them. These microprocessors will in future be programmed in what computer people call a higher-order language, such as Pascal. Many of the data highways will end up at flight-control surfaces, engines or weapons, while many others will arrive in the cockpit. Here they will feed large picture-type displays which can on occasion shout written (and audible) warnings. The warning will automatically trigger circuits giving the pilot command to input corrective action, if this is possible (if there is any doubt he can ask for further information). Among many other advantages, the computerized fighter will actually gain in engine power (without changing the engines) and in acceleration and turn rates (without changing the flight controls.)

Basic improvements in cockpit instruments include the development of comprehensive combined displays which, though to some degree derived from traditional instruments, yet offer far more information and, unlike traditional gyro instruments, cannot "topple" in manoeuvres. One common type is the ADI (attitude director indicator) which gives an indication of what is happening in the vertical plane, including accurate non-lag indication of bank or dive angle. A more complicated instrument is the HSD

Above: Currently the most important air-combat fighter in the Western world, the F-16A sets an extremely high standard in such matters as pilot posture (almost lying down), pilot view and the Hotas (hands on throttle and stick) technique. This cockpit is that of a Dutch aircraft, but it could be flown by any other F-16 pilot. The next generation is shown on page 74.

Below: The F-14A cockpit, planned in 1968, is dominated by a central VSI with an HSI below it. Three vertical tape instruments show engine rpm, temperature and fuel flow.

The F-15 – a Cockpit of the 1970 Era

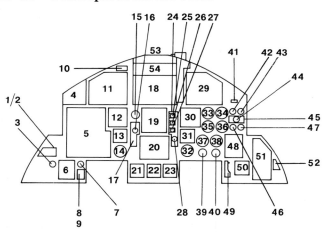

1. Hook switch
2. Hook panel
3. Flap indicator
4. Fire warn panel
5. Armt cont'r panel
6. Gear handle
7. Pitch ratio indicator
8. Pitch ratio switch
9. Pitch ratio panel
10. Radio call panel
11. Radar scope
12. Air speed indicator
13. Angle of attack indicator
14. G meter
15. Emer jett switch
16. Steer mode switch
17. Steer mode panel
18. Hud control panel
19. Altitude indicator
20. Horizontal situation indicator
21. Air speed (standby)
22. Attitude (standby)
23. Altimeter (standby)
24. Master mode panel
25. A/C mode button
26. ADI mode button
27. V1 mode button
28. Beacon light
29. Tews display
30. Altimeter
31. Vertical velocity
32. Clock
32. Left tachometer
34. Right tachometer
35. Left temperature
36. Right temperature
37. Left fuel flow
38. Left nozzle position
40. Right nozzle position
41. Canopy unlocked light
42. PC1 indicator
43. PC2 indicator
44. Utility indicator
45. Oil/hyd ind panel
46. Left oil press
47. Right oil press
48. Fuel oty indicator
49. JFS panel
50. Cabin press alt
51. Caution panel
52. Emer vent panel
53. IFF remote panel
54. UHF remote panel

Below: The main front panel of the F-15A would be familiar to a WWII pilot, except for the VSI and HSI in the centre and the HUD controls immediately above. This was the last major use of dials.

or HSI (horizontal situation display or indicator) which is basically a compass but also includes desired heading (course), actual heading, actual track, command track to the next radio beacon, magnetic bearing to the next Tacan beacon or ADF beacon, cross-track error, various range displays (usually distances to go) up to 999.9 nautical miles, and all necessary ILS radio-approach information for bad-weather landings.

The next stages were to provide such things as moving-map displays containing colour maps stored on film which could be driven past the screen at such a rate that the position of the aircraft remains at the same spot on the display, and then to combine this type of instrument with the main radar display so that the two more or less coincide. Then the electronics engineers went on to create even more versatile displays, but first a very important new instrument grew out of the traditional reflector sight. This is the HUD (head-up display).

First perfected in about 1961, the HUD consists of an optically transparent sheet, such as a sloping pane of glass, on to which can be projected symbology and alphanumerics without getting in the way of the pilot's view ahead. The symbols and written data tell the pilot such vital things as his speed, heading, height above ground, attitude, and relevant weapon status and aiming cues. The information appears in the form of bright lines all generated electronically and focussed at infinity. Thus the pilot can keep looking ahead, either at a hostile aircraft or searching for features on the ground speeding past immediately below, without having to refocus his eyes to glance at the HUD information.

At one stroke this showed how further development could virtually eliminate the need ever to look inside the cockpit, except for occasional low-priority tasks which are seldom time-critical. Looking inside the cockpit can cause fatal collision with the ground or other objects, induce vertigo, and not infrequently result in errors in the pilot's actions. Thus the HUD was from the start a development of enormous significance, even though the first examples were little more than a reflector sight with more information.

There were still many shortcomings in the typical fighter cockpit, resulting in a most imperfect man/machine interface. For one thing there were too many separate indicators and controls inside the cockpit; for example, in the front panel of an F-15A there are 34 dial instruments and 85 control inputs, while along the consoles on each side of the pilot are a veritable phalanx of switches, buttons and rotary knobs.

Another, arising from the first, is

Above: This view not only shows the left console of an F-15A, with its many traditional input devices, but also shows the hefty throttles (under the pink banner) with their pioneer Hotas (hands on throttle and stick) interfaces.

Below: F-16 radar display in air-to-air mode. W-like aircraft symbol at centre on horizon line (ie, level flight); target rectangle below, and what looks like II is acquisition symbol (which is not yet on target).

Below: F-16 radar (changed colour is night-time UV lighting), showing a ground map mode with DBS (doppler beam sharpening), a technique which gives improved angular resolution. The scan can be up to 60° left/right.

Above: Capt Doug Moss sets up his HUD before a mission from Kadena, Okinawa, in his F-15D. This has better radar and software than the F-15A, but a very similar cockpit. The photogrph emphasizes the pilot's tight fit inside.

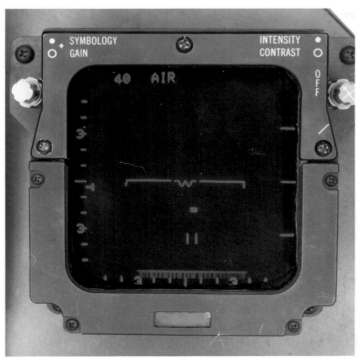

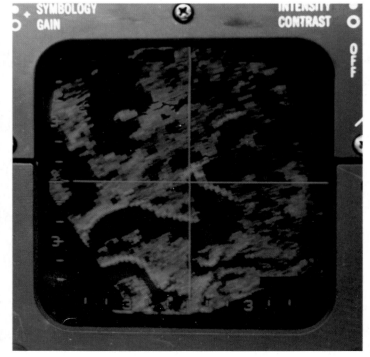

that the pilot had to look inside the cockpit in order to select the right control interface, even though some might be needed every few seconds in an attack or in combat (for example, airbrake, radar mode, weapon selection and sensor designation or hold).

A third shortcoming is that the real world seen through the HUD was not always bright and sunny; it might be thick fog, heavy rain or at night. Even the slightest overcast can turn the speeding landscape into a dull blur from which even an experienced pilot with good eyesight finds it extremely hard to pick out a single helpful object except by luck.

These problems have led to three routes towards solutions. One is replacement of traditional instruments and arrays of switches by extremely flexible displays

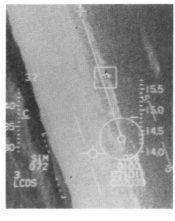

Above: F-16 HUD in LCOS (lead-computing optical sight) mode, with radar locked-on the target (in small square). Height 14,825ft, pulling 3.2g at 370kt ($C = 3.7$).

Above: Pipper on the target, so the pilot can open fire with the M61 gun and know most rounds will hit. Now 3.0g, up to 14,890ft but speed down to 3.4 (340kt).

which are based on digital electronics and quickly reprogrammable to show different things. The pilot of the F/A-18A Hornet, for example, faces hardly any ordinary instruments and controls, except for some on a small "back-up panel" at lower right. The scene is dominated by the HUD, a UFC (up-front control), and three CRT (cathode ray tube) displays which look like small colour TVs.

The UFC is the control for the often overlooked but vital CNI (communications, navigation, identification). It is a small panel, half the size of this page, which allows the pilot to use either hand (and without looking into the cockpit) to control the UHF/VHF radios, ILS, data link (to a carrier, airfield or AWACS aircraft), Tacan, beacons, ADF, IFF and autopilot

Gun (air-air) mode

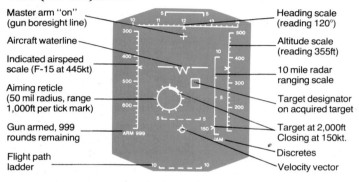

Master arm "on" (gun boresight line)
Aircraft waterline
Indicated airspeed scale (F-15 at 445kt)
Aiming reticle (50 mil radius, range 1,000ft per tick mark)
Gun armed, 999 rounds remaining
Flight path ladder

Heading scale (reading 120°)
Altitude scale (reading 355ft)
10 mile radar ranging scale
Target designator on acquired target
Target at 2,000ft Closing at 150kt.
Discretes
Velocity vector

Medium Range Missile (air-air) mode

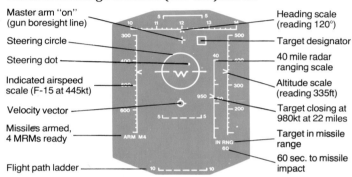

Master arm "on" (gun boresight line)
Steering circle
Steering dot
Indicated airspeed scale (F-15 at 445kt)
Velocity vector
Missiles armed, 4 MRMs ready
Flight path ladder

Heading scale (reading 120°)
Target designator
40 mile radar ranging scale
Altitude scale (reading 335ft)
Target closing at 980kt at 22 miles
Target in missile range
60 sec. to missile impact

Automatic (air-ground) mode

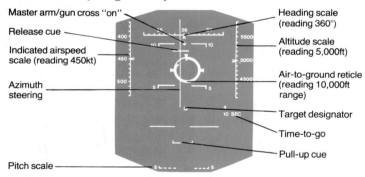

Master arm/gun cross "on"
Release cue
Indicated airspeed scale (reading 450kt)
Azimuth steering
Pitch scale

Heading scale (reading 360°)
Altitude scale (reading 5,000ft)
Air-to-ground reticle (reading 10,000ft range)
Target designator
Time-to-go
Pull-up cue

CDIP (air-ground) mode

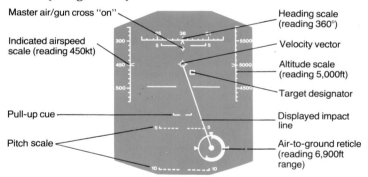

Master air/gun cross "on"
Indicated airspeed scale (reading 450kt)
Pull-up cue
Pitch scale

Heading scale (reading 360°)
Velocity vector
Altitude scale (reading 5,000ft)
Target designator
Displayed impact line
Air-to-ground reticle (reading 6,900ft range)

Above: A traditional non-holographic HUD is the McDonnell Douglas Electronics display fitted to the F-15 Eagle. There are more modes available than the ones shown here.

Below: McDonnell Douglas could well describe the F/A-18A Hornet as having tomorrow's cockpit today, the immediately striking feature being the near-absence of instruments.

Below: The Hornet's Ferranti Comed 2035 (Combined map/electronic display) displays radar images and much other information, called up with the 20 surrounding buttons.

Right: The contrailing target is seen in the target box in the HUD of an F-15 working in MRM (medium-range missile) mode. On page 200 is seen the MRM actually fired seconds later.

modes. It is especially useful in formation flight in bad weather or during carrier circuits at night or poor visibility, when the CNI workload is high and yet the eyes need to stay outside the cockpit.

As for the three prominent displays, these are generally known as MFDs (multifunction displays), but in the F/A-18 they are labelled MFD, MMD (master monitor display) and HSD. The MMD is the primary display for warnings (RWR etc), EW, EO/IR sensors, armament, BIT (built-in test) and scratch-pad display of other items. The HSD is the usual CRT-generated colour navigation picture superimposed on the moving map, to simplify navigation updates, radar map matching and input other tactical data such as EW threats, electronic orbat (order of battle) and details of

each navigation segment. The MFD is the primary display for the main radar and also backs up the MMD.

Each display is surrounded by 20 touch-switches whose functions change depending on what is being displayed. There is a quarter-inch strip around each sensor picture or other display telling the pilot the function of each switch. Thus in the example illustrated, in addition to the unchanging night/auto/day/off, brightness and contrast knobs, the buttons give such choices as wide or narrow FOV (field of view), positive or negative picture format, etc.

The Hotas (hands on throttle and stick) concept has already been mentioned. It is inconceivable that any fighter will ever again be designed without it. By grouping every commonly used control on

The Hotas Arrangement

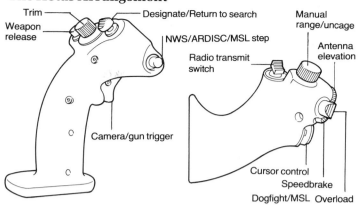

Above: The F-16 affords an excellent example of the Hotas (Hands on throttle and stick) philosophy. Any designer could stick a lot of switches and buttons on a handgrip, but it takes careful research to find the best Hotas arrangement that the pilot can operate instinctively and without needing huge hands.

either the throttle(s) or the stick the pilot is enabled to fly most of the time like a skilled pianist or typist, neither of whom ever needs to look at what his hands are doing.

Just how far we can go in interfacing perhaps 20 or 30 systems through two hand controllers is something we have to find out. It would be simplicity itself to provide a special button or other input on each controller which at a touch would alter the function of every other button, switch and trigger, thus doubling the number of functions literally at the pilot's fingertips. After a certain level of complexity is reached the Hotas idea probably becomes self-defeating.

The diagram shows a typical organization for a modern set of displays for combat aircraft. Data highways of standard type shuttle the billions of digital "bits" around in a highly flexible and mission-adaptive way, to give colour or monochrome pictures, instantly written calligraphic symbology, or mixes of moving maps, radar, video, IR and other sensor pictures.

The HUD today is invariably of the raster type (a raster is a picture made up of many parallel lines as in a TV) created by a FLIR or LLTV to give a bright and clear picture no matter what the actual world outside may be like. This has an obvious spin-off advantage in

giving the pilot much greater confidence in landing in a blizzard at night. In the FLIR mode the pilot sees the world ahead as an IR seeker sees it, so he cannot tell the colour of an aircraft parked on an airfield but can instantly spot such things as white engines (hot, therefore running) or black inner parts of the wings (filled with freezing cold fuel, so the aircraft has just landed from a high-level sortie with fuel left in the tanks).

Quite apart from being able to "see" in new ways, today's HUD has much larger FOV. The diagram shows that the FOV of the HUD in the F-16A is 13.5° left/right and 9° up/down, which is good by the standards of the 1970s. For the F-16AFTI, with CCV features, Marconi Avionics came up with a HUD then thought to be the limit to what could be achieved, 20° by 15°.

But the same company has now perfected a so-called diffractive-optics or holographic HUD of radically new design for the F-16C fitted with Lantirn sensor pods. This amazing HUD can see virtually the whole world ahead, 30° wide and 18° vertically, which can be used in bright sunlight, guide the aircraft in tight turns near the ground, present a selected holographic picture on one wavelength while portraying the real world on all other visual wavelengths, and provide a night

Above: The author regards the F-16C cockpit as the most modern of any fighter in the mid-1980s. The main differences compared with an F-16A are the two multifunction displays and the gigantic Marconi HUD.

Below: Newest of all the cockpits in this book, Sweden's JAS39 Gripen will have a giant HUD, with clear up-front controls, three MFDs and four genuine dial instruments. The MFDs are exceptionally large.

Helmet Pointing Gun System

Gun installation in typical early-1980s fighter, aligned with axis of fuselage

Gun installation of typical late-1980s fighter with rapid aiming through cone of about 30°

Above: Designers have been toying with fighter guns and sight systems which are not fixed along the axis of the fuselage. Now they are trying the more difficult task of arranging an HPS (helmet pointing system) linked to a trainable gun, as well as the seeker heads of AAMs. Thus, by merely spotting a hostile aircraft within a large cone of fire ahead of the fighter the weapons could automatically be aimed at it.

Above: Black boxes are not always black, like this one (the electronics unit for the Marconi Avionics Lantirn HUD for the F-16C) but all are densely packed with the devices that are increasingly at the heart of on-board systems. The microelectronic packages are soldered to pre-printed circuit boards which, if faulty, can be replaced in seconds without delaying the mission.

Below: Tomorrow's fighter pilot may have a helmet which not only copes with ejection into a 600-knot wind but also has CRT displays (red) to transmit exact "direction of look".

vision system which, though magnified, so completely fills the pilot's view ahead that he can fly at 200ft (60m) by night on this alone.

Since the mid-1960s many companies have researched helmet sights and displays, and a few are close to production. These vary in form, but a typical arrangement provides a sighting reticle (often a bright display formed by LEDs in a dot matrix) attached to the pilot's helmet, through which he looks at targets in any direction, a method of measuring the exact direction of the pilot's sightline, and a computerized output which is either displayed to the pilot or used to cue or aim a sensor or a weapon.

One system by Ferranti can project a TV-type picture, which is roll-stabilized to prevent pilot-disorientation, the FOV being 40° wide. Another system by Marconi Avionics measures sightline direction by three V-slit cameras which look at eight LEDs mounted in groups on each side of the helmet. Such a system can display flight information, threat warnings, energy-management

guidance, nav fixing, missile cueing and lock-on, ground-target designation, and, for helicopters, aiming of a gun turret.

Convinced that pilot workload has already reached saturation point, Crouzet in France has been developing a voice-command interface called EVA (équipement vocal pour aéronef). It responds only to the pilot assigned to the mission, who before takeoff carefully reads out all the input words he may use in calling up data (such as fuel remaining) or asking for a given weapon, height-hold, AOA, Mach, altitude or radio frequency. EVA responds in a synthesized voice output, not confusable with a radio call. The author doubts Crouzet's belief in this system, but would like every fighter to have a voice recorder into which the pilot could dictate information which at present he has to bring home in his head.

Looking ahead to the 1990s the FOV of new possibilities is limit-less. Nobody should appear to like weapons of war, but surely fighter aircraft do have as much appeal and technical interest as in the past?

The Aircraft and Their

Weapons

Though its basic design dates from almost 20 years ago the Grumman F-14 Tomcat still offers the greatest stand-off kill capability of any combat aircraft. Its Hughes AWG-9 radar can choose targets from a large formation at ranges of well over 100 miles (161km) and pick them off with up to six of these giant Phoenix missiles.

Introduction

It is important to appreciate that, though the title of this book is "Modern Air Combat", this does not explicitly mean combat between opposing aircraft. A book concerned exclusively with air-superiority fighters would be thinner and less interesting, and from the start we recognised the importance of including air/ground (or anti-ship) missions. Thus the following pages include such aircraft as the Buccaneer, F-111 and A-7, as well as both versions of Tornado. In general, attack aircraft try to avoid air combat in the narrow "Red Baron" sense, but play a central role in modern air warfare.

Most people like to imagine themselves cast in the role of a modern Red Baron, picking off foes almost like swatting flies. In fact, in today's world not even an agile fighter or alert pilot can offer much insurance against sudden destruction. Every aeroplane, no matter how exceptional an air-combat fighter it may be, is a potential target. It can suddenly succumb to air-to-air gunfire, AAMs, SAMs or triple-A – or to accidents, which claim the lives of scores of fighter pilots around the world each year. We must not forget that, though the following pages concentrate on firepower and offence, the other side of the coin is survival. Increasingly this is a matter of complicated and often very powerful electronics, system and engine redundancy, widely separated duplicated flight controls, dispensed chaff, flares and jammers, and even old-fashioned armour. Most of these items cannot readily be illustrated in these pages – they have been dealt

Above: An RAF Tornado GR.1 carrying giant JP.233 dispensers each packed with advanced runway-cratering munitions and area-denial mines. Note also ECM pods and the laser under the nose.

Below: Sweden's JA37 Viggen fighter pioneered pulse-doppler radar in Europe, as well as a full spectrum of gun and missiles. It can operate far enough from known airfields to survive in war.

with earlier – though in some cases active ECM jammer pods have been included.

Without doubt, the artwork on the following pages is visually striking. But, like the rest of this volume, this major section has been planned to be not only impressive but also highly informative. One's eye alights first on the illustrations, and the main drawings are unique. It was not possible or desirable to select one common overall scale, one aircraft to another, because each illustration was planned to make the best use of the available space, and the aircraft differ markedly in size and shape.

It will be obvious that in such cases as the F-16 and A-10 there was a superabundance of possible stores, and we made a choice governed mainly by the importance and technical interest of each store. In every case, the store has been publicly associated with the type of aircraft concerned, though in some cases only with particular versions of it. Thus, we have drawn a tactical attack F-111, but have illustrated weapons which are carried only by the strategic FB-111A version. In many cases gun ammunition and freeflight rockets have been shown, though not necessarily in the actual numbers carried. Where the number that can be carried of each item is not clear this information will normally be given in the text, in the section dealing with Armament, while details of underbelly pylon positions, and locations of guns, will be found in the plan view line drawing which also indicates the position of ammunition tanks. In a few cases, such as Jaguar and Harrier II,

there is a choice of gun and both types are illustrated.

Of course, inclusion of any particular weapon does not imply that all customers for the aircraft use that particular store. For example, the Matra 550 Magic AAM is used on the Sea Harrier only by the Indian Navy. In some instances stores have been included for interest which, though they have been flown on the type of aircraft, have not been put into service by regular units which fly that aircraft. Thus, there does not yet exist a production Wild Weasel version of F-16 Fighting Falcon armed with Shrike or Harm missiles, though GD is proposing such an aircraft and has been the subject of a USAF evaluation. Another new weapon is the BAe Dynamics Alarm, by far the most modern anti-radar missile in the world. While this book was in preparation Alarm was adopted for the RAF and Fleet Air Arm after a keen competitive battle with the older-technology American Harm, but it will be four years before it appears on operational aircraft.

Of course, in the case of Warsaw Pact aircraft it is accepted that the information is extremely incomplete. Even aircraft such as the specialized PVO interceptors – Su-11, Su-15 and Tu-128, for example – almost certainly can carry external stores other than AAMs and tanks, while it is reasonable to assume that the number of possible items carried by, say, the MiG-23BN/MiG-27 must be several times greater than those whose appearance is known in the West. Rather than make guesses, we thought it more useful to restrict our choice of weapons to those positively identified.

Above: Mirages laying down retarded bombs typify today's ground attack missions. Aiming is imprecise but putting a whole stick across a target is bound to cause damage.

Below: Sea Harriers of 801 Sqn, Royal Navy, give no obvious hint of their unique ability to operate from a forest clearing or the deck of a small frigate. This is the only way for airpower to survive in

future, because there is no way to protect immovable precisely-targeted airfields against destruction from long-ranged missiles with tactical nuclear warheads.

Above: The attack versions of F-111 combine heavy bombload with a range greater than that of any other tactical aircraft, but they are easy to destroy on their airfields.

Aeritalia/Aermacchi/EMBRAER AM-X

Origin: Joint programme by Italy and Brazil, first flight 1983.
Type: Single-seat attack.
Engine: One 11,030lb (5,003kg) thrust Rolls-Royce Spey 807 turbofan produced under licence by Alfa Romeo and Piaggio.
Dimensions: Span (excl AAMs and rails) 29ft 1½in (8.88m); length 44ft 6¼in (13.57m); wing area 226.0sq ft (21.0m²).
Weights: Empty 14,330lb (6,500kg); maximum 26,455lb (12,000kg).
Performance: (estimated) to fly lo-lo-lo mission with tanks plus 3,000lb (1,360kg) ordnance at Mach 0.75-plus, with dash at Mach 0.95 (722mph, 1,162km/h) with radius of 208 miles (335km); field length 3,000ft (914m).
Background: In the mid-1970s the Italian AF (AMI) studied the need to replace the G91 and G91Y in the fairly short term (from 1985) in the attack and reconnaissance roles, and by 1990 also to replace all versions of the F-104 in the same roles as well as long-range anti-ship attack and counter-air roles. In 1977 studies for an Italian aircraft to meet these needs began at Aeritalia, and a year later embraced Aermacchi, hence the designation AM-X for Aeritalia/Macchi Experimental. In 1980, following discussions with the FAB (Brazilian AF), EMBRAER became an industrial partner, and since then AM-X has been a two-nation programme to meet the needs of both air forces.
Design: From the start AM-X has been notable in avoiding the common temptation to aim for near Mach 2, though this still seems to appeal to some air forces with more money than sense. Instead the accent has been on the ability to carry a carefully selected spectrum of sensors and weapons, operate from small austere bases and fly with the greatest agility at the lowest cost.

At first glance the parameters appear to resemble those of the Hunter and similar aircraft of 30 years ago, but in fact every part of the design is totally modern. The wing is slightly swept, and has full-span slats, small outboard ailerons, large double-slotted flaps and two pairs of spoilers which can be used to augment roll. All movables are hydraulically powered, with manual reversion for the ailerons. The slab tailplanes incorporate small carbon-fibre elevators, the main surfaces being powered trimmers. The large vertical tail, with FBW rudder, is designed for good stability at very high AOA, and everything possible has been done to ensure the greatest possible manoeuvrability, augmented by the slats and flaps up to Mach 0.6.

Though there is a large tank between the simple inlets, most of the classified internal fuel capacity is in the sealed wing boxes, extending from the three-spar/three-frame root attachments to near the broad tips. Later the fin might be added. Apart from this almost everything is in the large

and shapely fuselage, which has carefully thought-out provisions for one or two guns and alternative suites of avionics. At present there are no airbrakes or braking parachute, and a slight complicating factor is that the rear fuselage and horizontal tail is removable for changing the engine. Later it is probable that direct side-force control, plus airbrakes, will be added by fitting split powered side doors to all four underwing pylons. The nosewheel is steerable, but the forward-retracting main units have tyres inflated to 140lb/sq in (9.65bars), compared with 95-115lb/sq in for equivalent Soviet types designed for use from unpaved surfaces.
Avionics: Final details were still uncertain in 1983, but everything is modular and pallet-mounted

Above: As this book went to press the first AM-X had not been flown, so this is an artist's impression.

and variable according to the mission. Basic navigation is by INS and VOR; no radar is fitted apart from a small ranging set, but there are two digital computers which control weapon delivery and also serve an advanced MFD facing the pilot and a HUD. Some of the aerial positions agreed in early 1983 are depicted on the three-view drawing. There will be a radar altimeter and probably Tacan and ILS, but the exact arrangement of sensors for the ADC system was awaiting the results of flight experience. Likewise there is bound to be some rethinking on the contents of the bay forward of the right main gear which may be occupied by any of several arrangements of reconnaissance cameras, or an LRMTS. For dedicated reconnaissance missions a multisensor pod would be carried externally. Passive EW systems in the Italian aircraft are expected to include fin-mounted RWR aerials, though Aeritalia removed these (and the VOR aerials) from a British cutaway drawing before using it in their brochures. Active ECM will certainly include external pods, though an internal installation has been studied. There will be an internal chaff/flare dispenser in the rear fuselage.
Armament: (Italy) One 20mm M61A-1 gun with 350 rounds, (Brazil) two 30mm DEFA 554 or similar, each with 125 rounds. Seven external points for weapons, with following ratings: fuselage and inboard wing 2,000lb (907kg); outboard wing 1,000lb (454kg); wingtip rails 188.5lb (85.5kg); total permissible load 8,377lb (3,800kg). The tip rails are for close-range AAMs, such as Sidewinder. A wide range of other ordnance can

be carried, especially including anti-ship missiles. Three alternative pallet-mounted reconnaissance systems or an LRTMS can be installed in the forward fuselage, without affecting weapon capability; a pod-mounted recon system, or EW pods, are other alternatives.
Future: Though there will continue to be minor differences between the Italian (initial buy expected to be 187) and Brazilian

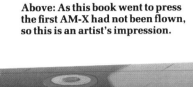

(about 80) aircraft, due to different mission requirements and NATO refusal to grant export licences for certain items such as the M61 gun, the commonality between the aircraft for the two air forces is about 97 per cent and this is unlikely to fall significantly. Space has been left for such items as an attack radar, which is needed for effective anti-ship missions, and for NIS, JTIDS, GPNS and similar desirable add-ons.

Weapon provisions:
A. 20mm M61 with 350 rounds (Italy).
B. LRMTS or camera bay.
C. Two 30mm DEFA each with 120 rounds (Brazil).
D. Single hardpoint with side-by-side ejector racks total 2,000lb (907kg).
E. Pylon 2,000lb (907kg).
F. Pylon 1,000lb (454kg).
G. Tip rail for AAM.

Combat avionics:
A. Range-only radar.
B. Avionics bays
C. HUD.
D. UHF.
E. UHF/VHF.
F. Radar warning receiver (RWR).
G. VHF.
H. VOR.
J. Tacan.

Key to stores:
1. AIM-9L Sidewinders.
2. Elettronica ELT-555 ECM jammer.
3. AGM-65A Maverick.
4. Durandal anti-runway bomb.
5. Kormoran anti-ship missile.
6. M61A1 gun with 20mm ammunition (Italy).
7. DEFA 554 gun with 30mm ammunition (Brazil).
8. Mk 84 GP bomb 2,000lb (907kg).
9. Thompson-Brandt BAP.1000 anti-runway weapons.
10. M117 GP bomb 750lb (340kg).
11 Mk 83 GP bomb 1,000lb (454kg).
12. Beluga cluster dispenser.

British Aerospace Buccaneer

Left: Buccaneers of RAF No 208 Sqn. Note how it is common to fold wings after landing to save room; in the same way USAF F–111s fold their wings fully back. The three seen on a training mission are practising how to make the best use of terrain to make life hard for hostile defences, ground and airborne

Origin: UK, first flight 30 April 1958.

Type: Two-seat attack and reconnaissance.

Engines: Two 11,030lb (5,003kg) Rolls-Royce Spey 101 turbofans; (50) in addition 8,000lb (3,628kg) BS.605 rocket.

Dimensions: Span 44ft (13.41m); length 63ft 5in (19.32m); height 16ft 3in (4.95m); wing area 514.7sq ft (47.83m²).

Weights: Empty about 30,000lb (13,610kg); loaded (clean) 46,000lb (20,865kg), (maximum) 62,000lb (28,123kg).

Performance: Maximum speed 645mph (1,038kmh, Mach 0.85) at sea level; tactical radius (hi-lo-lo-hi, no external fuel) 500 miles (804km); range on typical hi-lo-hi strike mission with weapon load 2,300 miles (3,700km).

Background: When in 1957 the UK Minister of Defence hit on the idea that all manned combat aircraft were obsolete he cancelled almost everything except the Lightning and Buccaneer. The latter was then frantically being readied for a first flight, and it managed not only to survive but, after more than a decade of derisive rejection by the RAF, in July 1968 was ordered for that service as well as for its original customer, the Royal Navy. The RAF accepted the "Bucc" reluctantly, only because the TSR.2, F-111K and AFVG had been successively cancelled. Thereafter the derision gradually turned to solid appreciation of what many now consider the finest attack bomber of its day. Unlike most British aircraft in the tactical class it has a large internal fuel capacity, which with efficient non-augmented fan engines gives range adequate for every necessary mission. A capacious internal bomb bay enables it to carry a 4,000lb (1,814kg) bombload whilst preserving a clean exterior and cruising significantly faster than a Mirage, F-4 or any other known attack aircraft with the same weapons, and for a fraction of the fuel consumption. Deck landing and low-level attack were built into the original specification in 1952, resulting in full-span boundary-layer blowing systems of great power which enable small wing and tail surfaces to behave like large ones in the slow-speed blowing regime. It follows that at high speed the ride is remarkably steady, and with up to 3,020gal

(13,728 litres) of fuel, consumption one-tenth that of several single-engined attack aircraft and a sea-level speed second to none, the Buccaneer has proved one of the most popular aircraft the RAF ever had. Like Israel with the very different Skyhawk, its crews cannot imagine how it can ever be replaced. Incidentally, the RAAF could have had over 100 for the price of its 24 F-111Cs, with individual aircraft capabilities strikingly similar, but at that time (1963) the air force of "the Home Country" regarded the Buccaneer as unworthy of consideration.

Design: Originally planned to be powered by two large Sapphire turbojets, mounted on the sides of the fuselage, the NA.39 (as the project was known) was refined to have an advanced blowing system and small Gyron Junior engines giving fuel burn reduced by 39 per cent. All central primary structure was sculpted from high-tensile steel, including the fuselage "spider" beams, engine rings and inner wing spars, and the wing skins were machined from plate. The whole aircraft was visibly area ruled to give minimum transonic drag, and features included tandem stepped cockpits, fully powered controls (including almost full-span ailerons and a small all-moving tailplane at the top of the fin) and extremely compact folded dimensions, folding including the radome and large split tailcone airbrakes.

Avionics: Abysmal lack of foresight has resulted in this superb aircraft having to soldier on with a nav/attack system planned in the 1950s. Ferranti's Blue Parrot is a good ship-attack radar for its era, but very far from the ideal for 1980s overland missions. Navigation is by twin-gyro platform and doppler, which had some advantages over inertial for shipboard use but few when flying from airfields. EW kit was non-existent at first but now includes ARI.18228 passive warning and second-hand (ex-USAF) ALQ-101 jammer pods.

Armament: Rotating bomb door carries four 1,000lb (454kg) bombs or multi-sensor reconnaissance pack or 440gal tank; four wing pylons each stressed to 3,000lb (1,361kg), compatible with very wide range of guided and/or free-fall missiles. Total stores load 16,000lb (7,257kg).

Key to stores:
1. ARI.18228 RWR receiver aerials (L/R wings, forward-facing).
2. AIM-9L Sidewinder self-defence AAM.
3. Data-link pod for guiding AJ.168 Martel (TV).
4. ALQ-101 ECM jammer pod.
5. ML Practice bomb carrier.
6. Practice bomb, 5lb (2.25kg).
7. Practice bomb, 4lb (1.8kg).
8. Slipper long-range tank, 430gal (1,955lit).
9. AS.30 air/surface missile (not AS.30L).
10. BAeD Sea Eagle long-range anti-ship missile.

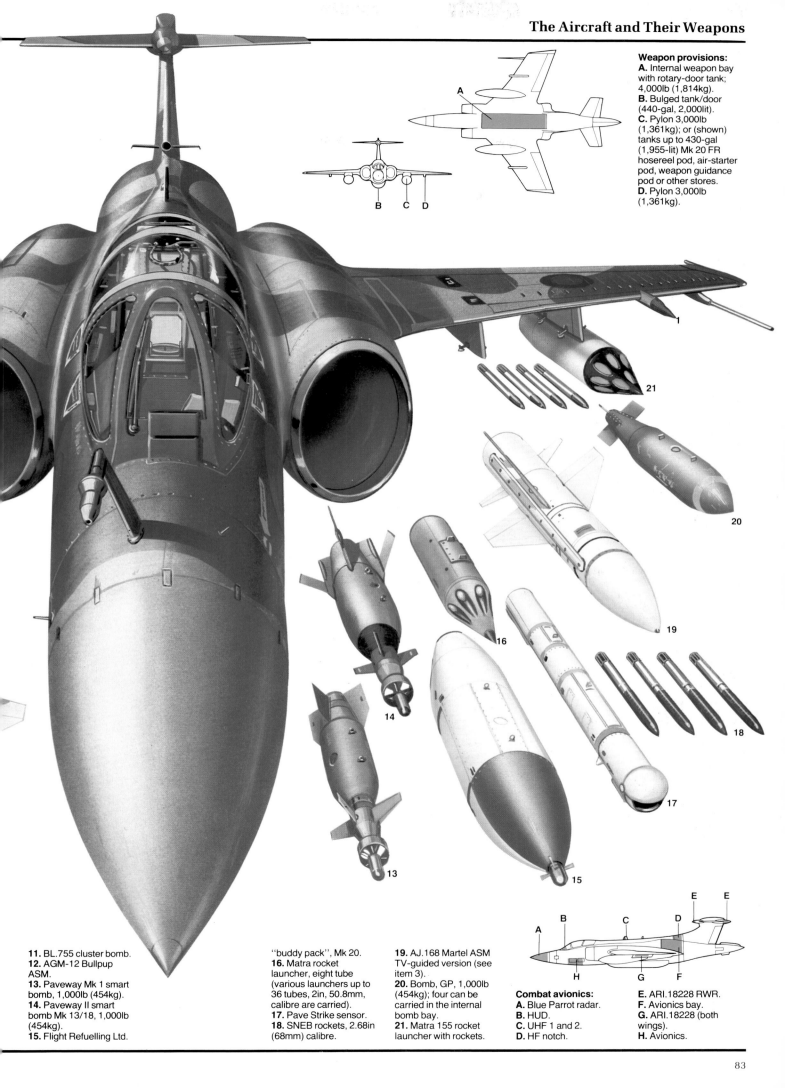

Weapon provisions:
A. Internal weapon bay with rotary-door tank; 4,000lb (1,814kg).
B. Bulged tank/door (440-gal, 2,000lit).
C. Pylon 3,000lb (1,361kg); or (shown) tanks up to 430-gal (1,955-lit) Mk 20 FR hosereel pod, air-starter pod, weapon guidance pod or other stores.
D. Pylon 3,000lb (1,361kg).

11. BL.755 cluster bomb.
12. AGM-12 Bullpup ASM.
13. Paveway Mk 1 smart bomb, 1,000lb (454kg).
14. Paveway II smart bomb Mk 13/18, 1,000lb (454kg).
15. Flight Refuelling Ltd.

"buddy pack", Mk 20.
16. Matra rocket launcher, eight tube (various launchers up to 36 tubes, 2in, 50.8mm, calibre are carried).
17. Pave Strike sensor.
18. SNEB rockets, 2.68in (68mm) calibre.

19. AJ.168 Martel ASM TV-guided version (see item 3).
20. Bomb, GP, 1,000lb (454kg); four can be carried in the internal bomb bay.
21. Matra 155 rocket launcher with rockets.

Combat avionics:
A. Blue Parrot radar.
B. HUD.
C. UHF 1 and 2.
D. HF notch.
E. ARI.18228 RWR.
F. Avionics bay.
G. ARI.18228 (both wings).
H. Avionics.

British Aerospace Harrier

Origin: UK, first flight (GR.1) 28 December 1967.
Type: Single-seat STOVL tactical attack and reconnaissance; (T.4) dual trainer or special missions.
Engine: One 21,500lb (9,752kg) thrust Rolls-Royce Pegasus 103 vectored-thrust turbofan.
Dimensions: Span 25ft 3in (7.6m), (with bolt-on tips, 29ft 8in/8.7m); length (GR.3) 47ft 2in (14.37m), (T.4) 57ft 3in (17.44m); height (GR.3) 11ft 3in (3.42m); (T.4) 13ft 8in (4.16m); wing area 201.1sq ft (18.68m^2).
Weights: Empty (GR.3) 12,200lb (5,533kg); (T.4) 13,600lb (6,168kg); maximum (non-VTOL) 26,000lb (11,793kg).
Performance: Maximum speed over 737mph (1,186km/h, Mach 0.972) at low level; maximum dive Mach number 1.3; initial climb (VTOL weight) 50,000ft (15,240m)/min; service ceiling, over 50,000ft (15,240m); tactical radius on strike mission without drop tanks (hi-lo-hi) 260 miles (418km); ferry range 2,070 miles (3,331km).
Background: The genesis of the Harrier, the world's first jet combat aircraft to escape from fixed-location airfields, lay in the farsighted appreciation of retired French aircraft designer Michel Wibault that such bases were totally vulnerable to nuclear missile attack. To give NATO a hope of future survivable airpower he made a proposal in 1956 for a complicated form of jet-lift V/STOL, which the engineers at Bristol Aero-Engines translated into the elegant Pegasus vectored-thrust engine, first used in the Hawker P.1127 of 1960. Via the tripartite (UK/US/Germany) Kestrel of 1963 and cancelled Mach 2 P.1154 the P.1127-RAF was permitted to go ahead in 1965 as the first new RAF fighter-like aircraft since such machines were declared no longer wanted in 1957. Named Harrier in 1966, it emerged as a new design with close family links with its predecessors and sharing their amazing simplicity, manifest in only one extra pilot control, a nozzle (angle) lever graduated from 0° (forward flight) to 110° for braking and lift.
Design: Tailored to tactical attack and reconnaissance missions, the Harrier was given a small wing for smooth flight at 700mph (1,126km/h) at tree-top height. Subsequently it was realised that

the normal takeoff would not be VTO but a rolling STO, and that a larger wing would enable heavier weapon loads to be lifted, improve combat manoeuvrability and provide room for more pylons. As the government decided in 1975 there was "not enough common ground" with the USA for a joint programme the next generation will be the US AV-8B, with British Aerospace a minority partner. Obviously the engine has to be amidships so that its four nozzles give thrust evenly disposed about the aircraft centre of gravity, with control provided by reaction control jets at the wingtips, nose and tail. With such a "tight" compact design all weapons have to be hung externally, including various stores under four wing pylons, two guns under the fuselge and a centreline hardpoint which can accept a recon pod.
Avionics: From the start the nav/attack system was an inertial (Ferranti INAS) installation, supplemented by a laser ranger and HUD; com radio comprises main and standby UHF plus VHF, with Tacan, IFF and ARI.18223 radar warning passive receivers. The US Marine Corps do not use the laser and removed the inertial system from the AV-8A Harrier I, and both are still absent from today's updated AV-8Cs which have passive warning receivers at the wingtips and in the tailcone, as well as improved UHF com and a secure voice data-link. GR.3s in the Falklands were fitted with I-band transponder compatible with RN ships.
Armament: All external, with many options. Under-fuselage strakes each replaceable by pod containing one 30mm Aden or similar gun, with 150 rounds. Five or seven stores pylons, centre and two inboard each rated at 2,000lb (907kg), outers at 650lb (295kg) and tips (if used) at 220lb (100kg) for Sidewinder AAMs, first fitted during the Falklands crisis. Normal load 5,300lb (2,400kg), but 8,000lb (3,630kg) has been flown.
Future: Plans to re-wing existing RAF Harriers are unlikely to be implemented; had the BAe Harrier GR.5 design been adopted this would have been a possibility. Future efforts are directed at extending safe airframe life of the existing structure; there are also several planned equipment updates.

Key to stores:
1. AIM-9B Sidewinder AAM (for the Falklands campaign the improved AIM-9L, now in production in Europe, was quickly made available, and a twin carrier was also cleared for use).
2. Hunting JP.233

dispenser (short type).
3. Lepus flare.
4. Drop tank, 100gal (455lit); for the Falklands conflict a 190gal (864lit) pattern was quickly cleared for use.
5. Wasp ASM launching pod (12 round).
6. Wasp ASM (unfolded).
7. Practice-bomb

dispenser with bombs installed.
8. BAe reconnaissance pod with horizon-to-horizon optical cameras, forward oblique and various low-level cameras, plus BAeD type 401 IR linescan.
9. Gun pod (one of two) containing 30mm Aden

Weapon provisions:
A. Two 30mm Aden each with 125 rounds (close-packed).
B. Hardpoint 1,000lb (454kg) or recon pod.
C. Pylon 2,000lb (907kg).
D. Pylon 1,000lb (454kg) or twin AAMs.

13

12

11

14

11

11

15

10

8

9

and ammunition.
10. Ammunition, typically 120-130 rounds per gun, maximum being 150.
11. Two Matra retarded bombs, 882lb (400kg).
12. ML twin carrier with

two GP bombs, 1,000lb (454kg).
13. Rocket launch pod and rockets; one common type is Matra 155 with 18 tubes of 2.68in (68mm) for SNEB rockets.

14. GBU-13/18 Paveway II smart (laser-guided) bomb which was based on the British 1,000lb (454kg).
15. Hunting BL.755 cluster bomb.

Combat avionics:
A. LRMTS.
B. IFF.
C. HUD.
D. UHF.
E. Avionics bay.
F. HF notch.

G. ARI.18223 RWR.
H. VHF.
J. UHF standby
K. Tacan.
L. I-band expdr (Falklands only)
M. Attack camera.

British Aerospace Hawk

Origin: UK, first flight 21 August 1974.

Type: Two-seat trainer and light interceptor.

Engine: One 5,340lb (2,422kg) Rolls-Royce/Turboméca Adour 151 turbofan (export versions, 5,700lb/2,586kg Adour 861).

Dimensions: Span 30ft 10in (9.39m); length (over probe) 39ft 2½in (11.95m); height 13ft 5in (4.08m); wing area 179.64sq ft (16.69m²).

Weights: Empty 7,450lb (3,379kg); loaded (trainer, clean) 12,000lb (5,443kg), (attack mission) 16,260lb (7,375kg).

Performance: Maximum speed 630mph (1,014km/h) at low level; Mach number in shallow dive 1.1; initial climb 6,000ft (1,830m)/min; service ceiling 50,000ft (15,240m); range on internal fuel 750 miles (1,207km); endurance with external fuel 3hr.

Background: The RAF's need for a new jet trainer in the mid-1960s was to have been met by the Jaguar, but this turned out to be far more capable than the trainer requirement called for and the two-seat version is used only for weapon instruction in Jaguar squadrons. Instead of continuing collaboration with France a new RAF trainer requirement was drawn up, while in 1969 France went ahead with West Germany on a rival design (see Alpha Jet). The RAF wished to replace the Jet Provost, Gnat Trainer and Hunter. Designs were proposed by BAC and Hawker Siddeley, and in October 1971 the latter's HS.1182 was chosen. The choice of engine lay between the Viper and Adour, the latter being more expensive but offering greater mission performance and weapon load with superior fuel economy, and it was selected in March 1972. Later in the same month the aircraft was named Hawk, and an order was placed for a prototype and 175 for the RAF inventory. Development was outstandingly fast and successful and has resulted in an aircraft which in the US Navy VT/XTS contest proved dramatically superior on all counts to any existing machine in the same category.

Design: In true Kingston tradition the Hawk is simple. The wing is in one piece, forming one integral tank, and there is a single tank in the fuselage. Features include large double-slotted flaps, powered ailerons and anhedral slab tailplanes, manual rudder and a large door-type airbrake under the rear fuselage. The main gears have a track of 11ft 5in (3.47m) and some customers have selected the optional braking parachute. The pressurized cockpits are deeply staggered and normally have Mk 10B zero/zero seats fired through the clamshell canopy which has previously been shattered by MDC (miniature detonating cord) which can also be fired from outside.

Avionics: In the standard aircraft these comprise typical nav/com systems, plus Tacan, ILS and IFF/SSR, and of course night and all-weather instrumentation. There are many additional options, some of them taken up by export customers. the T-45 family will have US Navy avionics, though not for all-weather weapon delivery or air combat.

Armament: One centreline hardpoint for pod containing loads to 1,000lb (454kg) or one 30mm Aden gun and up to 130 rounds; four underwing hardpoints each capable of carrying a pylon rated as shown with 3-view, maximum external load demonstrated being 6,800lb (3,084kg). RAF T.1 normal load 1,500lb (680kg) including two AIM-9L Sidewinders. T-45, normally unarmed.

Future: British Aerospace have recognized the Hawk's tremendous tactical capability by developing a completely new "100 Series" Hawk with an advanced nav/attack system derived from that of the F-16, with Singer-Kearfott INS, Smiths Hudwac and Hotas (hands on throttle and stick) controls. This version is tailored to attacks at very low level and will have a complete EW suite, both internal and external, as well as a laser ranger. There remains the possibility of a dedicated single-seat version with more internal fuel and perhaps CCV technology. The RB.199 engine would fit such an aircraft beautifully.

Above: Hawks in the RAF are assigned to No 4 FTS (in training red/white) and to Tac Weapons Units (in camouflage). This TWU aircraft is one of 72 armed with AIM-9B (later AIM-9L) in a local air-defence role.

Below: The Hawk demonstrator pictured with a weapon load of 6,800lb (3,084kg): four Mk 83 bombs of 1,000lb (454kg), four Mk 82 of 500lb (227kg) and the 30mm gun pod which, with its ammunition, weighs 800lb (363kg).

Key to stores:
1. Matra 155 rocket launcher.
2. Rockets for (1), 18 SNEB of 68mm calibre.
3. Practice bomb carrier, four bombs.
4. Practice bomb, British, 4lb (1.8kg).
5. Practice bomb, British, 5lb (2.27kg).
6. Practice bomb, British, 28lb (12.7kg).
7. GP bomb, 500lb (227kg); like the 1,000lb (454kg) can be carried in pairs.
8. Paveway II smart (laser-guided) bomb, Mk 13/18, based on British GP bomb, 1,000lb (454kg).
9. Gun pod (one only), Aden 30mm.
10. Ammunition for (9), up to 130 rounds.
11. Drop tank, 100 or

Weapon provisions:
A. 30mm Aden with 120 (tight packing 125) rounds.
B. Pylon 1,120lb (508kg) to 8g or gun pod (800lb, 363kg).
C. Pylon 1,120lb (508kg) to 8g or 1,500lb (680kg) to 5.5g.

130gal (455 or 592lit).
12. Hunting BL.755 cluster bomb.
13. AIM-9L Sidewinder close-range AAM (can be carried in pairs, though RAF emergency interceptors have single installation).

Combat avionics:
A. IFF/SSR.
B. HUD (option).
C. VHF/UHF.
D. ILS.
E. Tacan.
F. Laser ranger (option).

British Aerospace Lightning

Origin: UK, first flight (F.1) 1960, (F.6) 1964.

Type: Single-seat all-weather interceptor.

Engines: Two 15,680lb (7,112kg) thrust Rolls-Royce Avon 302 afterburning turbojets.

Dimensions: Span 34ft 10in (10.6m); length 53ft 3in (16.23m); height 19ft 7in (5.96m); wing area 380.1sq ft (35.32m²).

Weights: Empty about 28,000lb (12,700kg); loaded 50,000lb (22,680kg).

Performance: Maximum speed 1,500mph (2,415km/h) at 40,000ft (12,200m); initial climb 50,000ft (15,240m)/min; service ceiling over 60,000ft (18,290m); range without overwing tanks 800 miles (1,290km).

Background: Britain appeared to find the concept of a supersonic fighter difficult to grasp, and instead of (like other countries) just going ahead with such a project in 1949-50 the decision was taken to concentrate on research aircraft. One of these, the English Electric P.1, was then used in 1955 as the basis from which an interceptor for the RAF might be developed, and this was ordered as the P.1B in November 1956. The specification was amazingly restrictive, combining two very thirsty afterburning turbojets with extremely limited fuel capacity, and no requirement for any kind of air-to-ground capability. In 1957 manned fighters were in any case proclaimed obsolete, but the P.1B was allowed to continue because it had gone too far to cancel. The Lightning F.1 entered RAF service with 74 Sqn in 1960, and eventually English Electric and its successor BAC was allowed to make 338 production aircraft in six successively improved marks. The big prize of Germany and the other F-104 customers was lost by the government's total indifference to the concept of a Lightning with adequate fuel and air-to-ground weapons, but the company at last managed to develop this in the mid-1960s for Saudi Arabia and Kuwait.

Design: Unique in many respects the Lightning has two engines both fed by a two-shock nose inlet, with radar in the pointed centrebody, the lower engine being under the mid-mounted wing and the upper engine in the top of the rear fuselage, the lower needing a long pipe to reach the afterburner. The wing is almost a 60° delta with a notch removed at the trailing edge, and the same is true of the slab tailplanes. All surfaces are powered, lateral control being solely by the ailerons which are unswept and join the leading and trailing edges at the tips. Main landing gears retract outwards into the outer wings, and wing leading edges are fixed. An afterthought was a wing-mounted FR probe, and later marks carried later AAMs (with a larger vertical tail to preserve directional stability) and deleted the two 30mm guns originally mounted above the nose, the guns finally being restored in the front of the enlarged ventral tank of the F.6. In this location firing the guns at night does not result in the pilot having to close his eyes, or lose his night vision.

Avionics: Apart from basic 1950s-style nav/com, and Elliott autopilot with ILS coupling, the key installation in the original F.1 was Ferranti Airpass (Airborne Interception Radar and Pilot Attack Sight System), originally tailored to a traditional tail-on chase by night or in bad weather using guns or IR missiles. Later the system was updated for engagement from any aspect, and a wide range of stores was cleared, those above the wing being forcibly ejected for clean separation at low level.

Armament: Interchangeable packs for two all-attitude Red Top or stern-chase Firestreak guided missiles; option of two 30mm Aden cannon in forward part of belly tank; export versions up to 6,000lb (2,722kg) bombs or other offensive stores above and below wings.

Future: At all times the Lightning has been a viceless and exhilarating aircraft to fly. In Saudi Arabia the F.53 is being replaced by the F-15, while in the RAF Nos 5 and 11 Sqns at Binbrook are due to convert to the Tornado F.2 from mid-1984.

Key to stores:
1. GP bombs of 1,000lb (454kg) size. The Lightning was cleared to carry a wide range of GP bombs, including patterns not of UK manufacture.
2. Twin store carrier mating standard underwing pylon with two bombs of 1,000lb size.
3. Gun pod with two 30mm Aden cannon and ammunition, housed in the front of the ventral fuel-tank fairing. Earlier Lightnings had the same armament in the upper part of the nose. The ventral pack installation has the advantage that there is no visible flash in front of the pilot.
4. Ammunition feed system for one gun in the ventral pack.
5. 30mm ammunition, typically 130 rounds per gun.
6. As an alternative to the guns this reconnaissance pack can be installed, the conversion taking a matter of minutes.
7. Red Top IR-homing AAMs. Earlier marks of Lightning were armed with the previous-generation Firestreak △

Left: Of 332 Lightning fighters built only about 30 are still operational, almost all with the RAF. In 1980 British Aerospace carried out a detailed structural audit of a Lightning to verify the suitability of these popular aircraft to continue operating at low level in dense air, not envisaged when the aircraft was designed in the mid-1950s. These are Saudi two-seaters (far left) and an F.6 formerly flown by RAF No 23 Sqn.

(Blue Jay) IR-homing AAM but this is no longer in use.

8. Overwing ferry fuel tank of 260gal (1,182lit) capacity; can be jettisoned by cartridge ejector/release units but normally retained and reused.

9. Overwing pylon with twin store adapter carrying two Matra JL100 pods each comprising an 18-rocket launcher (see item 10) in front of a 50gal (227lit) fuel tank.

10. Matra launcher Type 155 each for 18 rockets of standard SNEB 68mm calibre; the outer pylon is shown with adapters for a pair of such launchers.

11. Flight refuelling probe. This is fixed but readily removable, and is ▽

Weapon provisions:
A. Two 30mm Aden each with 130 rounds.
B. Body pylons for two Red Top or Firestreak missiles.
C. Pylon 2,000lb (907kg).
D. Pylon above wing with cartridge ejectors, 1,000lb (454kg).

normally installed only for long-range positioning flights, such as UK to Cyprus.

12. Microcell rocket launcher, which in earlier marks was a common alternative to the AAM installation. Made of glassfibre, its two hinged sections each house 14 rockets of 50.8mm calibre.

Combat avionics:
A. Airpass radar.
B. IFF.
C. VHF 2.
D. VHF/UHF.
E. VHF.
F. Compass unit.
G. AAM avionics or 44 rockets of 2-in (50.8-mm) calibre.

British Aerospace Sea Harrier FRS.1

Origin: UK, first flight 20 August 1978.

Type: Single-seat STOVL multirole (including fighter, reconnaissance and strike) aircraft for deployment aboard surface ships.

Engine: One Rolls-Royce Pegasus 104 vectored-thrust turbofan rated at 21,500lb (9,752kg).

Dimensions: Span 25ft 3in (7.6m); length (including probe) 47ft 7in (14.5m); height 12ft 2in (3.71m); wing area 201.1sq ft (18.68m^2).

Weights: Empty about 13,000lb (5,896kg); max weapon load 8,000lb (3,628kg); max TO 26,000lb (11,793kg).

Performance: Max speed (clean, SL) 740mph (1,191km/h); dive limit Mach 1.29; high-altitude cruise, typically Mach 0.8 (530mph, 853km/h); service ceiling 51,200ft (15,604m); time from brakes release to 40,000ft (12,191m) at air-intercept weight about 2 min; time from alarm (cockpit alert, engine not running) to combat area at 35 miles (56km) under 6 min; hi-intercept radius (allowance for 3 min combat and VL on return) 460 miles (740km); strike radius (hi-lo-hi, unstated bombload) 288 miles (463km); ferry range unrefuelled 2,340 miles (3,766km).

Background: Though the P.1127 operated from HMS *Ark Royal* in May 1963, it took many further years before it was recognised that vectored-thrust STOVL aircraft enabled high-speed fixed-wing airpower to be deployed at sea without the need for large and extremely costly carriers. The Harrier could operate from helicopter platforms , but by 1972 the best platform was judged to be a purpose-designed ship of under 20,000 tons, needing neither catapults nor arrester gear and fitted with a curving 'ski jump' ramp giving a takeoff trajectory inclined upwards at about 12° to enable either the run to be shortened or the weapon/fuel load to be greatly increased. More recently schemes have been published for quickly fitting prefab ski jumps to merchant ships, together with containerized weapon systems for ship protection. After years of study a go-ahead for the Sea Harrier at last came in May 1975. An order was placed for 24, for operation from Invincible type ships. Subsequently 10 more were ordered (and six for the Indian Navy), and a further 14 after the Falklands campaign. In that campaign the Sea Harrier did all that was asked of it, both in intercepting a wide variety of hostile aircraft (for example supersonic Daggers, C-130s and helicopters) and in attack on heavily defended ground targets. Five were lost, one in a takeoff accident, two in a collision in fog, one to AAA and one (it is believed) to a SAM. Serviceability and operational readiness rates (80 per cent) were outstanding, in the most gruelling conditions.

Design: No attempt was made to alter the aerodynamics, propulsion (except to switch from magnesium or its alloys to aluminium alloys for exposed components) or basic systems. All major changes are in the nose, which is completely redesigned. It had long been obvious the Harrier cockpit was a severe limitation, and the need to accommodate a more comprehensive avionic fit resulted in the decision to raise the entire cockpit 11in (280mm). This has the incidental advantage of giving the pilot a fighter-like all-round view, but it was done in order that extra volume should be provided under the floor and extra console space around the pilot. The greater depth of nose also facilitates installation of the radar, which is compact and can be folded back 180° to reduce length to 41ft 9in (12.72m). Other changes include: fitting Martin-Baker Mk 10H zero/zero seat; switching to British Oxygen lox system (GO$_2$, gaseous oxygen, in Indian aircraft), increasing the power of the roll-control RCJs (reaction control jets) to handle severe turbulence in ship wakes; increasing fin height to counter the larger nose area; increasing tailplane travel +2° nose-up; adding an emergency wheel brake system for confined spaces; extending operating time of water injection; adding lashing lugs to the landing gears; fitting improved external-stores pylons; and making minor changes to the systems, including fitting an alternator with greater output.

Avionics: Though the entire nav/attack system is different from that of the RAF Harrier, the main new item is the radar, the Ferranti Blue Fox. Derived from the Seaspray (Navy Lynx) radar, this operates in I-band and is a small (186lb, 84kg) modular set able to operate in four main air modes: search, with B-type sector scan or PPI with multi-bar or single scan; attack, with lead/pursuit or chase in the air combat mission and weapon aiming via the HUD in attack; boresight for ranging on targets of opportunity, and xpdr (transponder) for identifying friendly echoes. Smiths provide the Hudwac (HUD/weapon-aiming computer), whose computer portion has 20k words and serves as a flexible generator of graphics and symbology for air/air or air/ground aiming. An 8k-word computer ties the various units of the Navhars (Nav and heading/attitude ref system), a Ferranti unit which, to avoid alignment inaccuracy at sea, is no longer pure inertial but comprises a lower-cost twin-gyro platform monitored by a Decca 72 doppler. The entire system is digital, self-monitoring and in most cases fitted with integral fault diagnosis. It is designed for easy updating or reprogramming to take in later weapons, new navaids (such as Omega) or changed tactics. The RWR uses similar geometry to that in the Harrier, with the aft hemisphere aerial in the tip of the tail boom and the forward receiver

Above: Since returning from the South Atlantic all Sea Harriers in the Royal Navy have been factory-painted in low-visibility colours, though 801 Sqn, seen here, has check-painted rudders.

on the fin, but the latter is inserted as an extra section which increases the fin height by 5in (127mm) as noted above, and the system itself is a later model which gives ranges, bearings and broadbrush identities of all perceived threats. To reduce pilot workload a simple autopilot function gives heading, height and turn hold. Other equipment includes U/VHF with VHF standby, IFF/SIF, an I-band xpdr to enhance signature for surface-control guidance, and (following two years of experience with the HAPI, Harrier approach path indicator, a red/white optical ship system) the Madge all-weather microwave landing system.

Armament: Normally fitted with two 30mm Aden Mk 4 each with 150 rounds; five hardpoints for max weapon load of 8,000lb (3,630kg) including Sea Eagle or Harpoon ASMs, Sidewinder AAMs and very wide range of other stores.

Future: In the Falklands US-supplied AIM-9L AAMs were carried as well as older RN-stock AIM-9Bs, and the usual air/ground ordnance comprised GP bombs and BL.755s. For the near future it is intended to give medium-range radar AAM capability by fitting Sky Flash, and later Amraam, with the CW illuminator in the nose of the right external tank.

Weapon provisions:
A. Two 30mm Aden each with 125 rounds (close-packed).
B. Hardpoint 1,000lb (454kg) or recon pod.
C. Pylon 2,000lb (907kg).
D. Pylon 1,000lb (454kg) or twin AAMs.

Key to stores:
1. Matra 550 Magic AAM.
2. AIM-9L Sidewinder AAM.
3. AIM-9B Sidewinder AAM.
4. Sea Eagle ASM.
5. Harpoon ASM.
6. 100gal tank (190gal, 864lit, is now used).
7. Lepus flare.
8. Reconnaissance pod.
9. 30mm Aden gun pod.
10. 30mm ammunition.
11. 1,000lb (454kg) GP bomb.
12. Matra retarded bomb.
13. ML twin carrier with Matra 155 launchers
14. RN 2in (50.4mm) rocket launcher.
15. BL.755 cluster bomb.

Combat avionics:
A. Blue Fox radar.
B. IFF.
C. HUD.
D. UHF.
E. HF notch.
F. ARI.18223 RWR.
G. IFF notch.
H. Radar altimeter.
J. UHF standby.
K. Tacan.

Dassault-Breguet/Dornier Alpha Jet

Far left: The first of the 33 Alpha Jets bought by Belgium, in whose manufacture Belgian industry had a share.

Left: The Federal German Luftwaffe uses Alpha Jets not only for training but also as light attack and reconnaissance aircraft. They have pointed noses.

Origin: Jointly France and W Germany, first flight 26 October 1973.

Type: Two-seat trainer and light strike/reconnaissance aircraft.

Engines: Two 2,976lb (1,350kg) thrust SNECMA/Turboméca Larzac 04 turbofans.

Dimensions: Span 29ft 10¾in (9.11m); length (excluding any probe) 40ft 3¾in (12.28m); height 13ft 9in (4.19m); wing area 188.4sq ft (17.5m²).

Weights: (Trainer) empty 7,374lb (3,345kg); loaded (clean) 11,023lb (5,000kg) (max) 16,535lb (7,500kg).

Performance: (Clean) maximum speed 576mph (927km/h) at sea level, 560mph (900km/h) (Mach 0.85) at altitude; climb to 39,370ft (12,000m), less than 10 minutes; service ceiling 48,000ft (14,630m); typical mission endurance 2hr 30min; ferry range with two external tanks 1,827 miles (2,940km).

Background: The Alpha Jet was designed jointly by Dassault-Breguet of France and Dornier of West Germany to meet the needs of the two countries for advanced trainers and light attack aircraft. Throughout, the German demand has been for an aircraft to replace the G91 in light attack and reconnaissance missions; other customers wanted a trainer, and to this end the design was configured with the rear cockpit steeply stepped up, though this is not needed in the tactical roles and increases drag. Later Belgium and Egypt came into the manufacturing programme, and though the start of deliveries was delayed from 1973 to 1978 the Alpha Jet has been forcefully marketed and is now available in a dedicated light attack form, designated NGEA (Nouvelle Génération Entraînement et Appui, new generation training and attack).

Design: It was primarily to give plenty of clearance for underwing stores that the unusual shoulder-high wing layout was adopted, which in turn forced the main gears to be attached to the fuselage. Another fundamental choice was twin engines, SNECMA and Turboméca jointly producing a small turbofan, carried on the sides of the fuselage with short inlet ducts and jetpipes on each side. Wing leading edge is fixed, the tailplane is a slab, and all flight controls are fully powered. The complex internal fuel system has six tanks, and a drop tank can be

carried on each outer pylon. The need of the Federal German Luftwaffe to operate the Alpha Jet in close support and reconnaissance roles led to a substantial amount of redesign and the installation of special role equipment. The only store normally carried under the fuselage is the Mauser gun pod, the gun being the same new model as fitted to the IDS Tornado. The rounded nose of the trainer is replaced by a pointed nose with pitot probe (overall aircraft length increased to 43ft 5in/13.23m), and the Martin-Baker seats (old Mk 4 series for France but new zero/zero rocket-assisted Mk 10 for export customers) are replaced by American Stencel seats built under licence by MBB. There has been prolonged argument about the original design feature of arranging for the seats to be fired through the canopy, and detonating cord to shatter the canopies is now being fitted.

Avionics: Non-German aircraft have the expected suite of VHF/UHF/Tacan, VOR/ILS, IFF/SIF and simple weapon-aiming sight and computer. The Luftwaffe's version has the 27mm gun pod and a HUD, radio altimeter, doppler nav with computer, attitude/heading reference, Teledyne Ryan APN-220 doppler velocity sensor and various Italian EW pods including the Elettronica ELT/460 and /555 and Selenia ALQ-234. The NGEA has a laser ranger in a 'chisel' nose, different HUD and radar altimeter, and a Sagem inertial platform.

Armament: Optional for weapon training or combat missions, detachable belly fairing housing one 30mm DEFA or 27mm Mauser cannon, with 125 rounds; same centreline hardpoint and either one or two under each wing (to maximum of five) can be provided with pylons for maximum external load of 5,510lb (2,500kg), made up of tanks, weapons, reconnaissance pod, ECM or other devices.

Future: The Alpha Jet NGEA could become an important light tactical aircraft despite its basic shortcomings. Sustained efforts are being made by both partners to update the aircraft, for example, by fitting a supercritical wing, manoeuvre flaps, carbon-fibre tail surfaces and direct side-force flight controls in the form of pilot-commanded split airbrakes mounted on the four wing pylons.

Key to stores:
1. Matra Magic AAM.
2. Quad MLMS (air-launched Stinger).
3. 68.2gal (310lit) drop tank.
4. Super Cyclope/camera pod.
5. 12-round Wasp pod.
6. Wasp ASM.
7. Selenia ALQ-234 jammer.
8. Alternative tank.
9. AGM-65 Maverick ASM.
10. Twin Durandal anti-runway weapons.
11. Target towing pod.
12. Mauser 27mm gun pod and ammunition.
13. Carrier for (14).
14. Practice bomb (6 in carrier).
15. SAMP 882lb (400kg) smart LGB.
16. DEFA 30mm gun pod and ammunition.
17. Twin Beluga cluster dispensers.
18. BL.755 cluster bomb.
19. Matra 440lb (200kg) retarded bomb.

Weapon provisions:
A. Pylon 500kg (1,102lb) shown with gun pod (30mm DEFA or 27mm Mauser).
B. Pylon 500kg (1,102lb).

23. Matra 155 launcher with 18 68mm rockets.
24. Practice bomb.
25. Practice-bomb and rocket carrier.
26. LAU (US) launcher.
27. Brandt BM 400 882lb (400kg) bomb.
28. Matra EU2 GP bomb, 551lb (250kg).

20. Snakeye Mk 82 bomb.
21. BL18 fragmentation bomb, 276lb (125kg).
22. Twin Mk 82 GP bombs.

Combat avionics:
A. UHF.
B. IFF/SIF.
C. VOR/ILS.
D. VHF/UHF.
E. Tacan.
F. Crash recorder.
G. Avionics compartment.

Dassault-Breguet Mirage III and 5

Origin: France, first flight 1956, (5) 1967, (NG) 1983.

Type: Single-seat or two-seat interceptor, tactical strike, trainer or reconnaissance aircraft (depending on sub-type).

Engine: (IIIC) 13,225lb (6,000kg) thrust (maximum afterburner) SNECMA Atar 9B turbojet; (most other III and some 5) 13,670lb (6,200kg) Atar 9C; (NG) 15,873lb (7,200kg) Atar 9K-50.

Dimensions: Span 27ft (8.22m); length (excl probe) (IIIC) 48ft 5in (14.75m), (IIIE) 49ft 3½in (15.02m), (5) 51ft 0¼in (15.55m); height 13ft 11½in (4.25m); wing area 375sq ft (34.85m²).

Weights: Empty (IIIC) 13,570lb (6,155kg); (IIIE) 15,540lb (7,050kg); (IIIR) 14,550lb (6,600kg); (IIIB) 13,820lb (6,270kg); (5) 14,550lb (6,600kg); loaded (IIIC) 19,700lb (8,935kg); (IIIE, IIIR, 5), 29,760lb (13,499kg), (IIIB) 26,455lb (11,999kg).

Performance: Maximum speed (all models, clean) 863mph (1,389km/h) (Mach 1.14) at sea level, 1,460mph (2,349km/h) (Mach 2.2) at altitude; initial climb, over 16,400ft (5,000m)/min (time to 36,090ft (11,000m), 3min); service ceiling (Mach 1.8) 55,775ft (17,000m) range (clean) at altitude about 1,000 miles (1,610km); combat radius in attack mission with bombs and tanks (mix not specified) 745 miles (1,200km); ferry range with three external tanks 2,485 miles (4,000km).

Background: The first Mirage was a small light interceptor powered by two British Viper engines plus a rocket, flown in 1955. Dassault wisely scaled it up, first to have two Gabizos (not flown) and then, as the Mirage III, a single Atar 101G. This aircraft flew on 17 November 1956, and led to the initial IIIC production version with the improved Atar 9B engine, optional booster rocket motor (whose fuel replaced the 30mm ammunition) and Cyrano radar. The IIIC was a short-range bomber interceptor, with intended attack capability, and it triggered export successes all over the world. Dassault emphasized Mach 2 performance and the ability to use short airstrips, though in practice Mach 2 could only be demonstrated very briefly in training and was never required in combat missions, and a safe landing (avoiding the back of the drag-curve) demanded a paved 6,000ft (1,829m) runway; indeed with any substantial attack load even the takeoff ground run exceeded 5,000ft (1,524m). The success of this aircraft, foundation of Dassault's pre-eminence as a builder of fighters, rested on attractive appearance, lack of competition, and success in the hands of Israeli pilots in 1967.

Design: As a tailless 60° delta with thickness from 4.5 to 3.5 per cent, the Mirage III suffers from fundamental limitations. It is probably the most inefficient production aircraft at low speeds and high angles of attack. In combat the wing has the ability to travel very fast in straight lines, but speed bleeds off violently in any tight manoeuvres, to the point where this can even be turned to advantage in that pulling a tight turn is almost a sure way to force an enemy astern to overshoot. It means dogfighting in any positive way is difficult, except against aircraft lacking in power and agility. At extreme high altitude the rocket does give the extra thrust needed to go round corners as well as most opponents. The entire design, including the variable inlets and aerodynamic shape, is tailored to the attainment of the highest possible Mach number. The original aircraft was almost as limited as the British Lightning in fuel capacity and mission weapon loads. By 1961 the longer IIIE opened the way to extra fuel, better avionics and a range of aircraft tailored to air combat, attack, recon or dual training.

Avionics: Key items comprise Cyrano II radar and the CSF97 sight, a very elementary HUD, which together provide most of the information needed for interception or ground attack. The radar affords limited help in the lo penetration, but this remains primarily a visual and manual task. In the Mirage 5 each mission is even more reliant on the human eyeball, though an inertial navigation system is usually fitted and in some aircraft the lightweight Agave radar or Aida radar-ranging set is fitted to give some capability for all-weather weapon delivery, in a few aircraft further assisted by a laser ranger. In many respects a Mirage 5 with Agave is superior to an early Mirage III with the large Cyrano radar, and it carries a much heavier external weapon load. The more powerful Mirage 50 has a further updated nav/attack system, with a HUD and either Agave or Cyrano IVM3 (a simplified form of the IVM used in Armée de l'Air Mirage F1s). The most modern system would be fitted to the Mirage IIING.

Armament: Two 30mm DEFA 5-52 cannon, each with 125 rounds (normally fitted to all versions except when IIIC carries rocket-boost pack); three 1,000lb (454kg) external pylons for bombs, missiles or tanks (Mirage 5, seven external pylons with maximum capacity of 9,260lb, 4,200kg).

Future: First flown on 21 December 1982 after being converted from the prototype Mirage 50, the IIING has an improved airframe with canards and LERX (leading-edge root extensions) and a largely new avionics system. The latter includes the Cyrano IVM and Mirage 5 inertial/HUD boxes, as well as digital FBW (fly-by-wire) flight controls. Precise details would be left to future customers.

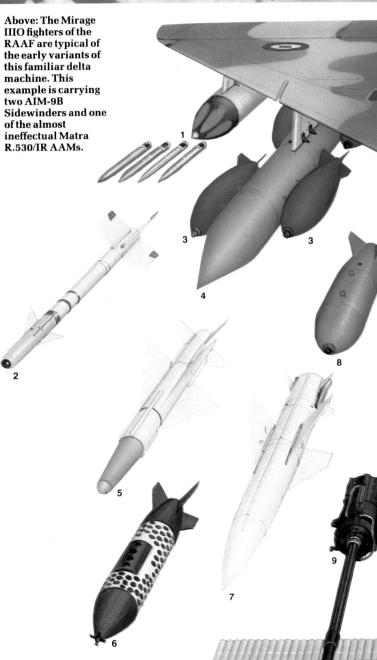

Above: The Mirage IIIO fighters of the RAAF are typical of the early variants of this familiar delta machine. This example is carrying two AIM-9B Sidewinders and one of the almost ineffectual Matra R.530/IR AAMs.

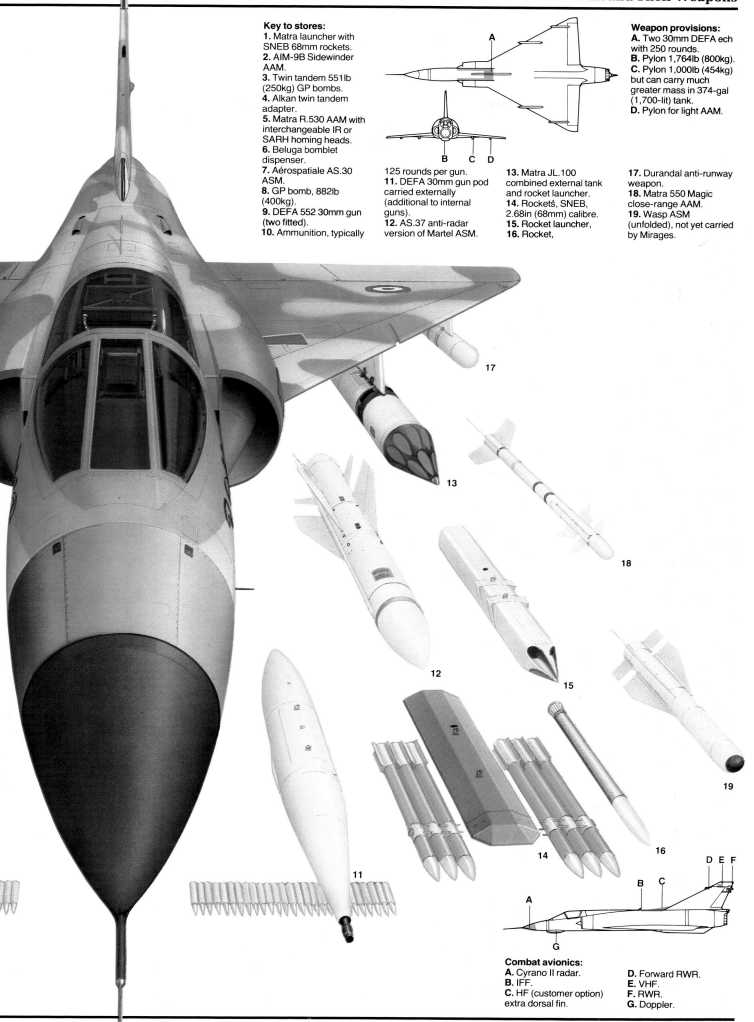

Key to stores:
1. Matra launcher with SNEB 68mm rockets.
2. AIM-9B Sidewinder AAM.
3. Twin tandem 551lb (250kg) GP bombs.
4. Alkan twin tandem adapter.
5. Matra R.530 AAM with interchangeable IR or SARH homing heads.
6. Beluga bomblet dispenser.
7. Aérospatiale AS.30 ASM.
8. GP bomb, 882lb (400kg).
9. DEFA 552 30mm gun (two fitted).
10. Ammunition, typically

125 rounds per gun.
11. DEFA 30mm gun pod carried externally (additional to internal guns).
12. AS.37 anti-radar version of Martel ASM.

13. Matra JL.100 combined external tank and rocket launcher.
14. Rockets, SNEB, 2.68in (68mm) calibre.
15. Rocket launcher,
16. Rocket,

17. Durandal anti-runway weapon.
18. Matra 550 Magic close-range AAM.
19. Wasp ASM (unfolded), not yet carried by Mirages.

Weapon provisions:
A. Two 30mm DEFA ech with 250 rounds.
B. Pylon 1,764lb (800kg).
C. Pylon 1,000lb (454kg) but can carry much greater mass in 374-gal (1,700-lit) tank.
D. Pylon for light AAM.

Combat avionics:
A. Cyrano II radar.
B. IFF.
C. HF (customer option) extra dorsal fin.
D. Forward RWR.
E. VHF.
F. RWR.
G. Doppler.

Dassault-Breguet Mirage F1

Origin: France, first flight 1966.
Type: Single-seat multimission fighter; (E) all-weather strike, (R) recon, (B) dual trainer.
Engine: 15,873lb (7,200kg) thrust (maximum afterburner) SNECMA Atar 9K-50 augmented turbojet.
Dimensions: Span 27ft 6¾in (8.4m); length (F1.C) 49ft 2½in (14.1m); (F1.E) 50ft 11in (15.51m); height (F1.C) 14ft 9in (4.49m), (F1.E) 14ft 10½in (4.53m); wing area 269.1sq ft (25.0m²).
Weights: Empty (F1.C) 16,314lb (7,400kg); (F1.E) 17,857lb (8,100kg); loaded (clean) (F1.C) 24,030lb (10,900kg), (F1.E) 25,450lb (11,540kg); (maximum) (F1.C) 32,850lb (14,900kg) (F1.E) 33,510lb (15,200kg).
Performance: Maximum speed (clean, both versions) 915mph (1,472km/h) (Mach 1.2) at sea level, 1,450mph (2,335km/h) (Mach 2.2) at altitude (with modification to cockpit transparency and airframe leading edges F1.E capable of 2.5); rate of climb (sustained to Mach 2 at 33,000ft/10,057m) (F1.C) 41,930-47,835ft (12,780-14,580m)/min, (F1.E) above 59,000ft (17,982m)/min; service ceiling (F1.C) 65,600ft (20,000m), (F.1E) 69,750ft (21,250m); range with maximum weapons (hi-lo-hi) (F1.C) 560 miles (900km), (F1.E) 621 miles (1,000km); ferry range (F1.C) 2,050 miles (3,300km), (F1.E) 2,340 miles (3,765km).
Background: By 1962 Dassault had been forced to recognise the limitations of the tailless delta. After prolonged study of variable-sweep the Armée de l'Air chose a shoulder-wing aircraft of conventional layout with the TF306 augmented turbofan in the 10t class. A contract was placed for the Mirage F2 in two-seat form in 1964, and the first flight was on 12 June 1966. But Dassault privately funded a smaller version, the F1, powered by a single Atar, the first flying on 23 December 1966. Dassault got this version selected instead of the large aircraft with the efficient turbofan engine. It is a very great improvement over the III/5 family, and it is amazing that the latter should have been preferred by so many air forces.
Design: Though the fuselage is derived from that of the III it is greatly refined and has integral fuel tankage throughout. The wing has LE sweep of 47.5° and is less than three-quarters the size of the delta,

thus giving a much better ride in the lo attack which has been reflected in pilot performance and delivery accuracy. Good high-lift systems dramatically reduce approach speed and field length needed, while slab tailplanes, large wing spoilers, ailerons and airbrakes ahead of the twin-wheel main gears all give superior agility. Compared with the III/5 series lo attack radius is doubled and hi patrol endurance trebled, while Dassault describes combat manoeuvrability as "more than 80 per cent increased".
Avionics: Dassault offers a spectrum of radars from the simple ranging set fitted to the F1.A series used for day ground attack by South Africa and Libya to the Cyrano IVM multimode monopulse set now standard in Armée de l'Air F1s. The F1.C originally used the IV-0 with no air/ground capability, and this is still used by many export customers. The IV-1 adds MTI for limited look-down capability against lo aircraft and the IV-2 has beam-sharpening for air/ground missions, but all displays are of the head-down type. The IVM is the most sophisticated radar for the F1 and the head-down display shows a B-type for interception and a PPI for attack. Other avionics include HF/VHF/UHF/Tacan, VOR/ILS, autopilot, IFF and optional

SAGEM inertial nav, doppler, terrain-avoidance radar (normally external), digital computer and laser ranger. The Thomson-CSF BF is the usual passive RWR, with four receivers giving 90° coverage each (all on the fin, conical fore/aft and flush discus type on each side). The jammer pods used by most customers are the DB 3163 and, for F1s earmarked as dedicated EW platforms, the Caiman. South African aircraft use the larger Alligator, with 6kVA ram-air generator for pulse and CW from 6 to 8GHz.
Armament: Two 30mm DEFA-5-53 cannon, each with 135 rounds; five pylons, rated at 4,500lb

(2,000kg) on centreline, 2,800lb (1,350kg) inners and 1,100lb (500kg) outers; launch rails on tips rated at 280lb (120kg) for air-to-air missiles; total weapon load 8,820lb (4,000kg).
Future: Though an excellent aircraft the F1 series have been to some extent bypassed by the continued sale of the older deltas, and in recent years by the development of the 2000. The latter is now regarded as the chief new product on which to build, and with the French government's support of the next-generation ACX the F1 is probably going to receive no more than cosmetic treatment.

Left: The Mirage F1 is an excellent aircraft which Dassault expected to succeed and ultimately replace the tailless delta Mirages. This example was one of the first F1.C fighters to enter service with the Armée de l'Air.

Weapon provisions:
A. Two 30mm DEFA each with 135 rounds.
B. Pylon 4,500lb (2,040kg).
C. Pylon 2,800lb (1,270kg).
D. Pylon 1,102lb (500kg).
E. Rail 280lb (127kg).

Key to stores:
1. Matra 550 Magic close-range AAM on tip rail.
2. Beluga cluster dispenser.
3. Wasp ASM (folded).
4. SAMP GP bomb, 551lb (250kg).
5. AS.37 anti-radar Martel ASM (carried on centreline only).
6. Durandal anti-runway weapon.
7. Matra R.530 AAM.
8. GP bomb, 1,102lb (500kg).
9. Largest-size drop tank, 374gal (1,700lit).

10. DEFA 553 gun with 30mm ammunition (60 rounds only shown).
11. Matra Super 530 advanced AAM.
12. Matra 155 rocket launcher.
13. SNEB rockets, 68mm (2.68in) calibre.
14. AS.30 attack missile (X35 warhead).
15. AS.30L missile (used with Atlis II guidance pod).
16. DB 3163 ECM jammer pod.
17. AIM-9L Sidewinder AAM.

Combat avionics:
A. Cyrano IV radar.
B. Avionics bay.
C. HF extra dorsal fin (Libya only).
D. RWR.
E. HF/UHF notch.
F. VHF 1.
G. IFF.
H. VOR/Loc.
J. VHF 2.
K. UHF Tacan.

Dassault-Breguet Mirage 2000

Origin: France, first flight 10 March 1978.
Type: Interceptor and air-superiority fighter, later to have air/ground attack capability.
Engine: One SNECMA M53-5 turbojet with ratings of 12,350lb (5,601kg) dry and 19,840lb (9,000kg) with afterburner; from 1985 M53-P2 of higher thrust may be used
Dimensions: Span 29ft 6in (8.99m); length 47ft 1in (14.35m) (with probe 50ft 3½in, (15.32m); two-seaters excluding probe 47ft 9in (14.55m); height, not stated; wing area 441sq ft (41.98m²).
Weights: Empty about 16,535lb (7,500kg); air combat 20,944lb (9,500kg); maximum 36,375lb (16,500kg).
Performance: Maximum speed (clean, hi, brief dash) 1,550mph (2,495km/h) (Mach 2.35); sustained speed (clean, hi, for limited period) 1,450mph (2,335km/h) (Mach 2.2); max at SL (clean) 915mph (1,472km/h) (Mach 1.2); max at SL with eight 250kg bombs 690mph (1,110km/h); max climb 49,000ft (14,934m)/min; time to 49,000ft (14,934m)at Mach 2, 4 min; operational ceiling 59,000ft (17,982m); tac radius 435 miles (700km); ferry range 1,118 miles (1,800km); approach speed 162mph (260km/h); takeoff run with AAMs 4,000ft (1,220m).
Background: By 1963 the Dassault project staff were trying to hedge all their bets, with improved plain deltas, the jet-lift Mirage IIIV, the IIIT and F series with conventional fixed wing and tail, and the IIIG family with swing-wings. By 1974 a belated go-ahead was given on the ACF (Avion de Combat Futur); the design had hardly been completed when, on 18 December 1975, the ACF was cancelled in favour of a Dassault proposal for a delta the same size as the Mirage III. Not only was this expected to be much cheaper (an expectation not realized) but because of the adoption of the latest technology it could be made dramatically better than all previous Mirages in the air combat role.
Design: The Mirage 2000 marks notable advances over earlier Mirages in structure, aerodynamics, propulsion and systems. Fundamentally, it represents the ideal modern application of the classic tailless delta configuration. Design uses CCV technology, which implies FBW flight controls with instant response to pilot input, the movable surfaces being continuously adjusted to give exactly the required aircraft trajectory. Thus, the aircraft can in some regimes be more or less unstable, but prevented from divergent accelerations by continuous positive control. CCV technology is especially well suited to the tailless delta because it overcomes the problem of severe trim drag. The Mirage 2000 in any case has a wing with full-span leading-edge slats in inboard and outboard sections and large full-

span elevons, again in inboard and outboard sections. Such a wing does not have variable camber in the same sense as, for example, the F-16, but the slats enable the wing to operate at high angles of attack and also serve the vital function of enabling the elevons to be driven downwards, giving extra lift, instead of in the opposite direction during high-AOA flight. Thus, in high-AOA manoeuvres, or on takeoff and landing, the elevons add significantly to lift instead of opposing it. Like most deltas the wing is large, giving low wing loading for relatively light weight and simple structure, and for the first time in the Mirage 2000 the common delta failings of high drag-at-lift and high trim drag are overcome. On the other hand the low wing loading is totally unsuited to the attack role and the number of 0.5g bumps per minute in the full-throttle sea-level mode verges on the unacceptable. Structure includes a proportion of CFC, BFC and titanium. Small strakes on the inlets improve high-AOA handling, and during flight development the Kármán fairings at the bulged wing roots (not quite a blended wing/body but responsible for extra internal fuel and reduced structure weight) were extended well aft of the trailing edge of the main part of the wing: other changes were to make the vertical tail much broader, lower and more sharply swept and install fully quadruplexed FBW with no mechanical reversion. Internal fuel is 835gal (3,795 litres, compared with 735gal (3,341 litres) for Mirage III.
Avionics: Even operating under close ground control a relatively short-endurance aircraft of this type needs a good radar, and the intention was to fit a new PD radar called RDI (radar doppler à impulsions). Development of this at Thomson-CSF in partnership with ESD has lagged, and until 1985 the only radar available will be the RDM (multifunctions) originally intended for export customers only. This is a generally improved version of the Cyrano IV (Mirage F1). Radar data appear on conventional HUD and HDD displays, and no major display change is envisaged when the RDI becomes available. Hopefully RDI will detect fighter targets at 55 nautical miles (100km) and certainly it is designed to be able to direct Super 530 missiles on to targets much lower at "treetop" height as well as against targets 33,000ft (10km) higher. The SAGEM Uliss 52 INS is a direct development of the set used in the F1. Two ESD computers, linked by a Digibus data highway, perform system-management and attack computations. Basic avionics include VOR/ILS, Tacan and radio altimeter. EW includes the Thomson-CSF Serval-B RWR, with passive receiver aerials facing to the rear from the tail and ahead from the wingtips. ESD is developing a classified internal ECM suite which in air-defence

Above: A prototype Mirage 2000 taking off with a heavy "attack load" (mostly dummies). In fact, though a good air-combat aircraft in many respects, the 2000 is fundamentally handicapped in the subsonic attack role by its large wing and high fuel burn.

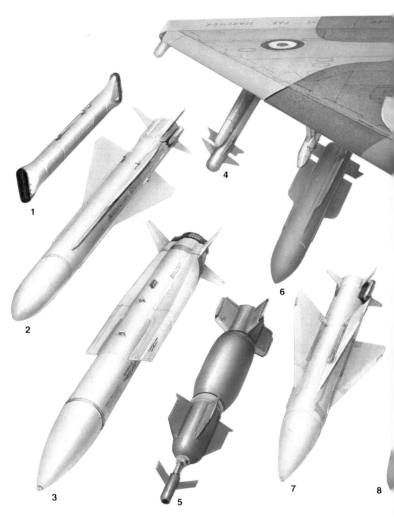

roles eliminates the need for an external pod such as Remora. For deep penetration Thomson-CSF is developing an ECM jammer pod, and the Atlis laser tracker can also be fitted.
Armament: Two DEFA 554 30mm guns, each with 125 rounds; nine external hardpoints, five under fuselage and two under each wing, for maximum total weapon load of 11,020lb (5,000kg).
Future: By the end of 1984 the first squadron should be equipping (2EC at Dijon) with the Dash-5 engine and RDM radar. The latter

has low PRF, can scan through various arcs to ±60° and has shown ability to track air targets at over 35 miles (56km); in the lo-attack mode against ground targets ranges up to 20 miles (32km) are achieved. For the attack aircraft, which will have numerous airframe and systems differences, a third radar is being developed. Called Antilope 5, this has a wide but shallow flat-plate aerial and is tailored especially to the terrain-following and lo-nav mode, updating the nav system either by manual inputs or by using terrain correlation.

Key to stores:
1. DB 3163 ECM jammer pod
2. AS.39 Exocet anti-ship missile.
3. ASMP cruise missile.
4. Matra 550 Magic AAM.
5. SAMP (Paveway derived) smart bomb.
6. Matra Super 530 AAM.
7. AS.30 (or laser-guided AS.30L) ASM.
8. Thomson-CSF/Martin Marietta Atlis II pod.
9. DEFA 554 30mm gun (internal mounted).
10. DEFA gun pod housing Type 554 gun.
11. 30mm ammunition for (9) and (10).

Weapon provisions:
A. Two 30mm DEFA each with 125 rounds.
B. Pylon 2,205lb (1,000kg).
C. Tandem pylons each 1,102lb (500kg).
D. Pylon 2,205lb (1000kg); can accept heavier 374-gal (1,700-lit) tank.
E. Pylon for light AAMs.

12. GP bomb, 1,102lb (500kg).
13. Durandal anti-runway weapon.
14. Twin carrier with GP bomb, 551lb (250kg).
15. Thomson-Brandt Type 100-6 rocket launcher.
16. Rockets, 3.94in (100mm) calibre.

17. Matra 155 rocket launcher.
18. Matra F1 36-tube rocket launcher.
19. Rockets, 2.68in (68mm) calibre.
20. Beluga cluster dispenser.
21. Thomson-CSF/Martin Marietta Atlis II pod.

Combat avionics:
A. RDM radar.
B. HUD.
C. IFF.
D. Avionics bay.
E. UHF.
F. RWR.
G. VOR.
H. VHF.
J. ECM jammer.
K. RWR (both tips).
L. VHF.
M. Radar altimeter.

Dassault-Breguet Super Etendard

Origin: France, first flight 28 October 1974.
Type: Single-seat carrier strike fighter.
Engine: 11,265lb (5,110kg) thrust SNECMA Atar 8K-50 turbojet.
Dimensions: Span 31ft 5¾in (9.5m); length 46ft 11½in (14.31m); height 12ft 8in (3.86m); wing area 305.7sq ft (28.4m²).
Weights: Empty 14,220lb (6,450kg); loaded 25,350lb (11,500kg).
Performance: Maximum speed 745mph (1,200km/h) at sea level, Mach 1 at altitude; initial climb 24,600ft (7,500m)/min; service ceiling 45,000ft (13,715m); radius (hi-lo-hi, one AM 39, one tank) 403 miles (650km).
Background: Basic design of the Etendard could hardly be more conventional, and dates from autumn 1955 when Dassault prepared the basic drawings for a NATO strike fighter. Prototypes flew with various engines from July 1956, and after adoption as a carrier-based type the IVM-01 flew in May 1958. Subsequently the IVM attack and IVP recon were standard Aéronavale types. The intended replacement was the Jaguar M, which was built and tested very satisfactorily in the Anglo-French programme, but Dassault succeeded in getting this rejected in favour of an improved Etendard with a completely new nav/attack system, slightly more powerful engine and improved wing high-lift features. Compared with the Jaguar the Super Etendard has much lower performance and carries less than half the weapon load, but is almost 100 per cent French. The planned 100 were cut to 71 by price-escalation.
Design: The basic 45° wing has been improved in detail with spoilers ahead of double-slotted flaps having greater travel and slightly different drooped dogtooth leading edges. Inset ailerons, spoilers, slab tailplanes and rudder are all powered. Fuel capacity is almost unchanged, though external fuel (at expense of weapons) can be much greater; Dassault claim the engine has reduced sfc compared with the original IVM but SNECMA's figures show consumption slightly higher at all throttle settings. The basic advantages of 11 per cent more thrust and a more efficient wing on accelerated takeoff enable the weapon load to be increased from 3,307 to 4,630lb (1,500 to 2,100kg), and by far the most important assets of the Super Etendard are its avionics and AM 39 anti-ship missile.
Avionics: Whereas the Etendard had only the fixed-18° cone of the tiny Aida ranging radar, the Super does have proper multimode radar, though the Thomson-CSF Agave is again a very small (106lb, 48kg) equipment which, though attractive and versatile, necessarily has limited power. Thomson-CSF's figure for range against small warships is 40-55km (25-34 miles), which is less than the effective range of the AM.39. A

HUD is fitted (Thomson-CSF VE 120), and so is an inertial system (though this is generally considered not the optimum solution for carrier-based aircraft, see Sea Harrier). Other equipment includes VHF/UHF/IFF/ Microtacan, VOR/ILS and a radio altimeter. There was from the start a scheme for a multisensor recon pod but this has not yet been funded. The usual Type BF passive RWR is fitted, though side-facing receiver disc aerials appear not to be fitted on the fin. The only jammer pod so far seen on Super Etendards is the common Thomson-CSF DB 3141, which can be carried on one of the side-by-side fuselage weapon pylons.
Armament: Two 30mm DEFA 553 guns each with 125 rounds; two fuselage hardpoints each rated at 551lb (250kg) with provision for a 132gal (600lit) tank or FR hosereel pod; four wing pylons each rated at 882lb (400kg), the inners plumbed for 242gal (1,100lit) tanks. Total external load 4,630lb (2,100kg), one option being one AM.39 Exocet (right) and one tank (left).
Future: Despite the great age of its basis, and its several severe shortcomings – such as the use of an obsolescent turbojet with double the weight and fuel consumption of modern engines – the Super Etendard demonstrated in the Falklands that against unprotected or unready ships it can be deadly. There is still much argument about whether or not the AM.39 that struck HMS Sheffield exploded, and mystery surrounds the ship's apparent failure to notice the fact that it was being illuminated by the radars of either the aircraft or its missile. The subject of the main illustration is Super Etendard 0753 of 2a Escuadrilla Aéronaval de Caza y Ataque (fighter bomber squadron) of the Argentine Navy. Of course the Argentine aircraft do not carry all the French missiles depicted,

Above: The Super Etendard is inevitably handicapped by being an improved version of an aircraft first flown in 1956. Thus it cannot equal modern aircraft in the same class such as the Italo-Brazilian AM-X, which has been designed from the start for a turbofan engine and modern avionics. Nevertheless it has shown in the most dramatic way that if it is allowed to it can inflict lethal wounds on major warships.

which include both the AN52 nuclear bomb and the projected ASMP long-range cruise missile. On the other hand the Argentine Martin Pescador (Kingfisher) is shown, even though this has not been identified on any operational Argentine aircraft. A locally developed ASM with a weight of 308lb (140kg) and range of up to 5½ miles (9km), it has simple radio command guidance and has been fired under test from MB.326 jet trainers and the A109A light helicopter. The colours of the missile are typical of test rounds, but when it is fully operational it will probably be finished in less conspicuous hues.

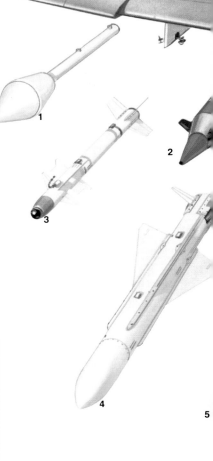

Left: One of the Super Etendard prototypes, pictured during carrier trials. Clearly visible are the lowered wing flaps, partly opened airbrakes and A-frame arrester hook. Because of the proven effectiveness of its Exocet missile in the South Atlantic (effectiveness increased by deficiencies in RN warships) Dassault Breguet has had several enquiries for further export sales, notable from Libya and Iraq.

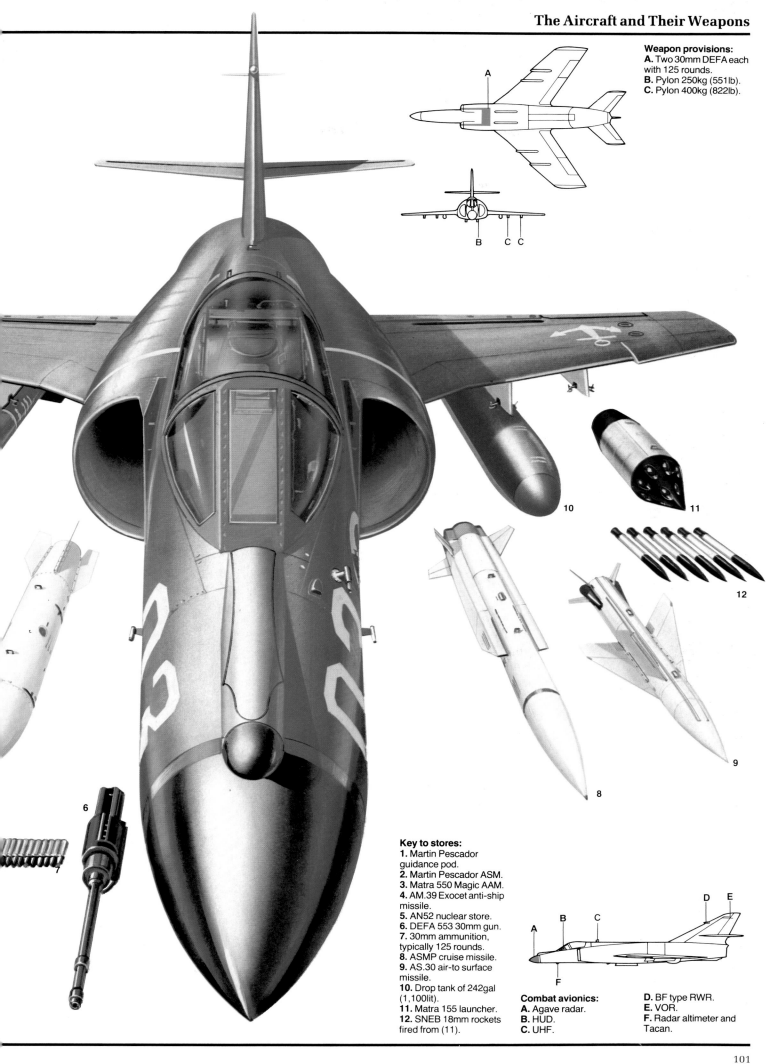

Weapon provisions:
A. Two 30mm DEFA each with 125 rounds.
B. Pylon 250kg (551lb).
C. Pylon 400kg (822lb).

A

B   C   C

10

11

12

9

8

6

7

Key to stores:
1. Martin Pescador guidance pod.
2. Martin Pescador ASM.
3. Matra 550 Magic AAM.
4. AM.39 Exocet anti-ship missile.
5. AN52 nuclear store.
6. DEFA 553 30mm gun.
7. 30mm ammunition, typically 125 rounds.
8. ASMP cruise missile.
9. AS.30 air-to surface missile.
10. Drop tank of 242gal (1,100lit).
11. Matra 155 launcher.
12. SNEB 18mm rockets fired from (11).

Combat avionics:
A. Agave radar.
B. HUD.
C. UHF.
D. BF type RWR.
E. VOR.
F. Radar altimeter and Tacan.

D   E

B   C

A

F

Fairchild Republic A-10 Thunderbolt II

Origin: USA, first flight 10 May 1972.
Type: Close-support attack aircraft.
Engines: Two 9,065lb (4,112kg) thrust General Electric TF34-100 turbofans.
Dimensions: Span 57ft 6in (17.52m); length 53ft 4in (16.25m); height (regular) 14ft 8in (4.47m); (NAW) 15ft 4in (4.67m); wing area 506sq ft (47.02m²).
Weights: Empty 21,519lb (9,761kg), forward airstrip weight (no fuel but four Mk 82 bombs and 750 rounds) 32,730lb (14,846kg),

Left: The USAF has tried very hard to evaluate the ability of the A-10A to survive in the environment of a land battle on NATO's Central Front; these aircraft are on an exercise. The overriding need to fly very low makes such training hazardous even in peacetime; attrition has been high.

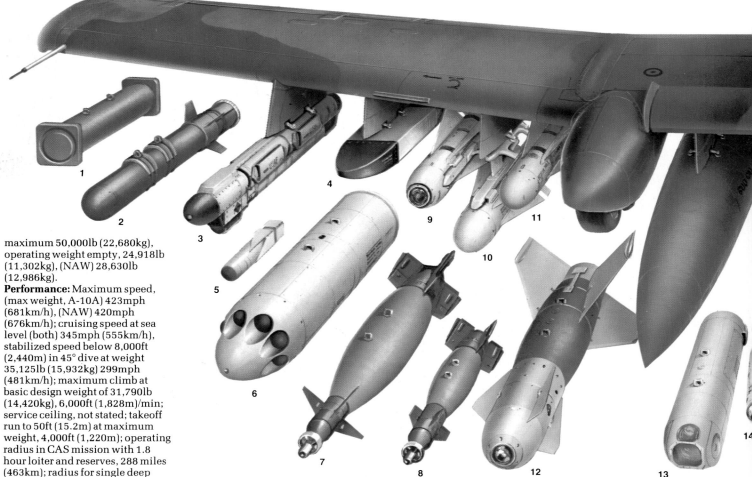

maximum 50,000lb (22,680kg), operating weight empty, 24,918lb (11,302kg), (NAW) 28,630lb (12,986kg).
Performance: Maximum speed, (max weight, A-10A) 423mph (681km/h), (NAW) 420mph (676km/h); cruising speed at sea level (both) 345mph (555km/h), stabilized speed below 8,000ft (2,440m) in 45° dive at weight 35,125lb (15,932kg) 299mph (481km/h); maximum climb at basic design weight of 31,790lb (14,420kg), 6,000ft (1,828m)/min; service ceiling, not stated; takeoff run to 50ft (15.2m) at maximum weight, 4,000ft (1,220m); operating radius in CAS mission with 1.8 hour loiter and reserves, 288 miles (463km); radius for single deep strike penetration, 620 miles (1,000km); ferry range 2,542 miles (4,091km).
Background: The AX specification of 1967 called for an aircraft to be powered by turboprop or fan engines. It was not required to have high speed but instead was to have the maximum lethality against hardened (armoured) targets, and to be able to achieve this lethality with the first round fired or the first store dropped. The primary weapon was to be a gun of greater muzzle horsepower than any previously flown. This was to be backed up by a heavy external weapon load. Avionics were hardly mentioned, the emphasis being laid on low cost, and short field length.
Design: Both the finalists in the AX competition were aircraft in the 20-ton loaded class, powered by two high-ratio turbofans. The winning design had these mounted high on the rear fuselage to

minimize IR signature. It was claimed that the A-10A could fly home after an engine had been shot completely off, or half the twin-finned tail or many other parts. Left/right interchangeability was stressed, control and system runs are duplicated and widely separated and the main wheels project when retracted. The wing has no sweep and deep NACA 6716 profile, and the large ailerons split into top/bottom halves opening as airbrakes. The cockpit is surrounded by a "bathtub" of titanium armour proof against 23mm fire, and fuel piping is tracked inside the reticulated foam tanks.
Avionics: The original avionics suite was officially described as "austere", despite the fact that the obvious main theatre of use has always been the Central Sector of the NATO front in Europe. Here neither offensive lethality nor survivability is possible without

the highest possible standard of weapon aiming sensors and defensive electronic systems, all-weather navigation for blind attack being taken for granted. Standard equipment today includes VHF/UHF/Tacan, IFF/SIF, INS, ILS, Kaiser HUD (recently updated with the ability to compute velocity vectors) and dual-reticle optical sight used in conjunction with the Pave Penny laser designation pod. The usual RHAW is the standard Itek ALR-46(V) and any of the common ECM jammer pods can be carried in lieu of a weapon. Another external option is the UTL ALQ-133 DF elint system, which measures threat bearings within about 0.5°. From 1977 Fairchild Republic worked on various augmented schemes and, built as a privately financed programme, a two-seat N/AW (Night/Adverse Weather) prototype with totally updated

avionics including Westinghouse (modified WX-50) radar, with ground MTI for mapping, terrain following/avoidance and threat detection: AAR-42 FLIR; Ferranti 105 laser ranger; new INS and new HUD: CRT display for the added backseat crew-member; and (for comparison with FLIR) LLLTV. This was never adopted, but the USAF has added a few sparsely equipped two-seaters with no better avionic fit than the A-10A.
Armament: One 30mm GE GAU-8/A high-velocity high-energy gun with 1,174 rounds; 11 pylons for maximum load (full internal fuel) of 14,341lb (6,505kg), or (reduced fuel) 16,000lb (7,258kg).
Future: Future developments are likely to be in the nature of retrofits, and by far the most important is likely to be fitting the LANTIRN (Low-Altitude Nav Targeting IR for Night) fire control pod.

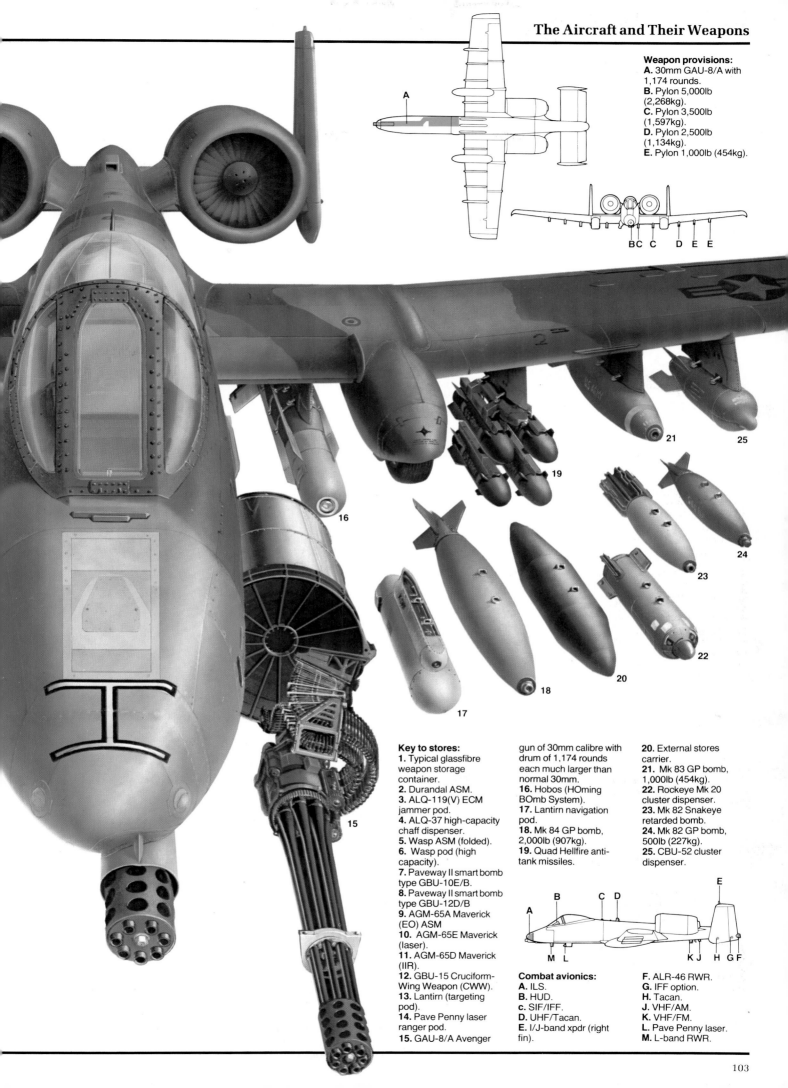

Weapon provisions:
A. 30mm GAU-8/A with 1,174 rounds.
B. Pylon 5,000lb (2,268kg).
C. Pylon 3,500lb (1,597kg).
D. Pylon 2,500lb (1,134kg).
E. Pylon 1,000lb (454kg).

B C   C   D E E

21
25
19
16
24
23
22
20
18
17
15

Key to stores:
1. Typical glassfibre weapon storage container.
2. Durandal ASM.
3. ALQ-119(V) ECM jammer pod.
4. ALQ-37 high-capacity chaff dispenser.
5. Wasp ASM (folded).
6. Wasp pod (high capacity).
7. Paveway II smart bomb type GBU-10E/B.
8. Paveway II smart bomb type GBU-12D/B
9. AGM-65A Maverick (EO) ASM
10. AGM-65E Maverick (laser).
11. AGM-65D Maverick (IIR).
12. GBU-15 Cruciform-Wing Weapon (CWW).
13. Lantirn (targeting pod).
14. Pave Penny laser ranger pod.
15. GAU-8/A Avenger

gun of 30mm calibre with drum of 1,174 rounds eacn much larger than normal 30mm.
16. Hobos (HOming BOmb System).
17. Lantirn navigation pod.
18. Mk 84 GP bomb, 2,000lb (907kg).
19. Quad Hellfire anti-tank missiles.

20. External stores carrier.
21. Mk 83 GP bomb, 1,000lb (454kg).
22. Rockeye Mk 20 cluster dispenser.
23. Mk 82 Snakeye retarded bomb.
24. Mk 82 GP bomb, 500lb (227kg).
25. CBU-52 cluster dispenser.

Combat avionics:
A. ILS.
B. HUD.
c. SIF/IFF.
D. UHF/Tacan.
E. I/J-band xpdr (right fin).

F. ALR-46 RWR.
G. IFF option.
H. Tacan.
J. VHF/AM.
K. VHF/FM.
L. Pave Penny laser.
M. L-band RWR.

FMA IA 58A Pucará

Left: In the Falklands campaign Pucarás of the IX and III Brigada Aerea suffered five losses in the air, and 14 on the ground.

Above: The Pucará was designed as a pure Co-In machine to put down uprisings by people not in possession of modern AA weapons.

Origin: Argentina, first flight 20 August 1969.
Type: Counter-insurgency attack.
Engines: Two 988shp (737kW) Turboméca Astazou XVIG turboprops.
Dimensions: Span 47ft 6¾in (14.4m); length 46ft 9¼in (14.255m); height 17ft 7.1in (5.361m); wing area 326.1sq ft (30.3m²).
Weights: Empty 8,900lb (4,037kg); maximum 14,991lb (6,800kg).
Performance: Maximum speed 310mph (500km/h) at 9,842ft (3km); initial climb at 12,125lb (5,500kg), 3,543ft (1,080m)/min; typical field length 3,300ft (1km); range with max internal fuel 845 miles (1,360km).
Background: Despite many changes of name the Fábrica Militar de Aviones at Córdoba has a history of over 50 years of designing its own military aircraft. The Pucará, named for a kind of early Indian fortress, was produced as a type optimised to Argentina's need for a Co-In aircraft to quell revolutionaries. The specification was similar to that formulated in the USA slightly earlier, in stressing the need for good short-field performance, good ground clearance for carrying external stores over rough surfaces, and such features as good crew visibility and inflight agility. It did not demand the ability to carry personnel, casualties, paratroops or cargo, as did the US requirement (which led to the OV-10).
Design: For short field-length and good low-level agility the IA 58 was designed with an efficient high-lift wing of quite large span. Later it might have spoilers and full-span flaps but all aircraft so far have played safe with large ailerons. Despite the slim fuselage there was ample room for fuel, in self-sealing tanks in the fuselage and inner wings. Despite their weight and cost it was considered worth fitting the very best zero/zero seats (Martin-Baker Mk 10), and the sharply stepped cockpits under a long clamshell canopy give an outstanding all-round view. Armour protection against ground

fire is provided under both cockpits and the engines, and US (MIL standard) practice was followed for structural design and system redundancy. Most services are hydraulic, but windscreen (the only) deicing is electrical and there is a Lox system. The main legs use steel ring-spring shock-absorption (as in the wartime Ju 88) with a very long stroke, and in emergency three ATO rockets can be bolted to the centreline pylon to give a takeoff run of only 262ft (80m). Flying controls are manual.
Avionics: These approximate to a typical top-drawer private-owner machine, with VHF nav/com, ADF, VOR/Loc/ILS and an HF/SSB long-range com set, together with full night and blind-flying equipment. The nose has provision for off-the-shelf weather radar but no Pucará has been seen thus fitted and there has never been any attempt at blind attack capability. The usual attack is a dive at an angle set up on the Matra reflector sight, with stores released by a Bendix programmer. At least one aircraft has been evaluated with a long dorsal blade aerial showing the use of a tactical VHF/FM radio, while there have been various temporary fits of ECM pods and IFF.
Armament: Two 20mm Hispano-Suiza HS 2804 guns each with 270 rounds plus four 7.62mm FN-Browning guns each with 900 rounds; centreline pylon rated at 2,205lb (1,000kg), two outer-wing pylons each rated at 1,102lb (500kg), for total external load of 3,571lb (1,620kg). All three hardpoints plumbed for tanks.
Future: The first 100 aircraft comprised 60 IA 58A (45 for the Fuerza Aérea Argentina and 15 for export, including 12 for Uruguay) and 40 IA 58B with 30mm DEFA guns instead of 20mm Hispano, 4 gal (18 litres) of fuel transferred from the fuselage to the wings and

dual avionics. In 1980 the IA 66 with 1,000shp (746kW) Garrett TPE331 engines began flight testing, and this may become the

standard model in the course of IA 58B production. A planned version with twin aft-mounted jets was abandoned.

Key to stores:
1. Rocket pods, LAU series.
2. Martin Pescador ASM.
3. Rocket pod, 19 tubes.

4. Tandem triplets of GP bombs (typically 110lb, 50kg, or various 115 or 120kg including fragmentation types)

shown on Aero 7A-1 tandem pylon.
5. Hispano-Suiza HS2804 gun with 270 rounds of 20mm (in some

Weapon provisions:
A. Two 20mm Hispano each with 270 rounds.
B. Four 7.62mm FN each with 900 rounds.
C. Pylon 2,205lb (1,000kg).
D. Pylon 1,102lb (500kg).

1

10

7

6

5

8

9

Combat avionics:
A. ILS.
B. Avionics.
C. HF/VHF.
D. VOR/Loc/ILS.

6. Centreline tank, 264gal (1,200lit).
7. JL100 rocket pod with

aircraft replaced by 30mm DEFA with 140 rounds).

68mm SNEB type rockets.
8. GP bomb, 265lb (120kg).
9. GP bomb, 882lb

(400kg).
10. F1 rocket pod with 68mm rockets.

General Dynamics F-16 Fighting Falcon

Origin: USA, first flight (Model 401) 2 February 1974, (F-16A) 8 December 1976.

Type: Multirole air-combat fighter with advanced ground attack capability.

Engine: One Pratt & Whitney F100-PW-200 augmented turbofan rated at 14,670lb (6,654kg) dry and 23,830lb (10,810kg) with max augmentation.

Dimensions: Span 31ft 0in (9.448m) 32ft 10in (102m) over missile fins); length (both versions, excl probe) 47ft 7.7in (14.52m); wing area 300.0sq ft (27.88m²).

Weights: Empty (A) 15,137lb (6,866kg), (B) 15,778lb (7,157kg); loaded (AAMs only) (A) 23,357lb (10,594kg), (B) 22,814lb (10,348kg), (max external load) (both) 35,400lb (16,057kg). (Block 25 on) 37,500lb (17,010kg).

Performance: Maximum speed (both, AAMs only) 1,350mph (2,172km/h, Mach 2.05) at 40,000ft (12,191m); maximum at SL, 915mph (1,472km/h, Mach 1.2); initial climb (AAMs only) 50,000ft (15.239m)/min; service ceiling, over 50,000ft (15,239m); tactical radius (A, six Mk 82, internal fuel, hi-lo-hi) 340 miles (547km); ferry range, 2,415 miles (3,890km).

Background: An LWF (lightweight fighter), competition was won in January 1975 by the YF-16 (previously the GD Model 401). The LWF had been launched as a technology demonstrator, but by 1975 it had been recast as a slightly larger and much more capable, multirole aircraft bought for TAC, and soon afterwards sold to four European nations. Subsequent development has today led to important new versions.

Design: From the start the emphasis was on CCV technology, with FBW controls without manual reversion. The configuration chosen had a single vertical tail, mid-mounted tailerons and a mid-mounted wing, with 40° taper on the leading edge, fitted with auto-scheduled variable camber provided by leading-edge flaps and trailing-edge flaperons. Features include forebody strakes to generate strong vortices and improve handling at high AOA, an ARI (auto aileron/rudder interconnect) and YRI (yaw-rate limiter) and, in normal service aircraft, an overall limitation to within 9g and 26° AOA. Thus the pilot can fly by Hotas techniques while ignoring the possibility of losing control or damaging the aircraft (but, so quiet is the ride, he must always have broad idea of AOA, airspeed and other parameters to avoid, for example, letting speed bleed right off at low level). The cockpit has an exceptional all-round view, the only canopy frame being behind the pilot (in the single-seat models) and the only obstruction ahead being pencil-thin AOA nosewheel steering indicators. Control inputs are by a force-sensing sidestick controller on the right console and force-sensing pedals, all ideally positioned for maximum application of force up to a point at which each control input comes up against a mechanical stop.

Avionics: The radar is the Westinghouse APG-66, an I/J-band pulse-doppler set, which was the most powerful that could be designed in 1975 without resorting to liquid cooling. Range scales are 10, 20, 40 and 80 nautical miles. The primary air-to-air mode is Downlook which gives end-on detection of fighter targets at over 30 nautical miles (56km) and shows them on a clutter-free display even when the target is at treetop height. There are 13 further modes, those vital in air combat all being controlled by thumb buttons on the throttle or stick; these include Dogfight, Radar Cursor, Designate, and Return to Search. Primary navigation system is the Singer-Kearfott SKN-2400 INS. Equipment includes UHF, VHF and Magnavox KY-58 secure voice, IFF, Tacan, ILS and Sperry air-data computer. EW includes the Dalmo Victor ALR-69 radar warning system with AEL aerials (antennae). Standard ECM pod is the ALQ-131 in various forms but other pods are used and Belgian F-16s have Loral Rapport III internal ECM housed in the extended tail compartment used to contain a drag chute in Norwegian F-16s.

Armament: One 20mm M61A-1 gun with 500 (tight pack, 515) rounds; ratings of pylons in 3-view are for 5.5g, giving theoretical weapon load with reduced internal fuel of 20,450lb (9,276kg). For 9g manoeuvres total load is reduced to 11,950lb (5,420kg).

Future: On 29 October 1980 the second F-16B two-seater was flown with the General Electric J79-119 engine rated at 18,730lb (8,496kg) max thrust, as the first F-16/79. This family was planned for export. On 19 December 1980 the first F-16A was flown after conversion to F-16/101 standard with the General Electric F101-DFE (F110) rated at over 28,000lb (12,700kg) max thrust. The basic F-16 is being enhanced over the next six years into the F-16C/D by the MSIP (multinational staged improvement programme) which initially cleared 37,500lb (17,009kg) MTOW with an enlarged tailplane, introduces structural changes for uprated pylon loads and two extra pylons on the sides of the engine inlet duct, a drag chute and increased internal avionic loads, and in later phases will introduce a new cockpit, fire-control avionics and sensors/weapons. The cockpit will replace many instruments by large electronic MFDs, and Marconi Avionics will provide a new holographic HUD with enhanced fov. For night and all-weather ground attack Lantirn pods will be carried on each side of the inlet, and new weapons will include Advanced Mavericks, Amraam radar AAMs, Wasp pods, LADs and 30mm Gepod guns. The fire-control computer will have double the memory and double the processing speed, the ASPJ will be

Above: Two early production Fighting Falcons of the USAF, with the original small tailplanes.

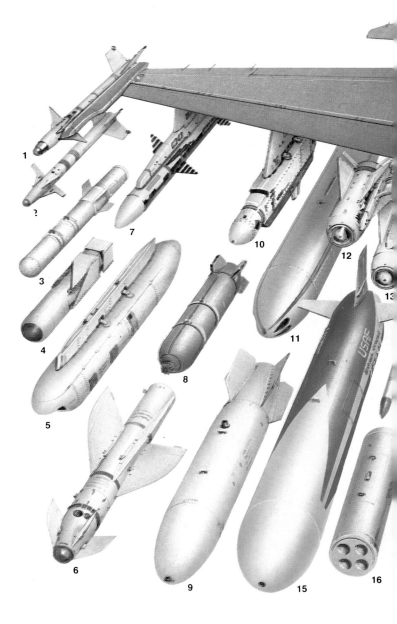

carried as standard, and Seek Talk secure voice will be fitted. The USAF is also studying a Wild Weasel defence-suppression version. More radical advances include the AFTI-16 (Advanced Fighter Technology Integration), first flown on 10 July 1982, and the F-16XL, which flew just a week earlier. The AFTI has twin inclined canard controls driven by a digital flight control system which among other things allows the fighter to move up, down or to either side instantly, without needing to bank or to alter the attitude of the aircraft. The XL, prototype of a planned F-16E, has a cranked-arrow wing of more than double the original area. It offers "substantially greater radius on internal fuel with twice the weapon load or more than double the radius with equal load"

Key to stores:
1. AIM-9L Sidewinder AAM.
2. AIM-9J Sidewinder AAM.
3. Durandal ASM.
4. Wasp ASM (folded).
5. Oldelft Orpheus reconnaissance pod.
6. Penguin Mk 3 ASM (Norway only).
7. AIM-120A Amraam.
8. CBU-528 dispenser.
9. B43 nuclear weapon.
10. ALQ-131 ECM jammer pod.
11. Gepod 30mm gun pod.

12. AGM-65A Maverick EO ASM.
13. AGM-65E Maverick laser ASM.
14. AGM-65D Maverick IIR ASM.
15. AGM-109H MRASM prototype.
16. SUU-25E flare pod.
17. LAU-3/A rocket pod.
18. SUU-20 practice dispenser.
19. EO-FLIR.
20. LST pod.
21. Atlis II pod.
22. Paveway I smart bomb KMU-351A/B.
23. M61 gun (internal). ▽

Weapon provisions:
A. 20mm M61 gun with 515 rounds.
B. Pylon 2,200lb (9,985kg).
C. Pylon 4,500lb (2,041kg).
D. Pylon 3,500lb (1,587kg).
E. Pylon 700lb (318kg).
F. 425lb (193kg).

24. Ammunition, 20mm, for (23).
25. Mk 82 bombs (one with stand-off fuze fitted).
26. Hobos (HOming BOmb System).
27. Mk 84 GP bomb, 2,000lb (907kg).
28. Mk 82 Snakeye.
29. AGM-78 Standard ARM (proposed Wild Weasel).
30. External carry pod.
31. Mk 83 GP bomb, 1,000lb (454kg).
32. Non-slick GP bomb, 750lb (340kg).
33. AGM-45 Shrike ASM (proposed Wild Weasel).
34. AGM-88A Harm ASM (proposed Wild Weasel).
35. Data link pod.

Combat avionics:
A. APG-66 radar.
B. HUD.
C. Tacan.
D. UHF/IFF.
E. RWR.
F. Rapport III ECM (FAN only).
G. Pave Penny or other sensor.
H. UHF/IFF.
J. Forward RWR.

General Dynamics F-111

Origin: USA, first flight 21 December 1964.
Type: A,D,E,F, all-weather attack; FB, strategic attack, EF, tactical ECM jammer.
Engines: Two Pratt & Whitney TF30 afterburning turbofans, as follows, (A,EF) 18,500lb (8,390kg) TF30-3, (D,E) 19,600lb (8,891kg) TF30-9, (FB) 20,350lb (9,231kg) TF30-7, (F) 25,100lb (11,385kg) TF30-100.
Dimensions: Span (fully spread) (A,D,E,F,EF) 63ft 0in (19.2m), (FB) 70ft 0in (21.33m), (fully swept) (A,D,E,F,EF) 31ft 11½in (9.74m) (FB) 33ft 11in (10.33m); length (except EF) 73ft 6in (22.4m), (EF) 77ft 1.6in (23.51m), wing area (A,D,E,F,EF, gross, 16°) 525sq ft (48.79m²).
Weights: Empty (A) 46,172lb (20,943kg), (D) 49,090lb (22,267kg) (E) about 47,000lb (21,319kg), (EF) 53,418lb (24,230kg), (F) 47,481lb (21,537kg), (FB) close to 50,000lb (22,680kg); loaded (A) 91,500lb (41,500kg), (D,E) 92,500lb (41,954kg), (F) 100,000lb (45,360kg), (FB) 114,300lb (51,846kg), (EF) 87,478lb (39,680kg).
Performance: Maximum speed at 36,000ft (10,972m), clean and with max afterburner, (A,D,E) Mach 2.2, 1,450mph (2,335km/h), (FB) Mach 2, 1,320mph (2,124km/h), (F) Mach 2.5, 1,653mph (2,660km/h), (EF) Mach 1.75; 1,160mph (1,865km/h); cruising speed, penetration, 571mph (919km/h); initial climb (EF) 3,592ft (1,094m)/min; service ceiling at combat weight, max afterburner, (A) 51,000ft (15,544m), (F) 60,000ft (18,290m), (EF) 54,700ft (16,670m); range with max internal fuel (A,D) 3,165 miles (5,093km), (F) 2,925 miles (4,707km), (EF) 2,484 miles (3,998km); takeoff run (A) 4,000ft (1,219m), (F) under 3,000ft (914m), (FB) 4,700ft (1,433m), (EF) 3,250ft (991m).
Background: The 1960 USAF specification for a new tactical fighter (TFX) reflected such new technology as titanium structure, variable-sweep "swing wings", high-lift airfoils, augmented turbofan engines, terrain-following radar and advanced AAM armament to permit stand-off interception without the need for dogfighting. The result was intended to be a gigantic programme to replace existing fighters and attack aircraft of the USAF, Navy and Marine Corps and most friendly air forces. The first of 18 F-111A (USAF) prototypes flew on 21 December 1964, and the first of five F-111B (Navy) fighters followed on 18 May 1965. The B programme collapsed but the A eventually overcame severe difficulties and entered USAF service as an attack bomber. Subsequent production totalled 537, subdivided into six versions, of which 42 of the earliest are being rebuilt as EW jamming platforms.
Design: Having accepted the configuration of a high-mounted swing-wing, slab tailerons for pitch and roll (plus wing spoilers augmenting roll at low speeds),

twin engines in a wide fuselage housing the retracted main gears, and side-by-side crew seats, GD then concentrated on the difficult attack and ferry missions and provided large internal fuel capacity, large multimode nose radar plus terrain-following radar linked through the autopilot to the flight controls, a very small weapon bay plus large external weapon pylon capacity (despite the entire underside of the fuselage being sterilized by the landing gears and air brake) and full-span vari-camber slats and double-slotted flaps on the outer wings to hold down field length despite the growing MTO weight. Problems with drag and engine mismatch led to further increases in fuel capacity and MTO weight, until the latter had climbed from the target 60,000lb (27,215kg) to more than 90,000lb (40,823kg). Successive versions introduced engine inlets of higher efficiency, engines of greater thrust, a new and very complex avionic fit and, finally, a better version of the same engine and a third state of avionics. SAC and the RAAF bought versions with long-span wings and strengthened landing gear.
Avionics: The colossal nose is filled with avionics, in standard racking for easy module replacement. The forward-looking radar was the first in a major GE family with designation APQ-113. A large liquid-cooled set operating in J-band (16-16.4GHz), it is used by the F-111A, C and E navigator (right-hand seat) for navigation, air/ground ranging and weapon delivery and (in theory) in the air/air mode using the 20mm gun (seldom fitted) or Sidewinders. In the "Mk II" avionic fit of the F-111D the main radar is the APQ-130, with MTI, doppler beam sharpening, illumination for radar-guided AAMs and many other advanced features. For the FB-111A bomber the radar is the APQ-114, derived from the -113 with added beacon mode, photo recording and a north-oriented display. The F-111F has the GE APQ-144 with a new 2.5 mile (4km) display ring made possible by a 0.2s pulse-width capability; digital MTI was tested but not built into production 144 sets. Under the main radars are TFRs, usually the TI APQ-110, which gave all tactical versions the unique ability of automatic terrain-following flight at a selected low height, in any weather. Other items include Litton INS, GPL doppler, Sanders ALQ-94 noise deception jammer, Dalmo-Victor ALR-62 RWR, Cincinnati Electronics AAR-44 IRWR, Textron RHAWS and Avco ECM receiver. Today the ALQ-94 is being replaced by the Sanders ALQ-137, though active jammer pods are carried under the rear fuselage, the usual pod being the ALQ-119(V) or ALQ-131. It is planned eventually to fit the ALQ-165 ASPJ. The most useful add-on to the F-111Fs of the 48th TFW is Ford's AVQ-26 Pave Tack which combines a laser with a FLIR both

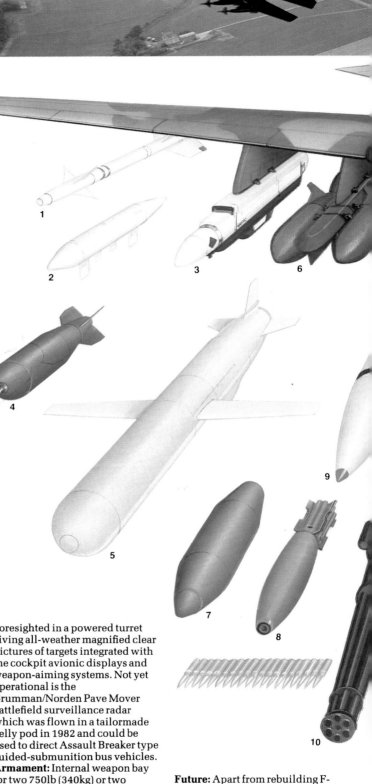

boresighted in a powered turret giving all-weather magnified clear pictures of targets integrated with the cockpit avionic displays and weapon-aiming systems. Not yet operational is the Grumman/Norden Pave Mover battlefield surveillance radar which was flown in a tailormade belly pod in 1982 and could be used to direct Assault Breaker type guided-submunition bus vehicles.
Armament: Internal weapon bay for two 750lb (340kg) or two (various) nuclear bombs or other loads, or one 20mm M61A-1 gun with 2,084 rounds. Four pivoting wing pylons for 24 bombs of 750lb (340kg), 500gal (2,273lit) tanks or other loads (see main illustration). Provision for four fixed pylons under outer wings, the inboard pair very occasionally being fitted (same ratings).

Future: Apart from rebuilding F-111A attack aircraft as EF-111A electronic jamming platforms, the main future plans concern updates to systems, weapons and avionics. Pave Mover is still a possibility, Pave Tack could be procured for the F-111E and possibly D, and the ASPJ and JTIDS are further additions which might be funded before 1985.

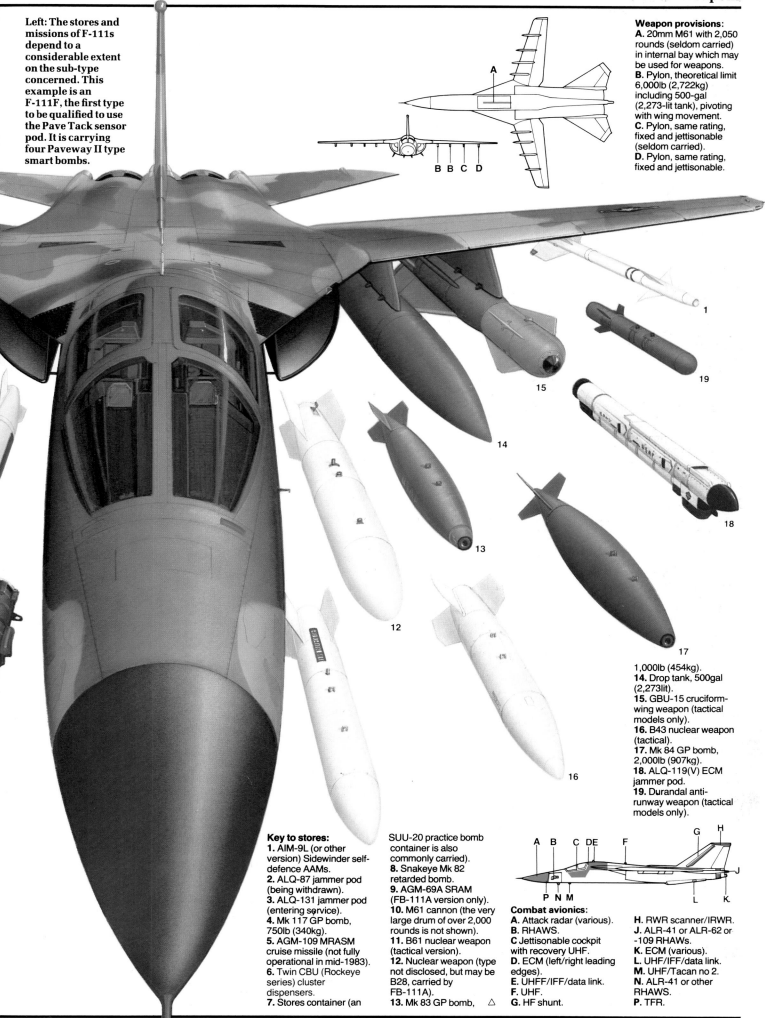

Left: The stores and missions of F-111s depend to a considerable extent on the sub-type concerned. This example is an F-111F, the first type to be qualified to use the Pave Tack sensor pod. It is carrying four Paveway II type smart bombs.

Weapon provisions:
A. 20mm M61 with 2,050 rounds (seldom carried) in internal bay which may be used for weapons.
B. Pylon, theoretical limit 6,000lb (2,722kg) including 500-gal (2,273-lit tank), pivoting with wing movement.
C. Pylon, same rating, fixed and jettisonable (seldom carried).
D. Pylon, same rating, fixed and jettisonable.

B B C D

1,000lb (454kg).
14. Drop tank, 500gal (2,273lit).
15. GBU-15 cruciform-wing weapon (tactical models only).
16. B43 nuclear weapon (tactical).
17. Mk 84 GP bomb, 2,000lb (907kg).
18. ALQ-119(V) ECM jammer pod.
19. Durandal anti-runway weapon (tactical models only).

Key to stores:
1. AIM-9L (or other version) Sidewinder self-defence AAMs.
2. ALQ-87 jammer pod (being withdrawn).
3. ALQ-131 jammer pod (entering service).
4. Mk 117 GP bomb, 750lb (340kg).
5. AGM-109 MRASM cruise missile (not fully operational in mid-1983).
6. Twin CBU (Rockeye series) cluster dispensers.
7. Stores container (an SUU-20 practice bomb container is also commonly carried).
8. Snakeye Mk 82 retarded bomb.
9. AGM-69A SRAM (FB-111A version only).
10. M61 cannon (the very large drum of over 2,000 rounds is not shown).
11. B61 nuclear weapon (tactical version).
12. Nuclear weapon (type not disclosed, but may be B28, carried by FB-111A).
13. Mk 83 GP bomb, △

Combat avionics:
A. Attack radar (various).
B. RHAWS.
C Jettisonable cockpit with recovery UHF.
D. ECM (left/right leading edges).
E. UHFF/IFF/data link.
F. UHF.
G. HF shunt.
H. RWR scanner/IRWR.
J. ALR-41 or ALR-62 or -109 RHAWs.
K. ECM (various).
L. UHF/IFF/data link.
M. UHF/Tacan no 2.
N. ALR-41 or other RHAWS.
P. TFR.

A B C DE F G H

P N M J L K

Gruman A-6 Intruder

Origin: USA, first flight 19 April 1960.
Type: Two-seat carrier-based all-weather attack.
Engines: Two 9,300lb (4,218kg) thrust Pratt & Whitney J52-8A turbojets.
Dimensions: Span 53ft (16.15m); length (except EA-6B) 54ft 7in (16.63m); height (A-6A, A-6C) 15ft 7in (4.74m); (A-6E, EA-6A) 16ft 3in (4.95m); wing area 528.9sq ft (49.15m²).
Weights: Empty (A-6A) 25,684lb (11,650kg); (EA-6A) 27,769lb (12,557kg); (A-6E) 25,630lb (11,625kg); maximum loaded (A-6A and E) 60,400lb (27,397kg).
Performance: Maximum speed (clean A-6A) 685mph (1,102km/h) at sea level or 625mph (1,006km/h, Mach 0.94) at height; (EA-6A) over 630mph (1,014km/h); (A-6E) 648mph (1,043km/h) at sea level; initial climb (A-6E, clean) 8,600ft (2,621m)/min; service ceiling (A-6A) 41,660ft (12,679m); (A-6E) 44,600ft (13,595m); range with full combat load (A-6E) 1,077 miles (1,733km); ferry range with external fuel (all) about 3,100 miles (4,989km).
Background: Despite the subsequent success of the A-4, experience in the Korean War had repeatedly demonstrated to the US Navy and Marine Corps the urgent need for a larger jet attack aircraft with all-weather avionics able to make blind first-pass bombing runs on point targets. A requirement was issued in 1956, and in December 1957 the Grumman G-128 proposal was accepted from 11 designs submitted by eight companies. The prototype flew as the YA2F-1 on 19 April 1960, and led not only to the mass-produced A-6A and updated A-6E attack versions but also to the Navy/Marines dedicated tanker aircraft (KA-6D rebuilds) and EW platforms (EA-6B Prowler, all new-builds).
Design: Though area-ruled, the A-6 has no pretensions at speed but concentrates on the much more important capabilities of flying low and flying accurately in bad weather or by night. The wing has surprisingly high aspect ratio and full-span leading- and trailing-edge flaps, roll control being by spoilers. Pure jet engines are on the flanks of the fuselge under the wing roots, the massive main gears retracting forwards into compartments in the lee of the inlets under the wing roots. Pilot and navigator sit almost side-by-side in Martin-Baker GRU.7 seats under a clamshell canopy, there is room for no less than 1,986 gal (9,028 litres) of internal fuel, and the entire nose is formed by a giant radome over a large search radar and small tracking radar, feeding an early digital computer and displays. Later this entire system was superseded, as outlined in the next section.
Avionics: The A-6A gave the Navy/Marines their first real all-weather capability against surface targets other than ships. This was done at the cost of severe

maintenance problems, high "down time" (unserviceability) and many other difficulties, most of which could be swept away by new solid-state microelectronics. Today's A-6E has a totally different Norden APQ-148 multi-mode radar replacing the two previous sets and vastly outperforming either except possibly in the mission against small vehicles and other moving targets against a land background, and AMTI (airborne moving target indication) has been added in 1981-83 for this purpose. There is no HUD but instead an HDD of remarkable character, the Kaiser AVA-1, which was the first display ever to use a CRT to show the pilot basic flight data such as aircraft attitude, nav information and weapon-delivery cues. The bright display includes synthetic terrain/sea and sky and can incorporate radar pictures and other data for use in basic all-weather flight, navigation, all forms of weapon delivery (including terrain following or terrain avoidance) and approach and landing. Basic navigation is by an INS updated by Litton's ASN-92 CAINS (carrier-aircraft INS). All A-6Es will have been fitted with TRAM (Target Recognition and Attack Multisensor) by 1985. This adds an under-nose turret containing a FLIR and a laser. The navigator flies on the main radar and AVA-1 VDI (vertical display indicator) on which he acquires targets. He switches to the FLIR, using optical zoom to give an enhanced and magnified image. He then uses the laser to mark the target for "smart" weapons; alternatively the laser can detect a target marked by other lasers.
Armament: All attack versions, including EA-6A, five stores locations each rated at 3,600lb (1,6333kg) with maximum total load of 15,000lb (6,804kg); typical load thirty 500lb (227kg) bombs; (EA-6B, KA-6D) none.
Future: Despite the attack

capability of the F/A-18A Hornet the A-6E/TRAM is expected to remain in low-rate production for the next several years, and existing aircraft continue to be updated, with at least four further add-on or improvement programmes planned. TRAM equipment should be with all embarked Fleet Attack wings (Medium) by early 1985, and additional sensor and navigation systems may be added, including the Awsacs (All-weather stand-off attack control system) which will

enhance the ability of the A-6E to operate autonomously in the most adverse weather against major targets including surface combatants. New weapons being introduced include AGM-84A Harpoon, six of which can be carried, and the AGM-109 MRASM in all three versions, and especially the sea-control missile AGM-109K. Normally four MRASMs would be carried, though for modest combat radii it is theoretically possible to carry six.

Left: Grumman built a straight run of 482 of the original A-6A model, followed by conversions to A-6B, A-6C and KA-6D standard. This is one of today's A-6Es, the definitive attack version, of which about 350 are to be delivered. Some 230 of these will be rebuilds of earlier models. All current aircraft are being delivered with the TRAM chin turret and capability to launch Harpoon anti-ship missiles.

The Aircraft and Their Weapons

Weapon provisions:
A. TRAM turret (IR, laser).
B. Pylon 3,600lb (1,633kg).
C. Pylon 3,600lb (1,633kg) or 250-gal (1,135-lit) tank.

Key to stores:
1. Forward emitting aerials of ALQ-41/ALQ-100 deception jamming system (not always carried).
2. Tandem triple low-drag GP bombs of 250 or 500lb (113 or 227kg) size.
3. 250gal (1,136lit) long-range tank.
4. AGM-65A standard Maverick; several other versions are compatible, and the Marine Corps uses the AGM-65E laser model.
5. AGM-109I dual-role version of MRASM with DSMAC II (digital scene-matching area correlation) and IIR guidance and large unitary warhead for anti-ship or land attack missions.
6. AGM-84A Harpoon long-range anti-ship missile
7. CBU Rockeye Mk 20 Mod 1 anti-armour cluster dispenser.
8. Mk 82 GP bomb of 500lb (227kg) with stand-off probe fuze.
9. Snakeye (Mk 92 GP bomb) fitted with tail retarder.
10. Mk 83 GP bomb, 500lb (227kg).

Combat avionics:
A. APQ-148 radar.
B. AVA-1 display.
C. ARA-48 UHF/ADF.
D. ARN-84 Tacan.
E. L-band UHF,
F. APN-153 doppler.
G. Jammer option ALQ-41 or -100.
H. L-band UHF.
J. FLIR and laser.

Grumman F-14 Tomcat

Origin: USA, first flight 21 December 1970.
Type: Two-seat carrier-based multi-role fighter.
Engines: (F-14A) two 20,900lb (9,480kg) thrust Pratt & Whitney TF30-412A afterburning turbofans; (C) two 20,900lb (9,480kg) thrust Pratt & Whitney TF30-414A afterburning turbofans.
Dimensions: Span (68° sweep) 38ft 2in (11.63m), (20° sweep) 64ft 1½in 919.54m); length 62ft 8in (19.1m); height 16ft (4.87m); wing area (spread) 565sqft (52.50m²).
Weights: Empty 37,500lb (17,010kg); loaded (fighter mission) 55,000lb (24,948kg), (maximum) 72,000lb (32,658kg).
Performance: Maximum speed, 1,564mph (2,517km/h, Mach 2.34) at height, 910mph (1,464km/h, Mach 1.2) at sea level; initial climb at normal gross weight, over 30,000ft (9,144m)/min; service ceiling over 56,000ft (17,067m); range (fighter with external fuel) about 2,000 miles (3,200km).
Background: Grumman was teamed with General Dynamics on the F-111B. When in 1968 it became evident that this programme might collapse work was urgently started on a possible replacement, starting from almost a clean sheet of paper. Items transferred bodily from the F-111B were the TF30 engine, Hughes AWG-9 radar and Hughes AIM-54 Phoenix long-range AAM. The F-14 itself was totally new and uncompromised, and was announced winner of the hastily contrived VFX competition on 15 January 1969. The first of six R&D prototypes flew on 21 December 1970. Unlike the F-111 no attempt was made to achieve commonality with any other aircraft, and the needs of the fighter sweep/escort, CAP (combat air patrol) and DLI (deck-launched intercept) missions were given priority.
Design: It is ironic that, though the F-14 has a swing wing able to take up any angle automatically between 20° and 68° according to the varying demands of the mission, its actual usage has been almost totally in the fighter/interceptor role. The main advantages of the swing wing for the F-14 are to reduce takeoff and landing speeds, facilitating cat (accelerated) launches at high gross weights, and to reduce fuel consumption in subsonic loiter and enable higher altitudes to be reached at low subsonic speeds. Though the two aircraft could

hardly be more different in other ways, the F-14 and A-6 share a similar inlet duct, wing and main landing gear geometry, the latter folding forwards alongside the duct into compartments faired under the wing roots. Unlike the A-6 the long fully augmented engines extend far downstream to variable nozzles at the extreme rear of the aircraft, widely separated throughout by fuselage tankage and with a canted vertical tail above each engine and with the airbrakes above and below in the wide gap between the nozzles. Pilot and naval flight officer sit well separated in capacious tandem cockpit with a long one-unit upward-hinged canopy. Aerodynamics are complex, with large fixed wing gloves carrying the outer-wing pivots 17ft 10in (5.43m) apart and incorporating retractable canards (called glove vanes) which are fully extended at maximum sweep of 68°.
Avionics: The F-14 is believed to have been the world's first production aircraft with a look-down shoot-down capability. Amply discussed earlier in this book, this capability against low-flying aircraft was the last major gap that had to be closed in air defence, and it is claimed the F-14 has almost total capability against not only hostile aircraft but also sea-skimming anti-ship missiles. The AWG-9 radar is a hefty (1,293lb/586.5kg; 28cuft/0.79m³) liquid-cooled package with the vital coherent pulse-doppler mode for look-down capability. It was also the first fighter radar with TWS (track while scan), enabling it at unprecedented range of well over 100 miles (161km) to detect, select and track more than 20 air targets, pick out the six most threatening and launch six Phoenix AAMs against these, each missile being code-keyed to its own target. The severe problem of long-range recognition is greatly assisted by the Northrop TCS, also discussed previously, though the rate of funding has been such that by mid-1983 more than seven out of eight F-14s in service had yet to receive it. With it fitted the only crippling shortcoming is the need to keep flying towards the enemy whilst providing target illumination for the AIM-7 medium-range AAMs. Kaiser provides the AVA-12 vertical situation display and electronically separate but mechanically integrated HUD, the latter having no combiner glass but

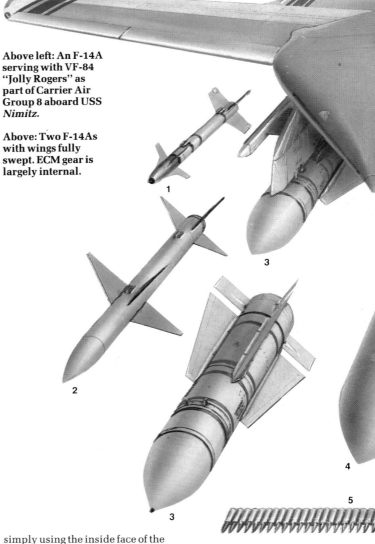

Above left: An F-14A serving with VF-84 "Jolly Rogers" as part of Carrier Air Group 8 aboard USS *Nimitz*.

Above: Two F-14As with wings fully swept. ECM gear is largely internal.

simply using the inside face of the windscreen. Other kit includes an expanded-memory digital computer, laser-gyro INS (being retrofitted when funds permit, and on the F-14C version) and, after long delays, the definitive Westinghouse/ITT ASPJ (airborne self-protection jammer) and Hughes-ITT JTIDS combined with the Itek ALR-67 threat-warning system. Since 1982 Hughes has been retrofitting a completely new backseat all-digital display and control system, with programmable signal processor. Pending development of a dedicated recon aircraft 49 F-14s have been fitted to carry the TARPS (Tac Air Recon Pod System) with cameras and IR linescan.
Armament: One 20mm M61A-1 gun; fuselage pallets for four AIM-54 Phoenix AAMs or recesses for

four AIM-7 Sparrow or AIM-120 Amraam; wing pylons for two Phoenix or Sparrow or AIM-120 plus two AIM-9 Sidewinders or four Sidewinders. Attack weapons can replace AAMs to limit of 14,500lb (6,577kg).
Future: The TF30 engine was accepted as interim propulsion pending development of the F401 engine. Every F-14 in service has had the TF30, and problems have been severe and prolonged. Even the F-14C now in production retains an improved TF30, but the Navy has never lost sight of the F110 (flown in an F-14 in 1981) as an alternative. An important gain will be replacement of AIM-7 by Amraam, which is a fire-and-forget missile.

Weapon provisions:
A. 20mm M61 with 675 rounds.
B. Chaff dispenser.
C. Hardpoints for tank, Tarps or tandem AIM-7 or -120.
D. Body pallets for tandem AIM-54 or AIM-7 or -120.
E. Pylons for 222-gal (1,011-lit) tanks.
F. Pylons for 3,000lb (1,361kg) various stores.

Key to stores:
1. AIM-9J Sidewinder AAM.
2. AIM-7 Sparrow radar guided AAM.
3. AIM-54A long-range AAMs.
4. Drop tank carried under inlet ducts, 222gal (1,011lit).
5. Ammunition, 20mm.

6. M61 gun, 20mm calibre.
7. Ammunition, 675 rounds.
8. Tarps reconnaissance pod.
9. AIM-120 Amraam AAMs.
10. AIM-9L Sidewinder.
11. AIM-7 training Sparrow AAM.

Combat avionics:
A. AWG-9 radar.
B. Avionics bay.
C. HUD.
D. UHF/Tacan.
E. UHF/IFF/data link.
F. ECM aerial (both fins).

G. ECM aerial.
H. ALR-45 RWR (both tailplanes).
J. ALQ-100 DECM, IR seeker or TCS.
K. ALE-39 chaff/flare/jammer dispenser.

Israel Aircraft Industries Kfir-C2

Origin: Israel, first flight (C1) 1972.
Type: Multi-role fighter and attack, (TC-2) trainer and EW.
Engine: One 17,900lb (8119kg) General Electric J79-J1E augmented turbojet.
Dimensions: Span 26ft 11½in (8.21m); length (C1, C2) 51ft 4¼in (15.65m), (C2 with Elta radar) 53ft 11¾in (16.45m); (TC2) 54ft 1¼in (16.49m); height 14ft 11¼in (4.55m); wing area 374.6sq ft (34.8m²); foreplane 17.87sq ft (1.66m²).
Weights: Empty (C2, interceptor) 16,060lb (7,285kg); loaded (C2, half internal fuel plus two Shafrir) 20,700lb (9,390kg), (C2, max with full internal fuel, two tanks, seven 500lb bombs and two Shafrir) 32,340lb (14,670kg).
Performance: (C2) Maximum speed (clean) 863mph (1,389km/h) at sea level, over Mach 2.3 (1,516mph, 2,440km/h) above 36,090ft (11km); initial climb 45,950ft/min (233m/s); service ceiling 58,000ft (17,680m); combat radius (20min reserve), (interceptor, two 110gal, 500 litre tanks plus two Shafrir) 215 miles (346km), (attack, three 330gal, 1,500 litre tanks plus seven bombs and two Shafrir, hi-lo-hi) 477 miles (768km).
Background: The Dassault Mirage 5 was developed at the suggestion of the Israeli Chel Ha'Avir (air force), which underpinned development with an order for 50. The French then switched their allegiance to the Arabs, put the same 50 aircraft into their own air force and cut off Israel from service support. The result was Israel's decision to become self-sufficient, initially by building a near-copy of the Mirage 5 called the Nesher and subsequently by carrying out a sweeping redesign to produce a superior combat aircraft powered by the American J79 engine. The Kfir (Lion Cub) was planned as a multi-role air-combat fighter, attack aircraft, recon platform and, in two-seat form, as an EW aircraft and conversion trainer. Almost every equipment item is of Israeli manufacture.
Design: Compared with the Mirage 5 the Kfir-C2 has three main differences: propulsion, aerodynamics and avionics, the last being discussed separately. The J79 engine is slightly heavier than the original Atar 9C but considerably shorter and more powerful. There was no severe problem with aircraft c.g. (centre of gravity) though the fuselage is considerably shorter and the nozzle face is a metre ahead of the trailing edge of the rudder. The engine bay had to be completely redesigned for an engine of different shape with differently located accessories, and with augmented cooling supplied by several new ram inlets including one at the front of a new dorsal fin. The main aerodynamic change is the addition of a swept fixed canard foreplane high on each inlet duct ahead of the main wing roots. This improves handling qualities, manoeuvrability and ride under

virtually all conditions. In particular it reduces takeoff and landing distances, increases sustained rate of turn at all heights and Mach numbers, and reduces gust response in the lo attack role. Further considerable improvements, especially at high angles of attack, stem from the extended-chord dogtooth outer wings and small strakes mounted horizontally on each side of the nose. The cockpit is largely redesigned, the seat is a Martin-Baker IL.10P (one of very few imported items) and the main gears are strengthened and of longer stroke to facilitate operations from unpaved strips.
Avionics: The first Kfirs of the interim Kfir-C1 type without canards were often fitted with large Cyrano-type radar, but the usual radar in today's C2s is the small range-only Elta EL/M-2001B, which fits in the tip of the slim and lengthened nose and looking through a small dielectric nosecone. This keeps the Kfir firmly in the same operational category as the original Mirage 5, with visual detection and identification of targets. The radar merely provides tracking and range information, which can be fed to the HUD now fitted to almost all Kfirs. Curiously Elta states the much larger EL/M-2021B radar is used on the Kfir, but the author has never seen this (this radar is certainly used on some Israeli Mirages and Phantoms). Apart from lack of a multi-mode radar the Kfir's avionic fit is comprehensive and wholly Israeli, including licensed INS, Elbit multifunction CRT display, a choice of two nav/weapon-delivery systems and extremely good autopilot and stability-augmentation systems. Israel Electro produce the HUD-sight, using a lot of borrowed technology, and there is no doubt the SIF/IFF and EW suite is to a high standard, though largely classified. At least one C2 was fitted with Thomson-CSF type BF RWR with small receivers on the fin and wingtips, but a different system is standard. There is reported to be provision for chaff/flare dispensing, and the most common ECM jammer pod is the Elta L-8202 which is an outstanding product giving high-power (2.3kVA) cover from 3 to 20GHz and with the threat library and responses reprogrammable on the flight-line. The tandem-seat Kfir-TC2 was announced as a dual trainer but clearly serves also as an EW aircraft, carrying additional avionics among which is the Elta L-8230 internal self-protection jammer. This is a major installation (93lb, 42kg) covering wavebands from 4 to 20GHz and putting out various forms of jamming to counter both surface and air radars. The TC2 has an overall length of 53ft 8in (16.36m) and the nose is tilted sharply down to maintain a reasonable forward view from both cockpits. Flight performance is little affected.
Armament: Two 30mm DEFA 553

Above: Kfir-C2s have established an enviable record in combat duty with Israel's Chel Ha'Avir. The C7 will follow it into service.

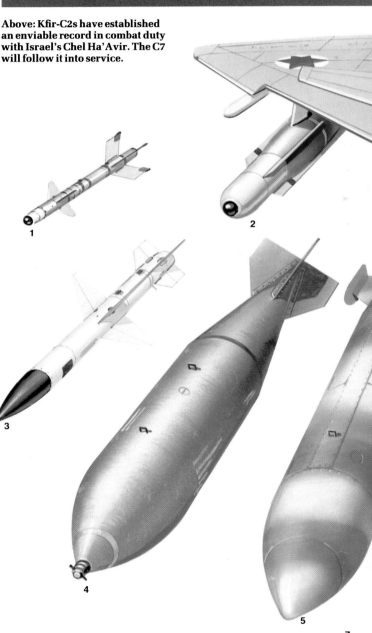

cannon, each with 150 rounds; external weapon load up to 8,500lb (3855kg), normally including one ECM pod and two Shafrir air/air missiles.
Future: Well over 200 Kfirs to various build-standards have gained enough experience in active service, including much combat action, to confirm hopes

that they will prove extremely cost/effective aircraft with capabilities substantially greater than any previous delta Mirage variant. Dassault have paid IAI the compliment of copying their rival to produce the Mirage IIING. At least one major updated form of Kfir is planned for use before the Lavi enters service in 1992-3.

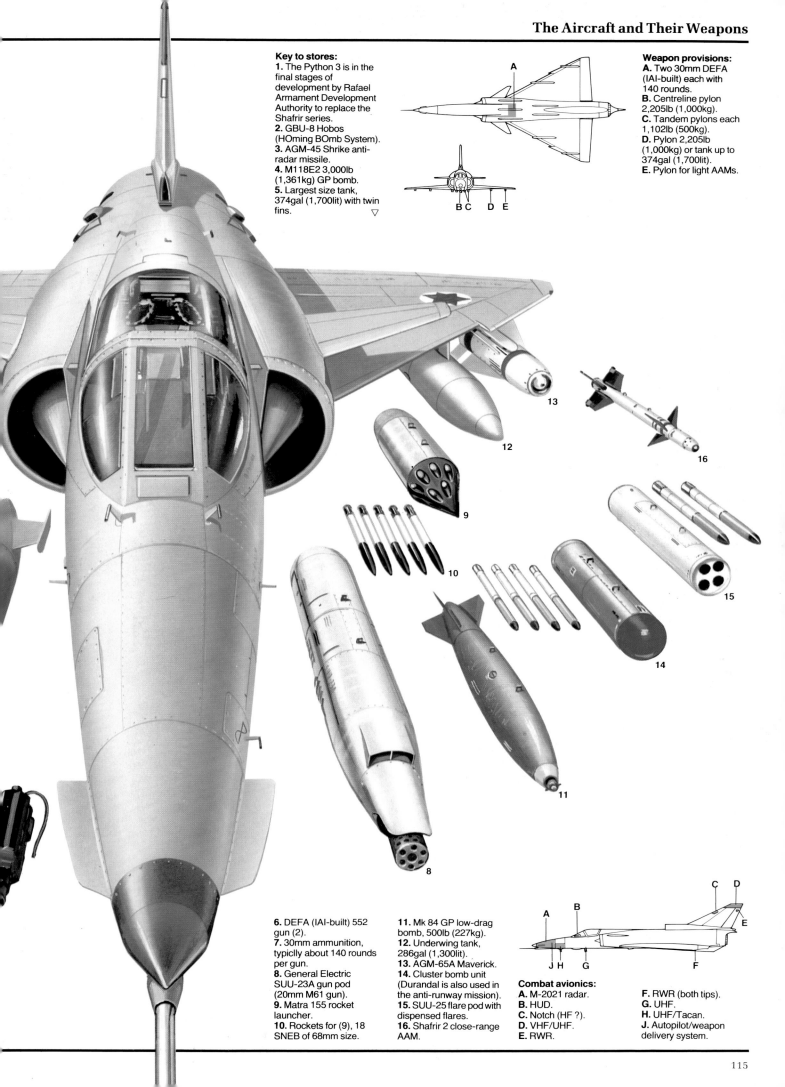

Key to stores:
1. The Python 3 is in the final stages of development by Rafael Armament Development Authority to replace the Shafrir series.
2. GBU-8 Hobos (HOming BOmb System).
3. AGM-45 Shrike anti-radar missile.
4. M118E2 3,000lb (1,361kg) GP bomb.
5. Largest size tank, 374gal (1,700lit) with twin fins.

Weapon provisions:
A. Two 30mm DEFA (IAI-built) each with 140 rounds.
B. Centreline pylon 2,205lb (1,000kg).
C. Tandem pylons each 1,102lb (500kg).
D. Pylon 2,205lb (1,000kg) or tank up to 374gal (1,700lit).
E. Pylon for light AAMs.

6. DEFA (IAI-built) 552 gun (2).
7. 30mm ammunition, typiclly about 140 rounds per gun.
8. General Electric SUU-23A gun pod (20mm M61 gun).
9. Matra 155 rocket launcher.
10. Rockets for (9), 18 SNEB of 68mm size.

11. Mk 84 GP low-drag bomb, 500lb (227kg).
12. Underwing tank, 286gal (1,300lit).
13. AGM-65A Maverick.
14. Cluster bomb unit (Durandal is also used in the anti-runway mission).
15. SUU-25 flare pod with dispensed flares.
16. Shafrir 2 close-range AAM.

Combat avionics:
A. M-2021 radar.
B. HUD.
C. Notch (HF ?).
D. VHF/UHF.
E. RWR.
F. RWR (both tips).
G. UHF.
H. UHF/Tacan.
J. Autopilot/weapon delivery system.

Lockheed F-104 Starfighter

Origin: USA, first flight (XF-104) 7 February 1954.
Type: (G) multimission strike fighter; (CF) strike-reconnaissance; (TF) dual trainer; (QF) drone RPV; (F-104S) all-weather interceptor; (RF and RTF) reconnaissance.
Engine: One General Electric J79 turbojet with afterburner; (G, RF/RTF, CF) 15,800lb (7,167kg) J79-11A; (S) 17,900lb (8,120kg) J79-19 or J1Q.
Dimensions: Span (without tip tanks) 21ft 11in (6.68m); length 54ft 9in (16.69m); height 13ft 6in (4.11m); wing area 196.1sq ft (18.22m²).
Weights: Empty 14,082lb (6,387kg), (F-104S, 14,900lb, 6,758kg); maximum loaded 28,779lb (13,054kg), (F-104S, 31,000lb, 14,060kg).
Performance: Maximum speed 1,450mph (2,334km/h, Mach 2.2); initial climb 50,000ft (15,239m)/min; service ceiling 58,000ft (17,677m) (zoom ceiling over 90,000ft, 27,430m); range with maximum weapons, about 300 miles (483km); range with four drop tanks (high altitude, subsonic) 1,815 miles (2,920km).
Background: The F-104, Lockheed Model 83, was designed by a team led by Clarence L. Johnson after the latter had been told by pilots fighting the MiG-15 in Korea in 1951-2 that they were prepared to sacrifice almost everything to get more performance. None of the Allied fighters had the speed, climb rate and angle and ceiling of the Soviet aircraft, and their pilots urged simplification and a reduction in size and weight. Johnson found that with the new J79 engine he could reach Mach 2, but though the F-104 offered a new realm of speed and height it proved far too limited in other ways. It is pure chance that it later proved to be an excellent basis for a low-level strike/recon aircraft, and later still a stand-off interceptor.
Design: At a time when the standard fighter wings were of swept or delta shape, the F-104 was made to ride on a stubby unswept wing of extraordinarily small span, thickness and area. The aileron power units, for example, had to fit within a maximum depth of 1in (25.4mm). Reasonable low-speed lift was achieved by blown flaps, blasted by HP air from the engine at the landing setting, and full-span drooped leading edges. The long needle-nose fuselage thus had to accommodate everything, including 746 gal (3,392 litres) fuel, the new M61 gun, the three units of the landing gear, all avionics and a downward-ejection seat. Small numbers were built as fighters, fighter/bombers and tandem trainers (583 gal, 2,650 litres, fuel), but shortcomings of poor turn radius, limited pylon space and totally unforgiving piloting qualities terminated the programme by 1959. By this time, however, Lockheed's proposal for a strengthened and avionically updated aircraft had been accepted by West Germany, leading to a family of aircraft based on the

F-104G which offered exceptional penetrative capability in the nuclear attack role, with the first INS in tactical use and speed at sea level close to Mach 1 combined with extremely small radar signature. Standard G pylon ratings are 2,000lb (907kg) under the fuselage, 1,000lb (454kg) under each wing and an AIM-9 Sidewinder on each wingtip. Upward-ejection seats were fitted, the standard for most customers being changed to the Martin-Baker Q7A. Lockheed and Fiat (now Aeritalia) produced the F-104S interceptor with a multimode radar, nine stores pylons including provision for radar-guided AAMs (medium-range Sparrow or Aspide) and a more powerful J79 engine giving even higher speed of Mach 2.4. In the stand-off kill mission turn radius is unimportant, and despite its obsolescent design and other short-comings the F-104S offers valuable air defence at modest cost.
Avionics: The main radar of current F-104 versions never received an "AN" standard designation because it is not used by the US services. Built by North American Aviation Autonetics (now Rockwell International Electronics) it was originally the F-15A Nasarr (North American Search And Ranging Radar) configured mainly for ground mapping, surface attack and maintaining terrain clearance. Subsequently in 1965-68 it was developed into the R21G/H with more advanced circuitry and configured primarily for use in the air-to-air interception role, with the added capability of providing CW illumination of targets for Sparrow or Aspide misiles. Litton got in on the ground floor of inertial navigation with the LN-3 system for the F-104G. Minneapolis-Honeywell provided the stick-steering autopilot which provided for holding a constant IAS, altitude, heading or rate of turn. Most other gear is similar

1950s technology, including a fixed-reticle sight for air/air or air/ground gunfire or weapon delivery, air-data computer, Tacan, DR nav device, Mergenthaler Linotype bombing computer (with over-the-shoulder toss mode) and standard "Jeep cans" for basic communications, IFF and early ECM warning and jamming. In 1974 Aeritalia and Rockwell improved the radar with an MTI and improved ECCM addition built under licence by CGE-Fiar. This does not really provide a "look-down shoot-down" capability against low-flying aircraft.
Future: So far as is known no development is taking place upon the F-104 today, though several operators will continue to use these high-performance aircraft for many years. This is especially the

case with Italy and Turkey, where future developments are aimed at continued updating of avionics and EW capability, and clearance of the F-104S with additional weapons. Slowly dwindling numbers of F-104G, TF-104G, RF-104G or RTF-104G aircraft remain in use in Europe, as well as Luftwaffe trainers in the USA. Japan is gradually replacing some F-104J and DJ aircraft with the F-15. There have been few buyers of the secondhand aircraft (not even Argentina).

Left: The newest and most important of all F-104 versions is the F-104S all-weather interceptor, produced in Italy and shown here in service with the AMI (Italian AF). Though still an unforgiving aircraft the S version has shown itself to be cost/effective, reliable and quite popular with its pilots.

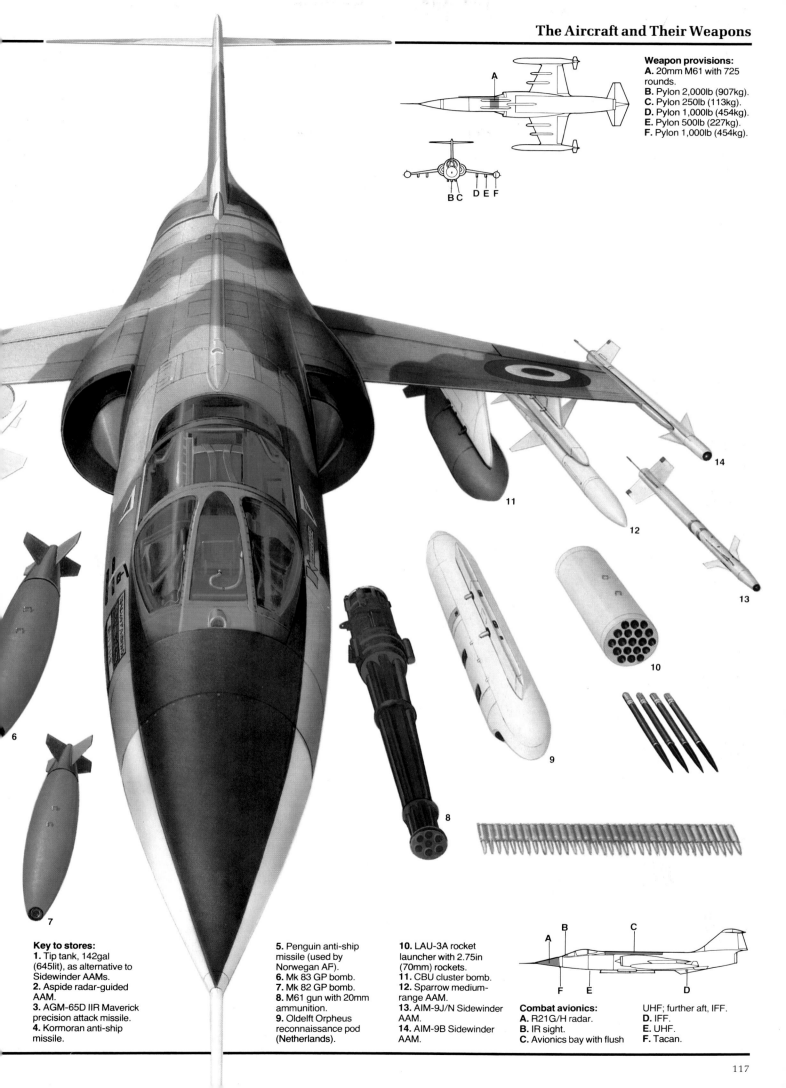

Weapon provisions:
A. 20mm M61 with 725 rounds.
B. Pylon 2,000lb (907kg).
C. Pylon 250lb (113kg).
D. Pylon 1,000lb (454kg).
E. Pylon 500lb (227kg).
F. Pylon 1,000lb (454kg).

Key to stores:
1. Tip tank, 142gal (645lit), as alternative to Sidewinder AAMs.
2. Aspide radar-guided AAM.
3. AGM-65D IIR Maverick precision attack missile.
4. Kormoran anti-ship missile.

5. Penguin anti-ship missile (used by Norwegan AF).
6. Mk 83 GP bomb.
7. Mk 82 GP bomb.
8. M61 gun with 20mm ammunition.
9. Oldelft Orpheus reconnaissance pod (Netherlands).

10. LAU-3A rocket launcher with 2.75in (70mm) rockets.
11. CBU cluster bomb.
12. Sparrow medium-range AAM.
13. AIM-9J/N Sidewinder AAM.
14. AIM-9B Sidewinder AAM.

Combat avionics:
A. R21G/H radar.
B. IR sight.
C. Avionics bay with flush

UHF; further aft, IFF.
D. IFF.
E. UHF.
F. Tacan.

McDonnell Douglas A-4 Skyhawk

Origin: USA, first flight 22 June 1954.

Type: Single-seat attack bomber; OA, two-seat FAC; TA, dual-control trainer.

Engine: (E, J) 8,500lb (3,856kg) Pratt & Whitney J52-6 turbojet; (F, G, H, K) 9,300lb (4,218kg) J52-8A; (M, N, Y) 11,200lb (5,080kg) J52-408A.

Dimensions: Span 27ft 6in (8.38m); length (E, F, G, H, K, L, P, Q, S) 40ft 1½in (12.22m), (M, N, Y) 40ft 3¼in (12.27m), (OA, and TA, excluding probe) 42ft 7¼in (12.98m); height 15ft (4.57m), (TA series 15ft 3in, 4.64m).

Weights: Empty (E) 9,284lb (4,211kg), (typical single-seat, eg Y) 10,465lb (4,747kg), (TA-4F) 10,602 (4,809kg); maximum loaded (shipboard) 24,500lb (11,113kg); (land-based) 27,420lb (12,437kg).

Performance: Maximum speed (clean) (E) 685mph (1,102km/h), (Y) 670mph (1,078km/h), (TA-4F) 675mph (1,086km/h); maximum speed (4,000lb 1,814kg bomb load) (Y) 645mph (1,038km/h); initial climb (Y) 8,440ft (2,572m)/min; service ceiling (all, clean) about 49,000ft (14,935m); range (clean, or with 4,000lb weapons and max fuel, all late versions) about 920 miles (1,480km); maximum range (Y) 2,055 miles (3,307km).

Background: Douglas Aircraft's El Segundo plant was awarded the prototype contract for a new tactical attack jet for the US Navy and Marine Corps in 1952 after chief engineer Ed Heinemann had convinced the Bureau of Aeronautics his design would meet the challenging specification and yet weigh just half the suggested 30,000lb (13,607kg). The prototype flew in June 1954 and not only fully met the requirements but set a world speed record and proved such a good basis for improvement that the A-4 remained in production 26 years.

Design: The requirements were based on Korean experience and called for the maximum payload/range and equipment for carrier operation, but not for all-weather avionics. The A-4 bristled with novel features intended to reduce weight and complexity. The main gears, tall enough for large underwing clearance, fold forwards to lie under the main wing box without cutting into it.

The wing is a curved-tip delta so small it does not need to fold, the entire box being an integral tank and the leading edges having full-span slats. The cockpit was put high above the nose for good view, and in the final versions the canopy was enlarged. There are large airbrakes on the rear fuselage, flight controls are powered, and the unique rudder hastily redesigned to eliminate "buzz" by having a single skin on the centreline with ribs on the outside remained in production to the 2,960th and last aircraft in 1980!

Avionics: The basic design was tailored to the attack mission exclusively, and concentration on saving weight and complexity resulted in an austere avionic fit in early versions, augmented later by simple nose radar offering mapping, ranging and terrain-avoidance, and later with Labs (for toss-bombing), improved auto flight control and heading references, doppler, tacan and radar altimeter. Many items of nav/com avionics had to be packaged in the added "camel hump" above the fuselage. The most important model, developed for the US Marines only, is the A-4M of 1970 with numerous improvements throughout the aircraft including the Hughes ARBS (Angle/Rate Bombing System), comprehensive radar warning, internal ECM jammers and payload dispensers and a modern HUD. The extra equipment called for an uprated engine-driven generator and a back-up windmill generator extended below the forward fuselage. Probably the most effective Skyhawks of all are the A-4Ns of Israel's air force, and the earlier Israeli aircraft which have been brought up to almost the same standard using Israeli avionics and airframe modifications. About 100 (of 267 single-seat and 27 two-seat) remain in Heyl Ha'Avir service. Their most obvious distinguishing feature is an extended jetpipe to reduce vulnerability to IR-homing missiles. Locally installed manoeuvre flaps are fitted under the wings.

Armament: Standard on most versions, two 20mm Mk 12 cannon, each with 200 rounds; (H, N, and optional on other export versions) two 30mm DEFA 553, each with 150 rounds. Pylons under fuselage and wings for total ordnance load of (E, F, G, H, K, L, P, Q, S) 8,200lb (3,720kg); (M, N, Y) 9,155lb (4,153kg).

Future: McDonnell Douglas have maintained a profitable business modifying or refurbishing A-4s for export, but this is a diminishing activity and the last US model, the conversion of TA-4F trainers into OA-4M FAC (Forward Air Control) models was handled in house by the US Navy. No funding exists for further updating of US Marine Corps aircraft, but substantial stocks of airworthy ex-US Navy and Marines aircraft exist and should they find customers they are almost certain to be updated. Post-Falklands approaches on behalf of Argentina appear not to have resulted in replacement of that country's A-4 losses, though this will probably be possible eventually. The A-4 did well in the Falklands campaign, flown on purely visual attacks against easily visible ships with free-fall bombs dropped from such low level they often failed to explode. The aircraft were refurbished A-4Bs and Cs with simple avionics, but with the important addition of Ferranti ISIS weapon-delivery sights.

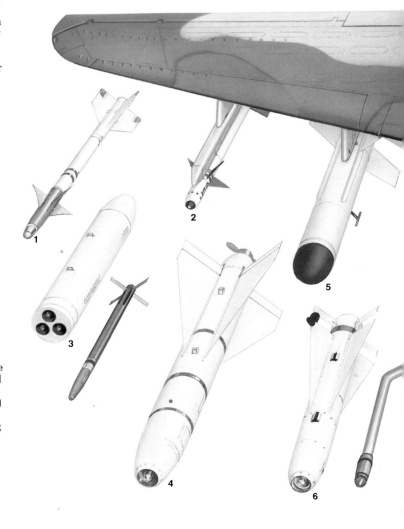

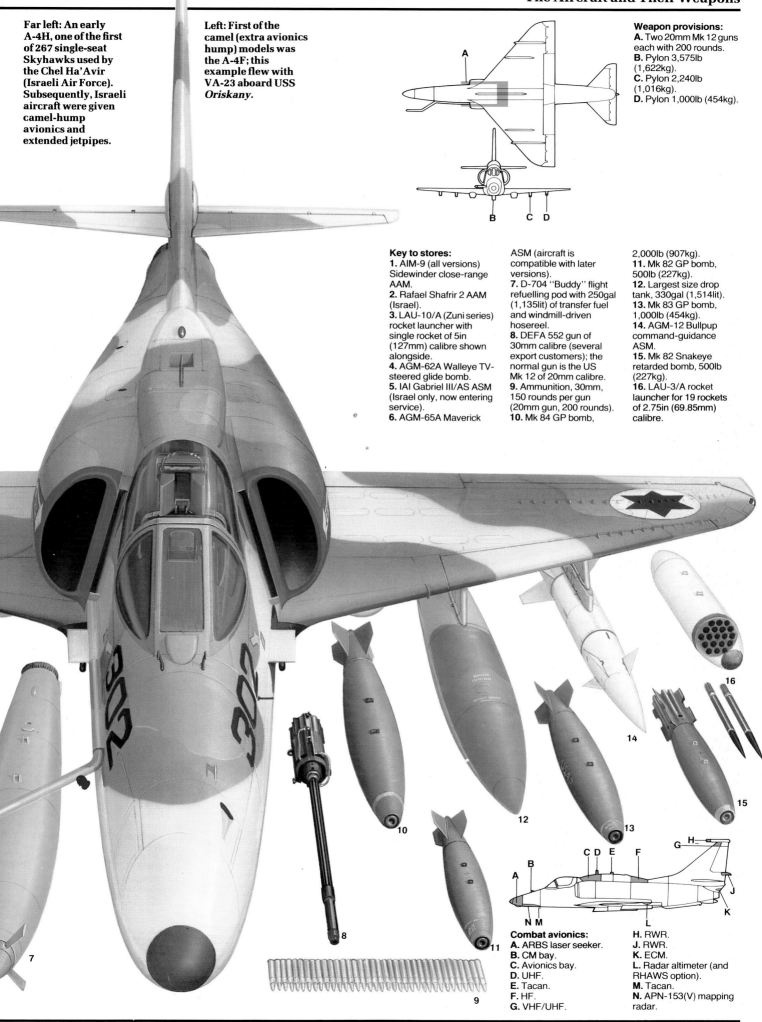

Far left: An early A-4H, one of the first of 267 single-seat Skyhawks used by the Chel Ha'Avir (Israeli Air Force). Subsequently, Israeli aircraft were given camel-hump avionics and extended jetpipes.

Left: First of the camel (extra avionics hump) models was the A-4F; this example flew with VA-23 aboard USS *Oriskany*.

Weapon provisions:
A. Two 20mm Mk 12 guns each with 200 rounds.
B. Pylon 3,575lb (1,622kg).
C. Pylon 2,240lb (1,016kg).
D. Pylon 1,000lb (454kg).

Key to stores:
1. AIM-9 (all versions) Sidewinder close-range AAM.
2. Rafael Shafrir 2 AAM (Israel).
3. LAU-10/A (Zuni series) rocket launcher with single rocket of 5in (127mm) calibre shown alongside.
4. AGM-62A Walleye TV-steered glide bomb.
5. IAI Gabriel III/AS ASM (Israel only, now entering service).
6. AGM-65A Maverick ASM (aircraft is compatible with later versions).
7. D-704 "Buddy" flight refuelling pod with 250gal (1,135lit) of transfer fuel and windmill-driven hosereel.
8. DEFA 552 gun of 30mm calibre (several export customers); the normal gun is the US Mk 12 of 20mm calibre.
9. Ammunition, 30mm, 150 rounds per gun (20mm gun, 200 rounds).
10. Mk 84 GP bomb, 2,000lb (907kg).
11. Mk 82 GP bomb, 500lb (227kg).
12. Largest size drop tank, 330gal (1,514lit).
13. Mk 83 GP bomb, 1,000lb (454kg).
14. AGM-12 Bullpup command-guidance ASM.
15. Mk 82 Snakeye retarded bomb, 500lb (227kg).
16. LAU-3/A rocket launcher for 19 rockets of 2.75in (69.85mm) calibre.

Combat avionics:
A. ARBS laser seeker.
B. CM bay.
C. Avionics bay.
D. UHF.
E. Tacan.
F. HF.
G. VHF/UHF.
H. RWR.
J. RWR.
K. ECM.
L. Radar altimeter (and RHAWS option).
M. Tacan.
N. APN-153(V) mapping radar.

McDonnell Douglas/BAe AV-8B Harrier II

Origin: USA with UK principal subcontractor, first flight 5 November 1981.
Type: STOVL multi-role attack (probably also reconnaissance).
Engine: One 22,000lb (9,979kg) thrust Pratt & Whitney F402-406 (RR Pegasus 11-21E) vectored-thrust turbofan.
Dimensions: Span 30ft 4in (9.25m); length 46ft 4in (14.12m); height 11ft 8in (3.56m); wing area 230sq ft (21.37m²).
Weights: Empty 12,750lb (5,783kg); maximum (VTO) 19,550 (8,867kg), (STO) 29,750lb (1,349kg).
Performance: Maximum Mach number in level flight 0.93 (at sea level, 673mph, 1,083km/h); combat radius (STO, seven Mk82 bombs plus tanks, lo profile, no loiter) 748 miles (1,204km); ferry range 3,310 miles (5,328km).
Background: One of the modern world's most significant warplanes, the AV-8B Harrier was developed at St Louis by McDonnell Douglas from the original British Harrier to meet the specific needs of the US Marine Corps. Until 1975 it had seemed obvious that further development of the Harrier would be either British or a 50/50 partnership with the USA, but unfortunately in that year the then British government said there was "not enough common ground" for collaboration. The inevitable result is that the Harrier II is a US programme, but because of its purchase for the RAF the UK industry does have a share (40 per cent in US/UK aircraft, 25 per cent in sales to other countries).
Design: The needs of the Marines revolved entirely around close support of friendly ground troops in amphibious landings. In contrast the RAF was extremely interested in air combat and reconnaissance and these were allowed to exert a small influence on the design, in particular in increasing instantaneous rate of turn. Almost every part of the original British design has been refined to improve vertical lift or reduce weight or the need for maintenance. Principal new item is the wing, a one-piece structure mainly of graphite-epoxy composite and with a deep supercritical section, increased span and area and reduced sweep. It gives better lift at all speeds, provides more pylon space and increases internal fuel capacity by 50 per cent. British Aerospace research added the curved LERX (leading-edge root extension) which increases rate of turn. McDonnell Douglas contributed the very large slotted flaps which are lowered for vertical lift, the rearranged geometry of the wing and extended zero-scarf (square-cut) nozzles giving a STOL lift gain of over 6,700lb (3,039kg). Other features include improved engine inlets, improved LIDs (lift-improved devices) under the belly, raised cockpit giving more interior space and better pilot view, and a generally strengthened structure.

Despite this the equipped empty weight is almost the same as the original Harrier's.
Avionics: The chief weapon-delivery system in both the AV-8B (USMC) and Harrier GR.5 (RAF) is the Hughes ARBS (angle/rate bombing system) in the nose, which comprises a dual TV/laser target seeker and tracker linked to the advanced Smiths HUD via a computer. Other new features are an advanced autopilot with two-axis stabilization computer which was used in December 1982 for an automatic vertical landing, Ferranti INS, Garrett digital air-data computer, Conrac fibre-optics CNI (com/nav/IFF) data converter, radar altimeter, Bendix APX-100 IFF, forward/rear RWR installation and Goodyear ALE-39 chaff/flare dispenser in the underside of the rear fuselage. In the greatly improved cockpit is a CRT multifunction display and (GR.5) moving-map nav display. The GR.5 has the usual nose-mounted camera and a British RWR and, it is expected, internal ECM.
Future: The Harrier II carries offensive loads that compare extremely favourably with any

Above: An AV-8B Harrier II operating from NAS Patuxent River on ordnance release tests. Many hundreds of Harrier IIs are likely to be built.

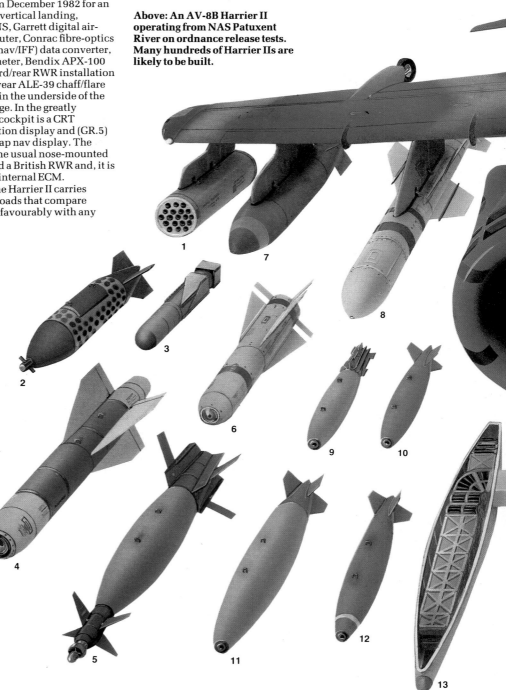

other attack aircraft. The Falklands campaign also showed the vital importance of V/STOL – or, more accurately, STOVL – airpower in being able to operate in the absence of airfields or fixed-wing carriers and also being able to operate in weather so severe that it would have prohibited flying by conventional aircraft. Details of the Harrier II's air-combat agility have not yet been published, but it meets the RAF's demand for instantaneous turn rate of 20°/s and has the added advantage of Viffing (vectoring the engine thrust in forward flight) which no conventional fighter can match. In the course of Harrier II development there is no doubt engine thrust will take its place as a primary flight control vector to be used under computer control for the maximum possible dogfight agility, not only in the vertical plane but also laterally. Studies have been made for different avionic fits including forward-looking and terrain-following radars, and there are various combat possibilities inherent in the two-seat TAV-8B now under development.

Key to stores:
1. LAU-3/19 rocket pod.
2. Beluga.
3. Wasp ASM (folded).
4. AGM-72 Walleye ASM.
5. GBU-10E/B Paveway II smart bomb.
6. Laser Maverick ASM.
7. UK GP bomb, 1,000lb (454kg).
8. AGM-84A Harpoon anti-ship missile.
9. Mk 82 Snakeye.
10. Mk 82 GP bomb.
11. Mk 84 2,000lb (907kg) GP bomb.

Weapon provisions:
A. GAU-12/U gun.
B. Fairing for 25mm ammunition.
C. Fuselage pylon, 1,000lb (454kg).
D. Inboard wing pylon, 2,000lb (907kg).
E. Centre wing pylon, 1,000lb (454kg).
F. Outboard wing pylon, 630lb (286kg).

12. Mk 83 GP bomb.
13. Gun magazine, 300 rounds (right pod).
14. GAU-12/U 25mm gun (left pod) (RAF Harrier GR.5 replaces items 13, 14 by 30mm Aden guns).
15. AGM-12 Bullpup ASM.
16. Combat tank, 100gal (455lit).

17. 30mm Gepod gun pod.
18. BAe Dynamics Sea Eagle anti-ship missile.
19. BL.755 cluster bomb.
20. AIM-9L Sidewinder AAM.
21. Durandal anti-runway weapon.
22. GBU-15CWW (cruciform wing weapon).

Combat avionics:
A. ARBS.
B. IFF.
C. RWR.
D. VHF/UHF CNI.
E. Radar altimeter (chaff dispenser is adjacent).
F. Tacan.
G. ILS.

McDonnell Douglas F-4 Phantom II

Origin: USA, first flight 27 May 1958.

Type: Originally carrier-based all-weather interceptor; now all-weather multi-role fighter for ship or land operation; (F-4G) EW defence suppression; (RF) all-weather reconnaissance.

Engines: (C, D, RF) two 17,000lb (7,711kg) General Electric J79-15 turbojets with afterburner; (E, F, G) 17,900lb (8,120kg) J79-17; (J, N, S) 17,900lb J79-10; (K, M) 20,515lb (9,305kg) Rolls-Royce Spey 202/203 augmented turbofans.

Dimensions: Span 38ft 5in (11.7m); length (C, D, J, N, S) 58ft 3in (17.76m), (E, G, F and all RF versions) 62ft 11in or 63ft (19.2m), (K, M) 57ft 7in (17.55m); height (all) 16ft 3in (4.96m); wing area 530sq ft (49.2m²).

Weights: Empty (C, D, J, N) 28,000lb (12,700kg), (E, F and RF) 29,000lb (13,150kg), (G, K, M) 31,00lb (14,060kg); maximum loaded (C, D, J, K, M, N, RF) 58,000lb (26,308kg), (E, G, F) 60,630lb (27,502kg).

Performance: Maximum speed with Sparrow missiles only (low) 910mph (1,464km/h, Mach 1.19) with J79 engines, 920mph (1,480km/h) with Spey, (high) 1,500mph (2,414km/h, Mach 2.27) with J79, 1,386mph (2,230km/h) with Spey; initial climb, typically 28,000ft (8,534m)/min with J79, 32,000ft (,753m)/min with Spey; service ceiling, over 60,000ft (18,287m) with J79, 60,000ft with Spey; range on internal fuel (no weapons) about 1,750 miles (2,816km); ferry range with external fuel, typically 2,300 miles (3,700km), (E and variants), 2,600 miles (4,184km).

Background: Company studies in the mid-1950s centred on the AH-1 attack aircraft with two of the new J79 engines and armed with cannon and a heavy ordnance load on 11 pylons. But in April 1955 the Navy had the project completely changed into the F4H fleet defence fighter with only a single pylon (for a large drop tank) and no guns, but equipped with a powerful radar, two seats and with belly recesses for four AAMs. In this form the prototype flew in May 1958, but the tremendous capability and performance cried out to be fully used and gradually the pylons were put back and, as late as 1967, an internal gun. Production totalled 5,211 airframes.

Design: Fundamental to the F-4 was the tremendous propulsion system of two afterburning J79s with optimized variable ramp inlets and fully controllable nozzles surrounding the variable primary afterburner nozzles. The disturbance caused by the installation in British Phantoms of the much more powerful Spey engine actually resulted in these versions being slower. The wing is so acutely tapered it is almost a delta, but divided into a flat centre section and sharply dihedralled outer panels with extended-chord leading edges and large dogtooth discontinuities. The F-4E and

related versions have powerful slats, and all have blown flaps and powered ailerons inboard of the hinge axis, the outer panels having fixed trailing edges. The fuselage is broad (even broader in British aircraft because of the greater airflow) with six or seven fuel cells filling the space between and above the engines (other tanks fill the wing between the front and main spars as far out as the hinge). The tail has a low aspect-ratio vertical surface, side area being augmented by the acute anhedral of the slab tailplanes.
US Navy/Marines F-4 J, N, S and variants, and RAF F-4K and M Phantoms have inflight-refuelling probes; USAF F-4E and G Phantoms, but not export versions or Japanese EJs, have a dorsal boom-receptacle.

Avionics: All Phantoms have nose radar, varying from giant liquid-cooled Westinghouse sets with 32in (813mm) dishes in Navy and RAF models, through the solid-state Hughes APQ-120 in the slimmer nose of the F-4E variants to the small APQ-99 in most RF recon models. Some have a sensitive IR detector in a pod under the nose, while other equipment includes autopilot, various nav systems, CNI package, radar altimeter, air-data computer, INS (RAF FGR.2) and such extra sensors as Northrop Tiseo and a succession of Pave-series laser designators culminating for the USAF in 180 F-4Es and 60 RF-4Cs being converted to carry the comprehensive Pave Tack with Flir for target acquisition and a laser for designation and ranging.

Armament: (All versions except RF models which have no armament) four AIM-7 Sparrow or Sky Flash (later Amraam) air-to-air missiles recessed under fuselage; inner wing pylons can carry two more AIM-7 or four AIM-9 Sidewinder missiles; in addition E versions except RF have internal 20mm M61 multi-barrel gun, and virtually all versions can carry the same gun in external centreline pod; all except RF have centreline and four wing pylons for tanks, bombs or other stores to total weight of 16,000lb (7,257kg).

Future: Today all F-4s, especially those based on the E, remain useful multirole aircraft with air-combat patrol endurance exceeding 3h, good stand-off kill capability, fair avionics and excellent capability to carry advanced sensors and weapons. The F-4G is the standard USAF Wild Weasel tactical defence-suppression aircraft with the APR-38 EW system for detecting, analysing and locating hostile emitters and with weapons such as Harm and Maverick for their suppression. It is probable that other air forces may use available F-4 airframes as the basis for their own future EW aircraft. In the surface-attack role the F-4 is still effective and lacks only modern cockpit display systems and, in the case of almost all existing aircraft, adequate sensors and aiming systems which, with

Above: Air-combat manoeuvrability of the F-4E was greatly improved by fitting large outer-wing slats, seen here open on a USAF aircraft with ALQ-119 ECM pod, data link and chaff dispenser. The main drawing at right shows only a selection of the vast range of stores.

Right: Subject of the main illustration is an F-4E, with slats extended.

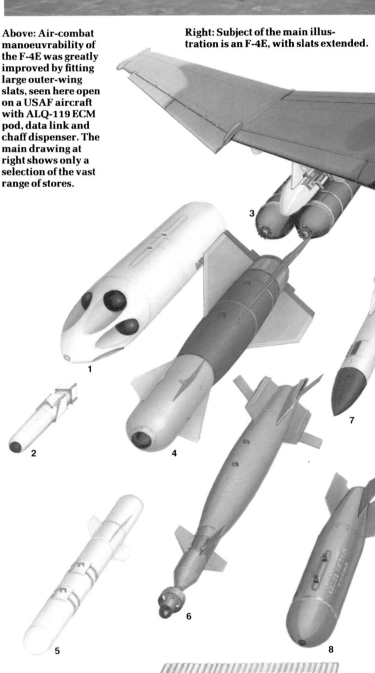

minor difficulties, can be added. It is only in the air-combat role that the basic outdated nature of the aircraft and engine is giving rise to problems. The F-4 has never been able to turn with a MiG-21 and the characteristics of most F-4 radars and AIM-7 missiles (which demand target illumination until impact) are no longer fully competitive. Possibilities long under discussion include retrofitting RAF aircraft with Foxhunter radar and Luftwaffe F-4Fs with APG-65 or APG-66, the latter with a small L-band illuminator matched to the future Amraam missile.

Key to stores:
1. Wasp tandem launch pod.
2. Wasp missile (folded).
3. British BL.755 cluster dispensers.
4. GBU-14 Cruciform-Wing Weapon. ▽

ammunition drum.
11. 20mm ammunition, typically about 639 rounds.
12. ALQ-119 jammer pod.
13. BAe Sky Flash AAM.
14. AGM-65D Maverick. ▽

Weapon provisions:
A. 20mm M61 gun with 639 rounds.
B. Pylon 3,500lb (1,588kg).
C. Recess for AIM-7 or -120.
D. Pylon 3,500lb 91,588kg0.
E. Pylon 2,240lb (1,016kg).

5. Durandal anti-airfield weapon.
6. GBU-16B/B (1,000lb) Paveway II smart bomb.
7. AGM-78 ARM anti-radar missile.
8. TAL cluster bomb, 551lb (250kg) (Israel).
9. AIM-9L Sidewinder.
10. M61 20mm gun with △

15. AIM-7 Sparrow medium-range AAM.
16. Mk 82 Snakeye retarded bomb.
17. AGM-88A Harm (Wild Weasel F-4G only).
18. AGM-12 Bullpup ASM.
19. GE 30mm Gepod (gun installation).

20. Mk 82 GP bomb of 500lb (227kg).
21. Mk 83 GP bomb of 1,000lb (454kg).
22. Mk 84 GP bomb of 2,000lb (907kg).
23. AGM-45 Shrike (F-4G only).
24. AIM-120A Amraam advanced AAM.

Combat avionics:
A. PQW-120 radar.
B. IFF.
C. Tacan.
D. VHF.
E. RWR.

F. Forward RWR.
G. Ranging aerial (right wing).
H. Avionics bays.
J. VHF/UHF.

McDonnell Douglas F-15 Eagle

Origin: USA, first flight 27 July 1972.

Type: Air-superiority fighter with secondary attack role.

Engines: Two 23,930lb (10,855kg) thrust Pratt & Whitney F100-100 afterburning turbofans.

Dimensions: Span 42ft 9¾in (13.05m); length (all) 63ft 9in (19.43m), height 18ft 7½in (5.68m); wing area 608sq ft (56.5m²)

Weights: Empty (basic equipped) 28,000lb (12,700kg); loaded (interception mission, max internal fuel plus four AIM-7, F-15A) 41,500lb (18,824kg), (C) 44,500lb (20,185kg); maximum with max external load (A) 56,500lb (25,628kg), (C) 68,000lb (30,845kg).

Performance: Maximum speed (over 36,000ft/10,973m with no external load except form AIM-7), 1,653mph (2,660km/h, Mach 2.5), with max external load or at low level, not published; initial climb (clean) over 50,000ft (15,239m)/min, (max wt) 29,000ft (8.8km)/min; service ceiling 65,000ft (19,811m); takeoff run (clean) 900ft (274m); landing run (clean, without brake chute) 2,500ft (762m); ferry range with three external tanks, over 2,878 miles (4,631km), (with Fast packs also) over 3,450 miles (5,562km).

Background: USAF funding for a new fighter was sought in 1965. McDonnell Douglas was selected on 23 December 1969, by which time the MiG-25 had thrown a scare into the Pentagon. Unlike the Soviet aircraft the F-15 was designed for unrivalled capability in close combat. Until 1976 there was hardly any attempt to explore missions other than air-to-air.

Design: Basic features include two new augmented turbofan engines in a wide body rear fuselage, a shoulder-high wing of 5.9/3 per cent thickness with sharp taper on the leading edge and conical camber outboard, a plain fixed leading edge, plain flaps and ailerons, structural beams projecting aft of the engine nozzles to carry the widely spaced vertical tails with fixed fins and low tailplanes with large inboard dogteeth (the latter become rolling stabilators at hi-AOA), and neat main gears with single high-pressure tyres. The two-dimensional external-compression inlets have automatically scheduled variable throats and spill doors, and at high AOA the entire inlet rotates nose-down about a hinge at the top. After landing the nose is held high with the large dorsal airbrake open; there is no braking parachute or any thrust-reverse. Some 26.5 per cent of the structure weight is titanium, including most of the rear fuselage whose engine bays are uncluttered and designed for easy maintenance and rapid engine changes. Even the original F-15A has no less than 11,635lb (5,277kg) internal fuel; the 600 US-gal drop tank was a new design, and the FAST (Fuel And Sensor, Tactical) packs shown in the main illustration are large containers which conform to the sides of the fuselage and add a further 9,750lb (4,423kg) of usable fuel as well as providing space for extra sensors and EW equipment. FAST packs were introduced with the F-15C which replaced the F-15A in June 1979 and apart from avionic improvements has 13,455lb (6,103kg) of internal fuel. The corresponding two-seaters, with unchanged internal fuel, are the F-15B and C.

Avionics: The Hughes APG-63 was designed for the F-15 as a multimode PD (pulse-doppler) radar optimised for A/A operation, and with all controls conforming to the concept of Hotas (hands on throttle and stick) which the F-15 pioneered. The main HDD is a VSD (vertical situation display), with a 4×4 graticule on which can be set various range scales and alphanumerical information together with digitally processed symbology showing targets and nothing else (unless the pilot calls up other pictorial information). The information is to a large extent repeated on the HUD which again can operate in various modes and in current aircraft serve vital functions in air/ground weapon delivery. Radar mode is selected by the AR (air refuelling disconnect) button, which in the forward position gives a boresight mode and when pulled aft gives Supersearch which scans the HUD field of view and locks on to the first detected target, which is likely to be the most threatening. Long-range search is the chief surveillance mode with distances to 160nm (296km) and interleaved high and medium PRFs. Pulse is a low-PRF non-doppler mode for shoot-up (anti-MiG-25) engagements. The outstanding CC (central computer) set a new standard in presenting processed information on the HUD and the F-15A was a revelation when it entered service in 1974 in enabling the pilot to fly Hotas and select any radar or HUD mode and any weapon (gun, SRMs or MRMs) without taking his eyes off the target. Today's F-15C has a programmable radar processor and larger radar memory (from 26K to 96K). All USAF F-15s have the Loral ALR-56 RWR system mounted internally, Northrop ALQ-135 internal counter-measures set and Hazeltine APX-76 IFF.

Armament: One 20mm M61A-1 gun with 940 rounds; fuselage flank ejectors for four AIM-7 Sparrows or AIM-120 Amraam; centreline pylon for 4,500lb (2,041kg) or 500gal (2,273lit) tank; other pylons rated as with 3-view, inboards having provision for paired AIM-9 Sidewinders and being plumbed for 500gal tanks. Total weapon load (excluding gun) 16,000lb (7,258kg). Enhanced Eagle F-15E has expanded capability and greater diversity of stores (see main illustration) to maximum of 24,000lb (10,885kg).

Future: Since 1981 testing has been completed on an updated avionic system with a new CC, new HUD processor, new flight/fire-control software, modified flight-control computers, added coupler linking flight and fire-control subsystems, and an Atlis II optical/laser tracking pod in the left forward MRM recess. A field mod allows MRMs (at present AIM-7F only) to be fired without looking at the VSD to check the hi-PRF mode, and the low velocity gate in the downlook mode has been raised to exclude fast motorway traffic. Not yet (mid-1983) committed to production are the Enhanced Eagle all-weather interdiction model with a SAR (synthetic-aperture radar) and 24,000lb (10,885kg) ordnance load, and a defence-suppression version with enhanced EW systems and Harm missiles.

Above: This F-15 was modified by McDD as the Enhanced Eagle, planned as the first of what the company hope will be the F-15E Enhanced Tactical Fighter; as this book went to press the USAF's choice could be the F-16XL.

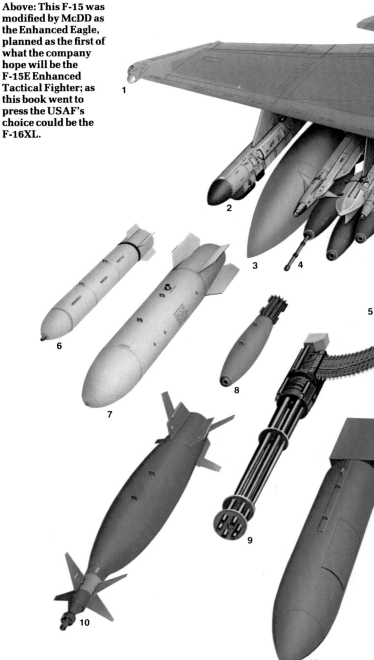

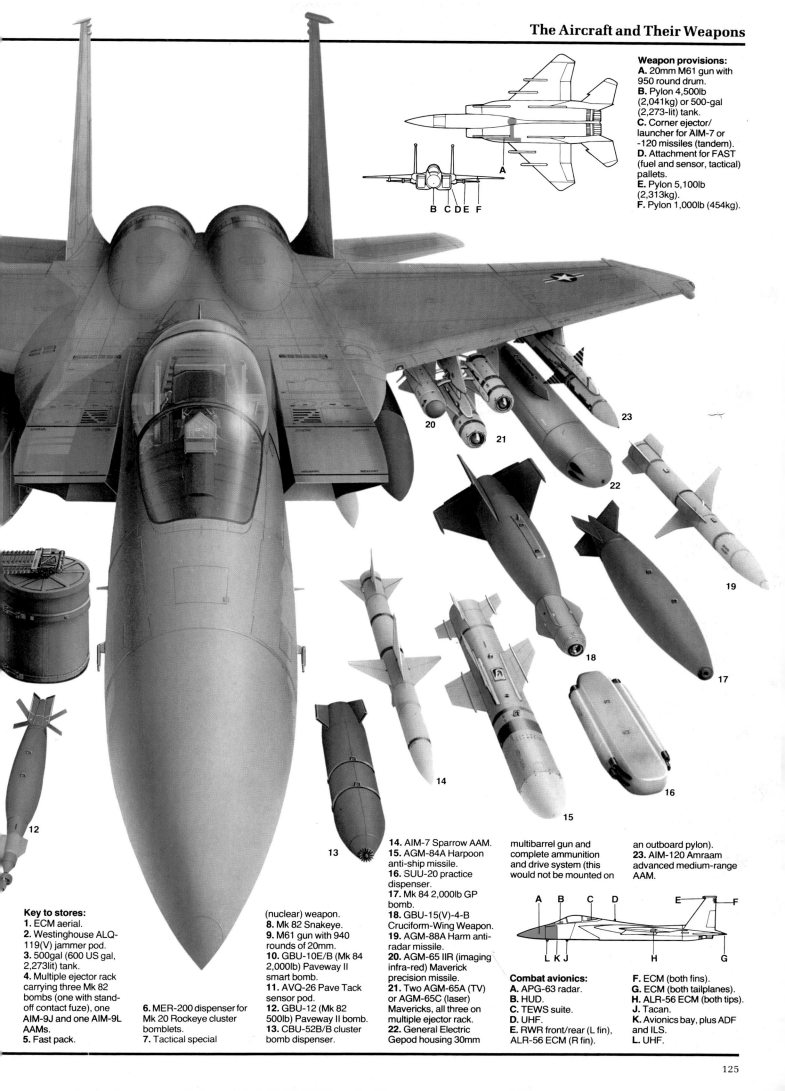

Weapon provisions:
A. 20mm M61 gun with 950 round drum.
B. Pylon 4,500lb (2,041kg) or 500-gal (2,273-lit) tank.
C. Corner ejector/launcher for AIM-7 or -120 missiles (tandem).
D. Attachment for FAST (fuel and sensor, tactical) pallets.
E. Pylon 5,100lb (2,313kg).
F. Pylon 1,000lb (454kg).

Key to stores:
1. ECM aerial.
2. Westinghouse ALQ-119(V) jammer pod.
3. 500gal (600 US gal, 2,273lit) tank.
4. Multiple ejector rack carrying three Mk 82 bombs (one with stand-off contact fuze), one AIM-9J and one AIM-9L AAMs.
5. Fast pack.
6. MER-200 dispenser for Mk 20 Rockeye cluster bomblets.
7. Tactical special (nuclear) weapon.
8. Mk 82 Snakeye.
9. M61 gun with 940 rounds of 20mm.
10. GBU-10E/B (Mk 84 2,000lb) Paveway II smart bomb.
11. AVQ-26 Pave Tack sensor pod.
12. GBU-12 (Mk 82 500lb) Paveway II bomb.
13. CBU-52B/B cluster bomb dispenser.
14. AIM-7 Sparrow AAM.
15. AGM-84A Harpoon anti-ship missile.
16. SUU-20 practice dispenser.
17. Mk 84 2,000lb GP bomb.
18. GBU-15(V)-4-B Cruciform-Wing Weapon.
19. AGM-88A Harm anti-radar missile.
20. AGM-65 IIR (imaging infra-red) Maverick precision missile.
21. Two AGM-65A (TV) or AGM-65C (laser) Mavericks, all three on multiple ejector rack.
22. General Electric Gepod housing 30mm multibarrel gun and complete ammunition and drive system (this would not be mounted on an outboard pylon).
23. AIM-120 Amraam advanced medium-range AAM.

Combat avionics:
A. APG-63 radar.
B. HUD.
C. TEWS suite.
D. UHF.
E. RWR front/rear (L fin), ALR-56 ECM (R fin).
F. ECM (both fins).
G. ECM (both tailplanes).
H. ALR-56 ECM (both tips).
J. Tacan.
K. Avionics bay, plus ADF and ILS.
L. UHF.

125

McDonnell Douglas/Northrop F/A-18 Hornet

Origin: USA, first flight
18 November 1978.
Type: (F/A) single-seat carrier-based multi-role fighter, (TF) dual trainer, (CF) single-seat land-based attack fighter.
Engines: Two 16,000lb (7,257kg) thrust General Electric F404-400 augmented turbofans.
Dimensions: Span (with missiles) 40ft 4¾in (12.31m), (without missiles) 37ft 6in (11.42m); length 56ft (17.07m); height 15ft 3½in (4.66m); wing area 400sq ft (37.16m²).
Weights: (Provisional) empty 20,583lb (9,336kg); loaded (clean) 33,642lb (15,260kg); loaded (attack mission) 48,253 (21,887kg); maximum loaded (catapult limit) 50,064lb (22,710kg).
Performance: Maximum speed (clean, at altitude) 1,190mph (1,915km/h, Mach 1.8), (maximum weight, sea level) subsonic; sustained combat manoeuvre ceiling, over 49,000ft (14,935m); combat radius (air-to-air mission, high, no external fuel) 461 miles (741km); ferry range, more than 2,300 miles (3,700km).
Background: Concerned at what then appeared to be the high cost of the F-14, the US Navy obtained DoD approval in spring 1974 for a VFAX lightweight multimission fighter. Six companies submitted bids, one being the McDonnell 263. In August 1974 Congress terminated VFAX, directing the Navy to look instead at the USAF YF-16 and YF-17. Neither was suitable, but Northrop entered discussison with an experienced builder of carrier aircraft, McDonnell Douglas, with a view to incorporting as much Model 263 as possible in the YF-17 to meet the NACF (Navy Air Combat Fighter) specification. The result was a total redesign with a wider fuselage, doubled internal fuel capacity, larger wing, strengthened structure and totally new avionics. After substantial further changes during prototype development the decision was taken to build a single basic single-seat model to fly both fighter and attack missions.
Design: The YF-17 of 1974 established the basic shape, with a 5/3 per cent thick wing with most taper on the leading edge, fully variable profile with powered leading and trailing edges, very large wing-root extensions and wingtip AAM rails, two slim engines with plain fixed inlets under the wing roots, large outward-canted vertical tails (fixed, with small inset rudders) mounted midway between the wing and the mid-mounted stabiliators (tailerons), and main gears retracting rearward to lie under the inlet ducts with the wheels turned through 90° to the horizontal position. Poor roll rate (Mach 0.9/10,000ft (3,047m) max 100°/s compared with 180° required) led to many changes including increasing inner and outer wing torsional stiffness, removing dogtooth snags from LE of both wings and tailplanes, increasing differential authority of

tailplane for roll and extending ailerons 20in (508mm) out to wingtips. These and other changes give 220°/s. Rudder toe-in reduces nosewheel liftoff speed by 35kt on takeoff, 45° aileron droop reduces approach speed 10kt, and drag is reduced by eliminating the axial slots along the wing roots. The tandem-seat TF/A-18A has 6 per cent less internal fuel (11,000lb/4,990kg in single-seater).
Avionics: Major challenges were optimizing design to equal capability in both fighter and attack missions with crew of one. Demand for radar-guide MRM capability (AIM-7F, later Amraam) met by Hughes APG-65 water-cooled PD multimode radar able to track 10 targets and display 8, has RAM (raid-assessment mode) and DBS (doppler beam sharpening) for good air/ground clarity. Cockpit claimed to be most advanced known, with three Kaiser CRT displays all used simultaneously in different modes plus advanced HUD to give exceptional info display power (though pilots take a long time to become proficient in system management). Large UFD (up-front display) keyboard serves as main man/machine interface, and one or more HDD can present radar, Flir, laser/EO (if fitted) and weapon-seeker images, while others show systems/engine health, RWR data and BITE information. Flight info also appears in cockpit, but pilot flies mainly on HUD symbology, with Hotas throughout a normal mission. Central HSI display is a moving map with superimposed symbology for nav, target data (including sensor FOVs) and location of defence threats. Three master avionic modes are Nav, A/A and A/G. In A/A main radar progresses through 80nm (148km) range-while-search mode, 40nm track-while-scan matched to MRMs, 30nm (55.59km) RAM (raid-assessment mode) and down to 20nm (37.06km) mode for AIM-9s and 5nm (9.26km) mode with pulse-to-pulse frequency agility for 20mm fire. In A/G the radar has exceptional ability to search for and define targets, lock-on and provide for multiple passes. Standard extra A/G sensors are Flir on left side of engine inlets and

Laser Spot Tracker and strike camera on right side.
Armament: One 20mm M61A-1 gun with 570 rounds; nine external weapon stations rated as shown with 3-view, with theoretical maximum load of 17,000lb (7,711kg), but in practice loads are much lower, eg maximum of 10 Mk 82 bombs, 9 Mk 83 or four Mk 84. Centreline and inboard wing hardpoints plumbed for 262gal (1,192lit) tanks.

Future: In late 1982 evaluation began of RF-18 with new nose without gun but accommodating recon sensor package looking through two bulged windows on underside. Sensors can include F-924 panoramic camera, KS-87B forward/oblique camera, KA-99 lo-altitude panoramic camera and AAD-5 IR linescan. Flight trials of RF-18 were due December 1983. Operational service began 7 January 1983 with VMF/A-314.

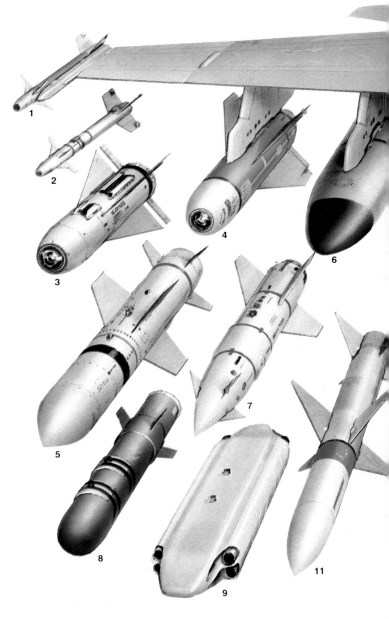

Below: One of the development prototypes during carrier qualification aboard USS America in November 1979.

Key to stores:
1. AIM-9L Sidewinder AAM.
2. AIM-9J Sidewinder AAM.
3. Maverick ASM (various models).
4. AGM-62 Walleye ASM.
5. AGM-109 Harpoon anti-ship missile (up to four).
6. Drop tank, 262gal (1,192lit).
7. AGM-12 Bullpup (no longer used by front-line units).
8. Durandal anti-runway weapon.

Weapon provisions:
A. 20mm M61 gun with 570 rounds.
B. Pylon (two Mk 82 or CBU-59, one tank or other conventional stores to 1,000lb).
C. Pylon (Sparrow AAM or FLIR or laser tracker/strike camera).
D. Pylon (bombs to 2,000lb, Maverick or Harm).
E. Pylon (bombs to 2,000lb including B57 or B61 nuclear).
F. Pylon (AIM-9).

AS missile.
13. Gun port.
14. M61 gun with 570 rounds of 20mm.
15. GBU-10E/B (Mk 84, 2,000lb, 907kg) LGB Paveway II series.
16. FLIR pod.
17. Mk 84 GP bomb, 2,000lb (907kg).
18. Triple Mk 82 GP bombs, 500lb (227kg).
19. Mk 82 Snakeye retarded bomb.
20. M117 GP bomb, 750lb (340kg).
21. Stores carrier.
22. Data-link container

(flight test and Walleye).
23. Rockeye II CBU-59.
24. Twin Mk 83 GP

bombs, 1,000lb (454kg).
25. LAU-61A/A and 68B/A rocket pods.

9. SUU-20 practice bomb/rocket dispenser.
10. ASQ-173 LST.
11. AIM-7 Sparrow medium-range AAM.
12. AGM-88A Harm

Combat avionics:
A. APG-65 radar.
B. HUD.
C. Tacan.
D. UHF/IFF.
E. Front hemisphere

ECM.
F. VHF.
G. RWR.
H. Main avionics bays.
J. UHF.
K. IR sensor.

Mikoyan/Gurevich MiG-21

Origin: Soviet Union, first flight (Ye-6 prototype) early 1957.

Type: (Most) fighter, (some) fighter/bomber or reconnaissance.

Engine: (21) one 11,243lb (5,5099kg) Tumanskii R-11 afterburning turbojet, (21F) 12,677lb (5,750kg) R-11F, (21PF) 13,120lb (5,951kg) R-11F2, (21FL, PFS, PFM, US) 13,668lb (6,199kg) R-11-300, (PFMA, M, R) R-11F2S-300, same rating, (MF, RF, SMT, UM, early 21bis) 14,550lb (6,599kg) R-13-300, (21bis) 16,535lb (7,500kg) R-25.

Dimensions: Span 23ft 5½in (7.15m); length (almost all versions, including instrumentation boom) 51ft 8½in (15.76m), (excluding boom and inlet centrebody) 44ft 11in (13.46m); wing area 247.57sq ft (23m²).

Weights: Empty (F) 12,440lb (5,643kg), (MF) about 12,300lb (5,580kg), (bis) 12,600lb (5,715kg); loaded (typical, half internal fuel and two K-13A) 15,000lb (6,800kg), (full internal fuel and four K-13A) 18,078lb (8,200kg), maximum (bis, two K-13A and three drop tanks) 20,725lb (9,400kg).

Performance: Maximum speed (typical of all, SL) 800mph (1,290km/h, Mach 1.05), (36,000ft/10,972m, clean) 1,385mph (2,230km/h, Mach 2.1), initial climb (F) about 30,000ft (9,144m)/min (bis) 58,000ft (17.677m)/min, service ceiling (bis, max) 59,055ft (17,999m); practical ceiling (all), rarely above 50,000ft (15,239m); range with internal fuel (F) 395 miles (635km), (bis) 683 miles (1,100km); max range with three tanks (bis) 1,118km.

Background: Soviet air staff and OKB leaders in 1954 studied Korean experience and TsAGI produced two optimised shapes for future fighters, similar except that one had swept wing (62°LE) and the other a delta (57°LE). MiG OKB evaluated prototypes of both from June 1956 and eventually chose Ye-5 delta which developed through refined Ye-6 variants into production MiG-21 of 1958. Original aircraft outstandingly light and agile, but extremely limited in weapons and load.

Design: Throughout 25 years of development basic wing never varied from 57° delta with 5/4.2 per cent thickness and plain "hard" LE with neither dogtooth nor camber. Flaps originally area-increasing slotted, from 1961 plain with SPS flap-blowing. Conventional ailerons sole roll control, slab tailplanes used for pitch only. Area of vertical tail progressively increased, along with engine thrust and fuel/weapons capacity. Forward view restricted in A/G mode by wide nose ducting engine airflow past centrebody with radar; rearwards view poor due to side-hinged canopy being followed by dorsal spine of same height and cross-section. Overall result was extremely high-performance and agile aircraft with enjoyable flying qualities but even in latest versions deficient in mission endurance, all-weather avionics, navigation (and in export versions ECM/IFF), weapon load and modern cockpit displays, but extremely good in reliability and availability (typically six sorties per day for several days) and, except in fuel burn, low cost of operation.

Avionics: All current single-seat models have simple search/track radar for A/A interception, but with very limited value in A/G role. From about 1961 to 1966 usual set was R1L or R2L "Spin Scan": I-band, 100kW, PRFs 925/950pps for search and 1,750/1,850pps for track, range in good weather 31 miles (50km), provides target illumination for AA-2-2 Advanced Atoll. Until 1979 no HUD radar symbology, but good HDD with three modes visible in bright sunlight. So far as known, no MiG-21 has had Hotas cockpit controls, radar having pushbuttons and rotary knobs around periphery of display. Sole radar input to HUD sight is target range. Since 1966 standard radar has been so-called Jay Bird: J-band, 100+ kW, 12.88/13.2GHz, PRFs various bands up to 2,724pps, max range again about 31 miles (50km), provides target illumination for AA-2-2. Still no advanced cockpit displays but post-1970 aircraft have improved radar with limited downlook and navigation capability, though not normally used in A/G role. Thus, so far as known, no MiG-21 has any all-weather capability except against aerial targets and with close ground control to vector close astern (in bad weather within 19 miles, 30km). All current single-seaters have VOR/ILS/ADF and standard SRO-2 IFF and Sirena III 360° RWR. Basic nav by twin-gyro platform, with doppler in most late versions, radar altimeter, MRP-56P beacon receiver, ARL-S data-link and provision for front/rear ECM jammers in removable wingtip pods (seldom seen in Soviet photos but supplied with many exported aircraft). Little has been seen of Soviet ECM jammer pods, though when an almost-new MiG-21bis was presented for inspection by a visiting air force the information was given that "different types" of pod are routinely carried by FA regiments using these aircraft. The only Western pod in full-scale service with MiG-21s appears to be the Italian Selenia ALQ-234, used by several Arab air forces including Egypt and Syria.

Armament: Varies greatly with model, but nearly all current tactical versions have one GP-9 comprising one 23mm GSh-23gun with 200 rounds; centreline pylon for reconnaissance pod or 108gal (490lit) tank; four wing pylons normally rated at 1,102lb (500kg) each, but aircraft has no effective radius with all at max load. Normal loads include FAB-500 (1,102lb) bombs or 108gal tanks on outer pylons and K-13A or twin AA-8 missiles on inners, or alternatively four FAB-250 (551lb) bombs.

Future: There will probably be no more new-build versions of Soviet MiG-21s, because of existence of MiG-23 family and MiG-29. With some 2,500 in the Soviet inventory, of which an estimated 1,300 are in front-line regiments, the MiG-21 remains a threat because of its sheer numbers, and there is no doubt that all active single-seaters are being subjected to routine update programmes. AA-8 Aphid AAMs have been carried since before 1980, and there are known to be major avionic update programmes on MiG-21s of the FA. Indian production of the bis-N until late 1984 has introduced no known major variation. Chinese production of the much older MiG-21F, with local designation J-7, was resumed in about 1980 after a gap of 14 years, with only minor changes. Some are being supplied to Egypt as operational trainers, where front-line MiG-21s – despite progressive replacement by the F-16 – are being retrofitted with Soviet-compatible Teledyne IFF and doppler, and (unconfirmed) a Smiths HUD and Ferranti INS. Egypt and India are expected to replace AA-2 and AA-2-2 AAMs by AIM-9s or other types.

Left: Like the French delta-wing Mirages, the MiG-21 is fundamentally extremely limited in almost all parts of its mission capability except speed and basic agility. Like the Mirage, it has proved a worldwide best-seller. This example is an obsolecent MiG-21PF used by Romania.

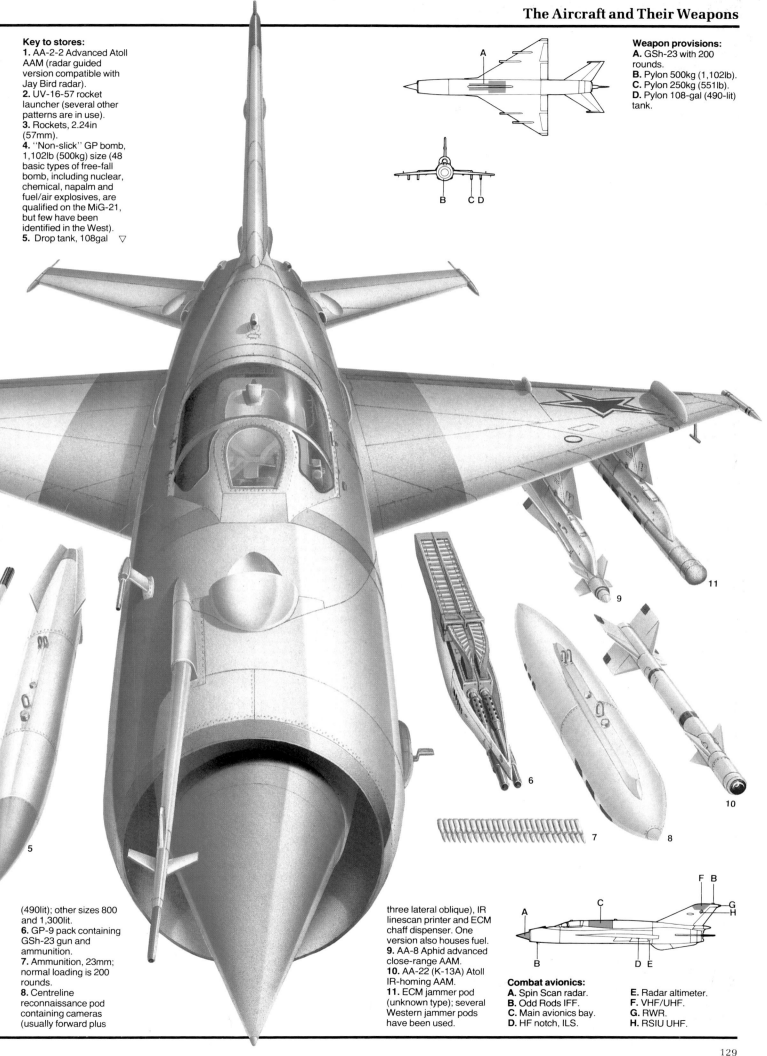

Key to stores:
1. AA-2-2 Advanced Atoll AAM (radar guided version compatible with Jay Bird radar).
2. UV-16-57 rocket launcher (several other patterns are in use).
3. Rockets, 2.24in (57mm).
4. "Non-slick" GP bomb, 1,102lb (500kg) size (48 basic types of free-fall bomb, including nuclear, chemical, napalm and fuel/air explosives, are qualified on the MiG-21, but few have been identified in the West).
5. Drop tank, 108gal ▽

Weapon provisions:
A. GSh-23 with 200 rounds.
B. Pylon 500kg (1,102lb).
C. Pylon 250kg (551lb).
D. Pylon 108-gal (490-lit) tank.

(490lit); other sizes 800 and 1,300lit.
6. GP-9 pack containing GSh-23 gun and ammunition.
7. Ammunition, 23mm; normal loading is 200 rounds.
8. Centreline reconnaissance pod containing cameras (usually forward plus

three lateral oblique), IR linescan printer and ECM chaff dispenser. One version also houses fuel.
9. AA-8 Aphid advanced close-range AAM.
10. AA-22 (K-13A) Atoll IR-homing AAM.
11. ECM jammer pod (unknown type); several Western jammer pods have been used.

Combat avionics:
A. Spin Scan radar.
B. Odd Rods IFF.
C. Main avionics bay.
D. HF notch, ILS.
E. Radar altimeter.
F. VHF/UHF.
G. RWR.
H. RSIU UHF.

Mikoyan/Gurevich MiG-23

Origin: Soviet Union, first flight (Ye-231 prototype) probably 1966.
Type: Multi-role fighter, attack and trainer.
Engine: (Early and most export fighters and all trainers) one Tumanskii R-27 afterburning turbofan rated at 15,430/22,485lb (7/10.2t) thrust; (all current Soviet operational versions) one Tumanskii R-29B afterburning turbofan rated at 27,500lb (12,475kg) with max augmentation.
Dimensions: Span (16° sweep) 46ft 9in (14.25m), (72°) 26ft 9½in (8.17m); length (all known variants, excl probe) 55ft 1½in (16.8m), (with instrument probe) 59ft 10in (18.23m); height 14ft 4in (4.36m); wing area (gross, 16°) about 400sq ft (37.17m²).
Weights: Empty (typical) 22,000lb (9,979kg); internal fuel 10,300lb (4,672kg), loaded (air/air mission) about 32,000lb (14,515kg; maximum (air/surface mission) about 41,000lb (18,597kg).
Performance: Maximum speed (clean, SL) 840mph (1,352km/h, Mach 1.1), (clean, 36,000ft/10,972m), 1,520mph (2,446km/h, Mach 2.31) initial climb (clean) about 50,000ft (15km)/min; service ceiling (afterburner) 61,000ft (18,591m); takeoff/landing runs, each about 2,950ft (899m), combat radius (hi, internal fuel) 560 miles (900km); ferry range, 1,740 miles (2,800km).
Background: Bearing not the slightest resemblance to the MiG-21, the next-generation MiG tactical fighter was designed around the TsAGI 1962 variable-geometry shape for unfettered new designs (also used for the Su-24), with outboard pivots on a minimal fixed glove (inboard portion of wing). Ye-231 prototype flown with Lyul'ka engine 1966 and substantial development batch included many aircraft (possibly 50) used in FA regiments to gain service experience. Aircraft largely redesigned with shorter and lighter Tumanskii engine and subsequently built in extremely large numbers in many single- and two-seat forms with interceptor or

attack nose and fixed- or variable-geometry engine installation, the latter being described separately as MiG-27. (All versions of -23 and -27 have the NATO name Flogger.)
Design: The wing is mounted in shoulder position, level with the top of the lateral inlet ducts to the single augmented turbofan engine but with a substantial fuselage spine passing above the upper surface. Wing and slab tailerons have no dihedral, and the fin area is the greatest that could be provided, even including a large ventral which is extended automatically by retracting the landing gear. Swing wings adjustable to 16°, 45° or 72°, sweep beyond 16° revealing the two largest leading-edge dogtooth vortex inducers on any aircraft. Leading-edge droop flaps automatically lowered with extension of three-section slotted flaps with wing at 16°. Upper-surface spoiler/dumpers can operate differentially as primary roll control together with differential tailerons. Four petal airbrakes around rear fuselage. Soft-surface landing gear with steerable twin-wheel nose unit with mudguard retracting to rear and main legs horizontal on ground carrying single wheels on long-stroke levered suspension. Fully variable Phantom-type inlets with large perforated splitter panels, and fully variable nozzle. Small framed canopy hinged up from opaque fuselge downstream with top level with top of fuselage, giving limited rear view either direct or via two mirrors facing pilot and one in blister above. Aircraft generally easy to fly, popular and said to be extremely reliable in adverse conditions.
Avionics: Usual radar in MiG-23MF called High Lark by NATO and said to have range of 53 miles (85km) for search and 34 miles (54km) in lock-on tracking mode. Can be used for ground mapping, surface search, terrain avoidance (not TFR) and all forms of interception against aerial targets including lookdown/shootdown against aircraft at very low level. Popular published account

Above: One of the best air-to-air photographs of any modern Soviet-built combat type, showing a Libyan-operated MiG-23 variant known to NATO as Flogger-E. The picture was taken by a US Navy aircraft over the Gulf of Sirte in August 1981.

implies usage against targets simulating Western cruise missiles. Laser ranger (possibly also used as marked surface-target seeker) under nose, doppler flush aerial further aft, and radar altimeter. Sirena 3 RWR aerials facing forward from leading edge of left and right gloves, just outboard of pylon, and astern from top of fin. Odd Rods SRO-3A IFF ahead of windscreen between additional pitots and yaw sensors, with AOA sensor on left side and Swift Rod ILS aerial on underside. CW illumination for radar-guided AAMs in all Soviet fighter versions, and many aircraft have small avionics blister on each side under nose ahead of nose gear (not the same as on the Flogger-H version of MiG-27). There are several small variations in avionic fit, and most recent aircraft have a blade (possibly VOR) aerial under the left taileron (which like its partner has a kinked trailing edge with reduced chord outboard). Export variants, whose designations are not known, have reduced avionic standard with a smaller radar (widely reported to be Jay Bird), no laser and little or no EW equipment. A similar reduced fit is usual on tandem-seat MiG-23U trainers, which also appear all to be powered by the R-27 engine used in first MiG-23s.

Armament: One GP-9 centreline installation of GSh-23 gun with 200 rounds; five pylons (centreline, under inlet ducts and under wing gloves) rated as shown by 3-view, centreline only plumbed for 176gal (800lit) tank. All have option of twin, triple or tandem twin stores ejector racks, eg for twin AA-8. Maximum load unknown but probably as MiG-27.
Future: With some 2,700 aircraft delivered to Soviet units (including MiG-27 versions) these aircraft are the most numerous in service with any air force, and will probably remain important until the end of the century. While production continues at a rate exceeding 600 per year, update programmes are producing numerous improvements to the airframe, avionics and other equipment. For several years a carrier-based version has been predicted, to form the fighter element of planned Soviet carriers in the 50,000-tonne class to embark an estimated 60 aircraft. A MiG-23 has been supplied from Egypt to the USA and another to China, and the latter country is reported to have used a great deal of MiG-23 engineering in its J-8 fighter (but with different propulsion).

2

Left: These six MiG-23MFs, with shorter dorsal fins and simpler avionics, made goodwill visits to Finland (seen here) and to France in the summer of 1978. Similar aircraft, with added undernose sensors and other equipment, are in Soviet service.

Weapon provisions:
A. GSh-23 with 200 rounds.
B. Pylon 176-gal (800-lit) tank.
C. Pylon 750 (possibly 1,000) kg.
D. Pylon 1,000kg (2,205lb).

Key to stores:
1. These drawings merely suggest possible appearance of Soviet tactical ASMs, including the elusive AS-7 Kerry (which is believed not to be the missile seen on an Su-22 in a released Soviet photograph).
2. Twin paired installation of AA-8 Aphid close-range AAMs.

3. GP-9 installation of GSh-23 gun and 23mm ammunition.
4. 176gal (800lit) tank normally carried on centreline pylon.
5. AA-2 Atoll IR-homing AAM (AA-2-2 Advanced Atoll can also be carried).

Combat avionics:
A. High Lark radar.
B. Main avionic compartments.
C. EO tracker (left wing), RHAWS (right).
D. VHF.

E. HF notch.
F. VHF/UHF.
G. ILS.
H. VOR.
J. Unknown.
K. LRMTS.
L. ILS.

Mikoyan/Gurevich MiG-25

Origin: Soviet Union, first flight (Ye-26 prototype) 1964 or early 1965.

Type: (25) high-altitude interceptor, (R) strategic reconnaissance, (U) trainer.

Engines: Two Tumanskii R-31 afterburning turbojets each rated at 16,755/24,250lb (7,600/10,999kg) thrust.

Dimensions: Span 45ft 9in (13.94m), (25R) 44ft 0in (13.49m); length (all known variants), (overall), 78ft 1¾in (23.82m), (fuselage only) 63ft 7¾in (19.39m); height 20ft 0¼in (6.10m); wing area, gross, 662sq ft (61.52m²). (25R) slightly less.

Weights: (typical) empty equipped (25) just over 44,090lb (19,999kg), (25R) 43,200lb (19,595kg); maximum loaded (25) 79,800lb (36,197kg), (25R) 73,635lb (33,400kg).

Performance: Maximum speed (low level) about 650mph (1,050km/h, Mach 0.85), (36,000ft/10,972m and above, MiG-25 clean), 2,115mph (3,400km/h, Mach 3.2), (36,089ft, 11,000m and above, 4 AAMs) 1,850mph (2,978km/h, Mach 2.8); maximum rate of climb 40,950ft (12,480km)/min; time to 36,090ft (10,999m) with sustained afterburner, 2.5min; service ceiling (25) 80,000ft (24,382m), (both 25R versions) 88,580ft (26,997m); combat radius (25) 700 miles (1,125km), (25R, max) 900 miles (1,448km); takeoff run (25, max weight) 4,525ft (1,380m); landing (25) touchdown 168mph (270km/h), run 7,150ft (2,180m).

Background: When the USAF planned its WS-110A strategic bomber in 1956-57 the Soviet Union studied possible defences against this vehicle with a high-altitude cruise speed of Mach 3. When the American XB-70 was contracted for in December 1957 Soviet contracts were immediately placed for a new super-long-range SAM system and a new super-fast interceptor. Mach 3 was attempted but in the event the MiG OKB settled for 2.8 in a combat mission, though 3.2 can be achieved in the clean configuration. Cancellation of the B-70 in 1961 did not halt the Ye-266 prototype programme, which led to a series of impressive world speed, height and climb records from April 1965. The definitive aircraft went into production as the MiG-25 interceptor and two forms of MiG-25R reconnaissance aircraft, as well as a dual trainer without combat equipment.

Design: The MiG-25 was designed as a single-mission aircraft to operate only from long paved runways and to fly at great speeds and altitudes. No attempt was made to operate at low levels or engage in any form of close combat, so while the propulsion system has fully variable inlets and nozzles, linked by a simple turbojet of low pressure-ratio, the wing has fixed geometry apart from plain ailerons and flaps. Design owed much to A-5 Vigilante and F-108, both by

the same company which built the B-70 (North American Aviation), with high-mounted wing with taper rather than sweep, twin canted vertical tails (but with fixed fins and separate rudders), a broad box-like fuselage flanked by large lateral air ducts, a slim nose for the pilot and radar, and main gears folding into the fuselage. Many items including engines, radar, hydraulic/fuel/environmental/WM-injection and electrics, missiles and reconnaissance systems, were specially designed for this aircraft, whose very high cost was considered worthwhile because of its ability to operate with virtually no chance of enemy fighter interception. In recent years new versions have brought lookdown/shootdown capability, much better manoeuvrability (with stronger structure, leading-edge root strakes and tailerons used as primary roll controls) and even greater engine thrust.

Avionics: For the necessary stand-off kill capability the main radar had to be large and powerful, and when it was designed in 1958-9 the Fox Fire radar was the most powerful for regular AI use with average electrical load of 600kW. Operating in I-band at frequencies near 9GHz, it is a typical thermionic-valve (vacuum-tube) set of this era, with Freon cooling and five operating modes which include ground mapping but offer no capability against low-flying aircraft. By modern standards it is bulky and lacking in sophistication, though of course it provides CW guidance for AAMs. Search range typically 75 miles (120km), with tracking of single targets reliably achieved at 43 miles (70km) in most weather conditions. The main computer is large and capable for a 1959 analog device, with automatic vectoring under guidance from the widespread Markham electronic environment and data-link (formerly operated by the IA-PVO) with reception by a blade aerial under the nose. Sirena 3 RWR with additional IR warning has 270° coverage from side-looking aerials in the wingtip antiflutter pods and rear of right fin tip, giving quadrantal cover for pulse/CW/TWS emitters. Active ECM jammer in each tip pod with horn emitter at front and rear. HF in left fin tip, VHF blade above fuselage and UHF below. IFF in right fin tip and ahead of windshield, ATC/SIF in right fin tip, and nose aerials for ILS, two beacons, doppler, radio compass and (usually removed) radar altimeter.

Armament: Four wing pylons, not plumbed for tanks; most common fit is four AA-6 Acrid AAMs (two SARH, two IR), but various single and paired installations have been seen of AA-7 Apex and even AA-8 Aphid. Later AAMs are entering service.

Future: New interceptor, possibly MiG-25M and called Foxbat-E, has completely new pulse-doppler radar with lookdown/shootdown

ability (said to display 20 targets and track any four), and many other improvements including ability to carry six AAMs of three (possibly four) types. Said in 1978 to have scored kill on target flying at below 197ft (60m) from 19,685ft (5,999m) at range of 12.5 miles (20km); later to have intercepted UR-1 target at 69,900ft (21,304m). Still later, considerably redesigned interceptor is called Foxhound by NATO. Few hard details, but has uprated engines and is said to have two crew and internal gun. Many

MiG-25 type aircraft have flown since the early 1970s with later Tumanskii engines each rated at 30,865lb (14,000kg) thrust, but these have been slow to get into production aircraft. To make sense, the extra thrust must be matched with a stronger airframe able to manoeuvre at low altitudes. Other unconfirmed reports claim there are now two body pylons to increase the number of weapon options and have greater combat persistence, engaging a greater number of targets.

Below: Libyan MiG-25 seen in August 1981. It has two giant AA-6 Acrid missiles, the right one being radar homing.

Weapon provisions:
A. Inboard wing missile pylons (various AAMs, but usually AA-6 of IR homing type).
B. Outboard wing missile pylons (various AAMs, but usually AA-6 of SARH type).
C. Unconfirmed report of internal gun in some aircraft.

Key to stores:
1. AA-6 Acrid AAM SARH (semi-active radar homing) version.
2. AA-6 Acrid AAM IR (infra-red) homing version.
3. AA-7 Apex medium-range AAMs. Note: early examples of MiG-25 frequently carried older AAMs, notably including AA-5 Ash (normally seen only on the Tu-128 Fiddler), and these are still in service.

Combat avionics:
A. Instrumentation pitot probe.
A. Main Fox Fire radar.
B. SLAR (MiG-25R versions only).
C. Odd Rods IFF.
D. Rear avionics bays.
E. VHF Tacan.
F. IFF and Sirena 3 RWR.
G. ATC/SIF and Sirena 3 RWR.
H. Sirena 3 RWR (dispensers added in MiG-25R).
J. UHF and marker beacon receiver.
K. Flush ILS.

Mikoyan/Gurevich MiG-27

Origin: Soviet Union, first flight (attack prototype) not later than 1970.

Type: Ground-attack aircraft.

Engine: One Tumanskii R-29 series augmented turbofan with maximum afterburning thrust of 25,353lb (11,500kg).

Dimensions: Span (16° sweep) 46ft 9in (14.24m), (72°) 26ft 9½in (8.17m); length (excl probe) about 53ft 5in (16.28m), (with probe) 55ft 6in (16.9m); height 14ft 4in (4.36m); wing area (gross, 16°) about 400sq ft (37.17m²).

Weights: Empty, about 22,000lb (9,979kg); maximum with no external weapons, 34,170lb (15,499kg); maximum takeoff, 44,310lb (20,098kg).

Performance: Maximum speed (SL) clean about Mach 1.1, with external weapons 723mph (1,163km/h, Mach 0.95); maximum speed at high altitude (clean) about 1,050mph (1,700km/h, Mach 1.6); service ceiling, about 50,000ft (15.24km); takeoff to 50ft (15m) at clean gross weight, 2,625ft (800m); combat radius (all lo, centreline tank, four FAB-500 bombs and two AAMs), 240 miles (386km); ferry range (three tanks) 1,550 miles (2,500km).

Background: The same TsAGI-developed aerodynamic shape was used in two MiG combat aircraft family for interception and the MiG-27 family for attack on surface targets. The MiG-27 ran a year or two later in timing than the -23, but major parts of the airframe and systems are common to both. In general the MiG-27 has a simpler propulsion system and different nose, but there are hybrid aircraft with the engine installation of the MiG-23, usually with the sub-type designation of MiG-23BN. These are described here because their role is that of the -27.

Design: Compared with the

Below: As in the West, Soviet swing-wing aircraft normally fold wings on the ground for easier taxiing and parking. Note nose.

MiG-23 the MiG-27 has virtually the same airframe, with the following known differences: revised stressing for operations at increased weight up to 18 tonnes but not normally exceeding 6g, compared with 7.5g of fighter (at max sweep in both cases); new forward fuselage, popularly called "ducknose", with no radar but broad flat downsloping profile ahead of cockpit containing various air/ground sensors, and with thick armour side panels; new cockpit raised 12in (30cm) with rearranged and modified displays and controls, less sharply raked and deeper windshield and canopy; new landing gear with very wide, larger-diameter low-pressure tyres, very small separate compartments for retracted nose- and mainwheels; deeper bulged compartments for nosewheels and mainwheels; numerous changes in avionic fit and armament, including widely spaced pylons under the air inlet ducts (which, like the centreline and glove hardpoints, are rated at 3117lb/700kg max each); and a six-barrel gun of 23mm calibre in place of the GSH-23 of the fighter.

Avionics: The only radars are an NI-50BM doppler, a nose terrain-avoidance radar, RV-5 radio altimeter, a missile-guidance radar (see later) and, in trials aircraft but not the Flogger-J (the latest variant identified in service in 1983) a TFR. Sirena 3 RWR has 180° rear cover from tip of fin and about 100° cover each side from dead ahead from blisters low on the forward fuselage just ahead of nose gear. Laser RMTS in chisel nose. In initial MiG-27 production two prominent tubular fairings project ahead of the wing glove above the stores pylons, that on the left housing a forward-emitting ECM jammer similar to the front of the MiG-25 wingtip pod, and that on the right housing a missile guidance system invariably associated with AS-7 ATC/SIF transponder near tip of fin, pitot on nose, pitot and yaw sensor ahead of windshield, VHF whip or blade aerial under fuselage, Swift Rod ILS under nose and SRO-2 IFF further aft under nose. MiG-23BN sub-family which combine attack nose and avionics with variable-geometry engine have been described as dual-role fighter/attack platforms, but attack certainly remains primary mission and they have virtually no bad-weather air combat capability despite greater power and speed. It is more significant that the so-called Flogger J has a new nose sensor arrangement, yet has no fairings projecting ahead of the wing glove. It is conceivable that the ''missile active jammer'' and forward active jammer may have been relocated in the tips of the added leading edge root extensions. No AOA sensor.

Armament: One 23mm six-barrel gun on centreline with unknown ammunition capacity (probably about 500 rounds); centreline pylon behind gun plumbed for 176gal (800lit) tank and rated at 1,000kg (2,205lb): pylons under inlet ducts, rear fuselage and glove vanes all believed rated at 1,102lb (500kg): fixed jettisonable pylons under outer wings rated at 2,205lb (1,000kg) and not normally used except for 176gal (800lit) tanks for ferry. Total load unknown but bombload of 6,614lb (3,000kg) is common.

Future: Flight time with MiG-23 and variants must far exceed one million hours, and the number built will exceed 4,000 by the end of 1984. Because of the scale of production the price is far less than that of any rival Western aircraft, but it is a reflection on official attitudes that many air forces have only lukewarm interest in such a serious attempt to fly real missions and prefer the "racy" appeal of a MIG-21 or Mirage 2000. Licence production in India of the Flogger-J, the latest known MiG-27 variant, could not be confirmed as this went to press. Not yet seen are advanced reconnaissance pods, air/ground ordnance (except traditional bombs and 57mm rockets), pod-mounted jammers and EW expendables.

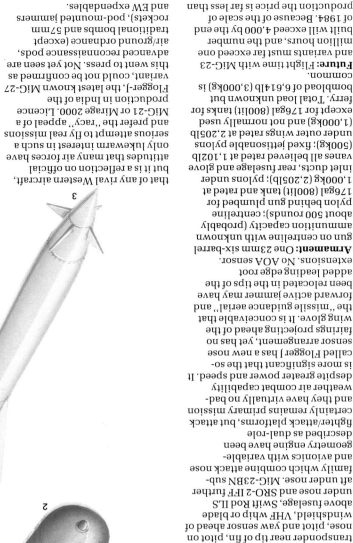

Left: From a distance this early MiG-27 is difficult to distinguish from the later variants with long leading-edge root strakes, modified nose sensors and kinked trailing edges to the tailerons. Note that with the main landing gears extended the ventral fin is folded to one side. Reports in the Soviet press indicate that serviceability and maintainability of these aircraft are setting national records.

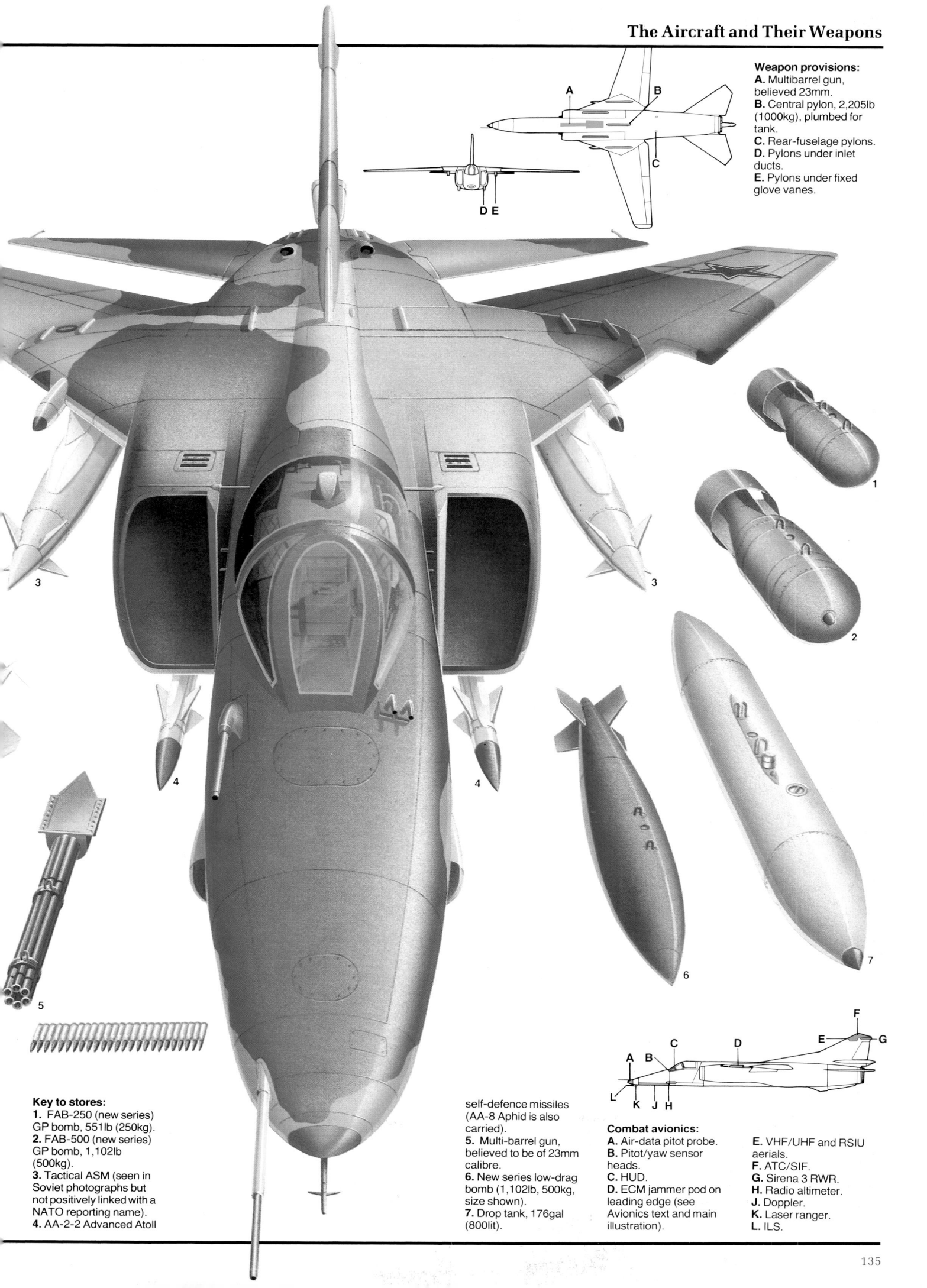

Weapon provisions:
A. Multibarrel gun, believed 23mm.
B. Central pylon, 2,205lb (1000kg), plumbed for tank.
C. Rear-fuselage pylons.
D. Pylons under inlet ducts.
E. Pylons under fixed glove vanes.

Key to stores:
1. FAB-250 (new series) GP bomb, 551lb (250kg).
2. FAB-500 (new series) GP bomb, 1,102lb (500kg).
3. Tactical ASM (seen in Soviet photographs but not positively linked with a NATO reporting name).
4. AA-2-2 Advanced Atoll

self-defence missiles (AA-8 Aphid is also carried).
5. Multi-barrel gun, believed to be of 23mm calibre.
6. New series low-drag bomb (1,102lb, 500kg, size shown).
7. Drop tank, 176gal (800lit).

Combat avionics:
A. Air-data pitot probe.
B. Pitot/yaw sensor heads.
C. HUD.
D. ECM jammer pod on leading edge (see Avionics text and main illustration).
E. VHF/UHF and RSIU aerials.
F. ATC/SIF.
G. Sirena 3 RWR.
H. Radio altimeter.
J. Doppler.
K. Laser ranger.
L. ILS.

Mitsubishi F-1

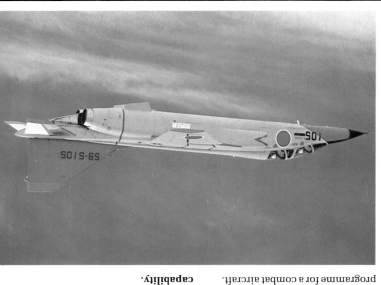

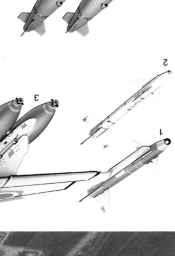

Type: (T-2A) two-seat supersonic trainer: (F-1) single-seat close-support fighter-bomber.
Engines: Two Ishikawajima-Harima TF40-801A (licence-built Rolls-Royce/Turboméca Adour 102) two-shaft augmented turbofans with maximum rating of 7,070lb (3,210kg).
Dimensions: Span 25ft 10in (7.87m); length 58ft 7in (17.85m); height 14ft 4in (4.368m).
Weights: Empty (T-2) 13,893lb (6,301kg); (F-1) 14,017lb (6,358kg); loaded (T-2, clean) 21,616lb (9,805kg); (T-2 maximum) 24,750lb (11,200kg); (F-1 maximum) 30,200lb (13,700kg).
Performance: Maximum speed (at clean gross weight) 1,056mph (1,700km/h, Mach 1.6); initial climb 19,680ft (6,000m)/min; service ceiling 50,025ft (15,246m); range (T-2 with external tanks) 1,610 miles (2,591km); (F-1 combat radius with eight 500lb bombs) 218 miles (350km).

Origin: Japan, first flight July 1971.

Background: In 1967 Mitsubishi was selected to build the T-2 supersonic trainer, with a design based on that of the Jaguar and powered by the same engines licence-made by IHI. In 1972 the design began of a derived single-seat "close-support fighter" to fly air defence, land attack and anti-ship missions. No requirement was stipulated for capability in the reconnaissance role, or for inflight refuelling.

Design: Closely based on the SEPECAT Jaguar, the Mitsubishi T-2 and F-1 have a high wing of 4.66 per cent thickness/chord ratio with full-span leading-edge droop flaps, the outer sections having increased chord with dogtooth discontinuities, and almost full-span slotted flaps. All these surfaces are electrically operated, the other main actuation tasks being hydraulic, including the two-section spoilers above each wing which are the only roll controls. Powered tailplanes have anhedral and the rudder is boosted. The lateral inlets have large splitter plates and four suck-in auxiliary doors, but are otherwise fixed geometry. As in the Jaguar there was no compromise in the design in order to reduce radar cross-section and radar energy can be reflected from the first-stage blading of the engines. There are two ventral airbrakes followed by two ventral fins. The single-wheel landing gears are not designed for off-runway operation but the nosewheel is steerable and the main gears have long-travel levered suspension. Equipment includes a drag chute and arrester hook. The pilot sits in a Weber zero/zero seat built by Daiseru in a cockpit with good forward view but extremely restricted view to the rear, the two small mirrors looking into the inlets. On the whole the F-1 is effective and popular and the two-seat T-2 equips the national aerobatic team.

Avionics: The basic fire-control system is the J/AWG-12, with a free-fall bombing computer and Mitsubishi Electric multimode radar with limited capability in ground mapping, terrain avoidance (not following) and attack on surface and aerial targets. Some radar data are passed to the J/AWG-12 HUD which is a Thomson-CSF pattern licensed to Mitsubishi. The primary navaid is the Ferranti 6TN/F-1 INS, backed up by Nippon Electric Tacan. Other equipment includes a Lear attitude/heading reference system, radio altimeter, dual UHF, IFF/SIF, the Tokyo Keiki APR-4 RWR, ASM-1 missile controls, strike camera and air-data computer. The APR-4 is a capable set whose receivers are located in the tube above the fin. The output is presented in graphic and alphanumeric form on a CRT display, and the system is controlled by a reprogrammable digital computer able to handle multiple threats simultaneously. The same company is developing the ALQ-6 active jammer which will handle wavelengths from 1 to about 18GHz and will almost certainly be pod-mounted.

Armament: One 20mm M61A-1 gun with 750 rounds; centreline and inboard wing stations plumbed for 182gal (821lit) tanks and rated for twin stores up to 1,543lb (700kg) total; outer wing pylons rated at 750lb (340kg); wingtip rails for Sidewinders. Normal maximum weapon load 6,000lb (2,722kg). ASM-1 anti-ship missile weighs 1,345lb (610kg).

Future: With a restricted budget and very limited production runs it is unlikely that any further aircraft will be constructed beyond the planned 80, over 75 of which had been delivered as this book went to press. Much thought has been given to the obvious possibility of introducing some of the available stages of uprating of the TF40 (Adour) engine, which could usefully improve inflight agility, especially with pylons loaded. There is no immediate intention to increase weapon load beyond the present 6,000lb (2,722kg), normally made up of 12 free-fall bombs of nominal 500lb (227kg). The locally developed ASM-1 anti-ship missile has also been working on an IR-homing AAM to replace Sidewinder but this has not reached the service test stage. Altogether the F-1 is a very adequate ground attack aircraft, with high speed and a satisfactory standard of avionics. Already its air-combat capability and offensive bombload are impressive, but Mitsubishi is unable to incur high costs in bringing in improvements. This could be the last all-Japanese programme for a combat aircraft.

Below: The two-seat T-2 has a simpler radar and cockpit displays than the F-1, and lacks an INS, but it has almost the same weapons and weapon-aiming capability.

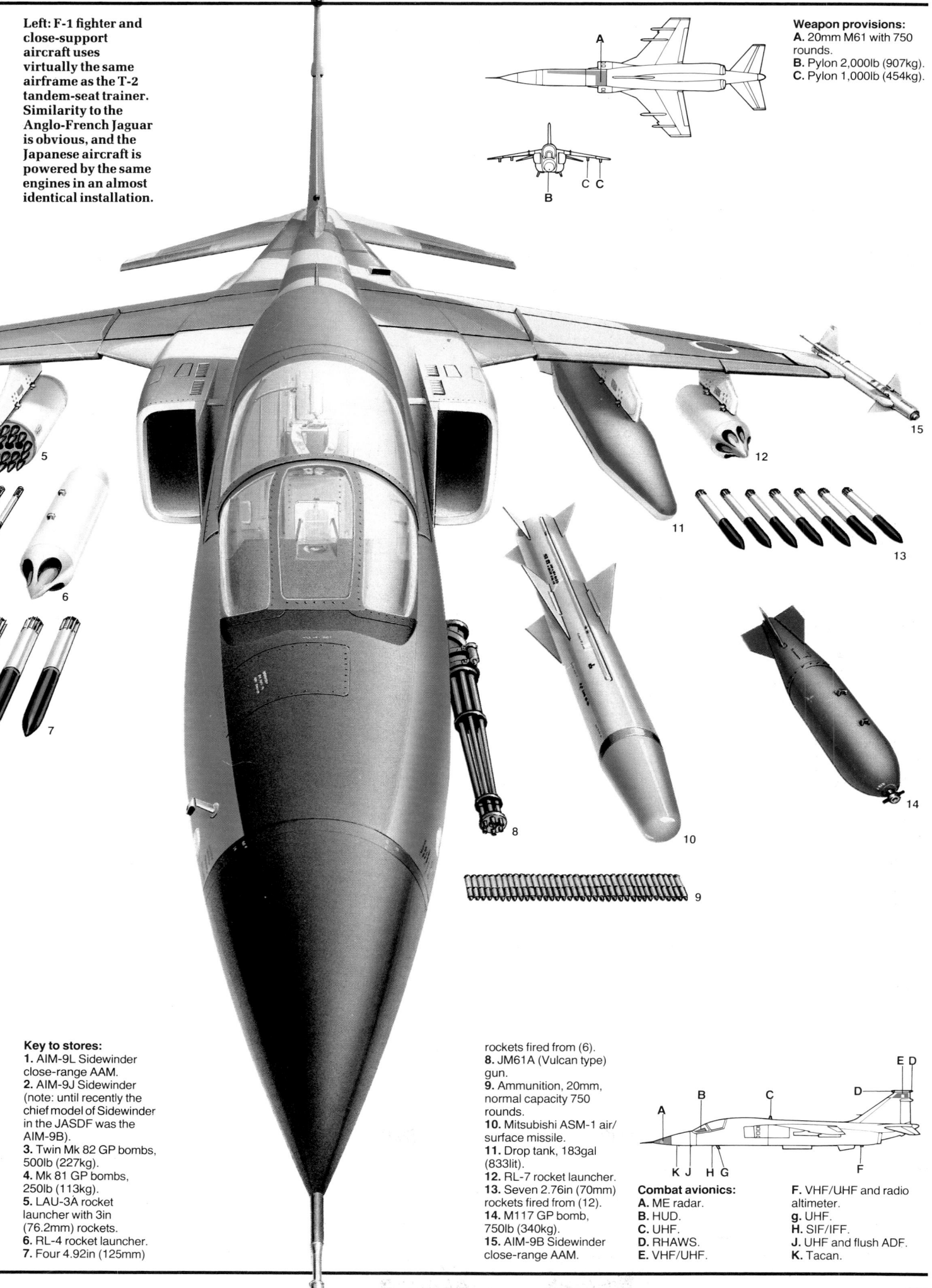

Left: F-1 fighter and close-support aircraft uses virtually the same airframe as the T-2 tandem-seat trainer. Similarity to the Anglo-French Jaguar is obvious, and the Japanese aircraft is powered by the same engines in an almost identical installation.

Weapon provisions:
A. 20mm M61 with 750 rounds.
B. Pylon 2,000lb (907kg).
C. Pylon 1,000lb (454kg).

Key to stores:
1. AIM-9L Sidewinder close-range AAM.
2. AIM-9J Sidewinder (note: until recently the chief model of Sidewinder in the JASDF was the AIM-9B).
3. Twin Mk 82 GP bombs, 500lb (227kg).
4. Mk 81 GP bombs, 250lb (113kg).
5. LAU-3A rocket launcher with 3in (76.2mm) rockets.
6. RL-4 rocket launcher.
7. Four 4.92in (125mm)

rockets fired from (6).
8. JM61A (Vulcan type) gun.
9. Ammunition, 20mm, normal capacity 750 rounds.
10. Mitsubishi ASM-1 air/surface missile.
11. Drop tank, 183gal (833lit).
12. RL-7 rocket launcher.
13. Seven 2.76in (70mm) rockets fired from (12).
14. M117 GP bomb, 750lb (340kg).
15. AIM-9B Sidewinder close-range AAM.

Combat avionics:
A. ME radar.
B. HUD.
C. UHF.
D. RHAWS.
E. VHF/UHF.
F. VHF/UHF and radio altimeter.
g. UHF.
H. SIF/IFF.
J. UHF and flush ADF.
K. Tacan.

Nanchang Q-5, Type 5 Qianjiji, also called A-5

Origin: China, first flight believed 1972.

Type: Attack aircraft.

Engines: Two Shenyang WP-6 (based on Tumanskii R-9BF-811) afterburning turbojets, each with max rating not less than 7,167lb (3,250kg) and probably 8,267lb (3,750kg).

Dimensions (estimated): Span 33ft 5in (10.1m); length 50ft 0in (15.23m); height 13ft 1½in (4.0m): wing area 355sq ft (32.9m²).

Weights (estimated): Empty 13,890lb (6,300kg); maximum 25,350lb (11,500kg).

Performance: Maximum speed above 36,000ft (10,972m) about 890mph (1,435km/h, Mach 1.35); at low level (internal bombload only) about 832mph (1,339km/h, Mach 1.09); field length, typically 4,900ft (1,493m); mission radius with max internal bombload and two tanks, hi-lo-hi, 400 miles (644km).

Background: Unlike other countries the Chinese recognised that the J-6 (MiG-19SF derived) single-seat fighter/bomber had some very good qualities, notably all-round combat agility in both horizontal and vertical planes, devastating firepower and inherent robust simplicity which translated into reliability in adverse environments. In the 1960s the Ministry of Defence and the 3rd Ministry of Machine Building decided to develop national trainer and dedicated attack versions. The latter became the Type 5 Attack aircraft (Qianjiji), and it virtually turns the basic machine into a '' poor man's Buccaneer'', identical in concept with the British aircraft but smaller and less-capable, and significantly lacking radar. An as-yet unseen interceptor version serves with the People's Navy.

Design: Having started with the J-6 the basic design was already settled, the outstanding feature being the amazing slender wing of 8 per cent thickness with leading-edge sweep close to 60° (55° at ¼-chord), yet with conventional outboard ailerons and large area-increasing flaps (the F-100, of the same 1949-50 design timeframe abandoned this for fear of aeroelastic twisting). Flight controls are all fully powered, including the slab tailplanes (which in the original Soviet aircraft were again a technical innovation). The main new feature introduced by the Chinese is an internal bomb bay, something rapidly becoming unknown in aircraft of other nations. This bay has resulted in stretched fuselage and increased span to maintain fuel capacity and field length on basically unchanged engines. Lateral inlets leave the nose free for what may eventually be a full spectrum of navaids and weapon-delivery systems, though Q-5s seen so far appear fairly sparsely equipped. Forward and downward view from the cockpit is dramatically better than in the J-6, though the long inlets do intrude upon lateral downwards vision (though not as much as in the original Harrier). The cockpit does not greatly differ from that of the J-6, and likewise has a Martin-Baker PKD.10 zero/zero seat, though a new feature is that the canopy is of the clamshell type (instead of sliding), and linked to the fly by a spine. The lateral ducts have allowed the fuselage to be area-ruled, and at low level speed is the same as for the smaller and lighter J-6 fighter. Extra side area forward is countered by a taller fin and ventral strakes.

Avionics: Though the interceptor is fitted with a multimode radar, believed to be a Western type, the basic Army machine has no radar, the avionic fit being very basic and comprising the usual nav/com/IFF sets, plus ILS, Tacan/DME, radio compass or ADF (the set varies) and at least one radio altimeter. There is no knowledge of passive warning receivers or any kind of ECM, but discussion with Western suppliers has been taking place over a long period.

Armament: Two wing-root guns, believed to be of Soviet 23mm type, ammunition capacity unknown. Internal bay for four bombs of 551lb (250kg) or other stores including nuclear weapons of up to 20KT yield; fuselage pylons each side of bomb bay each rated at 551lb (250kg); inboard wing pylons each rated at 551lb (250kg) at least and used for bombs (250kg), rocket pods or Harbin-built Sidewinder AAMs: outboard wing pylons can carry similar loads or 167gal (760lit) tanks (each about 1,500lb/680kg when filled).

Future: Pakistan, thwarted in its 1979 bid to buy the A-7 Corsair II, has become the first export customer for the Q-5 with a substantial purchase of 42.

Especially if its equipment fit can be updated, the considerable striking power of this aircraft combines with what is probably an extremely low price to yield a product that must look attractive to many air forces. There is no information on planned future versions, but later and more powerful engines would be an advantage; the next generation might even have a single Chinese-built afterburning Spey, the first of which ran in 1980.

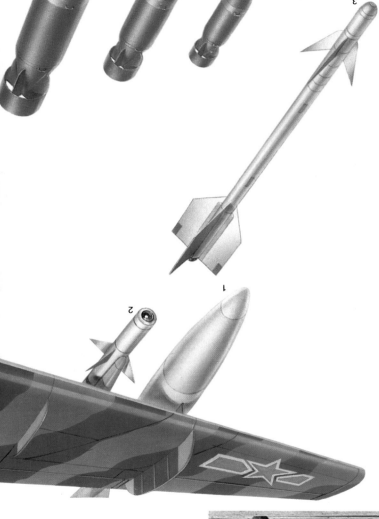

Left: The Q-5 represents an extremely successful attempt to capitalize on the proven low-cost simplicity of the MiG-19 yet acquire greatly enhanced effectiveness in the attack role. Aircraft so far seen are short of all-weather nav/attack avionics. It is believed that a radar-equipped interceptor version is used by the Chinese Navy; the first artist's impression to appear in the West showed such an aircraft.

The Aircraft and Their Weapons

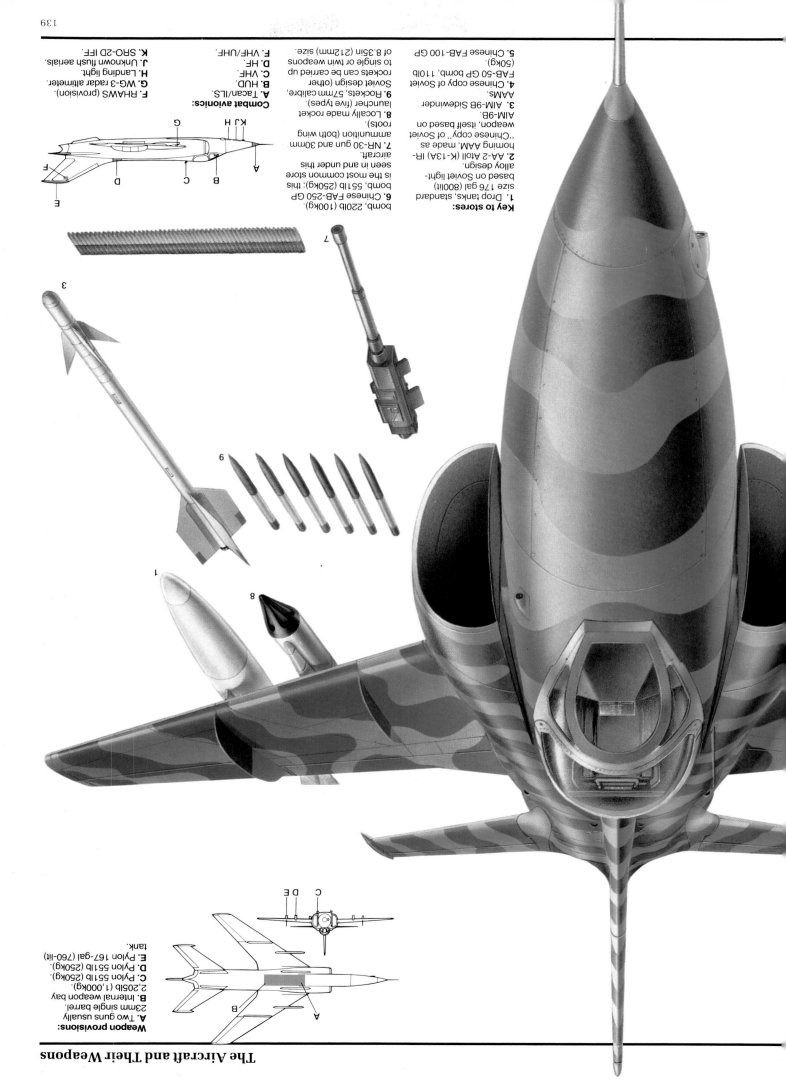

Weapon provisions:
A. Two guns usually 23mm single barrel.
B. Internal weapon bay 2,205lb (1,000kg).
C. Pylon 551lb (250kg).
D. Pylon 551lb (250kg).
E. Pylon 167-gal (760-lit) tank.

Combat avionics:
A. Tacan/ILS.
B. HUD.
C. VHF.
D. HF.
F. VHF/UHF.

F. RHAWS (provision).
G. WG-3 radar altimeter.
H. Landing light.
J. Unknown flush aerials.
K. SRO-2D IFF.

Key to stores:
1. Drop tanks, standard size 176 gal (800lit) based on Soviet light-alloy design.
2. AA-2 Atoll (K-13A) IR-homing AAM, made as "Chinese copy" of Soviet weapon, itself based on AIM-9B.
3. AIM-9B Sidewinder AAMs.
4. Chinese copy of Soviet AAMs.
5. Chinese FAB-100 GP bomb, 110lb (50kg).
6. Chinese FAB-250 GP bomb, 551lb (250kg); this is the most common store seen in and under this aircraft.
7. NR-30 gun and 30mm ammunition (both wing roots).
8. Locally made rocket launcher (five types).
9. Rockets, 57mm calibre. Soviet design (other rockets can be carried up to single or twin weapons of 8.35in (212mm) size).

Northrop F-5A Freedom Fighter, F-5E Tiger II

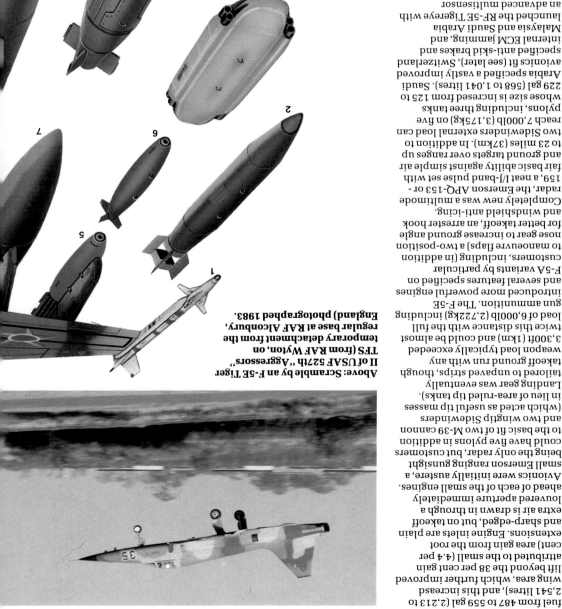

Above: Scramble by an F-5E Tiger II of USAF 527th "Aggressors" TFS (from RAF Wyton, on temporary detachment from the regular base at RAF Alconbury, England) photographed 1983.

Origin: USA, first flight (A) 30 July 1959, (E) 11 August 1972.

Type: Light tactical fighter and attack/recon.

Engines: Two General Electric J85 afterburning turbojets, (A/B) 4,080lb (1,850kg) thrust J85-13 or -13A, (E/F) 5,000lb (2,267kg) thrust -21A.

Dimensions: Span (A/B) 25ft 3in (7.6m) (A/B over tip tanks) 25ft 10in (7.87m), (E/F) 26ft 8in (8.12m), (E/F over AAMs) 27ft 11in (8.50m); length (A) 47ft 2in (14.37m), (B) 46ft 4in (14.12m), (E) 48ft 2in (14.68m), (F) 51ft 7in (15.72m); wing area (A/B) 170sq ft (15.79m²), (E/F) 186sq ft (17.2m²).

Weights: Empty (A) 8,085lb (3,667kg), (B) 8,361lb (3,792kg), (E) 9,683 lb (4,392kg), (F) 10,567lb (4,793kg); max loaded (A) 20,576lb (9,333kg), (B) 20,116lb (9,124kg), (E) 24,676lb (11,193kg), (F) 25,225lb (11,442kg).

Performance: Maximum speed at 36,000ft (10.97m), (A) 925mph (1,489km/h, Mach 1.4), (B) 886mph (1,425km/h, Mach 1.34), (E) 1,077mph (1,734km/h, Mach 1.63), (F) 1,011mph (1,628km/h, Mach 1.53); typical cruising speed 562mph (904km/h, Mach 0.85); initial climb (A/B) 28,700ft (8,750m)/min, (E) 34,500ft (10,516m)/min, (F) 32,890ft (10,025m)/min; service ceiling (all) about 51,000ft (15,544m), combat radius with max weapon load and allowances, (A, hi-lo-hi) 215 miles (346km), (E, lo-lo-lo) 138 miles (222km); range with max fuel, (A) 1,565 miles (2,518km), (E) 1,779 miles (2,863km).

Background: The F-5 is the outstanding example of how a well-managed programme can sustain large-scale production over a period which already exceeds 20 years, and with the F-20A will probably add at least another 15, despite absence of a home market. The original ''light fighter'' was planned by Welko Gasich in 1953-57, but found application first as a supersonic trainer. The N-156F Freedom Fighter, flown in 1959, was a company venture, but with US government support 879 were sold to 21 countries not including another 320 built under licence. This provided a base for the improved F-5E Tiger II first flown in 1972, which in turn has sold over 1,500 and provided a base for the powerful F-20A Tigershark (not included here as, as this went to press, it had not been sold).

Design: The wing has always had a thickness/chord ratio of 4.8 per cent and most of the sharp taper on the leading edge, there being no dihedral. Powered ailerons are well inboard, leaving room for simple slotted flaps inboard. The leading edge is straight, with no dogtooth, but has a full-span electrically driven flap. In the NF-5A this was given auto control for use in enhancing combat manoeuvres, and in the F-5E this feature was retained and used in conjunction with leading-edge root extensions. The F-5E fuselage was widened to increase internal fuel from 487 to 559 gal (2,213 to 2,541 litres), and this increased wing area, which further improved lift beyond the 38 per cent gain attributed to the small (4.4 per cent) area gain from the root extensions. Engine inlets are plain and sharp-edged, but on takeoff extra air is drawn in through a louvered aperture immediately ahead of each of the small engines. Avionics were initially austere, a small Emerson ranging gunsight being the only radar, but customers could have five pylons in addition to the basic fit of two M-39 cannon and two wingtip Sidewinders (which acted as useful tip masses in lieu of area-ruled tip tanks). Landing gear was eventually tailored to unpaved strips, though takeoff ground run with any weapon load typically exceeded 3,300ft (1km) and could be almost twice this distance with the full load of 6,000lb (2,722kg) including gun ammunition. The F-5E introduced more powerful engines and several features specified on F-5A variants by particular customers, including (in addition to manoeuvre flaps) a two-position nose gear to increase ground angle for better takeoff, an arrester hook and windshield anti-icing. Completely new was a multimode radar, the Emerson APQ-153 or -159, a neat J/I-band pulse set with fair basic ability against simple air and ground targets over ranges up to 23 miles (37km). In addition to two Sidewinders the external load can reach 7,000lb (3,175kg) on five pylons, including three tanks whose size is increased from 125 to 229 gal (568 to 1,041 litres). Saudi Arabia specified a vastly improved avionics fit (see later), Switzerland specified anti-skid brakes and internal ECM jamming, and Malaysia and Saudi Arabia launched the RF-5E Tigereye with an advanced multisensor reconnaissance nose which allows one gun to be retained.

Avionics: Most F-5As have only a UHF radio, IFF and a Tacan receiver. The F-5E has full blind-flight instruments, AOA sensor, air-data computer, improved nav/com (with optional INS), and options of VOR/DME, ADF (in a dorsal fin), ILS, flight-director computer and a CRT display for an AGM-65A or similar EO or radar ASM. Other options, taken up by few customers, include the widely used Itek ALR-46 programmable digital RWR and, for the Netherlands NF-5, two Tracer ALE-40 dispensers skin-mounted on each side of the fin ejecting 30 chaff cartridges or 15 flares. The tandem dual F-5F, which has one gun, can be fitted with the Northrop AVQ-27 laser designator.

Armament: (A) military load 6,200lb (2,812kg) including two 20mm M-39 guns and wide variety of underwing stores, plus AIM-9 AAMs for air combat; (E) wide range of ordnance to total of 7,000lb (3,175kg) not including two M-39A2 guns each with 280 rounds and two AIM-9 missiles on tip rails.

Future: Apart from the progressive introduction of new weapon and sensor options, many of which are now being discussed by Northrop with several customers, it is self-evident that air forces flying all versions of F-5 will increasingly recognise the need for proper EW suites. Northrop's own ALQ-171, is a neatly packaged RWR/processor/transmitter system in a conformal pod extending along one-third of the length of the ventral centreline.

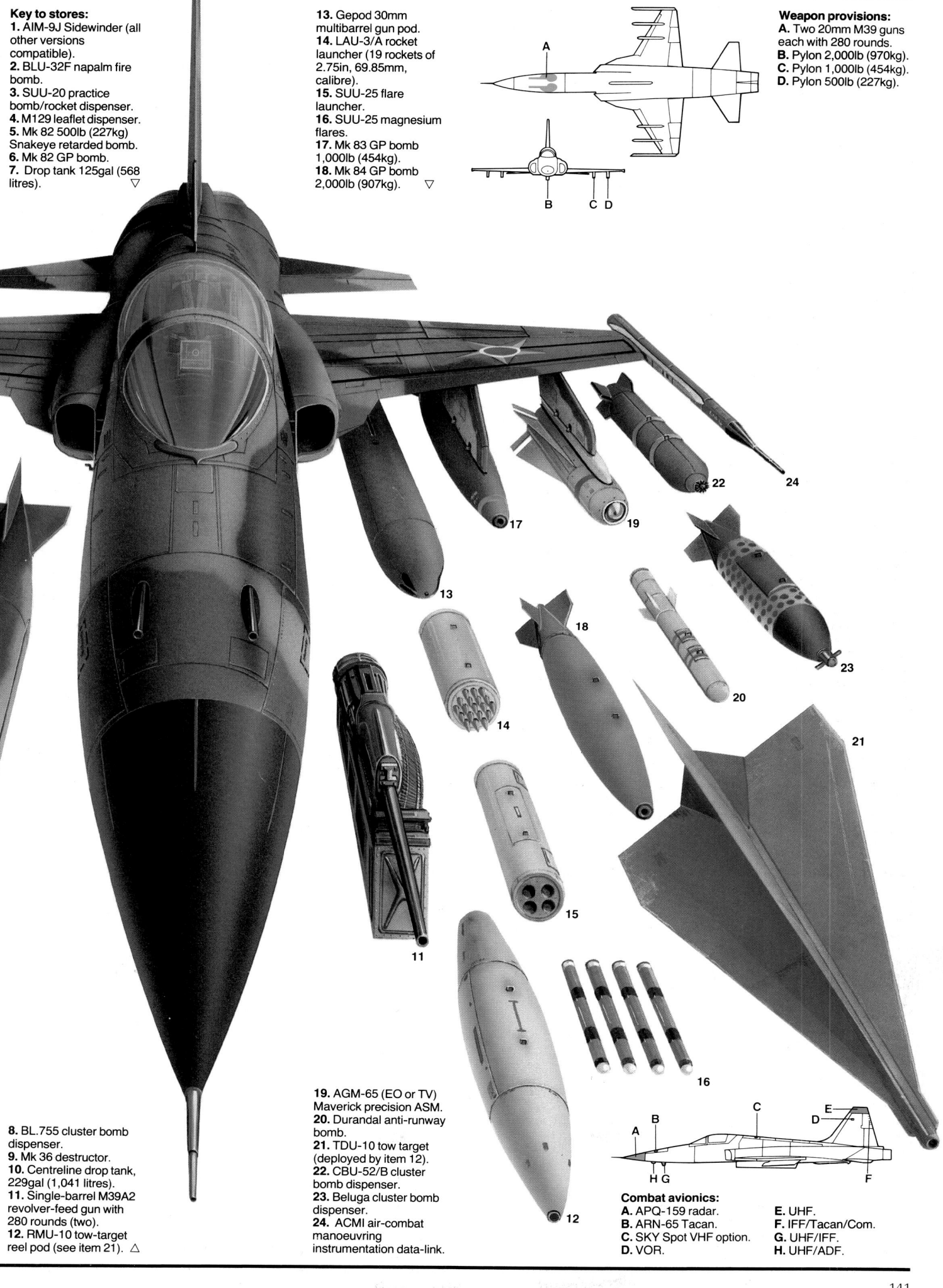

Key to stores:
1. AIM-9J Sidewinder (all other versions compatible).
2. BLU-32F napalm fire bomb.
3. SUU-20 practice bomb/rocket dispenser.
4. M129 leaflet dispenser.
5. Mk 82 500lb (227kg) Snakeye retarded bomb.
6. Mk 82 GP bomb.
7. Drop tank 125gal (568 litres). ▽

13. Gepod 30mm multibarrel gun pod.
14. LAU-3/A rocket launcher (19 rockets of 2.75in, 69.85mm, calibre).
15. SUU-25 flare launcher.
16. SUU-25 magnesium flares.
17. Mk 83 GP bomb 1,000lb (454kg).
18. Mk 84 GP bomb 2,000lb (907kg). ▽

Weapon provisions:
A. Two 20mm M39 guns each with 280 rounds.
B. Pylon 2,000lb (970kg).
C. Pylon 1,000lb (454kg).
D. Pylon 500lb (227kg).

8. BL.755 cluster bomb dispenser.
9. Mk 36 destructor.
10. Centreline drop tank, 229gal (1,041 litres).
11. Single-barrel M39A2 revolver-feed gun with 280 rounds (two).
12. RMU-10 tow-target reel pod (see item 21). △

19. AGM-65 (EO or TV) Maverick precision ASM.
20. Durandal anti-runway bomb.
21. TDU-10 tow target (deployed by item 12).
22. CBU-52/B cluster bomb dispenser.
23. Beluga cluster bomb dispenser.
24. ACMI air-combat manoeuvring instrumentation data-link.

Combat avionics:
A. APQ-159 radar.
B. ARN-65 Tacan.
C. SKY Spot VHF option.
D. VOR.
E. UHF.
F. IFF/Tacan/Com.
G. UHF/IFF.
H. UHF/ADF.

Panavia Tornado F.2

Origin: Germany/Italy/UK, with UK responsibility for assembly and test, first flight 27 October 1979.

Type: Two-seat long-range interceptor.

Engine: Two Turbo-Union RB.199 Mk 103 each rated at 16,000lb (7,258kg) thrust with maximum afterburner.

Dimensions: Span (25°) 45ft 7¼in (13.9m), (65°) 28ft 2½in (8.6m); length 59ft 3in (18.06m); height 18ft 8½in (5.7m); wing area not published.

Weights: Empty, equipped, about 31,500lb (14,290kg); takeoff weight (clean, max internal fuel) 47,500lb (21,546kg); maximum not published.

Performance: Maximum speed (clean, at height) about 1,500mph (2,414km/h, Mach 2.27); combat mission with max AAM load, 2h 20min on station at distance of 375 miles (602km) from base with allowance for combat.

Background: The UK bears a heavy responsibility in policing a block of airspace extending from the Arctic to Gibraltar and from Iceland to the Baltic. This calls for interceptors with long range and endurance, and exceptional avionic capabilities. From early in the Tornado programme it was evident that with minor modifications the basic aircraft could serve as the basis for an outstanding new interceptor to cover the UK Air Defence Region and replace first the Lightning and later the Phantom. Full-scale development on a one-nation basis was authorized on March 4, 1976. Though wholly a Panavia manufacturing programme the R&D was paid for by Britain, although there will be no problems in sorting out the financial side when several expected export orders materialise.

Design: Though in avionics and weapons the interceptor or ADV (Air Defence Variant) Tornado is a totally different aircraft, its basic airframe, propulsion and systems are those of the IDS version, and commonality is put at 80 per cent. The most significant change was the need to accommodate tandem pairs of Sky Flash (or Sparrow or later Amraam) AAMs recessed under the fuselage, and this demanded an increase in mid-fuselage length of 21.25in (539mm). This provides room for extra avionics in the side compartments. As in the RAF Tornado GR.1 the fin serves as an integral tank. Instead of a demountable FR probe housed in a bolt-on external box on the right side of the nose, a permanently installed FR probe is housed internally on the left side of the nose. The main nose radome is longer and more pointed, and the radar itself slightly longer, giving an overall increase in length of 53.5in (1.35m), which improves supersonic acceleration and reduces supersonic drag. To bring the centre of lift forward to match the forward migration of CG the

fixed wing ribs are extended forwards at 68° sweep, the Krüger flaps being deleted; this again happens to give a small bonus in reduced drag. To demonstrate CAP mission performance the A.01 prototype took off from the BAe base at Warton in early 1982 with two 330-gal (1,500-lit) subsonic tanks, four Sky Flash and two Sidewinders, transited to a patrol area 374 miles (603km) distant, flew CAP for 2h 20min, and on return loitered at Warton for 15min before landing after 4¼h with over 5 per cent internal fuel and less than one-eighth Lox consumed. Some of the 165 RAF interceptors are dual-pilot trainers.

Avionics: The main Marconi/Ferranti Foxhunter radar is a pulse-doppler FMICW (FM interrupted CW) set operating in I-band at 3cm. It has extremely advanced features and of course TWS (track while scan) for multiple (between 12 and 20) targets at ranges greater than 120 miles (193km), depending on cross-section, at any flight level. Special ECCM is provided to match any expected hostile ECM to the year 2000, and though an ECM-resistant data-link is provided the aircraft is designed for autonomous operation. Foxhunter continues to scan normally while storing hostile tracks in its computer, and after computer evaluation presents a TED (threat evaluation display) to the backseater. Interceptions are normally made on the HUD, and all displays may be recorded for subsequent replay. Advanced IFF is integrated with the radar, and a particular tactical feature is the way the entire tactical situation can be presented, if necessary in different ways, to both pilot and navigator. An extremely advanced RHWR is fitted, with its own processor. Since the start of the programme provision has been made for an EO VAS (visual augmentation system) for positive visual identifications at long range, but none has yet been fitted.

Armament: One 27mm IWKA-Mauser gun. Fuselage recesses for four Sky Flash, Sparrow or AIM-120 Amraam missiles. Four auto-swivelling wing pylons, the inners normally carrying two 330gal (1,500lit) tanks (each about 2,900lb filled) plus two or four Sidewinder or Asraam missiles. Outers often not fitted but can carry wide range of stores including electronic warfare pods.

Future: Slight reduction in delivery rates, to 42 per year, has caused the ADV programme to slip by what the UK Defence Minister called "a few months". The first Tornado F.2s should become operational in early 1985, by which time the US Amraam AIM-120 may have begun to replace the British Sky Flash AAM. By this time the standard F.2 will have engines with afterburners 14in (35cm) longer, giving greater thrust; this modification is fitted to all aircraft beyond No 19, first of the second batch of 52 of the interceptor version. Another major update due at about that time is a digital electronic engine/inlet/nozzle control system. There are various plans for continuing avionics system and propulsion improvements, but it is curious that there has been no recent news of the visual augmentation system because, especially in peacetime, it will be an important part of the F.2's task to make positive visual identification of distant targets. Certainly the RAF and Ministry of Defence are keenly aware of the prospects for using a wide range of different EM frequencies for this task. Satellite links, improved software and extended digital highways throughout the aircraft are all basic design features.

The Aircraft and Their Weapons

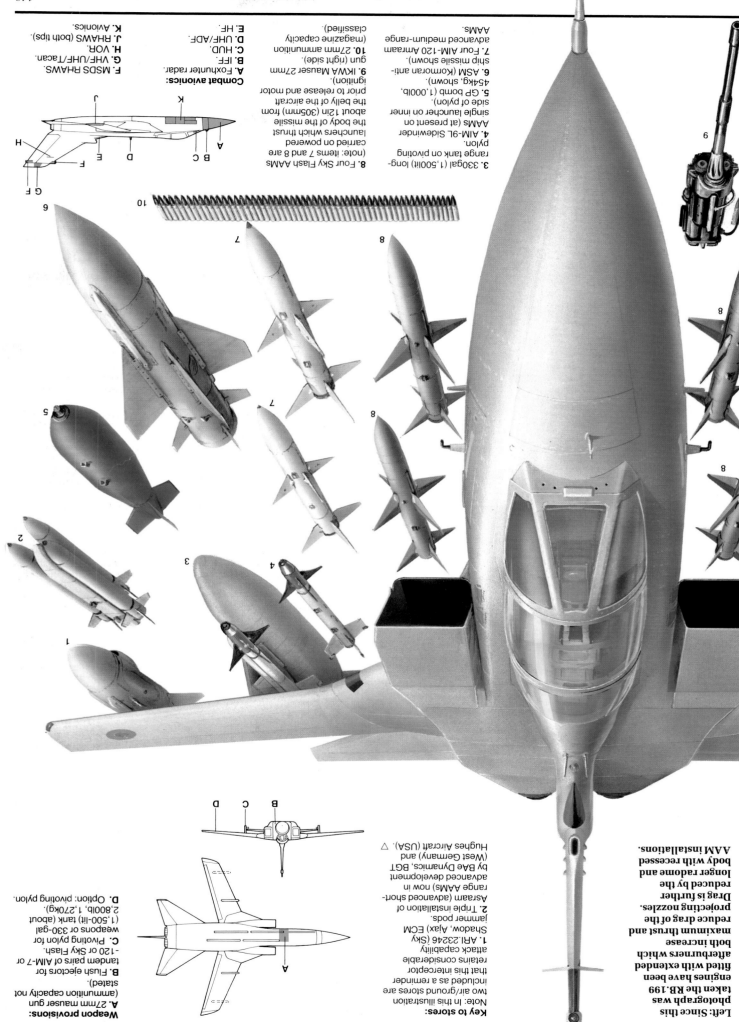

Weapon provisions:
A. 27mm mauser gun (ammunition capacity not stated).
B. Flush ejectors for tandem pairs of AIM-7 or -120 or Sky Flash.
C. Pivoting pylon for weapons or 330-gal (1,500-lit) tank (about 2,800lb, 1,270kg).
D. Option: pivoting pylon.

Key to stores:
Note: In this illustration two air/ground stores are included as a reminder that this interceptor retains considerable attack capability.
1. ARI.23246 (Sky Shadow, Ajax) ECM jammer pods.
2. Triple installation of Asraam (advanced short-range AAMs) now in advanced development by BAe Dynamics, BGT (West Germany) and Hughes Aircraft (USA). △
3. 330gal (1,500lit) long-range tank on pivoting pylon.
4. AIM-9L Sidewinder AAM (at present on single launcher on inner side of pylon).
5. GP bomb (1,000lb, 454kg, shown).
6. ASM (Kormoran anti-ship missile shown).
7. Four AIM-120 Amraam advanced medium-range AAMs.
8. Four Sky Flash AAMs (note: items 7 and 8 are carried on powered launchers which thrust the body of the missile about 12in (305mm) from the belly of the aircraft prior to release and motor ignition).
9. IKWA Mauser 27mm gun (right side).
10. 27mm ammunition (magazine capacity classified).

Combat avionics:
A. Foxhunter radar.
B. IFF.
C. HUD.
D. UHF/ADF.
E. HF.
F. MSDS RHAWS.
G. VHF/UHF/Tacan.
H. VOR.
J. RHAWS (both tips).
K. Avionics.

Left: Since this photograph was taken the RB.199 engines have been fitted with extended afterburners which both increase maximum thrust and reduce drag of the projecting nozzles. Drag is further reduced by the longer radome and body with recessed AAM installations.

Panavia Tornado IDS

Origin: Germany/Italy, UK, first flight 14 August 1974.

Type: Two-seat multi-role combat aircraft optimised for strike, (T) dual trainer.

Engines: Two Turbo-Union RB.199 Mk 101 or 103 augmented turbofans each rated at 15,800lb (7,167kg) with full afterburner.

Dimensions: Span (25°) 45ft 7¼in (13.90m), (65°) 28ft 2½in (8.60m); length 54ft 9¾in (16.7m), height 18ft 8½in (5.7m); wing area not published

Weights: Empty, equipped, 31,065lb (14,091kg); loaded (clean) about 45,000lb (20,411kg); maximum loaded, about 60,000lb (27,215kg).

Performance: Maximum speed (clean) at sea level, over 920mph (1,480km/h, Mach 1.2), at height, over 1,452mph (2,337km/h, Mach 2.2); service ceiling over 50,000ft (15,240m); combat radius (8,000lb/3,629kg bombs, hi-lo-hi) 863 miles (1,390km); ferry range 2,420 miles (3,895km).

Background: This extremely advanced blind first-pass attack IDS (interdiction strike) aircraft was designed jointly by the member-companies of Panavia (BAe, MBB and Aeritalia) to meet the specified demands of the Federal German Luftwaffe and Marineflieger, the RAF and the Aeronautica Militare Italiano. All agreed on a tandem two-seat aircraft, which with no significant changes except minor parts of the avionic fit serves with all four customers, and also serves in a dual-pilot version with small cockpit changes. The RAF also required a new long-range interceptor, and this variant is dealt with separately. The first IDS prototype flew in 1974, the first production aircraft in July 1979, and the first deliveries were to a tri-national training unit in July 1980. By mid-1983 some 220 had been delivered.

Design: Despite having to carry weapons of more different types than any other tactical aircraft in history, the Tornado is also amazingly compact; and at sea level in clean condition it is the fastest combat aircraft ever built. The wing probably has the highest lift coefficient of any fitted to a supersonic aircraft, for at minimum sweep of 25° it can extend full-span double-slotted trailing-edge flaps and full-span slats, plus Krugers on the 60° fixed glove portions. Taillerons are used for roll control, augmented at low sweep angles by large wing spoilers which also serve as lift dumpers. Some 14,000lb (6,350kg) of fuel is housed in fuselage cells and the integral-tank wings, the latter also carrying four auto-pivoting pylons which are plumbed for 330 gal (1,500-litre) tanks. There is provision for a detachable package along the right of the cockpit housing a retractable inflight-refuelling probe. Engine inlets are fully variable, and the engines incorporate full augmentation, reversers and variable nozzles. A large airbrake is

fitted on each side of the vertical tail. The landing gear is designed for soft semi-prepared strips, and an arrester hook is standard.

Avionics: No aircraft of this size has ever been more richly equipped for all-weather penetration of hostile airspace. TI provides (with European licensees) the main forward radar, which comprises a GMR (ground-mapping radar) and TFR, both operating in Ku band. The GMR is the primary attack sensor but can also operate in an air/air mode, and provides various modes for high-resolution nav update, target identification and fire control. The TFR can fly the aircraft automatically, at heights known to go below 200ft (61m), or the pilot can fly manually via the HUD, selecting any level of ride comfort. Primary nav mode is by digital INS plus doppler with Kalman filtering of both outputs. The triplex fly-by-wire flight-control system and, with the autopilot/flight director provides for any combination of attitude, barometric-height or heading hold, radar height lock, Mach/airspeed with autothrottle,

track acquisition and auto-approach and blind ILS. RWR is always internal and jamming is always (at present) pod mounted. RAF Tornado GR.1 aircraft have a modular RWR supplied by MSDS and the ARI.23246 modular jammer pod. German and Italian aircraft use the EL/73 deception jammer by Elettronica and AEG-Telefunken.

Armament: Two 27mm IWKA-Mauser guns. Centreline pylon (Germany/Italy) equipped for recon pod or MW-1 dispenser, (UK) many alternatives; two tandem fuselage pylons each rated at 2,205lb (1,000kg) fore and the same aft, so that with twin carriers eight 1,000lb (454kg) bombs can be carried under the fuselage; alternate fuselage load is two JP233 dispensers of double-length type. Four auto-swivelling wing pylons, unknown rating but inners can carry 330gal (1,500lit) tanks.

Future: There are numerous possible avionic augmentations, including Radpac (radar package) which gives enhanced performance in the air-combat role. RAF is have a Ferranti laser RMTS but are also expected to use the Westinghouse Pave Spike, despite the fact the Ferranti unit can guide Paveway II smart bombs and other known laser weapons.

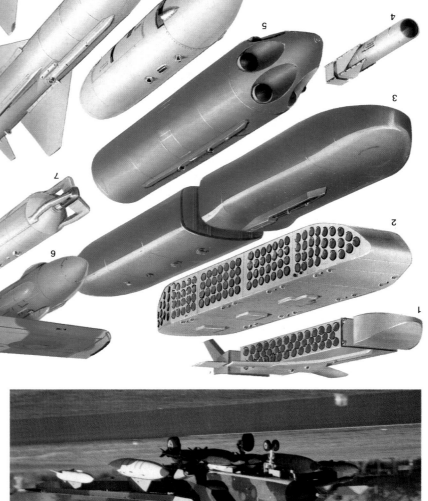

Left: The basic Tornado has the highest ratio of empty weight of any combat aircraft with supersonic performance, apart from the F-16. The main illustration shows only a selection of the more than 90 types of external store carried. Here an RAF Tornado takes off with JP.233 dispensers, tanks and jammer pods.

Nominal weapon load 18,000lb (8,165kg). Nominal weapon load 2,900lb each, weighing about 2,900lb each.

Key to stores:
1. MBB CWS (Container Weapon System), with front and rear modules shown detached.
2. MBB MW-1 lateral dispenser.
3. Hunting JP.233 dispenser (large tandem model).
4. Wasp ASM (folded).
5. Wasp pod (12 rounds).
6. ARI.23246 Sky Shadow ECM jammer.
7. ALQ-234 (now superseded by Zeus) jammer.
8. MBB reconnaissance pod. ▽

14. AS.30 (AS.30L can also be carried) ASM.
15. Low-drag cluster dispenser.
16. BAe Alarm anti-radar missile.
17. BAe Sea Eagle anti-ship missile.
18. Pave Spike laser pod.
19. IKWA-Mauser gun with 27mm ammunition (number of rounds classified).
20. CBLS 200-series carrier for (21-24).
21. Practice bomb, 28lb (12.7kg).
22. Practice bomb, 4lb (1.8kg). ▽

Weapon provisions:
A. Two 27mm Mauser guns (ammunition capacity not stated)
B. Pylon 2,000lb (907kg) or recon pod.
C. Four tandem twin pylons each 2,000lb (907kg)
D. Pivoting pylons, 3,000lb (1,361kg) or 330-gal (1,500-lit) tank.
E. Pivoting pylon, 1,000lb (454kg).

9. Kormoran anti-ship missile.
10. Tank (various to 330gal, 1,500lit).
11. AIM-9L Sidewinder AAM.
12. AIM-9B Sidewinder AAM.
13. AGM-65A Maverick ASM. △

23. Pactice bomb, 20lb (9kg).
24. Practice bomb, 5lb (2.27kg).
25. LGB smart bomb, 1,102lb (500kg).
26. Paveway II Mk 13/18 British, 1,000lb (454kg).
27. Napalm dispenser.
28. GBU-15 CWW (Cruciform-Wing Weapon).
29. Store carrier.
30. GP bomb, 1,000lb (454kg).
31. Special-weapon twin carrier.
32. Beluga dispenser.
33. BL.755 dispenser.
34. Lepus flare.
35. LR.25 rocket pod.

Combat avionics:
A. TI main radar.
B. IFF.
C. HUD.
D. UHF/ADF.
E. HF.
F. RHAWS (various).
G. VHF/UHF/Tacan.
H. RHAWS (both tips).
J. LRMTS.
K. Doppler.
L. Other sensor options and radar altimeter
M. TFR.

Saab 35 Draken

Origin: Sweden, first flight 25 October 1955.

Type: (J35) single-seat all-weather fighter-bomber; (Sk35) dual trainer; (S35) single-seat all-weather reconnaissance.

Engine: One Svenska Flygmotor RM6 (licence-built Rolls-Royce Avon with SFA afterburner): (A, B, C) 15,000lb (6804kg) RM6B; (D, E, F and export) 17,635lb (8t) RM6C.

Dimensions: Span 30ft 10in (9.4m); length 50ft 4in (15.4m) (S35E, 52ft); height 12ft 9in (3.9m); wing area 529.6 sq ft (49.2m^2).

Weights: Empty (D) 16,017lb (7,265kg); (F) 18,180lb (8,250kg); maximum loaded (A) 18,200lb (8,255kg); (D) 22,663lb (10,279kg); (F) 27,050lb (12,270kg); (F-35) 35,275lb (16,000kg).

Performance: Maximum speed (D onwards, clean) 1,320mph (2,125km/h), Mach 2.0), (with two drop tanks and two 1,000lb bombs) 924mph (1,487km/h), Mach 1.4); initial climb (D onwards, clean) 34,450ft (10,500m)/min; service ceiling (D onwards, clean) about 65,000ft (20,000m); range (internal fuel plus external weapons, typical) 800 miles (1,300km), (maximum fuel) 2,020 miles (3,250km).

Background: Thanks to sound policymaking and brilliant engineering, Sweden has sustained an unbroken succession of extremely successful combat-aircraft programmes which have fully met the national need and in general have been superior to competition elsewhere. The Saab 35 Draken stemmed from a 1949 requirement for a radar-equipped interceptor able to reach Mach 1.4+ in level flight while using 1949 runways. At first there was no surface-attack requirement. Erik Bratt's team created the boldest of all designs for production fighters of the 1950s, the packaging being from front to rear. Britain supplied the basis for the propulsion system.

Design: The so-called double-delta wing comprises conventional delta outer panels joined to a large inboard portion lying in the lee of fixed-geometry oval engine inlets and extending all the way back to the engine nozzle in the prototype flown in October 1955. Trailing-edge surfaces comprised four elevons, which in production J35s are fully powered and fitted with sensitive autostabilization. Much of the skin is adhesive-bonded honeycomb which has stood up well to combat service in harsh environments. No attempt was made to operate from wholly unprepared surfaces, but it has always been the sensible practice of the Flygvapen to disperse away from airfields and operate from country roads and other strips too numerous for them to be worth targeting with large missiles. Flared nose-high landings are made with airbrakes, antiskid brakes and drag chute, with accurate nosewheel steering at lower speeds. Draken production of 606 aircraft was divided into six Swedish and two export models,

all with basically the same airframe but with different avionics and mission equipment and from the J35D of 1960 introducing a more powerful engine. A rocket-boosted Saab zero/zero seat – developed from a British Folland type – is fitted.

Avionics: The original equipment fit included an Ericsson radar derived from an early CSF Cyrano, and Saab S6 fire-control linked to the Lear autopilot. This suited a lead-pursuit aircraft with guns. The J35B introduced a new radar and fire-control for collision-course attacks with rockets. The J35D, a few of which are still used for training, introduced a further improved radar, autopilot and fire-control, and reached Mach 2 without the US-licensed AAMs that could be carried. Both the S35E recon aircraft and J35F interceptor are still in use, with advanced avionics, comprehensive ECM and dispenser systems. The F (popularly called Filip) has a long-range PS-Ø1 radar, S7B fire control, Hughes IR sensor under the nose, nav/attack system, cockpit displays and EW provisions and very advanced for an aircraft of the mid-1960s era. Denmark and Finland use export versions with basically unchanged avionics from Filip, but lacking Falcon RB27 and RB28 AAMs or a data-link which in Swedish aircraft ties in to the national STRIL 60 air-defence system. The Filip marked a switch towards multirole capability in having up to 11 stores pylons, five of them rated at 1,102lb (500kg) each. Danish F-35s have nine pylons each rated at 1,102lb (500kg), and have demonstrated good airframe fatigue life in largely low-level operation.

Armament: (F) one 30mm Aden plus two RB27 Falcon (radar) and two RB28 Falcon (infra-red) missiles, plus two or four RB24; (F-35) two 30mm Aden plus nine stores pylons each rated at 1,000lb (454kg) all usable simultaneously, plus four RB24.

Future: Though they suffer from no fatigue problem, Drakens are progressively being phased out of service with Sweden's Flygvapen, and it is probable that all will have

left first-line units by 1985. The Royal Danish AF (Flyvevabnet), however, is retaining all its F-35 fighters, RF-35 recon aircraft and TF-35 trainers until after 1985, the F-16 force having been used to replace the F-100 and F-104. Introduction of the F-16 has resulted in the Danish Drakens being assigned principally to the ground-attack role, and they are being refurbished and updated with new HUD sights, improved

nav/attack systems, cockpit displays and EW installations including RWRs, active jammer pods (not yet seen in service) and ECM dispensers, which are carried externally. Finland is likewise retaining its Drakens, despite the introduction of Hawks and new MiGs, though the Ilmavoimat (Finnish AF) has not yet decided on the exact update programmes for maintaining their combat effectiveness.

Left: Though the original design dates from over 30 years ago, the Saab 35 is still an extremely effective air-combat and attack/recon aircraft, whose original price was much less than that of typical fighters of today. These J35F interceptors of the Swedish AF regularly practise sustained operations away from vulnerable airfields. The type is popular with pilots.

Weapon provisions:
A. Two 30mm Aden each with 100 rounds.
B. Pylon 1,000lb (454kg).

Key to stores:
1. Saab rocket launcher 19×75 (19 rockets of 75mm calibre).
2. Bofors 75mm rockets.
3. RB24 licence-produced AIM-9B type Sidewinder AAM.
4. Bofors heavy attack rocket of 135mm calibre, not fired from a launcher.

5. Muzzle port of 30mm gun.
6. Aden M/55 gun with 100-round magazine (right side of aircraft only).
7. Ammunition 30mm.
8. L. M. Ericsson (Hughes licence) IR seeker under nose.
9. RB28 licence-produced Hughes IR-

homing Falcon AAM.
10. RB27 licence-produced Hughes semi-active radar Falcon AAM.
11. GP bomb, 1,102lb (500kg) size.
12. Drop tank of 280gal (1,275 litres) capacity, two hung under fuselage side-by-side.

Combat avionics:
A. S7 radar.
B. HF/VHF.
C. Fire-control computer.
D. VHF.
E. UHF/Tacan.
F. Avionics bays.
G. DME.
H. IR seeker.

Saab 37 Viggen

Origin: Sweden, first flight 8 February 1967.

Type: (AJ) single-seat all-weather attack; (JA) all-weather fighter; (SF) armed photo-reconnaissance; (SH) armed sea surveillance; (SK) dual trainer.

Engine: One Svenska Flygmotor RM8 (licence-built Pratt & Whitney JT8D two-shaft turbofan redesigned in Sweden for Mach 2 and fitted with SFA afterburner); (AJ, SF, SH and Sk) 25,970lb (11,790kg) RM8A; (JA) 28,086lb (12,750kg) RM8B.

Dimensions: Span of main wing 34ft 9¼in (10.6m); length (AJ) 53ft 5¾in (16.3m), (JA37 with probe) 53ft 11in; height 18ft 4½in (5.6m); main-wing area 495 sq ft (46.0m²).

Weights: "Normal armament" gross weight, (AJ) 35,275lb (16t), (JA) 37,478lb (17t).

Performance: Maximum speed (clean) about 1,320mph (2,135km/h, Mach 2), or Mach 1.1 at sea level; initial climb, about 40,000ft (12,200m)/min (time from start of take-off run to 32,800ft-10,000m = 100sec); service ceiling, 60,000ft (18,300m); tactical radius with external stores (not drop tanks), hi-lo-hi profile, (AJ, JA) over 620 miles (1,000km), (lo-lo-lo) 310 miles (500km).

Background: System 37, later named Viggen (Thunderbolt) was launched in 1960 at the same time as the USAF's TFX; but unlike that unhappy project it was broadly based and called for a family of four closely related aircraft able to operate from short stretches of highway and fly fighter (JA), attack (AJ), recon (SF, SH) and training (SK) missions, each variant having a secondary role that was one of the others. Despite severe requirements for avionics, flight performance, weapons and the ability to sustain high sortie rates while maintained by short-service conscripts, the overall programme could hardly have been more successful.

Design: Like the previous generation System 35 Draken, the Viggen is a "double delta", but in this case there are two separate surfaces, the forward one being a flapped foreplane which generates powerful vortices to scrub the wing in tight manoeuvres and on the amazingly slow landing approaches. The latter are flown at constant attitude, the tandem-wheel main gears accepting the brutal no-flare landing followed by the shortest run of any modern combat aircraft with full reverse thrust and antiskid brakes. The main drawing shows the AJ37, compared with which the fighter Viggen JA37 is a very different aircraft, with a restressed structure, four (instead of three) elevon power units on each side, a taller fin with swept tip (also used on the tandem SK37 trainer), a more powerful engine with different compressor spools, largely changed systems and, of course, totally revised avionics and weapons. JA37 development started in 1968 but the first production aircraft did not fly until

1977, when AJ deliveries were complete. In almost all respects the Viggen is an outstanding aircraft, with all-round air combat qualities surpassing those of any West European aircraft in service and not far short of the latest US fighters which cost from four to 11 times as much. Turn radius, field length and low-speed qualities are as good as those of any other fighter in the world, and better than almost all; no other conventional (ie, not vectored-thrust) fighter can equal the Viggen's ability to use short austere airstrips, which in time of war would unquestionably mean the difference between elimination and survival. The only slightly adverse feature is high fuel consumption, especially in afterburner, but the lo-lo-lo radius is claimed to be 311 miles (500km) and high-altitude patrol endurance 1.5 to 2h, which is adequate for useful missions.

Avionics: The LM Ericsson UAP-1023 (PS-46/A) radar, used in the JA37, was the world's first multimode pulse-doppler set to go into production. Operating in I-band, it has fair lookdown capability (with ranges greater than 30 miles/48km, in this mode) and high resistance to ECM. It has multi-target capability, with display on the HUD or head-down, and TWS plus CW illumination for the Sky Flash RB71 missiles. An especially remarkable claim is the MTBF of over 100h in service, a reliability significantly better than that of comparably sophisticated sets with other air forces. Smiths provide the electronic HUD and Honeywell/Saab the digital flight control system, while other units draw on US experience, such as the Singer-Kearfott INS and Garrett digital ADC (air-data computer) developed from that in the F-14. Singer also licensed Saab to make the main digital computer, and because of its speed and capacity this may be retrofitted to the AJ37. The latter was the first variant to be produced, and 180 first-generation AJ, SF/SH and SK versions were delivered in 1971-77, since when they have performed outstandingly well. Substantial updating has already taken place, structural trouble has for several years been conspicuously absent, and a very high level of reliability has been reached. The AJ has an earlier Ericsson radar, Marconi-Elliott HUD, Phillips ADC and many other equipment differences.

Armament: Seven pylons, three under the fuselage and four under the wings, for total external load published as 13,228lb (6,000kg) which can include RBO4E or RBS15 anti-ship missiles, multisensor recon pods or various EW and ECM jammer pods. The centreline pylon is plumbed for a fuel tank. In addition the JA37 interceptor has a permanently installed belly pack housing a 30mm Oerlikon KCA gun with 150 rounds; AAMs include RB71 Sky Flash and RB24 Sidewinder.

Future: The general standard of the JA37 is so high that no major

change is expected in the immediate future, but the AJ has already been successively updated and it is likely to receive further new equipment fits including instrumentation, new passive receivers and improved active ECM and dispensing installations. Details of what is planned are classified, but a few possibilities are obvious. One of the most important would appear to be a switch late in the decade to the American AIM-120A (Amraam) as a successor to the licensed British Sky Flash. Sweden is extremely satisfied with the BAe Dynamics missile, and has already placed one large follow-on order, but the British government itself has terminated the promising Sky Flash Mk 2 in favour of the American weapon, so Sweden has no obvious alternative to following suit. Almost certainly an updated sensor fit for the SF and SH versions will later be introduced.

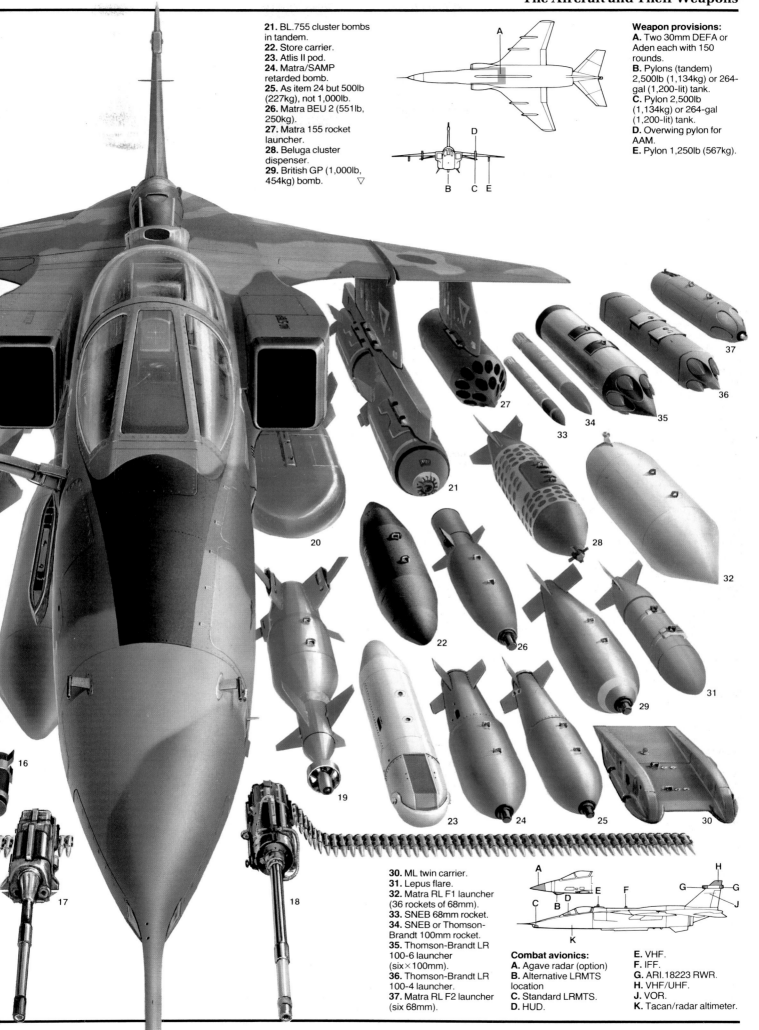

21. BL.755 cluster bombs in tandem.
22. Store carrier.
23. Atlis II pod.
24. Matra/SAMP retarded bomb.
25. As item 24 but 500lb (227kg), not 1,000lb.
26. Matra BEU 2 (551lb, 250kg).
27. Matra 155 rocket launcher.
28. Beluga cluster dispenser.
29. British GP (1,000lb, 454kg) bomb. ▽

Weapon provisions:
A. Two 30mm DEFA or Aden each with 150 rounds.
B. Pylons (tandem) 2,500lb (1,134kg) or 264-gal (1,200-lit) tank.
C. Pylon 2,500lb (1,134kg) or 264-gal (1,200-lit) tank.
D. Overwing pylon for AAM.
E. Pylon 1,250lb (567kg).

30. ML twin carrier.
31. Lepus flare.
32. Matra RL F1 launcher (36 rockets of 68mm).
33. SNEB 68mm rocket.
34. SNEB or Thomson-Brandt 100mm rocket.
35. Thomson-Brandt LR 100-6 launcher (six×100mm).
36. Thomson-Brandt LR 100-4 launcher.
37. Matra RL F2 launcher (six 68mm).

Combat avionics:
A. Agave radar (option)
B. Alternative LRMTS location
C. Standard LRMTS.
D. HUD.
E. VHF.
F. IFF.
G. ARI.18223 RWR.
H. VHF/UHF.
J. VOR.
K. Tacan/radar altimeter.

SOKO/CNIAR IAR-93 Orao

Origin: Joint 50/50 programme by Romania and Yugoslavia, first flight (both countries, same day) 31 October 1974.

Type: Single-seat attack aircraft.

Engines: Two Rolls-Royce Viper turbojets; current production (Type A) has 4,000lb (1,814kg) Mk 632-41, IAR-93B and corresponding Orao has 5,000lb (2,268kg) Mk 633-47.

Dimensions: Span 31ft 6¾in (9.62m); length 48ft 10⅝in (14.9m); height 14ft 7¼in (4.45m); wing area 279.86sq ft (26.0m²).

Weights: Empty (A) 13,007lb (5,007kg); maximum takeoff (A) 22,765lb (10,326kg).

Performance: Maximum speed (A, sea level) 665mph (1,070km/h), (B) 721mph (1,160km/h); initial climb (A) 6,693ft (2,040m)/min, (B) 12,992ft (3,960m)/min; takeoff and landing to/from 50ft (15m) (A) 5,400ft (1,650m).

Background: In one of the most remarkable of modern collaborative programmes, Romania (within the Warsaw Pact) is partnering Yugoslavia in the development and production of a totally homegrown attack fighter which uses licensed British engines and a great deal of licensed or imported equipment. The programme has been kept rigidly 50/50 to a degree that clearly has caused delays and increased costs. Thus CNIAR in Romania and SOKO in Yugoslavia each simultaneously flew a single-seat prototype on 31 October 1974, four years after the programme start, and each country then followed with a first flight of a two-seat prototype simultaneously on 29 January 1977! Primary mission is close air support, with secondary low/medium-altitude interception, the tandem-seat version also being used for dual training.

Design: Like the Japanese T-2/F-1 the Orao/IAR-93 (the former is the Yugoslav name and the latter the Romanian designation) shows signs of Jaguar influence, though it is a less-ambitious aircraft with turbojet engines for lower cost at the expense of higher fuel consumption. Yugoslavia has used the Viper engine for 25 years, and it was reasonable to use a pair of these tough and low-risk engines, with a second-generation version (called IAR-93B in Romania) with afterburning engines which, though they do not confer supersonic speed, more than double rate of climb and greatly reduce takeoff run and generally enhance inflight agility, especially with a bombload. Plain inlets are used, leaving the nose free for what is hoped eventually to be an effective nav/attack fit for all-weather operation. The wings have powered slats and conventional ailerons outboard of area-increasing flaps; slab tailplanes are used for control in pitch only. Two perforated airbrakes are mounted upstream of the main gears, which like Jaguar have twin wheels with low-pressure tyres suited for off-runway operation. Landing roll is reduced by antiskid brakes and a drag chute. Production aircraft have small strakes along the nose sides and large leading-edge root extensions, the A-series (non-afterburning) two-seater having stepped cockpits with side-hinged canopies and reduced internal fuel in the wings (677.5gal/3,080lit, reduced to 594gal/2,700lit). All models have pressurized cockpits with a Martin-Baker Mk 10 seat.

Avionics: The considerable number of aircraft flying in 1983 have a comprehensive fit for basic all-weather flight and communication, but nothing has been disclosed concerning weapon-aiming and EW equipment. A simple stability-augmentation system is fitted, and a more advanced autopilot may be installed later. Apart from basic communications radio and IFF, equipment in all aircraft includes a radio compass, beacon receiver (Tacan, probably with DME, will be standard) and radar altimeter. There is no intention to fit radar, but VOR/ILS might be provided, together with a twin-gyro platform or, possibly, a full INS. No details have emerged concerning the form of pilot sight fitted, and it is likely that a modern HUD will eventually become standard. There is no internal provision for a laser ranger, FLIR or any other sensor, and superficial examination of 1983 production aircraft did not disclose any obvious RWR or other EW protective receiver system.

Armament: Two Soviet twin-barrel GSh-23 guns are installed in the bottom of the fuselage, with 200-round magazines similar to those used with this gun in the MiG-21. There are five stores pylons, that on the centreline and the inboard wing pylons being plumbed for tanks of 119-gal (540-lit) capacity. Each pylon is rated at 1,102lb (500kg) to a reduced g-limit, but the normal maximum load is just half this. Loads cleared for use include the UV-16-57 rocket pod, the Soviet and SAMP 551lb (250kg) GP bombs, expendable bomblet containers weighing 331 or 661lb (150 or 300kg) and triplets of 220lb (100kg) bombs on the wing pylons only.

Future: In 1983 some dozens of the non-afterburning A-series aircraft were in service, mainly in the pilot-training role, with both air forces. The more advanced B-series aircraft has greater fuel capacity of 722gal (3,282lit) in integral-tank wings, the two-seater having the same capacity, to give adequate endurance with the afterburning engines; another change is that the tailplanes are of bonded honeycomb construction. Probably the B-series will become the future standard; for example Romania is following its 20 A-models (single- and two-seat) with a run of 165 B-type. By 1990 there is every intention of progressively updating the in-service aircraft with additional sensors and weapons. Great benefits would accrue from a switch to the Adour engine, which with structural reinforcement would enable mission load to be roughly quadrupled while holding field length and range at about their present values. This is unlikely to be possible, and a more likely switch would be to the Viper 680 engine which is almost installationally interchangeable with the Mk 632 but provides up to 14.4 per cent more thrust in its dry version. Rolls-Royce have stated that the 680 should be available for use in 1984.

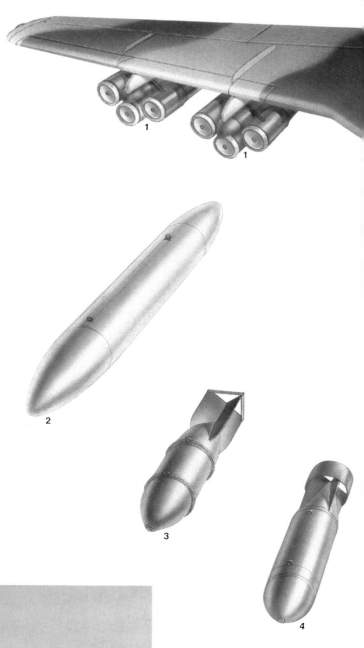

1
1
2
3
4

Left: One of the first photographs of a prototype, at a time early in the programme when almost all the publicity emanated from Yugoslavia. Today almost all the new photographs are being issued by Romania, possibly to balance out the credits in a programme where precise 50/50 shares have been taken to lengths which have certainly caused delays which could have been avoided!

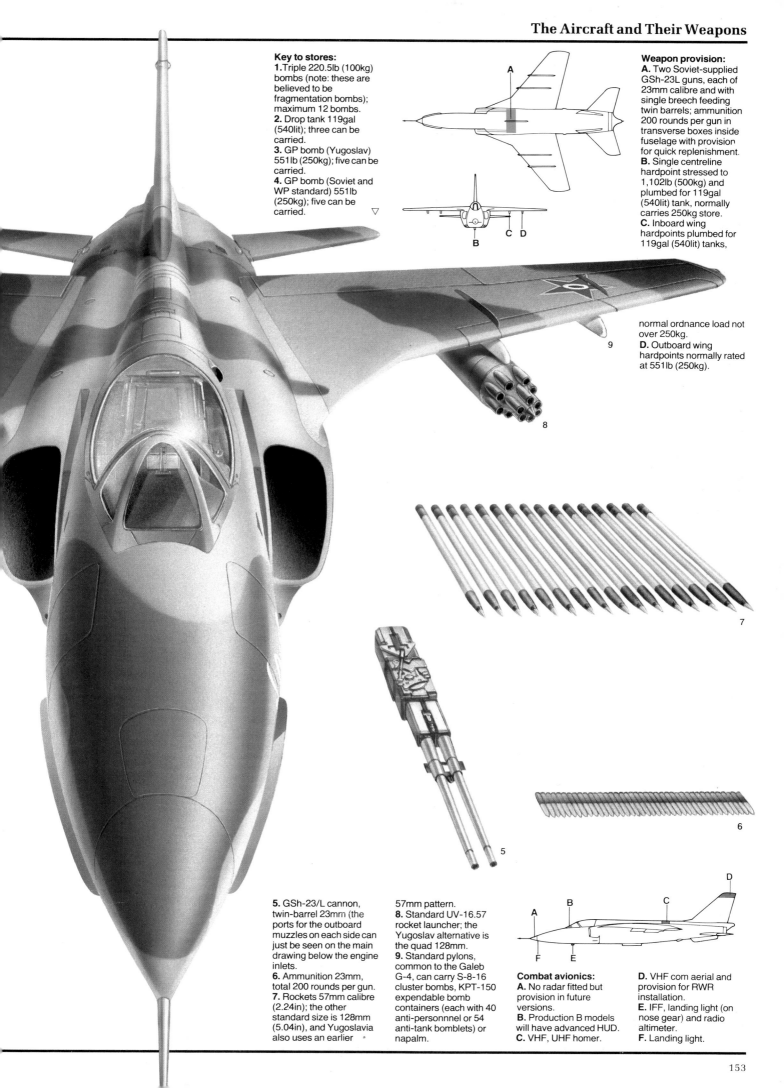

Key to stores:
1. Triple 220.5lb (100kg) bombs (note: these are believed to be fragmentation bombs); maximum 12 bombs.
2. Drop tank 119gal (540lit); three can be carried.
3. GP bomb (Yugoslav) 551lb (250kg); five can be carried.
4. GP bomb (Soviet and WP standard) 551lb (250kg); five can be carried.

Weapon provision:
A. Two Soviet-supplied GSh-23L guns, each of 23mm calibre and with single breech feeding twin barrels; ammunition 200 rounds per gun in transverse boxes inside fuselage with provision for quick replenishment.
B. Single centreline hardpoint stressed to 1,102lb (500kg) and plumbed for 119gal (540lit) tank, normally carries 250kg store.
C. Inboard wing hardpoints plumbed for 119gal (540lit) tanks, normal ordnance load not over 250kg.
D. Outboard wing hardpoints normally rated at 551lb (250kg).

5. GSh-23/L cannon, twin-barrel 23mm (the ports for the outboard muzzles on each side can just be seen on the main drawing below the engine inlets.
6. Ammunition 23mm, total 200 rounds per gun.
7. Rockets 57mm calibre (2.24in); the other standard size is 128mm (5.04in), and Yugoslavia also uses an earlier

57mm pattern.
8. Standard UV-16.57 rocket launcher; the Yugoslav alternative is the quad 128mm.
9. Standard pylons, common to the Galeb G-4, can carry S-8-16 cluster bombs, KPT-150 expendable bomb containers (each with 40 anti-personnnel or 54 anti-tank bomblets) or napalm.

Combat avionics:
A. No radar fitted but provision in future versions.
B. Production B models will have advanced HUD.
C. VHF, UHF homer.

D. VHF com aerial and provision for RWR installation.
E. IFF, landing light (on nose gear) and radio altimeter.
F. Landing light.

Sukhoi Su-7

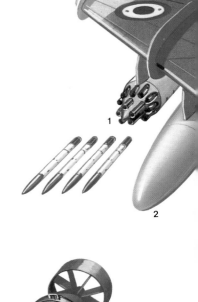

Origin: Soviet Union, first flight (S-1 research aircraft) late 1955.
Type: Ground-attack fighter.
Engine: One Lyul'ka afterburning turbojet, (7, 7B) 19,841lb (9t) AL-7F (later variants) AL-7F-1 rated at 14,990/21,164lb (6.8/9.6t).
Dimensions: Span 29ft 3½in (8.93m); length (incl probe) 57ft 0in (17.37m), (7U) 58ft 8½in (17.7m); height 15ft 5in (4.7m); wing area 297sq ft (27.6m²).
Weights: (BMK, typical) empty 19,000lb (8,620kg); normal loaded 26,455lb (12,000kg); maximum 29,750lb (13,495kg).
Performance: Maximum speed (36,000ft/11km), clean 1,055mph (1,700km/h, Mach 1.6), (four loaded pylons) 788mph (1,270km/h, Mach 1.2); (SL) max afterburner 837mph (1,345km/h, Mach 1.1, (dry) 530mph (850km/h); max initial climb (afterburner, clean) 29,000ft (8,840m)/min; service ceiling 49,700ft (15.15km); combat radius (with tanks, hi-lo-hi) 200/300 miles (322/480km); range (two tanks) 900 miles (1,450km).
Background: Together with the delta-winged interceptors (see next two pages) the Su-7 was one of the production aircraft stemming from prototypes flown by the reopened Sukhoi OKB in 1955. The Su-7 stemmed from the S-1 and its successors which had a 62° swept wing, and this was deemed the best choice for ground-attack missions. From the start the sheer size and power of the aircraft were impressive, but mission load and range were quite the opposite.
Design: Though an immense amount of detail tinkering was done in 1955-58, the basic design of the Su-7 (the Soviet military designation) could hardly have been more simple. The wing has a straight fixed leading edge, conventional outboard powered ailerons and large slotted (not Fowler) flaps, the innermost sections being at 90° to the fuselage. There are prominent

fences at mid-span and at the tip. The tail has slab tailplanes used for pitch only. The vast tube-like body has a plain nose inlet with a conical centrebody housing a small ranging radar, and the outer walls have auxiliary suck-in inlet doors for use on takeoff and at low speeds. Fuselage cells and a large integral tank in each wing provide 647gal (2,940lit) of internal fuel, and twin fuselage pylons are plumbed for two 132gal (600lit) drop tanks. Such is the fuel consumption that with full afterburner endurance at low level is a mere eight minutes! All units of the landing gear have long-stroke levered suspension and large soft-field tyres (in one version, the 7BKL, supplemented by metal skis outboard of each mainwheel for extra flotation on soft surfaces). Twin drag chutes are housed in a compartment at the base of the rudder above the large fully variable engine nozzle. Like all Sukhoi production aircraft of this generation, there are four airbrakes around the rear fuselage. Altogether the Su-7 added up to a very large aircraft for the job it does, which in terms of weapon load and mission radius is less than half that of the much smaller Jaguar. What is not immediately obvious are the inherent good qualities of amazing toughness, extending to every part of the structure and equipment, and docile flying qualities which have endeared it to its many thousands of pilots. Conversely, pilot control forces are so high (described by an Indian test pilot as "like a Hunter in the manual reversion mode") that the Su-7 would not have been accepted by any major Western air force, and despite the very limited weapon load the takeoff field length is 7,875ft (2,400m) to rotation speed at 224mph (360km/h), the same as the brochure-stated approach speed.
Avionics: Though the Su-7, in all versions, is an impressively large

and powerful aircraft, internal stowage space is hard to find. To a remarkable degree the aircraft still in service in various countries have the same avionic fit as the original production Su-7 of 1959, though there have been small improvements in the individual boxes. VHF, UHF and EHF com radios are grouped behind the rocket-assisted seat, where accessibility is poor. The SRD-5M (High Fix) range-only radar is typical of the sets fitted to the Hunter and F-86, but has greater radiated power. There is room for this to be replaced by a modern radar with a search capability, and there would be no difficulty in accommodating either an HDD radar display or a HUD in place of the ASP-5F gyro sight, which would give this otherwise well-liked aircraft some limited all-weather attack capability. Another possibility would be to add the undernose installation of modern air/ground sensors and TFR as fitted to the swing-wing developments of this aircraft in the Soviet Union, but this is not known to have been done. There is a simple stick-steering autopilot with a self-levelling mode, again typical of 1950s practice and similar to the installation in the first Yugoslav/Romanian Orao prototypes. There is the usual fit of ADF, ILS, IFF, Sirena 3 RWR (which gives no information on threat type or direction) and radar altimeter. An option is a vertical camera aft of the nose gear.
Armament: All versions have two NR-30 guns in the wing roots, each with a small box of 70 rounds (though these rounds are very hard-hitting indeed), the fuselage skin being reinforced near the muzzles by heavy plate. The side-by-side fuselage hardpoints are plumbed for tanks, and it is rare to fly without them. This leaves four (in a few early 7B aircraft, two) underwing pylons each rated at 1,102lb (500kg) inboard and 551lb

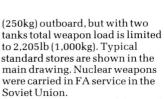

(250kg) outboard, but with two tanks total weapon load is limited to 2,205lb (1,000kg). Typical standard stores are shown in the main drawing. Nuclear weapons were carried in FA service in the Soviet Union.
Future: It is many years (about 13) since any Su-7s were built, and it is not believed that any have been converted into a swing-wing Su-17/20/22. Thus the only possibility is for operators to update their avionic/weapon fits, and it is known that some (notably India) are exploring what can be done.

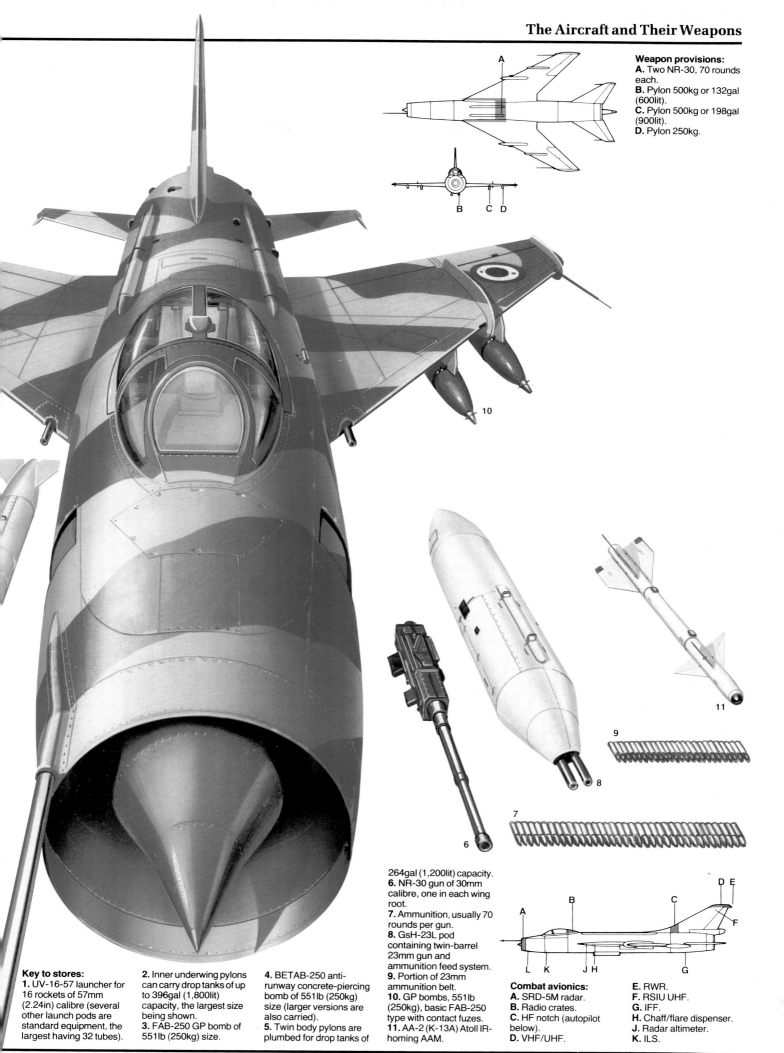

Weapon provisions:
A. Two NR-30, 70 rounds
each.
B. Pylon 500kg or 132gal
(600lit).
C. Pylon 500kg or 198gal
(900lit).
D. Pylon 250kg.

Key to stores:
1. UV-16-57 launcher for
16 rockets of 57mm
(2.24in) calibre (several
other launch pods are
standard equipment, the
largest having 32 tubes).
2. Inner underwing pylons
can carry drop tanks of up
to 396gal (1,800lit)
capacity, the largest size
being shown.
3. FAB-250 GP bomb of
551lb (250kg) size.
4. BETAB-250 anti-
runway concrete-piercing
bomb of 551lb (250kg)
size (larger versions are
also carried).
5. Twin body pylons are
plumbed for drop tanks of
264gal (1,200lit) capacity.
6. NR-30 gun of 30mm
calibre, one in each wing
root.
7. Ammunition, usually 70
rounds per gun.
8. GsH-23L pod
containing twin-barrel
23mm gun and
ammunition feed system.
9. Portion of 23mm
ammunition belt.
10. GP bombs, 551lb
(250kg), basic FAB-250
type with contact fuzes.
11. AA-2 (K-13A) Atoll IR-
homing AAM.

Combat avionics:
A. SRD-5M radar.
B. Radio crates.
C. HF notch (autopilot
below).
D. VHF/UHF.
E. RWR.
F. RSIU UHF.
G. IFF.
H. Chaff/flare dispenser.
J. Radar altimeter.
K. ILS.

Sukhoi Su-11

Origin: Soviet Union, first flight (Su-11) probably 1961.
Type: All-weather interceptor.
Engine: (9) one 19,840lb (9t) Lyul'ka AL-7 afterburning turbojet, (11) one 21,164 (9.6t) AL-7F-1.
Dimensions: Span 27ft 8in (8.43m); length (incl probe) (9) about 57ft 0in (17.37m), (11) 60ft 0in (18.29m); height 16ft 0in (4.88m); wing area about 366sq ft (34m²).
Weights: Empty (9) about 19,000lb (8,620kg), (11) about 20,000lb (9t); loaded (9) about 27,000lb (12.25t), (11) 30,000lb (13.6t).
Performance: Maximum speed (both, clean, 36,000ft/11km) about 1,320mph (2,125km/h, Mach 2). (two tanks and AAMs), (Su-9) about 750mph (1,200km/h, Mach 1.14), (11) 840mph (1,350km/h, Mach 1.27); max initial climb (both) about 27,000ft (8.2km)/min; service ceiling, from about 55,000ft (16.76km) for Su-9 with AAMs to 62,000ft (18.9km) for Su-11 (clean); range (both, high-altitude, two tanks and AAMs) about 700 miles (1,125km).
Background: During the Korean War the Soviet aerodynamic centre, TsAGI, worked on the problem of finding the best shapes for future supersonic fighters. One turned out to be the 62° swept wing, used in the Su-7 already described and in various MiGs. The other was the tailed delta with the leading edge swept at 53°. Again, both the Su and MiG OKBs built prototypes, the former being given various numbers in the T (triangular) series. Eventually, via the T-405 prototype flown in 1956,

a production all-weather interceptor was produced designated Su-9.
Design: The first production aircraft, the Su-9, was broadly like an Su-7 with a short-span delta wing and large interception radar. Alternatively it resembled a MiG-21 scaled up to fit the large and very powerful Lyul'ka engine. Compared with the Su-7 the wing has larger area, but this does not result in shorter field length nor in reduced turn radius. It was adopted mainly because it has lower supersonic wave-drag and results in slightly higher maximum speed. Like other interceptors of the PVO – the Soviet air defence forces, until 1983 a separate branch of the armed forces – the Su-9 was not required to operate from rough front-line bases but could count on good paved runways. Thus it has small wheels with high-pressure tyres and no drag chute. Internal fuel capacity is fractionally greater than for the Su-7, largely because of the greater available volume in the wings resulting from their larger area and the absence of guns and ammunition. Fully powered flight controls and large plain flaps are used, though design details are totally unlike those of the Su-7 which has aileron power units in the inboard leading edge, driving via rods and bellcranks, the interceptor having neat power units close to the ailerons

themselves. The structure of the slab tailplanes is again different, though external shape is little different and anti-flutter masses on forward-pointing tip rods are again needed. The cockpit is similar only in overall geometry to that of the attack aircraft, instruments and displays being quite different and no rear-view mirror being required. There is little first-hand information in the West about what the Sukhoi interceptors are like to fly, but there is every indication that, while the Su-7 had sweet and forgiving qualities combined with tiringly high control forces, the delta interceptors were quite the reverse, with quickly responsive controls but rather hard and demanding flying charcteristics and spinning prohibited. The original Su-9, powered by the AL-7 engine and armed with four early AAMs, was replaced in production in 1967 by the Su-11, and it is believed some of the earlier aircraft were retroactively modified to Su-11 standard. This has the slightly more powerful AL-7F-1 engine, with external fuel-pipes along the top of the fuselage, and a completely new combination of radar and weapons.
Avionics: Whereas the Su-9 had the R1L (High Fix) radar and four of the K-5 (AA-1 Alkali) AAMs on separate wing pylons, the second-generation Su-11 introduced the

Uragan 5B (Skip Spin) radar matched with the much more powerful AA-3 Anab AAM. This radar has considerably greater power than the short-range R1L; one Western report gives its power as 100kW but in fact it is more than 200kW and needed a large cooling airflow bled from the engine inlet duct. This feeds a large vizor type cockpit display, more typical of the 1950s than of later, with which the pilot makes his closure on air targets after initial positioning under ground control via an HF link with a whip aerial under the nose. There is a simple stability-augmentation system, ILS, beacon receiver and the usual SRO-2M IFF installation. The small radome above the jet nozzle has been described in the West as an RWR, though it does not appear to be one of the Sirena family. Altogether the avionic fit is adequate but austere by modern standards, and probably all-weather operations depend crucially upon ground control and navigation assistance.
Armament: Whereas the Su-9 was armed with four AA-1 missiles, the Su-11 has just two wing pylons each able to carry a single AA-3 Anab. The usual load is one AA-3 with semi-active radar homing and one with IR homing. This is normally combined with twin fuselage drop tanks.
Future: During the past several years the once very large force of Su-9 and Su-11 interceptors has been progressively whittled down and the type may vanish from Soviet service within the next year.

Below: Now withdrawn from combat duty the earlier Su-9 is being used in the role of target RPV and for trials.

Below: There is a slight kink in the outline to the nose of the Su-11 which is also seen in the main illustration at right.

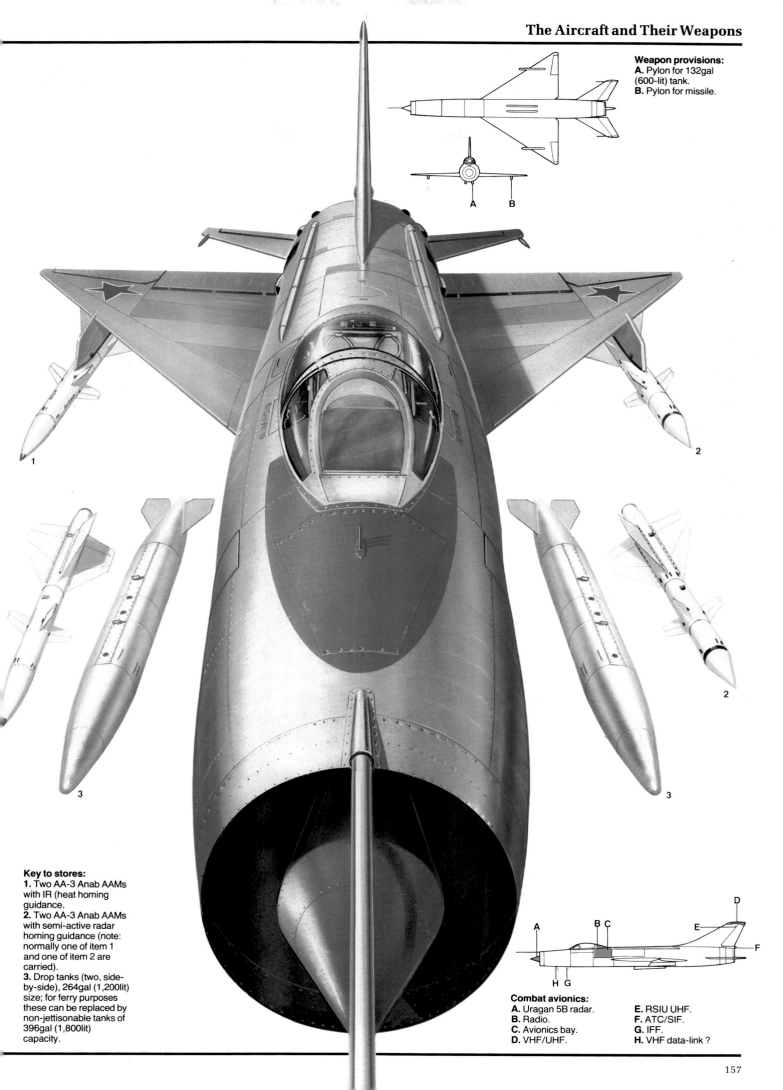

Weapon provisions:
A. Pylon for 132gal (600-lit) tank.
B. Pylon for missile.

Key to stores:
1. Two AA-3 Anab AAMs with IR (heat homing guidance.
2. Two AA-3 Anab AAMs with semi-active radar homing guidance (note: normally one of item 1 and one of item 2 are carried).
3. Drop tanks (two, side-by-side), 264gal (1,200lit) size; for ferry purposes these can be replaced by non-jettisonable tanks of 396gal (1,800lit) capacity.

Combat avionics:
A. Uragan 5B radar.
B. Radio.
C. Avionics bay.
D. VHF/UHF.
E. RSIU UHF.
F. ATC/SIF.
G. IFF.
H. VHF data-link ?

Sukhoi Su-15

Origin: Soviet Union, first flight believed 1965.
Type: All-weather interceptor.
Engines: Two Tumanskii afterburning turbojets, (A to D) 13,668lb (6.2t) R-11F2-300, (E, F) 15,875lb (7.2t) R-13F2-300.
Dimensions: Span (A) about 30ft 0in (9.14m), (others) 34ft 6in (10.5m); length (excluding probe) 72ft (22.0m); height 16ft 6in 95.0m); wing area 385sq ft (35.7m²).
Weights: Empty (A) about 25,000lb (11.34t), (F) about 27,000lb (12.25t); loaded (A) about 35,275lb (16t), (F) about 40,000lb (18t), (F, max with external tanks) 44,900lb (20t).
Performance: Maximum speed (clean, 36,000ft/11km), (A) about 1,520mph (2,450km/h, Mach 2.3), (F) about 1,650mph (2,655km/h, Mach 2.5); (with AAMs) (A) about 1,400mph (2,250km/h, Mach 2.1), (F) about 1,520mph (2,450km/h, Mach 2.3); initial climb about 45,000ft (13.7km)/min; service ceiling about 65,600ft (20km); combat radius (hi) about 450 miles (725km); ferry range about 1,400 miles (2,250km).
Background: The Sukhoi OKB devoted prolonged effort in the 1950s to devising a nose inlet that would be efficient for supersonic flight and still accommodate a powerful AI radar. In 1959 a requirement was issued for a new interceptor which, while having the most powerful radar available, would fly considerably faster than any known enemy aircraft (except for the XB-70, for which the MiG-25 was being designed). The design team then elected to return to lateral inlets, previously flown on several experimental types, but to use them to take air direct to two engines mounted side by side. Many portions, including major parts of the wing, vertical and horizontal tail, landing gear and even rear fuselalge panels and airbrakes, are closely related to corresponding parts of the Su-11.
Design: With this impressive series of interceptors the Su OKB capitalized to the limit upon the availability of good PVO runways and produced an aircraft whose rotation speed on takeoff, and speed on the approach, was 248mph (400km/h). Wing loading was high by any standard, and in

fact the original Su-15 was reminiscent of a larger F-104, with tremendous speed but only limited agility and large turn radius. The original inlets were sharp-edged but relatively simple, the only variable geometry being suck-in auxiliary doors in the side walls similar to those in the sides of the nose of the single-engined Su types. By 1970 the standard inlet had been altered to match the more powerful R13 series engine (the early subtypes are believed to have the R-11) and incorporating infinitely variable inner walls and throat profile downstream of large splitter plates incorporating perforations to extract boundary-layer air. Three years earlier, in 1967, the original small delta wing had been replaced by a wing of increased span with outer portions of reduced sweep joined to the original inner section by a short unswept link aligned with a weapon pylon and upper-surface fence. The kinks at this junction have almost the same vortex-generating effect as an axial "sawcut" or a drag-inducing leading-edge fence. Other features of the current Su-15 family include slight anhedral on the tailplanes, extremely broad rectangular slotted flaps, curved (ogival) nose radome replacing the original conical type, and a single large braking parachute streamed from beneath the rudder. Though obviously a "hot ship" in every sense, the Su-15 appears to be a beautiful machine to fly and it is regarded as a very great improvement over every preceding PVO interceptor. The final production model, called Flagon-F by NATO, will continue in service together with the tandem dual trainer (Flagon-C) until at least the end of the 1980s, the force being steady at about 700 aircraft throughout 1983.
Avionics: Full details of the current radar fit on the Su-15 are not known openly in the West, but – though often said still to be the rather old Uragan 5B called Skip Spin by NATO – the main radar is certainly large and powerful, with 200kW sent out via inverted Cassegrain aerials with hydraulic scanning and a CW illumination mode for use with radar-guided AAMs. It is assumed in the West

that the size of radome, combined with the extremely high flight performance and erosion by rain and hail, combined to lead to a conical design for all Su-15s seen prior to 1974. The subsequent replacement by ogival radomes is said to be purely for aerodynamic reasons and not in order to accommodate a different radar or larger aerial. The radar operates in I-band (3.3cm) with PRF said to be in the band 2.7 to 3.0kHz. Range in good weather is typically 50 miles (80km) against fighter size targets, and since 1982 there is evidence that a VAS (visual augmentation system) has been added. No IR sensor has been seen on Su-15s. The rest of the avionic suite comprises the usual ILS, ADF, beacon receivers, IFF, Sirena 3 RWR, ATC/SIF ground-control nav system and exceptionally comprehensive communications from HF to EHF.
Armament: Four wing pylons normally carry two radar AA-3 Anab AAMs and two with IR homing, but since 1981 Su-15s have been seen with close-range AA-8 missiles. The large AA-6 Acrid has not been seen on them, however, which in view of the radar power and very high flight performance is surprising. It has been speculated a gun pod can be carried on a fuselage pylon, these two locations normally being empty or used for tanks. AA-3 Anab has long been regarded as obsolescent.
Future: With so large a force, avionic updating is certain to be taking place, and may be expected to lead to new sensors and weapons during at least the rest of the 1980s.

Below: This much later Su-15 is of the variety known to NATO as Flagon-F. It was photographed by a neutral reconnaissance aircraft on which the Sukhoi formated with airbrakes open. Note the mix of large AA-3 Anab and small AA-8 Aphid missiles.

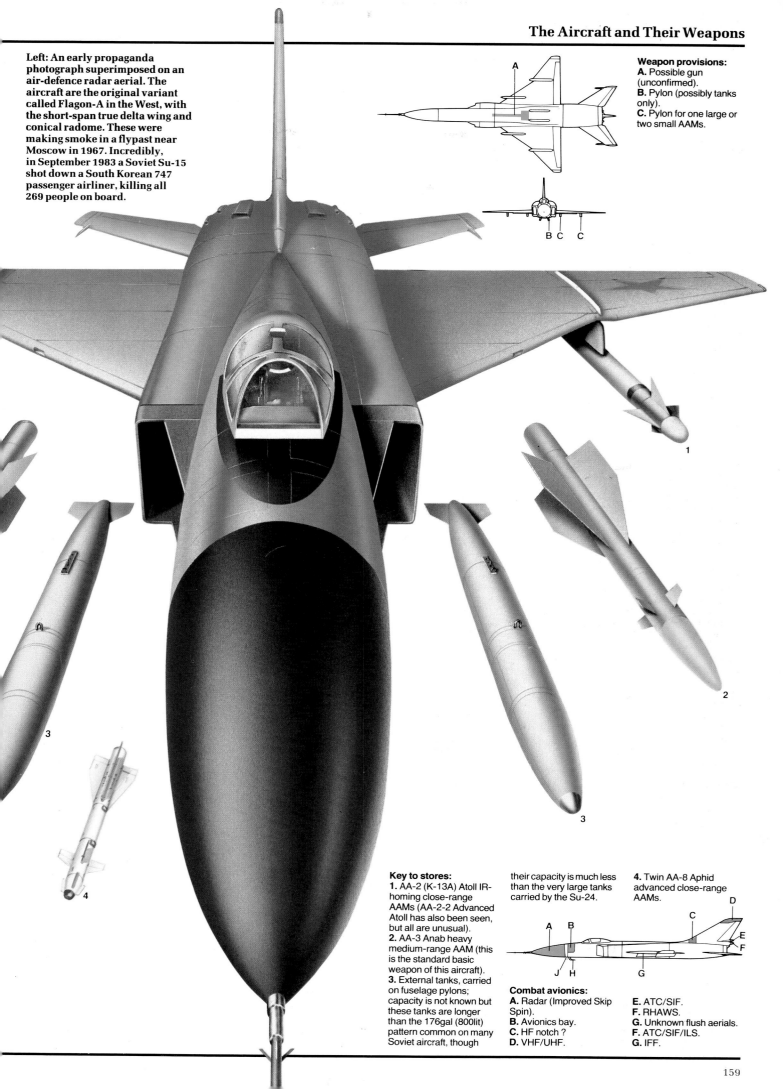

Left: An early propaganda photograph superimposed on an air-defence radar aerial. The aircraft are the original variant called Flagon-A in the West, with the short-span true delta wing and conical radome. These were making smoke in a flypast near Moscow in 1967. Incredibly, in September 1983 a Soviet Su-15 shot down a South Korean 747 passenger airliner, killing all 269 people on board.

Weapon provisions:
A. Possible gun (unconfirmed).
B. Pylon (possibly tanks only).
C. Pylon for one large or two small AAMs.

Key to stores:
1. AA-2 (K-13A) Atoll IR-homing close-range AAMs (AA-2-2 Advanced Atoll has also been seen, but all are unusual).
2. AA-3 Anab heavy medium-range AAM (this is the standard basic weapon of this aircraft).
3. External tanks, carried on fuselage pylons; capacity is not known but these tanks are longer than the 176gal (800lit) pattern common on many Soviet aircraft, though their capacity is much less than the very large tanks carried by the Su-24.
4. Twin AA-8 Aphid advanced close-range AAMs.

Combat avionics:
A. Radar (Improved Skip Spin).
B. Avionics bay.
C. HF notch ?
D. VHF/UHF.
E. ATC/SIF.
F. RHAWS.
G. Unknown flush aerials.
F. ATC/SIF/ILS.
G. IFF.

Sukhoi Su-17/-22

Origin: Soviet Union, first flight (Su-22IG) 1966.
Type: Ground-attack fighter.
Engine: (most) one Lyul'ka AL-21F-3 afterburning turbojet with ratings of 17,200/24,700lb (7.8/11.2t); (current variants) one Tumanskii R-29B afterburning turbojet with ratings of 17,635/25,350lb (8.0/11.5t) (estimated).
Dimensions: Span (28°) 45ft 11½in (14.0m), (62°) 32ft 6in (9.9m); length (basic-17 incl nose probes) 61ft 6¼in (18.75m), length of fuselage (inlet lip to nozzle) (-17) 50ft 6½in 915.4m), later 51ft 10in (15.78m); wing area (28°) 431.6sq ft (40.1m²).
Weights: (estimated): Empty (Fitter-C) 22,050lb (10t), (-H) 22,500lb (10.2t); loaded (clean) (-C) 30,865lb (14t), (-H) 34,170lb (15.5t); max loaded (-C) 39,020lb (17.7t), (-H) 42,330lb (19.2t).
Performance: maximum speed (clean, typical), (SL) 800mph (1,290km/h, Mach 1.05), (36,000ft/11km) 1,435mph (2,300km/h); initial climb (clean) 45,275ft 913.8km)/min; service ceiling 59,050ft (18km); take-off run at 17 weight, 2,035ft (620m); combat rdius (-C, 2t bombload, hi-lo-hi) 391 miles (630km), (-H, 3t bombload, hi-lo-hi) 435 miles (700km); ferry range, four tanks (-C) 1,400 miles (2,250km), (-HO) 1,700miles (2,750km).
Background: At the 1967 Aviation Day show at Moscow Domodyedovo, the last public air display of its kind in the Soviet Union, one of the new prototypes was an Su-7 with the outer portions of the wings pivoted in what appeared to be a rather primitive and ineffectual form of variable geometry. It was later learned that this was the Su-7IG (IG, Russian for variable geometry) or Su-22IG. In view of the apparently limited gains from such a modification this aircraft was assessed as a purely experimental type. It was a major surprise when what appeared to be complete regiments of this type were seen from 1972. In fact the production VG subtypes all incorporate considerable further improvement.
Design: Though based squarely on the later models of Su-7, the Su-17 (Fitter-C to NATO), the first VG production version, has numerous aerodynamic refinements which together probably improve maximum low-speed lift coefficient by a further 20 per cent to more than double that of the original Su-7. At speeds below about 200 knots (230mph, 370km/h) the Su-17 and its successors are as much like an Su-7 as chalk is like cheese. Turn radius is roughly halved, control forces dramatically reduced and approach speed can be brought down from 224mph (360km/h) to below 186mph (300km/h). It is possible to make an impressive slow flypast, which in an Su-7 is quite out of the question. Details of the manoeuvre envelope are not publicly known, but are probably

better than for the original fixed-wing machine. Inflight agility, range and field length have all benefited from the new Lyulka engine, which though more powerful actually burns fuel rather less rapidly than the Al-7F-1; and there has been a modest increase in internal fuel capacity, to 1,001gal (4,550lit). Not least, all VG production versions have eight highly rated pylons (see line drawings), giving a tremendous increase in mission payloads. From the original Su-17 the Su OKB has subsequently derived a succession of further upgraded aircraft with additional sensors (see Avionics, below), additional internal fuel, new and even more efficient turbofan engines which also reduce drag, improved pilot view and various tandem-seat versions some of which are not dual-pilot but use the backseater as a weapon-system officer.
Avionics: The basic Su-17 Fitter-C differs little from late Su-7 versions but from the start had the Sirena-3 RWR giving 360° coverage, with aerials in the left/right wing centre section and tail. Fitter-D has a longer nose, probably to accommodate extra avionics, with a ventral fairing for a TFR (some reports suggest merely a terrain-avoidance radar) and a forward-looking RWR. In the bottom of the inlet cone is an LRMTS looking through a small transparent window. Subsequent versions have a HUD, improved RWR and EW provisions, which include an internal ECM dispenser and what may be either of two types of pylon-mounted jammer pod, and various other new avionics which have not yet been identified.

Conversely, early export aircraft, to Peru in particular, were poorly equipped in almost every respect, particularly in the matter of attack sensors, navaids and IFF compatible with other anti-air weapons supplied by the Soviet Union at the same time! No aircraft of this family has been seen with any search radar or any significant air-to-air capability.
Armament: Most versions have the same two 30mm NR-30 guns, each with 70 rounds, as the Su-7; most two-seaters, however, have the right-hand gun only, and there is reason to believe that a newer gun may be fitted to some of these aircraft, though details are lacking. The eight pylons comprise four (tandem pairs) under the fuselage, two far forward under the wing gloves and two under giant fences aligned with the wing pivots. The rear body pylons and outer-wing pylons are all plumbed for 176gal (800lit) drop tanks, maximum weapon load with four tanks being only 2,205lb (1,000kg) in the original Su-17. Without tanks the maximum weapon load is normally 8,820lb (4,000kg), though according to some reports it can be 11,023lb (5,000kg). Among stores carried are nine types of GP bomb, retarded and anti-runway bombs, 16- and 32-tube rocket pods, the AS-7 Kerry and other (not yet known) missiles including smart bombs, and the 240mm anti-HAS (hardened aircraft shelter) rocket. Clearly, in war nuclear bombs would figure prominently in aircraft of the Soviet FA.
Future: Production of this prolific family was completed in 1977, but large numbers will continue in worldwide service until the 1990s.

Above: An early production Su-17 of the Polish air force; NATO designation is Fitter-C.

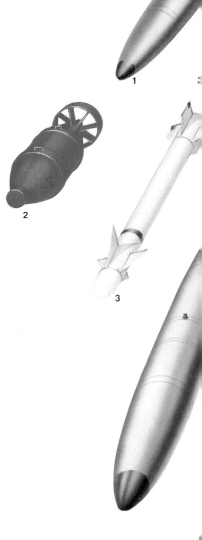

Left: Su-22 of the Libyan Arabic Republic, photographed in 1981 with AA-2-2 Advanced Atoll AAMs.

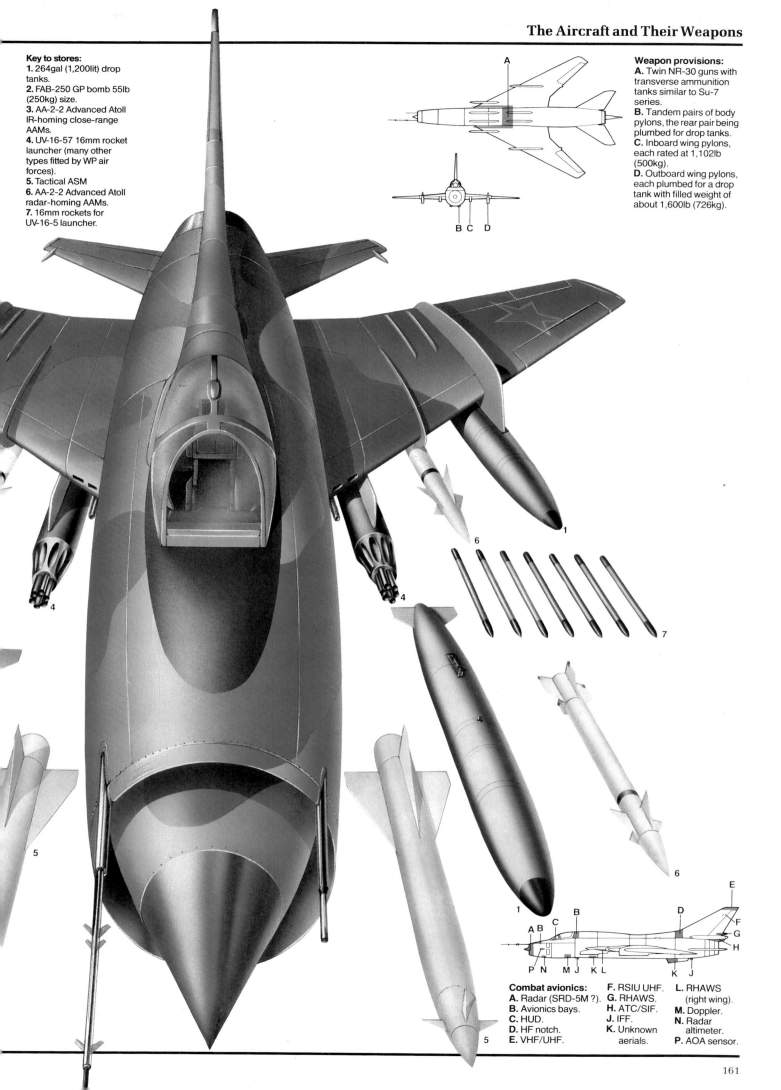

Key to stores:
1. 264gal (1,200lit) drop tanks.
2. FAB-250 GP bomb 55lb (250kg) size.
3. AA-2-2 Advanced Atoll IR-homing close-range AAMs.
4. UV-16-57 16mm rocket launcher (many other types fitted by WP air forces).
5. Tactical ASM
6. AA-2-2 Advanced Atoll radar-homing AAMs.
7. 16mm rockets for UV-16-5 launcher.

Weapon provisions:
A. Twin NR-30 guns with transverse ammunition tanks similar to Su-7 series.
B. Tandem pairs of body pylons, the rear pair being plumbed for drop tanks.
C. Inboard wing pylons, each rated at 1,102lb (500kg).
D. Outboard wing pylons, each plumbed for a drop tank with filled weight of about 1,600lb (726kg).

Combat avionics:
A. Radar (SRD-5M ?).
B. Avionics bays.
C. HUD.
D. HF notch.
E. VHF/UHF.
F. RSIU UHF.
G. RHAWS.
H. ATC/SIF.
J. IFF.
K. Unknown aerials.
L. RHAWS (right wing).
M. Doppler.
N. Radar altimeter.
P. AOA sensor.

Sukhoi Su-24

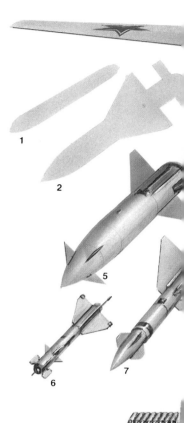

Origin: Soviet Union, first flight possibly 1970.

Type: All-weather attack and reconnaissance.

Engines: Two afterburning engines, almost certainly Tumanskii R-29B each rated at 17,635/25,350lb (8.0/11.5t).

Dimensions: (estimated): Span (16°) 56ft 6in (17.25m), (68°) 33ft 9in (10.3m); length overall 69ft 10in (21.29m); height 18ft 0in (5.5m); wing area (16°) 500sqft (46.4m²).

Weights: (estimated): Empty 41,890lb (19t); loaded (clean) 64,000lb (29t); maximum loaded 87,080lb (39.5t).

Performance: Maximum speed (clean, 36,000ft/11km) 1,590mph (2,560km/h, Mach 2.4), (clean, SL) about 870mph (1,400km/h, Mach 1.14); (max external load, hi) about 1,000mph (1,600km/h, Mach 1.5); (max external load, SL) about 620mph (1,000mph (1,600km/h, Mach 1.5), (max external load, SL) about 620mph (1,000km/h, Mach 0.815); service ceiling (with weapons) 57,400ft 917.5km); combat radius (lo-lo-lo, 8t bombload) 200 miles (322km), (hi-lo-hi, 2.5t bombload) 1,115miles (1,800km); ferry range (six tanks) about 4,000 miles (6,440km).

Background: Though it uses the same TsAGI-developed aerodynamics as the much smaller MiG-23, this long-range interdiction aircraft is one of the Soviet Union's rare examples of a totally new design owing no direct relationship to any existing type from the same OKB. Indeed, it owes more to the American F-111 than to any other single type, even to the almost certainly mistaken use of side-by-side seats. The mission was to carry a far greater load of more types of attack weapons and deliver them with pinpoint (180ft, 55m) accuracy over ranges never previously approached by any FA aircraft. The Su-24, even in its initial production form, can deliver heavy bombloads from WP airbases to Scotland or Brittany on a round trip with a substantial part flown at treetop height.

Design: General design closely follows that of the F-111 except in the important respects of air inlets and landing gear. The former were brought well forward ahead of the wing to give enough length to avoid grossly distorted airflow into the engines (which caused such prolonged trouble on the US aircraft). The main landing gears fold into the fuselage and offer ample track for stability on rough ground, but are so arranged that heavy weapon loads can be carried on four fuselage pylons. The swinging outer wings are particularly efficient and of high aspect ratio, with almost zero sweep in the low-speed regime (max is 68°), with full-span slats and powerful flaps, roll control being by a combination of spoilers and tailerons (for the first time on a Soviet aircraft). The wing is at the same level as the tail, and at maximum sweep lies closer to the tailplane than in the MiG-23, though not as near as in the F-111. A single vertical tail is used, backed up by ventral fins at the corners of the very wide and flat underside, without the need for a folding ventral surface. All units of the landing gear have twin wheels, probably sized to permit operation away from runways, though this is not certain. The steerable nose unit has a mudguard and retracts to the rear. The extremely large inlets are fully variable and their inboard ramp plates stand well away from the large vertical-walled fuselage. There are probably two conventional ejection seats, behind an extremely strong multi-panel curved windscreen and with a large one-piece clamshell canopy. There appears to be plenty of room for internal fuel, possibly including the fin, and the glove pylons can carry the largest drop tanks seen on any Soviet aircraft (about 650gal, 3,000lit).

Avionics: There is no doubt that the main radar is a completely new type, and it almost certainly has more operating modes than any previous Soviet set. Below it are probably dual TFRs. There is likewise no doubt that the Su-24 is packed from nose to tail with avionics, and there is abundant evidence that the entire fit was designed in parallel with the aircraft so that little has to be hung externally. During the past several years each new and improved photograph that has become available has revealed more and more comprehensive avionics, invariably with flush aerials. Especially at the tail early Su-24s showed an amazing absence of RWRs, IRWRs, drag chute containers and active jammers, yet all these are carried and more evidence keeps appearing. So far more than 20 flush aerials have been seen, but trying to identify their function would be guesswork. It is highly likely that the entire suite of ECM active jammers and payload dispensers is internal. Almost the only excrescences are around the nose: air-data sensors, AOA probe, ice probe, pitots, CW blister and laser. Everything else appears to be flush, though a good view from above has not yet emerged in the West.

Armament: Two prominent blisters under the fuselage have given rise to controversy. Some observers, including the author, at one time inclined to the view that these covered two guns of different calibre. That on the left is certainly a gun, generally regarded as a six-barrel 23mm type also carried by the MiG-27 on the centreline. The other installation has been given various explanations, but from its appearance it is a multisensor weapon-delivery system resembling the American Pave Tack. Weapons are carried on eight pylons, each rated at not less than 2,205lb (1,000kg), giving a total weapon load of 17,635lb (7,999kg). The pylons on the swing wings pivot to remain aligned with the airflow, and are the first of this type seen on a Soviet aircraft. Fairings over the two blisters on the underside are airbrakes, and they appear to preclude the carriage of more than one of the giant drop tanks under the fuselage. Every species of store issued to the FA can probably be carried, especially including all ASMs and nuclear free-fall bombs.

Future: By the time this book appears about 650 of these very formidable aircraft will be in service, 300 with five regiments of the 24th Air Army in Poland and another 300 with the 4th Air Army in Hungary and the Ukraine. Production is continuing at maximum rate, and no indication can be given of the eventual establishment planned.

Weapon provisions:
A. Multi-barrel gun ?
B. FLIR/EC sensor ?
C. Pylons (8) each 1,000kg (2,205lb).

Combat avionics:
A. Pulse dopper radar.
B. HUD.
C. CW illuminator ?
D. HF ?
E. RWR ?
F. VHF/UHF.
G. IRWS.
H. RHAWS.
J. ECM ?
K. Unknown.
L. Doppler ?
M. AOA sensor.
N. Air-data.
P. LRMTS.

Key to stores:
Note: It is possible to illustrate only a selection of stores whose appearance has become known; the very important AS-7 Kerry missile and several theatre (FA) nuclear weapons cannot be included.
1. ECM jammer pod, type unknown.
2. ASM, NATO reporting designation uncertain.
3. AA-2 Atoll AAM.
4. AA-2-2 Advanced Atoll.
5. Tactical ASM (believed not to be AS-7 Kerry) seen on Su-22.
6. AA-8 Aphid advanced snapshoot dogfight AAM.

7. AA-7 Apex medium-range AAM.
8. Giant drop tanks (about 650gal, 3,000lit, size).
9. 23mm twin-barrel gun pod (not positively identified on Su-24).
10. Unknown installation, believed to be dual-sensor weapon aiming system similar to Pave Spike or Pave Tack.
11. Multi-barrel gun of 23 or 30mm calibre.
12. Ammunition for (11), probably over 1,000 rounds.
13. GP bomb, 2,205lb (1,000kg).
14. Standard UV-16-57 launchers with 57mm rockets.

15. GP bomb, 1,102lb (500kg).
16. Alternative 500kg bomb.

17. Concrete-destroying bomb, believed of BETAB-250 (551lb) type.

Tupolev Tu-128

Origin: Soviet Union, first flight late 1950s.

Type: Long-range interceptor.

Engines: Two afterburning turbojets, almost certainly Lyul'ka AL-21F-3 with max afterburning rating of 24,250lb (11t).

Dimensions: (estimated): Span 59ft 0in (18.0m); length 89ft 3in (27.2m); height 23ft 0in (7m); wing area 860sq ft (80m²).

Weights: (estimated): empty 54,000lb (24.5t); internal fuel 30,000lb (13t); loaded 88,000lb (40t).

Performance: (estimated) Maximum speed (36,000ft/11km), (clean) 1,090mph (1,755km/h, Mach 1.65), (4 AAMs) 950mph (1,530km/h, Mach 1.44); initial climb 25,000ft (7.5km)/min; service ceiling 60,000ft (18.3km); combat radius 777 miles (1,250km); ferry range 2,000 miles (3,200km).

Background: Some understanding of this aircraft may be gained by looking at an atlas. Far larger than any other country, the Soviet Union poses an air-defence problem of gigantic proportions, and no budget could provide totally comprehensive defence of the entire frontier. The IA-PVO (air defence forces, manned interceptors) thus did the next-best thing and procured the world's largest and longest-ranged interceptor so that circles of the largest possible size could be drawn around each of a small number of major PVO airbases in several important but relatively remote regions. The requirement was raised in about 1955 but it took a long time to develop this aircraft, which was intended to replace the Yak-25 and operate with greater autonomy (though obviously ground surveillance radars are needed to provide warning of hostile tracks). The original Tu-102 (Tu-28) built in 1960 carried a giant ventral surveillance radar and two AAMs but gave way to the Tu-28P of the mid-1960s with a smaller (but still very large) nose radar and four missiles.

Design: Based on the Tu-98 supersonic bomber, the Tu-28 airframe was slightly smaller and provided tandem cockpits for a pilot and radar operator, each with an upward-hinged canopy. The wing is typical of the TsAGI-developed family used in eight Tu aircraft of the late 1950s, another being the Tu-105 (Tu-22 bomber), with track-mounted slotted flaps inboard and outboard of the characteristic main-gear pods, a fixed leading edge with no droops, dogteeth or fences, and powered ailerons well inboard from the tips. The production interceptor has slab tailplanes, originally with hinged "elevators" used only as trimming surfaces. The extremely large fuselage is area-ruled and contains more than half the total of about 4,600gal (21,000lit) of internal fuel, most of it between and beneath the very long inlet ducts. The inlets stand well away from the fuselage and have translating shock-cones but no other variable geometry. The low/mid position of the wing derives from the Tu-98 ancestry with a weapon bay; to reduce drag internal missile stowage was examined for the interceptor, but precluded by the large span of the missiles. The steerable nose gear retracts forwards, but the four-wheel bogie main gears fold rearwards in typical Tu style. Provision was to have been made for RWR, ECM dispensers and other installations in the bogie fairings, but nothing has been seen in photographs reaching the West. The pilot has a deep vee windscreen but no control over the radar and weapons. Both crew board via a large wheeled ladder platform.

Avionics: Called Big Nose by NATO, the main radar is a massive set possibly descended from the Scan Three used in the Yak-25; it operates in I-band and has a lock-on track range against small fighter targets of 50 miles (80km) presumably in clear weather. Detection range has been unofficially described by former Tu-128 pilots as "getting on for 200km" (124 miles). The usual kit of ADF, beacon receivers and ILS is carried, but almost nothing is known of mission equipment and no RWR has been identified. A long HF rail aerial runs along the right side under the nose.

Armament: The only weapons ever associated with these aircraft are the two sub-types of AA-5 Ash AAM, a large but quite old missile whose original design dates from the late 1950s. One pair of the SARH (semi-active radar homing) version was carried by the original Tu-28P, but the production Tu-128 has four underwing launch pylons and normally flies with two of each type of missile, the SARH type with a conical radome (usually coloured red) being on the outer pylons and the IR model, introduced in about 1965, being on the inners. There must have been other weapon fits, but nothing is known in the West.

Future: It is believed that about 300 of these giant interceptors entered service, and because of the unique mission radius and quite good endurance of 3h 30min on internal fuel almost the whole PVO force of some 180 remained in service into the 1980s. There must have been prolonged study of new avionic and weapon fits, and a switch to modern engines offering much reduced fuel burn, but nothing is known to have been done, and by 1983 the force was rapidly being reduced in size. According to one report the type was to be withdrawn in that year, in parallel with the closure of several former independent PVO district HQs.

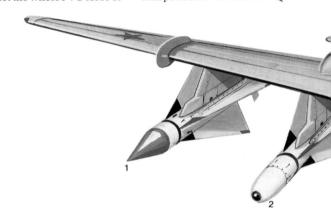

Below: Now gradually being withdrawn from operational service with the PVO the Tu-128 offered a combination of mission radius and flight performance that is difficult to sustain by later types (though we in the West know little about the so-called Su-27 Flanker). These Tu-128s are shrouded, perhaps against duststorms or severe weather?

Weapon provisions:
A. Missile pylon.

A A

1

2

2

2

Key to stores:
1. AA-5 Ash AAMs with semi-active radar homing guidance.
2. AA-5 Ash AAMs with IR (heat) homing guidance (note; normally two of item one and two of item 2 are carried on the four underwing pylons).

Combat avionics:
A. Big Nose radar.
B. HF notch ?
C. VHF/UHF.
D. RSIU UHF ?
E. doppler.
F. ATC/SIF/ILS.
G. HF rail.
H. Unknown.

A

B C D

H G F E

Vought A-7 Corsair II

Origin: USA, first flight 27 September 1965.

Type: (except K) attack, (K) combat trainer.

Engine: (D, H, K) one 14,250lb (6,465kg) thrust Allison TF41-1 turbofan; (E) one 15,000lb (6,804kg) TF41-2; (P) one 12,200lb (5,543kg) Pratt & Whitney TF30-408 turbofan.

Dimensions: Span 38ft 9in (11.8m); length (D) 46ft 1½in (14.06m), (K) 48ft 11½in (14.92m); wing area 375sq ft (34.83m²).

Weights: Empty (D) 19,781lb (8,972kg), loaded (D) 42,000lb (19,050kg).

Performance: Maximum speed (D, clean, SL) 690mph (1,110km/h); (5,000ft/1,525m, with 12 Mk 82 bombs) 646mph 91,040km/h); tactical radius (with unspecified weapon load at unspecified height), 715 miles (1,151km); ferry range (internal fuel) 2,281 miles (3,671km), (max with external tanks) 2,861 miles (4,604km).

Background: In the quickest development programme for a new combat aircraft since 1945, Vought (then LTV) were contracted in February 1964 to build a new carrier-based attack aircraft for the US Navy to replace the A-4, carrying more bombs over greater ranges. The design was based on the F-8 supersonic fighter, but with major changes to fit it to subsonic attack missions. Within three years of the initial contract large numbers were in operational service.

Design: The F-8 had a unique pivoted variable-incidence wing, but the A-7 wing is conventional and attached slightly below the high position, though leaving ample room for deep loaded pylons. The wing folds in line with the leading-edge dogtooth, with powered ailerons outboard and slotted flaps inboard preceded by symmetric-only spoilers; the entire leading edge droops. The slab tailplanes have slight dihedral and are below mid-position, and a large door airbrake is fitted under the fuselage. The fuselage is shorter than the F-8 but has a large cross-section giving ample volume for fuel, avionics and systems, the short landing gears and the non-augmented turbofan engine. There are comprehensive armour and damage-resistant systems, as well as an exceptionally advanced autopilot and flight system for all-weather operation including automatic carrier landing. In Navy versions there is a retractable flight refuelling probe on the right side of the forward fuselage; USAF A-7Ds have a refuelling boom receptacle above the left wing root (the A-7K has a universal fitting on the centreline). Emergency systems power is provided by a ram-air turbine.

Avionics: The original A-7A and B variants had basic 1960s-style equipment including doppler, multimode radar, nav computer, attitude reference system, roller-map display, Tacan and a weapon-aiming computer and optical sight. In 1968 Vought flew the A-7D for

the USAF and the Navy's A-7E, both with a totally new nav/attack system. The ASN-91 computer is an advanced and versatile processor providing all nav information, guidance for the target run and weapon-release cues. It integrates inputs from an ASN-90 INS, ASN-190 doppler, APQ-126 radar with ten operating modes including TFR, an air-data computer, radar altimeter and a very wide range of basic navigation and communications equipment. Cockpit displays include the AVQ-7(V) HUD and ASU-99 projected-map display, while the ASCU (armament station control unit) provides complete management of all weapons. ECM includes the ALR-45/50 internal RHAW, ALQ-126 active ECM, chaff/flare dispensers of different kinds for the two US services, and provision for a range of jammer pods compatible with the internal ECM/EW systems. Since 1978 Navy A-7Es have been progressively equipped to carry a 720lb (327kg) FLIR pod under the right wing with a TI gimballed sensor feeding pictorial information to a new Marconi Avionics raster HUD to give greatly enhanced attack capability by night. Only 91 pods can be afforded, aircraft thus equipped acting as "mission leaders", though it has not been explained how their presence will increase attack accuracy of the other A-7Es.

Armament: The original A and B models had two Mk 12 cannon of 20mm calibre in the sides of the air inlet in the nose, each with 250 rounds. In the D and E and derived export models these are replaced by a single M61A-1 20mm gun with a tank of 1,032 rounds, though 500 rounds is the normal loading. All versions have four outboard wing pylons, each with 3,500lb (1,587kg) capacity, all plumbed for tanks. The innermost wing pylons are not plumbed, and are rated at 2,500lb (1,134kg). Fuselage side pylons each rated at 500lb (227kg) are normally used for Sidewinder self-defence AAMs. All pylons cannot simultaneously be loaded to their limit; with max internal fuel the weapon load is limited to 9,500lb (4,309kg) which brings gross weight to the limit of 42,000lb (19,051kg) at a permitted manoeuvre load factor of 4.9g. With much reduced internal fuel the external stores load can reach just over 15,000lb (6,804kg).

Future: Production of two-seat A-7Ks for the ANG and conversion of Navy aircraft to two-seat TA-7C standard is complete. Many plans exist for updating, but money remains the pacing item and in 1983 there was no sign of early implementation of any of them. This is despite prolonged lobbying by avionics and accessory companies and, above all, by the US engine builders who have for years tried to oust the British-derived TF41 engine. A major effort was mounted by GE to get a twin F404 (unaugmented version of the Hornet engine) accepted.

Key to stores:
1. Durandal anti-runway weapon.
2. CBU cluster bomb.
3. Triple AGM-65 Mavericks (three different models).
4. AGM-88A Harm anti-radar missile.
5. AGM-45A Shrike anti-radar missile.
6. 250gal (1,137lit) tank.

Left: Shallow dive attack by a USAF A-7D with Snakeye retarded bombs. At the time of its introduction the A-7D and very similar A-7E set new standards of bombing accuracy.

Weapon provisions:
A. 20mm M61 with 500 rounds.
B. Body pylon, 500lb (227kg).
C. Pylon 2,500lb (1,134kg).
D. Pylon 3,500lb (1,588kg).

B C D D

A

7. Wasp anti-tank missile.
8. Paveway II GBU-10 E/ B (laser-homing 2,000lb, 907kg bomb).
9. AIM-9L Sidewinder AAMs.
10. 20mm M61 gun and short length of ammunition.
11. FLIR pod (A-7E only, under right wing).
12. AGM-62 Walleye

ASM.
13. Triple 250lb (113kg) GP bombs.
14. Triple Snakeye retarded bombs.
15. 1AGM-109 Harpoon.

16. GBU-15 CWW (Cruciform-Wing Weapon) for stand-off attack.
17. Matra RL 100 (six 100mm rockets).

Combat avionics:
A. APQ-126 radar.
B. HUD.
C. Tacan.
D. HF shunt.
E. UHF/IFF.
F. RWR.

G. VOR.
H. Chaff/flare dispenser.
J. Strike camera.
K. ASN-190 doppler.
L. Pave Penny laser.
M. ILS.

Yakovlev Yak-28

Origin: Soviet Union; first flight (28) believed 1959, (28P) probably 1960.

Type: (28P) two-seat interceptor.

Engines: (Most) Two 10,140/13,670lb (4.6/6.2t) thrust Tumanskii R-11 afterburning turbojets.

Dimensions: Span (most) 41ft 0in (12.5m); length overall, from 71ft 0in (21.6m) to (28P) 75ft 0in (22.9m); height 12ft 11½in (3.95m); wing area 405sq ft (37.6m²).

Weights: (estimated) Empty (28U) 23,000lb (10.4t), (28P) 29,000lb (13.15t), maximum loaded (28U) 33,000lb (15t), (28P) 44,000lb (20t).

Performance: (estimated) Maximum speed (hi, typical, clean) 750mph (1,200km/h Mach 1.14), (SL) 646mph (1,040km/h, Mach 0.85); service ceiling (afterburner) 55,000ft (16.75km); combat radius (all-hi) 560 miles (900km); ferry range 1,550 miles (2,500km).

Background: Though the total numbers built are not large by Soviet standards, the subtypes derived from the Yak-25 tandem-seat night fighter are many and diverse. In general each successive major redesign opened out the aerodynamic limitations, and increased internal fuel capacity, gross weight and cost. The Yak-28, stemming from prototypes flown in 1959-60, introduced the R-11 engine in a new underwing nacelle hung under a greatly developed wing moved up to almost the very top of the fuselage. Variants of this series were built for seven types of mission, the Yak-28P being an all-weather interceptor.

Design: Like all the Yak twin-jets of the late 1950s the 28P has a long fuselage of almost perfectly streamlined form and circular cross-section. The 45°-swept high wing has an inboard section sharply increased in chord at both front and rear, and outer sections with an extended leading edge in the form of powered droop flaps, outboard of a dogtooth discontinuity. Slotted flaps occupy all available trailing edge except for small powered ailerons at the tips which are the only roll controls. The slab tailplane is mounted half-way up the fin and has cutouts to allow the powered rudder to move. Unlike the Yak-25 and immediate offshoots, the wheelbase of the tandem "bicycle" main gears is enormous, and the front unit has twin wheels (like the rear) and is steerable. Outrigger gears fold rearwards into fairings near the wingtips which extend forwards to house anti-flutter masses. Fuel capacity in the fuselage and wing is limited by weight rather than space, yet some versions (usually not the 28P) can carry slipper tanks under the outer wings. Pilot and radar operator sit in tandem ejection seats under a large one-piece canopy which slides far to the rear. Unlike most other versions the 28P has no internal weapon bay, and since the mid-1960s guns have not been carried. Compared with the MiG-25 and Su-15 flight performance is on a much lower level, though Mach 1 can be exceeded at altitudes above about 13,000ft (3,962m). Flight endurance is better than in either of those interceptors, though because of lower speeds this does not quite translate into greater combat radius.

Avionics: The main radar is believed to be the same large I-band set as fitted to the Su-15, with the NATO name Skip Spin. Operating frequencies are 8,690 to 8,995MHz, with other data as given under the Su-15. It has five operating modes, one of which provides target illumination matched to the homing requirements of the missiles. Most 28Ps have an optical sight for the pilot, and this may be a relic from the time when a 30mm gun was fitted on the right side. The radar is managed by the backseater, though it is possible that its information may be presented directly to the pilot. Since 1977 the radome usually fitted has been considerably longer and more pointed than the original pattern, and though this may not have been the reason it would certainly reduce transonic drag and acceleration time. Few other details are known, though the usual VHF/UHF, Tacan, ATC/SIF and IFF aerials have been identified. The prominent quartet of aft-facing rod aerials at the tail (at least the upper and lower pair) may be Swift Rod ILS receivers, though this is unconfirmed. They may serve an RWR function, no RWR installation having been positively identified.

Armament: All Yak-28P aircraft have a pylon beneath each wing for an AA-3 Anab AAM. The usual fit is one of the SARH (radar homing) type under each wing; alternatively, the weapon under the left wing may be replaced by an AA-3 with IR homing. Since about 1977 two additional pylons have sometimes, but not always, been installed under the outer wings for two K-13A (AA-2 Anab), or presumably also AA-2-2 Advanced Anab or AA-8 Aphid. These are all close-range dogfight AAMs and the Yak-28P is at a severe disadvantage in this situation.

Future: Rather surprisingly, an estimated 300 Yak-28Ps were still in the active inventory in 1983, most of them in the IA-PVO in the remaining rather remote air defence districts. About the same number are probably available for training and trials purposes, for which their generally pleasant handling and good reliability are major assets. Some 28Ps are probably used as a final stage of training for pilots before they join Su-15 regiments which use almost the same radar/weapon combination. Nevertheless, this weapon system is to be regarded as obsolescent, and like the much larger and longer-ranged Tu-128 the Yak-28P was being withdrawn in 1983.

1

2

3

Below: Likely to remain in operational service much longer than the Yak-28P, the original Yak-28 versions with glazed noses for a navigator or systems operator are still quite numerous. These are "Brewer-C" EW/attack aircraft, with two radars, extensive EW suites, an internal bomb bay and forward-firing 30mm gun.

Weapon provisions:
A. Main wing pylons, always fitted, matched to AA-3 Anab medium-range AAM (see text for details).
B. Auxiliary wing pylons, sometimes fitted, matched to K-13A (AA-2 Atoll) and related close-range AAMs, and possibly to AA-8 Aphid.

A B

3

4

1

D

A   B   C

H   G   F   E

Key to stores:
1. AA-3 Anab medium-range AAM (IR-homing version).
2. AA-2 (K-13A) Atoll IR heat-homing dogfight AAM, not often carried.
3. AA-3 Anab medium-range AAM (semi-active

radar guided version).
4. AA-2-2 Advanced Atoll Radar-guided close-range AAM (not often carried).
Note: The Yak-28P interceptor is normally not fitted with the fixed forward-firing 30mm gun.

Combat avionics:
A. Main radar (believed to be Skip Spin).
B. Traditional reflector sight for visual alignment behind target, though no gun fitted.
C. Believed VHF blade aerial with Tacan

function.
D. VHF/UHF communications.
E. Believed to be Swift Rods ILS aerials.
F. Unconfirmed report of RWR.
G. Main avionics bays.
H. Air-data pitot probe.

Yakovlev Yak-36MP

Origin: Soviet Union, first flight believed 1971.
Type: Ship-based VTOL strike/fighter.
Engines: Vectored-thrust Turbofan(s) or turbojet(s) with total takeoff thrust of about 16,500lb (7,484kg); two lift jets ahead of wing with thrust of about 7,700lb (3,492kg) each.
Dimensions: (estimated) Span 24ft 0in (7.32m); length (A) 52ft 6in (16.0m), (B) 58ft 0in (17.68m); wing area 170sq ft (15.8m²).
Weights: (estimated) Empty (A) 15,000lb (6,804kg), (B) 15,500lb (7,030kg), maximum loaded (both) 23,700lb (10,750kg).
Performance: (estimated) Maximum speed (hi, clean) 725mph (1,170km/h, Mach 1.1), (SL, clean) 700mph (1,125km/h, Mach 0.9); initial climb, Western figure of 14,750ft (4.5m)/min appears rather low; service ceiling about 40,000ft (12.2km); combat radius (attack mission, hi-lo-hi) 230 miles (370km); ferry range (4 tanks) 1,800 miles (2,900km).
Background: From the late 1950s the Soviet Union carefully studied Western V/STOLs and flew several jet-lift research aircraft, of which two examples of one type, the Yak-36, were publicly shown in 1967. No aircraft in this category has appeared for use in land war, but in the early 1970s the Yak OKB was assigned the task of creating a jet-lift aircraft for deployment aboard the four large multirole ships of the Kiev class. Their chief role is to maintain air supremacy over Soviet fleets, and in particular to destroy ASW and patrol aircraft, EW and Awacs platforms and anti-ship helicopters. Secondary tasks include reconnaissance and anti-ship strike.
Design: From the start it was accepted that the aircraft would be a pure VTOL, unable to reap the benefits of rolling takeoffs and ski-jump decks. The design was derived from that of the Yak-36, hence the designation, but it departed so far that resemblance became slight. The main lift/cruise engine (it is generally assumed that, unlike the Yak-36, there is only one) is sized for cruise, the power for VTOL being made up by adding two lift jets further forward aft of the cockpit and between the inlet ducts. This gives more than thrice the likelihood of engine

failure than for a single-engined aircraft, because the lift jets are started and stopped twice on each mission. Though the lift-jet nozzles incorporate limited vectoring in the fore/aft plane, their centrelines are angled to the rear and the thrust component must be countered by rotating the main-engine nozzles to the 100 or 105° position, well forward of vertical. Reaction jets are provided on the wingtips for roll and at the tail for yaw; pitch appears to be by varying lift thrusts. There are plain lateral inlets to the main engine, the only variable geometry being six (originally three) suck-in auxiliary inlets which open at high power and low airspeed. There is no evidence of afterburning, though supersonic speed can be achieved at altitude. The small wings are tapered only on the leading edge and fold upwards halfway from root to tip. The leading edge is fixed; the trailing edge has plain flaps inboard and ailerons outboard, with no spoilers. The tail is said to have variable-incidence tailplanes, but the only certain fact is that, unusually, it has separate elevators (which according to some authorities have tabs). Simple conventional landing gear allows the wing to fold yet gives adequate deck stability; no hook or hold-down device has been seen. Structurally it is assumed the mid-fuselage is built up on massive rings to which the wings are attached. How the main engine is changed is unknown.
Avionics: These are conspicuously absent, the only visible aerials being for Tacan, beacon, IFF, ILS and various com frequencies. The dielectric nosecap is assumed to cover the aerial of a ranging radar for the optical sight, and nothing is known of what must be fully adequate all-weather navigation and attack systems. In particular the precisely repeated demonstration of apparently perfect stability and guidance in the takeoff and landing modes makes it clear there is a high-authority flight control system which converts these modes into a fully automatic procedure. Indeed there is abundant evidence for the 36MP being unflyable in any manual mode, because of the sheer complexity of the various thrusts, torques and gyroscopic effect.

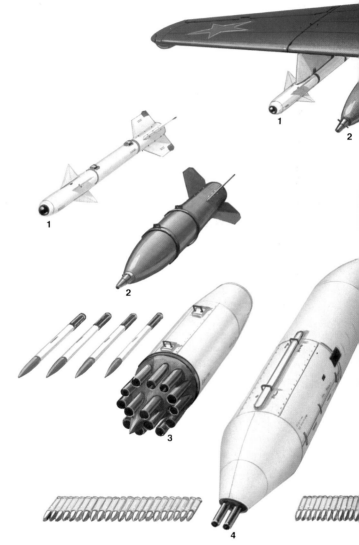

Armament: No internal armament has been seen in any 36MP, and the only known external hardpoints are four wing pylons all inboard of the fold and constricted to the extent that the main gears interfere with all except very slim stores on the inboard pylons. Weapons known to be carried include the K-13A family (AA-2 and 2-2 Atoll series) and AA-8 Aphid AAMs, GSh-23 gun pods, bombs up to 1,102lb (500kg) size, rocket pods with 16 or 32 tubes, large anti-ship rockets, practice-bomb carriers and 132gal (600lit) drop tanks. Items almost certainly carried include jammer pods, multisensor reconnaissance pods and various air-to-surface missiles, including sea skimmers for use against small ships. Total external load with 5,000lb (2,268kg) internal fuel is estimated at 3,000lb (1,361kg), though estimates give a margin of 6,000lb (2,722kg) between clean gross and MTO weight of about 28,660lb (13t).
Future: For several years a next-generation shipboard combat aircraft has been predicted. It is doubtful that the Yak-36MP has ever been intended as more than an interim type.

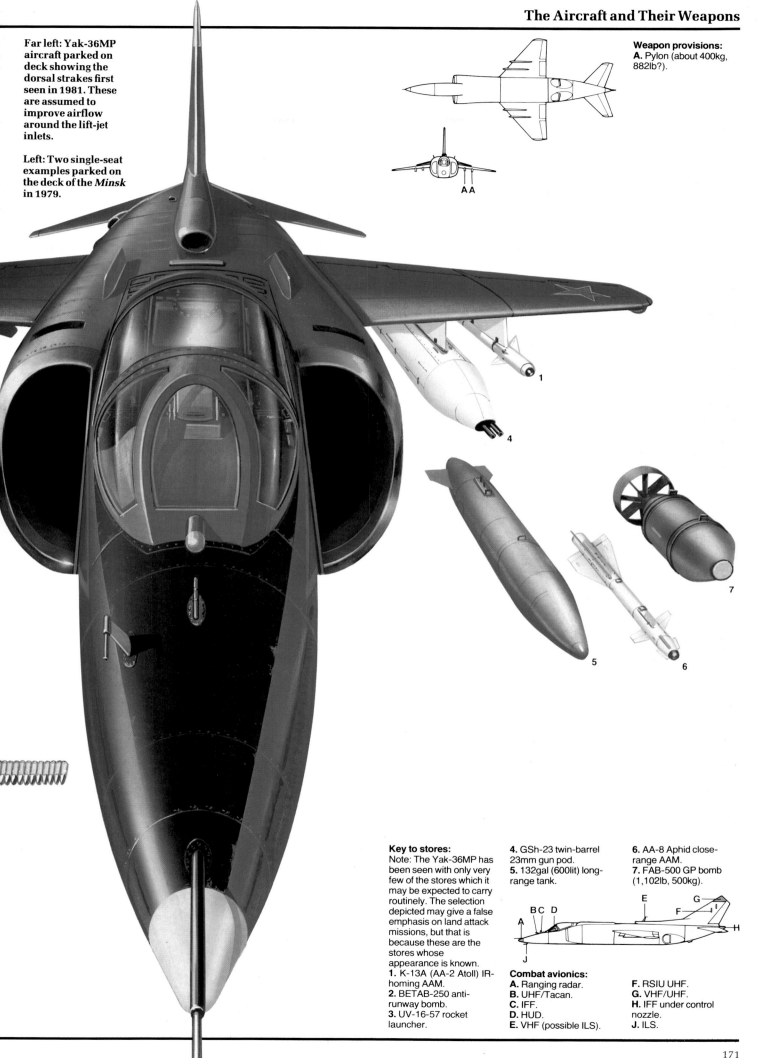

Far left: Yak-36MP aircraft parked on deck showing the dorsal strakes first seen in 1981. These are assumed to improve airflow around the lift-jet inlets.

Left: Two single-seat examples parked on the deck of the *Minsk* in 1979.

Weapon provisions:
A. Pylon (about 400kg, 882lb?).

A A

1

4

5

6

7

Key to stores:
Note: The Yak-36MP has been seen with only very few of the stores which it may be expected to carry routinely. The selection depicted may give a false emphasis on land attack missions, but that is because these are the stores whose appearance is known.
1. K-13A (AA-2 Atoll) IR-homing AAM.
2. BETAB-250 anti-runway bomb.
3. UV-16-57 rocket launcher.

4. GSh-23 twin-barrel 23mm gun pod.
5. 132gal (600lit) long-range tank.

6. AA-8 Aphid close-range AAM.
7. FAB-500 GP bomb (1,102lb, 500kg).

B C D   E   G
A   F

J   H

Combat avionics:
A. Ranging radar.
B. UHF/Tacan.
C. IFF.
D. HUD.
E. VHF (possible ILS).

F. RSIU UHF.
G. VHF/UHF.
H. IFF under control nozzle.
J. ILS.

Air Combat Tactics

Below: The excellent view astern in the US Air Force F-15 Eagle is a direct result of old lessons relearned in the unforgiving skies of the Middle East and Vietnam.

The F-15 carries a formidable array of active and passive detection devices, but it is still necessary for the pilot to search visually astern during combat.

Introduction

Air warfare does not occur in isolation, but is part of a much larger pattern. Consequently we must view air combat in its correct context: as part of a general conflict. Perhaps we should briefly examine the nature of war.

War is a state which occurs when politicians start losing an argument and resort to violence. The object of war is to achieve the desired result. Despite the evidence of the two World Wars in the first half of this century the desired result is not necessarily total military victory. The Korean War was successfully concluded (from the United Nations viewpoint) by saving South Korea from North Korean domination. Israel inflicted crushing military defeats on her Arab neighbours with the aim of preserving her independence. However, in no case did Israel attempt complete conquest of any of the opposing states, although once or twice this seemed a distinct possibility. The United States intervened in Vietnam with the stated aim of preventing the South being over-run by the North. In the Falkland Islands dispute, in which Great Britain was technically at war with Argentina, hostilities were confined to the area around the Falklands; although the stated objective was to restore the status quo to the Falkland islanders this was done without striking at the Argentine mainland, although it seems that this was within British capabilities.

One lesson to be learned from these conflicts is that the desired result can be achieved by eroding both the ability and the will of the enemy to continue the struggle. Another is that, in war, ground forces are paramount: wars are primarily about territory and only the foot soldier can hold territory. Sea power can dominate territory, as was shown in the Falklands dispute in April 1982, but only where geographical circumstances permit. Air power can dominate territory but, unless there is a tremendous disparity between the opposing air forces, such domination is usually of very brief duration.

A further lesson is not to attempt to fight a war with one hand tied behind your back. This was the mistake made by the United States in Vietnam. The Americans tried to fight a war of containment and attrition and in doing so they surrendered the initiative and paid heavily in consequence. The classic example was the initial prohibition of strikes against North Vietnamese

Above: An F-4 Phantom hurtles in to attack a North Vietnamese position. Support for the ground troops is an essential function of all air forces. Concentrated firepower is readily delivered from the air, affecting the morale of both sides.

airfields when North Vietnamese MiGs could be destroyed in the air but not on the ground!

If conventional war is concerned with the possession of territory, a task for surface forces, the role of air power can only be to aid the surface forces in their task. Modern battles are fought and won by surface and air forces working together. Air forces may be in support of ground forces, but with the firepower and mobility of aircraft they can make a direct contribution to the land battle. If there is one thing aircraft can do superlatively well it is to make life miserable for enemy soldiers and sailors.

Battlefield interdiction, cutting of supplies, and intelligence gathering are the *raison d'être* of an air force. If the war is protracted, reducing enemy potential to make war by striking at his centres of production may be added to the list.

AIR DEFENCE: AN ESSENTIAL FUNCTION

In any conflict, the air forces of both sides will be attempting all these things. Air defence arises from the need to prevent enemy aircraft from carrying out these tasks, and thwarting their attempts to spoil one's own strikes. Air defence is therefore preventative action and is an essential function of air power: the need to counter the opposing air force. Air defence is one role or function of an air force; although it can be a secondary role, it will take on differing priorities during the battle.

Defensive air combat is the reaction to attack; a series of defensive manoeuvres follows until the enemy make a successful escape is achieved, or the offensive is gained and the attacker shot down.

Offensive manoeuvring air combat occurs when the attacker has been detected by the target, and the attacker is forced to manoeuvre offensively to achieve the kill.

In any appreciation of air combat tactics it is necessary to consider both the tasks to be carried out and the nature of possible

The Five Phases of Air Combat

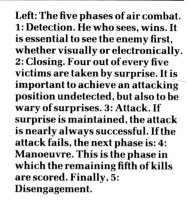

3: Attack

5: Disengagement

4: Manoeuvre

2: Closing

1: Detection

Left: The five phases of air combat. 1: Detection. He who sees, wins. It is essential to see the enemy first, whether visually or electronically. 2: Closing. Four out of every five victims are taken by surprise. It is important to achieve an attacking position undetected, but also to be wary of surprises. 3: Attack. If surprise is maintained, the attack is nearly always successful. If the attack fails, the next phase is: 4: Manoeuvre. This is the phase in which the remaining fifth of kills are scored. Finally, 5: Disengagement.

threats. This assessment must be made against a background of numerical strength and available technology. Nor can ground-based detection and counter-air measures be ignored.

Because flying is a three-dimensional activity, at first sight the combinations of manoeuvre appear to be unlimited. Such is not the case. All machines have their limitations. These are limitations of position (of which more later) and limitations of performance. Some performance limitations – maximum speed, altitude, and so on – are apparent from the aircraft section of this book. Other limitations are not so apparent. To help the reader understand these we have included a short section on basic aerodynamics, covering simply some of the whys and wherefores of aircraft capabilities and limitations.

What makes a good fighter is the next question we have tried to answer. Lots of first-class technology helps; in fact it sometimes seems that the main function of the pilot is to stop the computers getting bored! On the other hand technology can be counter-productive. An advanced technology fighter equipped with all the "nice to have" gadgets, is large, easier to detect, a bigger target and very expensive. A school of thought exists which advocates the austere (cheap) fighter, compensating with greater numbers for its lack of all-round ability. Is it better to have lots of cheap fighters or a few very expensive ones? Both solutions have their advocates. All we can do is to hope that we never have to find out.

THE FIVE PHASES OF AIR COMBAT

Air combat breaks down into five phases. The first is *detection* (and its corollary, avoidance of detection). Aircraft can be detected by three means; electronically, visually, and by their heat emissions. In a crowded sky identification is a problem of major proportions.

The next phase of air combat is *closing*. This involves reaching a favourable position from which to launch an attack. *Attack* is the third and often decisive phase, and is conditioned by relative positions and weaponry. (Some experts consider the closing and attack phases to be only one, in which case there would be just four phases of combat.) The fourth phase of air combat is *manoeuvre*. This is the glamorous part of air warfare; the domain of the aces. However, its importance is often over-rated. If the attack phase is successful, manoeuvre is of purely academic interest. It is nevertheless a subject of consuming interest and we have treated it in detail. The final phase of air combat is *disengagement*. Modern detection systems and weaponry have made this difficult to achieve, but considering the rate at which the modern fighter gulps fuel it is of ever-increasing importance.

Finally we cover the most important piece of software; the pilot. Training is an important factor, as is the psychology of the fighter pilot. So is the equipment, the "nuts and bolts".

SPEED IN KNOTS

The nautical mile per hour or knot is the standard measure of speed among Western nations; all speeds in this section are therefore given in knots. The knot has been gradually standardised over the last few decades as an aid to navigation. The nautical mile is one sixtieth of a degree of longitude, 6,080 feet (1,853 metres). It is thus about 15 per cent longer than one statute mile (1.6km); ie 1.15 miles (1.85km). It has a small extra value in combat in that at medium altitudes the Mach number multiplied by 10 gives a fairly close approximation of the distance travelled per minute in nautical miles.

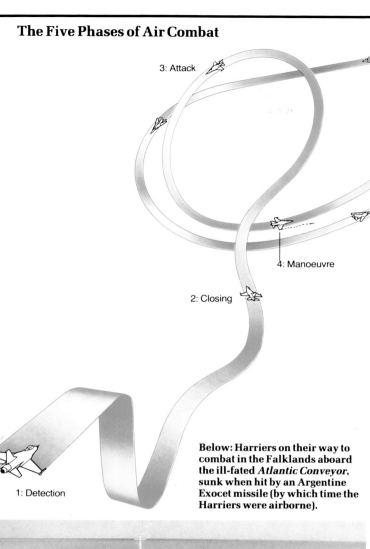

Below: Harriers on their way to combat in the Falklands aboard the ill-fated *Atlantic Conveyor*, sunk when hit by an Argentine Exocet missile (by which time the Harriers were airborne).

Basic Aerodynamics

A fighter is a series of compromises, a machine built to fly and to fight. It needs to have good acceleration, a high rate of climb and excellent manoeuvrability. These qualities oppose each other to a certain extent. Perhaps we should start by examining the medium in which it operates: the air.

Atmospheric conditions vary widely according to climate, season, and even the local weather. To avoid confusion, a standard atmosphere is adopted for aerodynamic calculations. Commonly used is the International Civil Aviation Organisation (ICAO) Standard Atmosphere. This assumes an atmospheric pressure of 29.92 inches (75.99cm) of mercury and a temperature of 15° Centigrade at sea level. The temperature is assumed to lapse at 1.98°C for each thousand feet (300m) of altitude above sea level, until at a height of 36,090ft (11,000m) a temperature of minus 56.5°C is reached. This height forms a hypothetical boundary called the tropopause; the region beneath it is known as the troposphere. Above the troposphere is a region called the stratosphere, in which the temperature remains at a constant minus 56.5°C.

The distinction between the troposphere and the stratosphere is important because it relates to the speed of sound. The local speed of sound is often referred to as Mach 1, called after mathematician Professor Ernst Mach. Aircraft speeds are often given in terms of the Mach number. The speed of sound varies considerably in the troposphere. At sea level Mach 1 is 661 knots (higher in summer, less in winter), reducing to 638 knots at 10,000ft (3,050m), 614 knots at 20,000ft (6,100m) and 589 knots at 30,000ft (9,150m). From the tropopause upwards it remains constant at 573 knots. As the speed of sound varies so widely at differing altitudes, it would be irrelevant were it not for the fact that certain phenomena occur in what is known as the transonic region, which will be discussed when we reach the subject of drag.

Above: The primary task of the A-10 Thunderbolt II is to destroy tanks. In battle it will spend much of its time flying at low altitudes. Its high aspect ratio wing confers a good rate of turn at low speeds.

The only other things we need to know about the atmosphere are that air pressure reduces with height, and that the oxygen content progressively diminishes until at 100,000ft (30,478m) there is insufficient to sustain combustion in even the most advanced jet engines.

Power is supplied by the gas turbine, or jet engine. In very crude terms, this sucks air in at the front, mixes it with fuel, burns it and shoves the resultant superheated gases out at the back much faster than the original air came in. This produces thrust which, applied to the aeroplane, starts it moving forward. To accelerate, thrust has to overcome two factors; inertia, or mass of the aeroplane, and drag. Drag can be roughly defined as the resistance of the air to the aeroplane, and at subsonic speeds it increases in proportion to the square of the speed. Thus the drag of an aeroplane moving at 150 knots becomes four times greater at 300 knots and *nine times* greater at 450 knots.

In subsonic flight, the air flows smoothly out of the way of the aeroplane, which creates a disturbance in the air ahead of it rather like the bow-wave of a ship. This bow-wave travels at the local speed of sound. In the case of an aeroplane flying at 36,090ft (11,000m) at a speed of 500 knots (Mach 0.87) the disturbance reaches out to about 120ft (36m) ahead of the aeroplane. At 550 knots (Mach 0.96) the disturbance is only 40ft (12.19m) ahead.

The air has insufficient time to flow smoothly out of the way and is roughly forced aside. The molecules of air are compressed together in an uneven manner (an aeroplane is an uneven shape). The aeroplane becomes surrounded by air of uneven density which sets up a shock wave. This in turn gives rise to an extra form of drag called "wave drag"; something more for thrust to overcome. At about Mach 1.2 wave drag dies away and the normal increase of drag to speed becomes almost constant again.

To overcome the effect of wave drag, afterburning is employed. Few aircraft are even marginally supersonic without the extra thrust supplied by afterburning. In essence, afterburning employs rings of nozzles which spray fuel into the already superheated exhaust gases, where it is burnt, creating even more thrust. It is, however, very prodigal of fuel and must be used sparingly.

Afterburning is often called "wet thrust" as opposed to "dry thrust", or maximum power as opposed to military power. Some idea of the effect may be given by comparing the afterburning and non-afterburning performance of an F-4E Phantom at sea level. Using normal engine power (military thrust) it takes 54 seconds to accelerate from Mach 0.5 (330 knots) to Mach 0.9 (595 knots). Average acceleration is 5 knots per second, during which time our Phantom consumes 57 gallons (259 litres) of fuel. With 'burners blazing it takes just over 22 seconds to accelerate the same

Right: The atmosphere consists of two regions. The troposphere is the lower of the two, where the temperature steadily reduces from 15°C at sea level to minus 56.5°C at the tropopause. Above this level lies the stratosphere, where the temperature remains constant to a great height. As climatic conditions vary widely, a Standard Atmosphere is used for calculation purposes.

Far right: The speed of sound varies with height in the troposphere, and comparison with the previous diagram shows a direct relationship to air temperature. Fighters usually reach their maximum speed at or around the tropopause, which theoretically occurs at 36,090ft (11,000m).

The Troposphere, Tropopause and the Speed of Sound

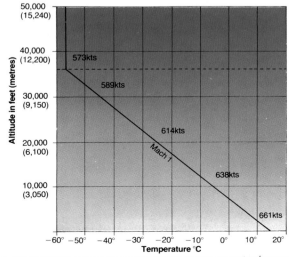

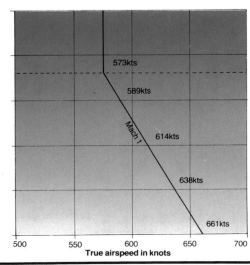

Fuel Cost of Using Afterburner

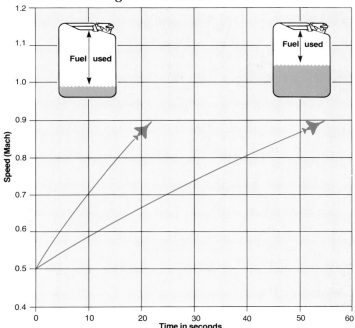

Above: Some idea of the effects of afterburning is shown here. An F-4E Phantom at sea level accelerates from Mach 0.5 to Mach 0.9, a speed increase of 265 knots. Using 'burner it takes 22 seconds, **compared with 54 seconds using dry thrust, a 145 per cent increase in acceleration. This advantage is bought at a cost of nearly 30 extra gallons of fuel, consumption rising to nearly four gallons per second.**

Afterburner Effect on Distance Travelled

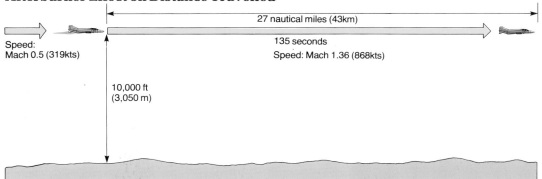

Below: An F-4 with afterburners blazing. Afterburning is the injection of fuel directly into the hot exhaust gases of the engine where it is burnt to produce extra thrust. It also makes an excellent infra-red target.

Above: "Speed is Life" is a truism of the fighter world. Speed, once lost, takes a great deal of time and even more distance to recover. Here, an F-4 loses contact with the enemy. Heading homewards at maximum power he will take 135 **seconds to work up to maximum speed (Mach 1.36/868 knots) at this altitude, and cover a horizontal distance of nearly 27 nautical miles. As speed increases, vulnerability to attack decreases.**

Below: Two fighters are at equal speed and height. On zoom climbing the heavier of the two pulls ahead because it has more kinetic energy. After the surplus energy has been expended, the best-climbing machine will win.

Effect of Kinetic Energy

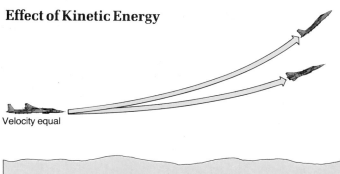

amount at an average acceleration of 12 knots per second. For this startling increase in performance it uses nearly 30 extra gallons (136l) of fuel at nearly 4 gallons (18l) per second!

Thrust decreases with altitude as the oxygen content of the atmosphere diminishes. Drag also reduces with height as the air density lessens. The tropopause is normally the optimum point for maximum speed, since the best compromise for thrust/drag is achieved at this level.

However, there are other factors which influence maximum speed. One is the structural strength of the airframe or engine. A factor creeping in at speeds in excess of Mach 2 is the effect of kinetic heating caused by the friction of the air, creating temperatures high enough to weaken aluminium alloys. Aircraft in this category are known as strength-limited. Others are persistence-limited. Climbing to the tropopause, and then accelerating to Mach 2 takes a long time and uses an enormous quantity of fuel. While certain aircraft may be quite capable of attaining twice the speed of sound, to do so would leave them dangerously low on fuel.

At low level almost all fighters are strength-limited. The Mach 2 capable fighter is restricted to between Mach 1.05 and Mach 1.2 at sea level. This was greatly to the Americans' advantage over Vietnam; their rugged Phantoms and Thunderchiefs were almost 100 knots faster than the more delicate MiG-21 at low altitude.

Finally, the enormous distances involved during prolonged acceleration need to be stressed. Let us assume that a Phantom has been involved in combat and that contact with the enemy is lost at 10,000ft (3,047m) and Mach 0.5 (319 knots). The terrain below is mountainous and hidden by cloud. It is enemy-dominated territory and hostile aircraft may reappear at any second. Fuel is somewhat low, so the pilot decides to leave the area as rapidly as possible. With full 'burner he makes a beeline for home. Two and a quarter minutes later he has attained his maximum speed for the altitude of Mach 1.36 (868 knots). The distance covered during this acceleration phase is nearly 27 nautical miles (50km). In any considerations of combat techniques the time and distance factors in recovering lost speed cannot be ignored.

In acceleration, the thrust/weight ratio is considered very important, but drag cannot be ignored. The F-104G Starfighter and the Phantom have similar thrust/weight ratios, but the Starfighter is much the cleaner aeroplane aerodynamically of the two, and consequently its acceleration is considerably better up to 600 knots. Thrust must first overcome drag, then the surplus can be used to increase the velocity of many tons of metal flying through the sky.

A device that can be used to increase acceleration is called "unloading". A falling object accelerates at 32.2ft (9.8m) per second. An aircraft can use this factor by nosing down in a shallow dive. A dive angle of 10° at 520 knots gives a rate of descent of 100ft (30.4m) per second. Gravity is thus used to overcome inertia and speed is gained more quickly than in level flight. Moreover, nosing over to zero-g (weightless) removes the drag caused by the wings having to support the overall weight.

This brings us to the subject of energy. An aeroplane in flight contains two forms of energy: positional and kinetic. Positional energy is the weight of the machine times altitude. It was noted as far back as October 1914 that an aeroplane with an altitude advantage over an opponent possessed a reservoir of energy in the form of height which could be converted into speed for escape or attack. The speed gained in this manner could be converted back into height.

Kinetic energy is the dynamic motion of the aircraft. If two fighters are travelling at the same speed, the heavier of the two will possess the most kinetic energy. If both pull up into a climb, the heavier machine will at first outclimb its lighter counterpart until its excess energy is used up. After this point, the thrust/weight plus drag ratio will become the dominant factor.

The total energy of an aeroplane is thus variable, and is generally measured in units of length called the "energy state". These units of length represent the height which the aeroplane could theoretically attain if the total of both its positional and kinetic energy could be converted into positional energy only. The importance of this is that performance and manoeuvrability are related to the energy state and how well that energy is used. In combat, energy is frequently used much faster than the available thrust can replace it.

CREATING LIFT

We can now consider the nature of lift. Velocity imparted to the air above a cambered (arched) surface causes a reduction in pressure. As the aeroplane speeds through the air, low-pressure areas form above the wings. The air pressure on the underside of the wing is normal, or slightly higher than normal. The difference in air pressure between the upper and lower surfaces of the wings tends

Converting Energy-gained Speed into Height

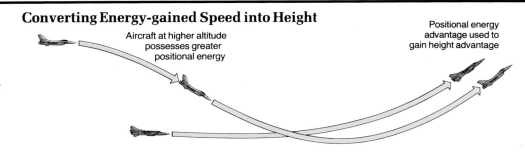

Aircraft at higher altitude possesses greater positional energy

Positional energy advantage used to gain height advantage

Above: Combat manoeuvrability is the art of energy management. A height advantage may be thought of in terms of positional energy. By

Lift and Angle of Attack

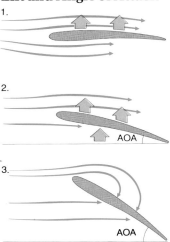

Above: 1. Air flowing smoothly over a plane surface creates an area of low pressure, or lift. 2. Increased angle of attack (AOA) creates extra lift. 3. In a stall, AOA becomes too steep and lift is lost.

diving, height can be exchanged for speed (kinetic energy), either for attack or escape. Here the attacker has a height (positional)

to push the wings upwards, thus creating lift. Provided that the aeroplane is securely attached to the wings, it will rise with them. For a practical demonstration of lift, hold a sheet of paper horizontally beneath your *bottom* lip and blow hard across its surface. The paper will rise to fill the low pressure area thus formed.

Several factors contribute to the amount of lift created by the wings. A narrow thick wing creates more lift per square foot of area (square metre) than a broad thin one. But at very high speeds a narrow thick wing creates a lot of drag, so modern fighters have wings which are very thin in relation to their width. The measure of this is called the thickness/chord ratio.

Two interlinked factors which

advantage which he trades for speed to overhaul the target. If the attack fails, he is able to convert surplus speed back into height.

affect lift are the velocity of the air flowing past the wing, and the air pressure, or density. An aeroplane with a minimum flying speed (stalling speed) of 150 knots at sea level has a minimum speed of 175 knots at 10,000ft (3,048m), 206 knots at 20,000ft (6,096m), 245 knots at 30,000ft (9,144m) and 384 knots at 50,000ft (15,240m). This is due to the air getting thinner at altitude.

The final major factor in creating lift is the angle of attack (AOA). This is the angle at which the wing meets the airflow. As the angle of attack is increased, so is lift. But lift is dependent on the air flowing smoothly over the surface of the wing. If the wing meets the air at too steep an AOA, the air will "burble" down as it flows past and

Minimum Flying Speeds at Altitudes

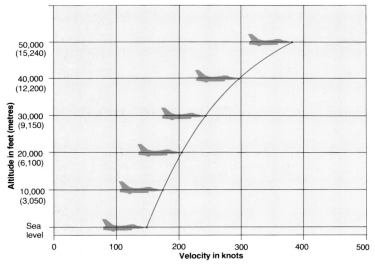

Above: As altitude increases, the air pressure diminishes, resulting in a reduced lift/velocity ratio. Here we illustrate the reduction, a minimum flying speed of 150 knots at sea level increasing to 384 knots at 50,000ft (15,240m). The indicated speed would, however, still show 150 knots.

Right: Two F-16 Fighting Falcons demonstrate their manoeuvrability. The F-16 was designed for the fair weather air superiority role, with the accent on sustained turning performance. Transient performance suffered slightly as a result, but the F-16 is a formidable opponent.

destroy the low-pressure area.

Lift is lost and the aeroplane will stall or, to use the modern term, "depart controlled flight".

In level flight, the weight of the aeroplane is exactly balanced by the lift created by the wing. In order to climb, more lift must be generated – the nose is pulled up, which increases the AOA of attack and creates more lift.

The minimum speed at which an aeroplane will fly is partly determined by its efficiency (coefficient of lift) but mainly by the load to be carried. This is generally expressed as total weight divided by wing area in pounds per square foot (kg per square metre). The wing loading of modern fighters varies from about 60lb/ft² (292.8kg/m²) to well over 100lb/ft²

(488.14kg/m²). As a generalisation, the higher the wing loading, the higher the minimum flying speed.

As air combat is a three-dimensional activity, fighters need to manoeuvre. Except for a few new prototypes they need to roll about their axis to change direction laterally; to pitch up or down to climb or dive, and they need to turn. There are three measures of turn – radius of turn, rate of turn, and "g". Both radius and rate of turn are a function of speed and "g".

"G" is an acceleration, often called centrifugal force, expressed in terms of the acceleration of gravity. At the time of writing the maximum practicable application of g is about 9, so we shall calculate up to that. The amount of g pulled in a turn is dependent on the angle

of bank, and is expressed by the equation

$$n = \frac{1}{\text{cosine}}$$

where n is the number of gs and ϕ is the angle of bank. The result can be seen in the diagram. As g is a multiple of the force of gravity, a hard-turning fighter has to create extra lift to sustain flight. This is done by increasing the AOA at the cost of incurring extra drag. If there is insufficient excess thrust to overcome the total drag, energy, in the form of speed, is rapidly lost. Positional energy (height) can be traded for speed to offset the loss. To complicate matters, the stall speed increases by the square root of the g being pulled; 4g is thus enough to double the minimum flying speed. Therefore high-g

manouevres can only be attempted when there is a sufficient margin of energy in hand; otherwise the turn must be eased as the fighter approaches the area of lost control.

The radius of turn is determined by the speed (velocity) and g of the aeroplane, and is calculated using the formula

$$R = \frac{V^2}{g \tan \phi}$$

where R = radius of turn in feet (metres)
V = velocity in feet (metres) per second
g = gravity (32.2ft/sec² or 9.81m/sec²)
ϕ = angle of bank (directly related to g).

The table below gives turn radii in thousnds of feet for various combinations of speed and g.

Effect of "G"

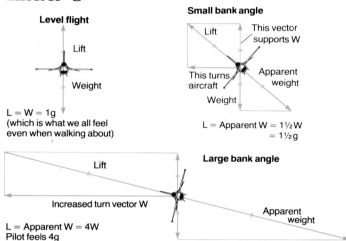

Level flight

Lift

Weight

L = W = 1g
(which is what we all feel even when walking about)

Lift

Increased turn vector W

L = Apparent W = 4W
Pilot feels 4g

Small bank angle

Lift

This vector supports W

This turns aircraft

Apparent weight

Weight

L = Apparent W = 1½W
= 1½g

Large bank angle

Apparent weight

Top left: In level flight, the 1g of gravity acts vertically down, and is balanced by lift acting upwards. **Top right:** in a turn, a sideways motion is imparted, which combines with gravity to produce a force vector. The weight of the aeroplane appears to increase as a result of the sideways force acting on it. To hold the turn, the aeroplane is banked to an angle at which lift directly opposes the combined pulls of turn and gravity. **Above:** the tighter the turn, the greater the sideways force imparted.

Speed in knots	Acceleration (g)							
	2g	3g	4g	5g	6g	7g	8g	9g
100	.51	.31	.23	.18				
200	2.05	1.25	.92	.72	.60			
300	4.60	2.82	2.06	1.63	1.35	1.15		
400	8.18	5.01	3.66	2.89	2.40	2.05	1.79	
500	12.79	7.83	5.72	4.52	3.75	3.20	2.79	2.48
600	18.41	11.27	8.24	6.51	5.39	4.61	4.02	3.57
700	25.06	15.34	11.21	8.86	7.34	6.27	5.47	4.86
800	32.73	20.04	14.64	11.57	9.59	8.19	7.15	6.34
900	41.42	25.36	18.53	14.64	12.14	10.36	9.04	8.03
1,000	51.14	31.31	22.88	18.08	14.98	12.79	11.16	9.91

Radius of Turn/Rate of Turn

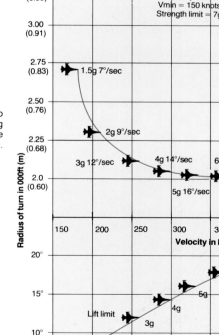

Angles of Bank for G Forces

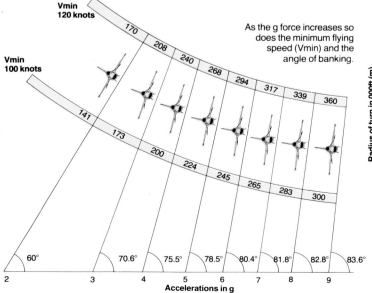

Vmin 120 knots

170 208 240 268 294 317 339 360

Vmin 100 knots

141 173 200 224 245 265 283 300

As the g force increases so does the minimum flying speed (Vmin) and the angle of banking.

60° 70.6° 75.5° 78.5° 80.4° 81.8° 82.8° 83.6°

2   3   4   5   6   7   8   9
Accelerations in g

Above: The forces encountered in a turn are measured as multiples of the force of gravity, or g. As g increases, so does the angle of

bank and the apparent weight of the aeroplane. More lift is needed to maintain flight and at high g loads minimum speed increases.

Above: Here we compare turn radius and turn rate for a fighter with a minimum flying speed of 150 knots and a strength limit of

7g. Both radius and rate of turn are best at around 400 knots; this is called corner velocity. The best speed for manoeuvre is 400-450kts.

Examination of the table shows a law of diminishing returns. The radius does not decrease in direct proportion to g. At 500 knots the 1g difference between 4g and 5g gives a radius advantage of about 1,200ft (365m), whereas the 1g difference between 8g and 9g at the same speed reduces to barely 300ft (91m). The most critical factor in turn radius is thus initial speed. More important than radius of turn, for reasons which will become clear later, is rate of turn. The following table shows rate of turn in degrees per second (rounded off) and that the rate of

Speed in knots	Acceleration							
	2g	3g	4g	5g	6g	7g	8g	9g
100	19	31	42	53				
200	9	15	21	27	32			
300	6	10	14	18	22	25		
400	5	8	11	13	16	19	22	
500	4	6	8	11	13	15	17	20
600	3	5	7	9	11	13	14	16
700	3	4	6	8	9	11	12	14
800	2	4	5	7	8	9	11	12
900	2	3	5	6	7	8	10	11
1,000	2	3	4	5	6	8	9	10

turn also operates on a law of diminishing returns. Its importance is, however, shown in the fig. 3 graph of turning radius against speed for a fighter with a minimum flying speed of 150 knots and a strength limitation of 7g. The initial downward curve is the aerodynamic limit imposed by the minimum flying speed. It is very noticeable that the radius of turn decreases slowly with

increased g, reducing from 2,700ft (823m) at 1.5g to just over 2,000ft (609m) at 7g, where structural strength becomes the limiting factor. From this point the radius of turn increases very sharply indeed.

What is significant is the rate of turn, which rises rapidly from 7°/sec at 1.5g at 184 knots to 19°/sec at 7g and 397 knots. Once at the structural limit, the rate of turn decreases, but slowly compared with the increase in turn radius, to 17°/sec at 450 knots and 15°/sec at 500 knots. Provided that the fighter has sufficient specific excess power to sustain the turn at 7g it can be seen that its best speed in a dogfight lies in the 400 to 450 knots region, where both radius and rate of turn are at their best. This is known as the "corner velocity".

The reason that rate of turn is usually more important than radius of turn is that an attacking fighter pilot needs to pull lead (pronounced leed) (aiming the nose of the aircraft ahead of the enemy) long enough to track his target and open fire, while in defence he needs to generate as much angle-off as possible to make himself a difficult target. In either case he is trying to haul the nose of his fighter around the horizon as fast as possible. (However, a missile-equipped fighter with a small radius of turn may be as well off as a high wing loaded aircraft with high rate of turn but enormous radius; weapon fit and capability are factors here.)

Having dealt with horizontal turns, we must now consider the vertical. A fighter performing a horizontal turn in which both velocity and g remain constant will describe a perfect circle. In the vertical, this will be affected by gravity, producing an egg-shaped figure. The 1g of gravity will reduce the radius of the top and increase it

Flight Performance Envelope

(Typical minimum flying speed at sea level 120 knots without using flaps or other high lift devices)

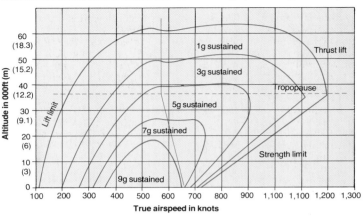

at the bottom, although the loading on the aeroplane remains the same. In practice the egg-shape will become even more pronounced, as the fighter will lose speed as it climbs towards the top, and gain speed going down the other side. Thus the velocity component of this manoeuvre will change and the consequent variations in turn radii at top and bottom will

Above: The abilities of a fighter are often illustrated in the form of a flight performance envelope. Here we show a series of envelopes for sustained performance at various g loadings. It will be noticed that there is a distinct "kink" in the envelopes in the transonic region. This is due to the slowing effects of wave drag. The normal limits are lift, thrust, and strength.

Manoeuvre Envelope 4g at 400 Knots Showing Effects of Gravity

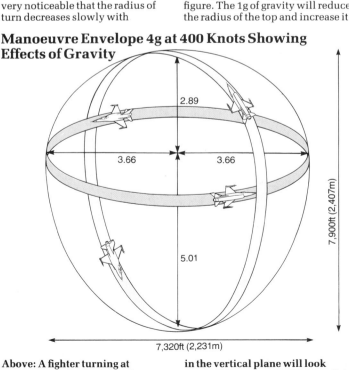

Above: A fighter turning at constant g and velocity in the horizontal plane through 360° will fly around a perfect circle. The same manoeuvre performed in the vertical plane will look much different, as the flight path is distorted by gravity. The radius of turn over the top reduces and the radius underneath increases.

become even more pronounced.

It would be helpful now to examine the chart of a flight performance envelope. This is a chart of speed/height on which are plotted lines which define the performance boundaries of a particular aircraft. In fact there is a series of performance boundaries, or envelopes, contained one within the other. These outline the g limitations, starting with 1g, which is essentially straight and level flight, through to 9g, which covers a small low-level area in the high transonic speed range.

Starting from the left hand, low speed area, we have an ascending line curving upwards. This is the line denoting minimum flying speed and is an aerodynamic limitation. As it curves over the top, it outlines the maximum altitude that can be achieved in normal flight. The line then curves down towards the point where maximum speed is achieved. This limitation is caused by lack of thrust. We then reach the point at which maximum speed is achieved. This is where thrust equals drag and the aeroplane can

go no faster. In some cases the thrust/drag curves cross at higher speeds, but structural and kinetic heating considerations come into play. Finally the line breaks sharply back on itself, down to sea level. This is a strength limitation. The average Mach 2-capable fighter cannot be allowed to exceed Mach 1.05 to Mach 1.25 at sea level.

The inner envelopes outlining sustained g limits show how the flight performance envelope is reduced by the need to manoeuvre. Another factor which considerably reduces overall limits is the amount of ironmongery hung beneath the fighter. A Phantom carrying four Sparrow AAMs is capable of Mach 2 at the tropopause. Hang one centreline and two underwing fuel tanks on it and the maximum speed reduces to Mach 1.7; at the same time its ceiling is reduced by nearly 10,000ft (3,047m).

All flight performance envelopes should be examined with caution. As we have just seen, external stores reduce maximum performance. In addition they can reduce the maximum g limit which

restricts manoeuvre capability. Finally, a Phantom equipped for a patrol demanding long endurance can carry nearly 22,046lbs (10 tonnes) of fuel. Having burnt off say 17,636lbs (8 tonnes) its wing loading towards the end of the mission will be considerably lighter and its performance much improved, especially if it has jettisoned the drag-inducing external tanks along the way.

Above and below: The F-4 Phantom is an incredibly versatile piece of hardware. It is rapidly convertible from strike to reconnaissance to interceptor roles, and can carry a vast and varied array of weaponry over considerable distances. Though designed mainly as a jack of all trades, it has proved surprisingly successful in the air superiority role when correct tactics are used.

Threats and Tasks

It is very easy to think of air fighting as an end in itself. After all, if one country is at war with another it obviously behoves the air forces on both sides to inflict as much damage on each other as possible at every opportunity. Or does it?

History seems to indicate that it does not. In the early summer of 1940, the *Luftwaffe* mounted *Frei-jagd*, or fighter sweeps over southern England, with the intention of tempting the Royal Air Force to come up and fight. In the summer of 1941, the Royal Air Force flew *Rodeos* over Northern France. A *Rodeo* was a fighter sweep of up to 72 aircraft. Neither *Frei-jagd* nor *Rodeo* was accompanied by bombers. The result in both instances was the same: the defending fighters stayed out of harm's way and let the intruders wear out their engines

without interruption. The fighter sweeps used valuable fuel and suffered attrition from accidents. They also provided target practice for the ground defences. The defending fighters could thus deplete the enemy at no risk by not accepting battle, whereas had they intercepted they would certainly have caused more damage but at great risk to themselves.

The same principle holds good today. The main difference is in the vastly increased effectiveness of the ground defences, which would make the old-fashioned fighter sweep prohibitively expensive.

This bears out our contention in the introduction that the role of air power is to support surface forces by causing as much damage to the other side and preventing them doing the same to you. One man's task is another man's threat, tasks and threats being the opposite

sides of the same coin. Air combat arises from the need to assist tasks and counter threats.

TASKS OF AN AIR FORCE

What are the tasks of an air force in wartime? First, reconnaissance. This is required to give timely (whether in the stratetic or tactical sense) and accurate information on the location, composition and activities of enemy forces. Ideally, it should cover the areas of interest of the ground and air commanders, and be of continuous nature to build up an intelligence picture, to gather information on potential targets and to help in deciding what to do next.

Information is gathered by three means: photography, electronic surveillance, and infra-red detection. Satellites in space can be of assistance but obviously have

limitations, otherwise the United States and the Soviet Union would have phased out their reconnaissance aircraft by now. Reconnaissance sorties fall into two groups: Mach 3 at 70,000ft (21,334m) or more and Mach 1 at 250ft (76m) or less. Both categories demand interception; and the second category might need fighter protection.

Secondly comes battlefield interdiction and close air support. This implies decisive intervention in the land battle, even though modern surface to air missiles make this an extremely risky proposition. Battlefield interdiction, whether by fixed-wing aircraft or helicopters, will be with us for some time yet.

The third task is supply route interdiction. Modern mechanised armies are very dependent on their supplies, particularly POL (petrol,

Above: One thing that aeroplanes do superlatively well is to make life miserable for enemy ground forces. Here a Mirage F1 demonstrates its awesome firepower at a ground target, letting fly with a devastating salvoe of unguided rockets. Troops would feel most unhappy on the receiving end!

Below: The most specialised tank destroyer ever built, the A-10 Thunderbolt II is capable of adding its quota of mayhem to the enemy on the ground. It can deliver an incredible variety of ordnance. Criticised for its lack of round-the-clock capability, experiments have been made with infra-red detection for night use.

oil, lubricants). The most efficient method of bulk supply is by rail, but not only are railways extremely vulnerable to air attack (to say nothing of the trains themselves) but they often do not go to where they are most wanted. Roads are less vulnerable to air attack; makeshift repairs are easy and quick and short detours around damaged areas are often possible. Furthermore, road traffic can theoretically travel well spaced to present a poor target to an attacker, although in practice this is difficult to achieve. Roads are most vulnerable where they cross a natural obstacle such as a river, or where several routes converge. These form "choke points" where attacks will be most effective.

The greatest obstacle to the performance of all tasks is opposition from the enemy air force. The fourth task, then, is to

Above: Paveway is a system of laser guidance for the precision delivery of munitions. The attacking aircraft can release from further away than would be the case with iron bombs and its exposure to defensive fire is thus lessened. Here a KMU-351 guided bomb hits a truck driver in the left ear.

Below: The prime task of any air force in wartime is the support of the surface forces. Support takes many forms: 1: Reconnaissance is carried out at ultra-low or very high levels. 2: Close air support and battlefield interdiction, giving direct aid to the fighting troops on the ground. 3: Interdiction of enemy supply routes in the rear of the battle area. 4: Airfield strikes to reduce enemy air capability. 5: Deep penetration strikes on oil refineries, supply depots, and communication centres, also stretching air defences. 6: Anti-shipping and anti-submarine patrols, both by fixed wing aircraft and helicopters. 7: Troop carrying and air supply, which may also cover airborne operations. 8: Finally, the enemy must be hindered in, if not prevented from, carrying out all these functions by the attainment of air superiority.

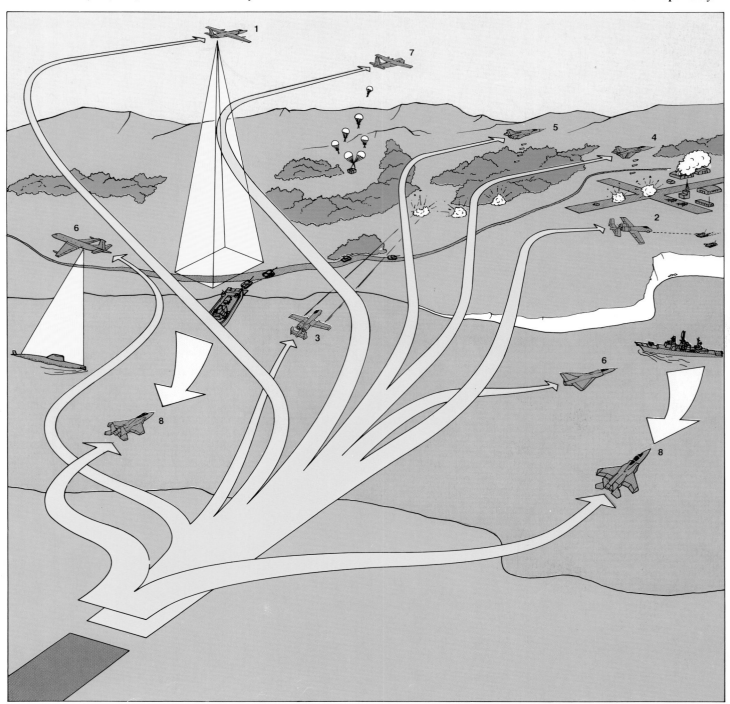

Above: The vulnerability of runways to air attack and the proliferation of airfield denial weapons has led to alternatives being sought. Here a Jaguar fighter-bomber takes off from a British motorway.

Below: USAF F-4 Phantoms take off from a highway. This will serve as a temporary expedient, but the logistics problems of operating large numbers of fighters from such temporary bases is formidable indeed.

Above: Swedish Viggens on a snow-covered road. Operation away from fixed bases was part of the original Viggen concept. It was therefore designed to embody exceptional short-field performance.

Below: Su-24 Fencers of Frontal Aviation are depicted taking out a runway. Often described as the most lethal warplane in the inventory of the Soviets, the Su-24 has much the same capability as the US Air Force's F-111.

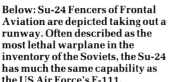

knock out his airfields. Unless the enemy uses nuclear rockets, this is easier said than done; perhaps "disrupt" would be a better term. Even in wartime, aircraft spend far more time on the ground than off it. Consequently airfields are the most heavily defended and protected targets. Aircraft are hidden in hardened shelters which are so spaced that an attacker can go for only one at a time. A series of attacks is necessary, and likely to prove expensive. Hitting a hardened shelter is no guarantee of success; it may be empty.

Runways are much easier to hit, but apart from the unlikely event of catastrophic damage being caused, quick reaction repair teams can have them serviceable again within hours. Besides which, many aircraft in service today can operate from half a runway, taxiways at a pinch, or even firm surfaces. It has been suggested that motorways could be used to

operate jets; this might be a desperation measure indeed, as the logistic problems of keeping even a small detachment of modern aircraft operational away from a fully equipped airfield are thought – maybe wrongly – to be formidable. It has often been suggested that the Harrier could be operated away from anything remotely resembling an airfield, but the logistic problems still apply. The logistic problems of supporting any fixed base are many; the Harrier retains the option of deploying dispersed as a survival measure.

Possibly the Harrier's greatest operational strength is that it is virtually impossible to render its airfield unusable by any means. But having said all this, rendering an enemy airfield unusable for several hours may well prove profitable in a critical situation if it can be carried out economically. The Harrier's vital difference is

Above: Two multi-million-dollar F-15 Eagles being afforded about as much protection as if they were in a garden shed! Air base dispersal is arguably more cost-effective than mere shelter-hardening.

Below: Who needs runways? The ultra-short takeoff, vertical landing Harrier can operate from anywhere able to supply it with fuel, weapons and spares. The Harrier can keep flying when all others are grounded.

that the enemy cannot know where it is.

Both supply route interdiction and airfield attacks are likely to take place simultaneously, crossing the enemy lines on a narrow frontage to swamp the ground defences on a local basis before fanning out to strike at individual targets. The entire flight is likely to be made at very low level.

The fifth task of an air force is deep penetration bombing. Profitable targets are oil refineries, transport and communications centres, munition factories and military bases. Low level flight consumes fuel at an enormous rate; part of a deep penetration flight must therefore be made at high level to attain the necessary range, even though the final dash to the target may well be made at low level. This is known as a Hi-Lo-Hi flight profile.

The sixth task is anti-shipping

and anti-submarine operations. Anti-shipping strike profiles depend entirely on the distance between base and target; low and fast at short range; high and fast at long range with possibly a low level attack at the end. Anti-submarine operations are by their very nature flown at economical altitudes and speeds on the way to the patrol area, reducing to low and slow when they reach it.

The seventh task of an air force is the unglamorous but vital job of troop and supply carrying. There is little to be added to this brief statement, except that it needs to be done rapidly, economically and safely.

The eighth and final task is a dual one: hinder the enemy from carrying out the first seven, and supply every assistance to friendly forces in their tasks. It can be seen that this is a tall order. The following pages show methods used in carrying it out.

Fighting Effectiveness

Having examined the threats to be countered and the tasks to be assisted we must now consider the qualities which make an outstanding fighter. The first question that arises is the combat environment in which the fighter will be called upon to operate.

The term "air combat" conjures up a vision of aircraft wheeling and darting against a clear blue sky to the accompaniment of thunderous afterburners, with smoky missile trails curving relentlessly in pursuit of their prey. If this was the whole picture, fighter characteristics could be clearly and easily defined.

Unfortunately the overall picture is much more complicated. The cloud-laden skies of Central Europe would, for example, restrict visual fighting. Even on the clearest day, night must fall. But come rain, shine or darkness, the war must go on. Poor weather conditions or darkness will assist attackers to penetrate defences undetected. Fighters must therefore have sufficient capability to operate effectively at night or in marginal weather conditions. The term "all-weather fighter" has been with us many years. In practice the aircraft that can fly and fight in all weather conditions, including blizzards, has yet to be designed; but if the enemy can fly, the defending fighters must be able to counter his aircraft.

DETECTION AND IDENTIFICATION

Timely interception is totally dependent on two factors: early detection and positive identification. Defence against air attack consists not only of fighters in the air, but a fully integrated system which combines radar detection and ground control, not to mention air-to-ground defences, which are outside our scope.

The speed of modern aircraft makes early detection vital if a threat is to be met in the time available. An overlapping chain of ground radar stations is thus essential. Airborne Warning and Control System (AWACS) aircraft provide a valuable extra facility with their ability to peer far over the normal horizon to detect low-level incoming raids. In theory nothing should slip through the net. But, to misquote Robbie Burns, "the best laid plans of mice, men, and Air Force Commanders gang oft agley!"

Radar detection systems are vulnerable. Their very value makes them prime targets for conventional air attack or surface to surface missile attack. Electronic countermeasures (ECM) will also be used against detection and communication systems. The air battle will therefore be preceded by and fought against the background of the invisible battle of the black boxes. Electronic systems and counter systems are now very clever indeed. Opinions differ as to the effectiveness of current ECM against the

Above: Three Eagles overfly a fairy-tale Schloss in a typical Central European scene. But even the best all-round fighter has problems in Europe's weather.

Below: The Boeing E-3A AWACS is the eyes of NATO and a prime target for the WARPAC forces. Its cost and potential (and problems) are enormous.

tremendously sophisticated computerised detection systems of the present day, but it would probably be fair to speculate that the performance of both detection and communication systems is likely to be degraded in a major war.

Running detection a very close second in priority is positive identification. This can be done electronically by the detection system which automatically interrogates the Identification Friend or Foe (IFF) system of the unidentified machine (bogey). If the correct response is received it can be positively identified as friendly. If not, it is enemy. Or is it? Could it not be a friendly aircraft with a damaged or unserviceable transponder? A device called TISEO (Target Identification System Electro-Optical) might be able to supply the answer. Slaved to the radar, it uses televisual and light enhancement techniques to project an image of the bogey onto a small screen, from well beyond normal visual range. From this,

positive visual identification may be made. Unless a dense cloud is in the way!

AWACS may well be better. Flying at medium/high altitudes well back from the battle area, its 240-mile-plus (400km+) radar reach might have tracked the intruder from a start point well beyond where any friendly machine could be, which would give positive identification as hostile.

AWACS aircraft are the most expensive flying machines ever built and they have a tremendous capability to influence events. Thus they also form prime targets and must be protected by fighter cover. They also have a certain measure of self-protective capability. Mainly this is in the form of countermeasures, but if a direct threat can be identified, AWACS simply turns and beetles off in the opposite direction at over 500 knots. Just five minutes or so gives an extra pursuit distance of 50 miles (80km), or 100 miles

(160km) on the round trip for a manned attacker. This has two effects: it may run the attacker dangerously low on fuel and it increases enormously the chance of him being intercepted. Long-range SAMs, such as SA-5 and SA-10, are another matter.

One factor which militates against electronic wizardry is confusion. Let us take the worst case – a full scale war in Central Europe. Dozens if not hundreds of aircraft will be flying in a relatively small space of air at the same time. As the first attack materialises the situation will be clear cut; friendlies over here, the enemy over there. Within minutes the two opposing air forces will merge and the situation will become confused. It is tempting to speculate that the confusion will be in direct proportion to the numbers of aircraft involved. Whether AWACS, with all its electronic magic working overtime, will be able to keep track of this complex situation in the face of intense ECM must be open to question.

This is the environment in which a modern fighter must operate; in all possible weather conditions night or day, to a sustained background of ECM and in a confused situation.

What then are the requirements of a modern fighter? Modern combat aircraft are extremely costly. One type of aeroplane for one job is no longer a viable proposition for even the richest air force. The most successful aircraft of recent times has been the Phantom, which successfully filled the interception, strike, interdiction and reconnaissance roles for many years, operating from aircraft carriers as well as land bases. Designed as an "all-rounder", its weakness was exposed in the Vietnam War; as an air superiority fighter it was not so effective particularly in the

case of the F-4B and C versions.

Nowadays the priorities have altered. Air superiority has moved ahead of strike capability. Two distinct trends have emerged: the long-range stand-off interceptor and the dedicated air superiority fighter, both with secondary capabilities as strike aircraft. These are typified by the F-14 Tomcat and Tornado F.2 in the first category, and the F-15 Eagle and F-16 Fighting Falcon in the second.

To see how these trends have emerged, it is necessary to start with the saying, "Combat is the ultimate (and the unkindest) judge". If the history of air combat illustrates one thing clearly, it is that the theoreticians usually get it wrong! It is therefore unsound to draw conclusions from contemporary hardware capabilities, since an enemy usually has ideas of his own! From the "stick-and-string" era to the present day, do any consistent trends emerge? And if so, is there any justification for saying that they no longer apply?

VALUE OF SURPRISE

A detailed examination of aerial victories from 1914 to the present day reveals one startling fact. Something like four out of every five aircraft shot down by fighters never saw their assailant until too late, if at all! During World War I a pilot frequently knew he was in a fight but failed to see his assailant pull in behind him. Many of the early aces, and McCudden in particular, told of carefully stalking an unsuspecting victim. In the skies over Vietnam, a pilot's first intimation that he was under attack was often when his tailpipe blew up! An exception was the massed daylight bomber raids of World War II, when bomber pilots almost always knew that they were under attack but were not free to manoeuvre against it.

Above: Prototype Tornado F-2 seen here armed with Skyflash AAMs. The RAF needs a long-range interceptor able to engage multiple targets at a distance.

Below: The F-14 Tomcat represents the top end of the fighter market. Its greatest strength lies in its over 100 miles (160km) range AIM-54 Phoenix.

The most important attribute of a modern fighter is its ability to achieve surprise. Its second most important attribute is to avoid being surprised. The third most important requirement is to have sufficient strength numerically to match the enemy in the air. Numerical parity on the ground is not enough. Many instances have occurred in the past where qualitatively superior fighters have been vanquished by superior numbers. The classic historical example was the German Me 262 jet fighter in 1944-5. It totally outclassed anything in the Allied inventory, yet was clawed from the skies by lots of inferior hardware.

Western theory has for many years gone for quality rather than quantity. This is sound provided that the numerical imbalance is not too great. The weapons fit also affects the balance: a Lightning with two missiles is outclassed by an F-15 or F-4 with eight. And the quality of the weapons carried can also affect the balance.

The fourth requirement is the ability to outmanoeuvre an opponent to gain a firing position. The historical justification for this is that, whereas only one-fifth of aerial victories are gained at this stage (which accounts for it being so low in the order of priorities), one-fifth of all aerial victories still adds up to a considerable total. The ability to outmanoeuvre an opponent is probably the most discussed area of air combat, and includes all the exciting factors such as speed, rate of climb and so on. The fact that it comes only fourth in the order of priorities does not mean that it is unimportant, just that it is not as important as is popularly supposed. To put matters into their

Below: The F-16 Fighting Falcon was an attempt to break out of the circle of rising costs. The "nice to have" gadgets were eliminated and a fine dogfighter emerged.

correct perspective, the capability of the aeroplane in the manoeuvre phase is nowhere near as important as the capability of the pilot to make the best use of the aeroplane he has been given.

The final requirement is the ability to obtain kills from fleeting chances. Historically this ability has always existed, even if few pilots were marksmen enough to exploit it fully. When fighters began to be armed with missiles only, much of this capability was lost. The semi-active radar homing Sparrow achieved a probability of kill (PK) per launch of 8 to 10 per cent in Vietnam, and was difficult if not impossible to use in close combat. The heat-seeking Sidewinder was better with a PK of about 15 per cent, but also suffered from a minimum range limitation.

The latest version of Sidewinder, AIM-9L, scored nearly 70 per cent in the Falklands, although it should be remembered that there were no big fighter-versus-fighter engagements; no dogfights as such. No firm data areavailable from the Arab/Israeli wars, but missile PKs there are believed to be higher than the Americans achieved over Vietnam. With no gun, some fighters, particularly the early USAF and late USN Phantoms, lost much of their effectiveness.

The weaponry of a fighter should be usable at all ranges and all opportunities.

We can examine the prime requirements of a modern fighter in order, taking the ability to achieve surprise and the ability to avoid being surprised together, as they too are the opposite sides of the same coin.

ACHIEVING AND AVOIDING SURPRISE

The perfect way of achieving surprise would be to have an invisible aeroplane. Unfortunately this not only means invisible to the human eye but also invisible to electronic and infra-red detection. Invisiblity to human sight is easily achieved using radar for detection and long-range missiles as weapons. A hostile aeroplane can then be killed from beyond visual distance. But there are snags.

Firstly, the missiles. Ideally these should be "fire-and-forget" weapons which home onto their targets without further assistance from the launching aircraft, which then becomes free to manoeuvre as necessary. The AIM-54 Phoenix carried by the F-14 Tomcat is a good example of this type and has on test shot down drones at ranges exceeding 100 miles (160km). Its drawbacks are twofold. It is an active radar homer; its emissions can be detected by the target and appropriate action taken. It is also the most costly air-to-air missile ever built. To fight a war entirely with AIM-54s would be prohibitively expensive.

Shorter-ranged and much less expensive is the Sparrow which uses semi-active radar homing

Above: The "fire and forget" AIM-54 Phoenix. Shooting down unseen targets would appear to lack job satisfaction.

Missile Homing Methods

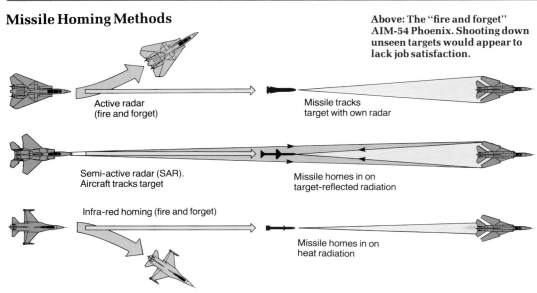

Active radar (fire and forget)

Missile tracks target with own radar

Semi-active radar (SAR). Aircraft tracks target

Missile homes in on target-reflected radiation

Infra-red homing (fire and forget)

Missile homes in on heat radiation

Above: The three types of missile homing. Top: the active radar homer is a "fire and forget" weapon, has long range and is costly. Centre: the semi-active radar homer needs tracking by the launching aircraft to home. This makes the launching fighter vulnerable. Bottom: the heat homer is a "fire and forget" weapon, very accurate, and relatively cheap. **Below: The drawback to semi-active radar homing is the need for target illumination by the fighter's radar. The attacker becomes vulnerable to a "fire and forget" missile in return.**

Radar-homing Hazards

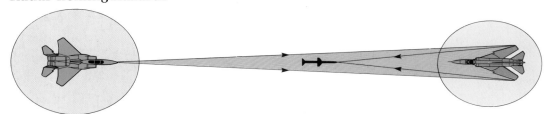

Fighter beyond visual distance tracks SARH missile, illuminating itself to enemy detectors

ECM may enable enemy fighter to avoid missile. Also could have time to launch missile counter-attack

(SARH) and relies on the parent fighter to illuminate the target by radar during the time of flight. The missile then homes on the reflected radiation emissions. For many reasons this may be tactically undesirable, not least if the target is carrying a "fire-and-forget" missile: in the case of a head-on attack it may acquire its attacker visually and launch its weapon just a second or two before being itself destroyed. Swapping one for one is not the best way to fight a war!

It is possible to build an infra-red homing missile for beyond visual distance interception. This would be ideal except for target discrimination. With the flight time exceeding one minute, a friendly aircraft could stray across its path and present a bigger infra-

red source than the original, thereby probably causing the missile to switch targets. So far, no-one has designed a missile which can distinguish between the various national insignia!

Invisibility lies in the use of radar for detection. While the fighter pilot maintains invisibility by remaining out of visual range, directly he switches on the radar, he lights up a huge electronic beacon which informs enemy detectors of his position, his identity, and possibly even his intentions. Physically he is invisible: electronically he is revealing himself to all.

The obvious conclusion is that much air fighting is likely to take place visually. After all, even if ECM were successful enough to negate all electronic detection and

communication systems (hardly likely), nothing would stop a fighter pilot strapping his aeroplane on his back and seeking out the enemy as did Bishop or McCudden during World War I. Fighters therefore need to remain undetected at visual ranges.

SMALL IS BEAUTIFUL

A priority is to have the smallest aeroplane capable of doing the job. From the head-on aspect, a MiG-21 is nearly invisible at two miles (3.2km). Not so the mighty F-15 Eagle, which by fighter standards is enormous. Even more important than size is smoke. Some western engines at certain settings emit a distinct smoke trail which can be seen from great distances. Even worse, it is a direct aid to

identified by the enemy.

Various tactical ploys can be used to reduce the chance of visual acquisition. These will be considered later. The next most important factor affecting surprise is to have a fast cruising speed in the battle area. Thirty years ago, maximum speeds of Mach 2 were in the offing, and the experts were generally agreed that Mach 5 was just around the corner. At the time this seemed very important. During World War II and the Korean War maximum speeds were frequently used in combat. There was little difference between maximum speed and combat cruising speed. Then almost overnight maximum speeds more than doubled. More importantly, the difference between combat cruise and maximum speed became a factor of between two and three instead of the previous 20 per cent or so. However, in practice the colossal top speeds proved unusable in combat. Top speeds take time to attain and, in doing so, aircraft guzzle fuel at an alarming rate. Maximum speeds can only be sustained for a few minutes at most. Even worse, the fighter at maximum speed can do little other than fly in a straight line. Manoeuvre becomes practically impossible.

What fighters need is the highest possible cruising speed which can be sustained without depleting fuel reserves too rapidly. As a generalisation the average cruising speed of just about all modern fighters lies between Mach 0.8 and Mach 0.9. Tailless deltas seem to have a slight edge in this department; maybe the French

Head-on Visibility Comparison

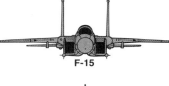

Above: The MiG-21 from head-on is nearly invisible at two miles. Not so the mighty F-15 Eagle. In the dogfight small is beautiful.

Above and below: The A-4 Skyhawk is often used as a threat aircraft in dissimilar air combat training. Top, an F-14 of VF 126 adjusts its wing sweep for maximum rate turn. Below, it

have the right idea.

Perhaps this is the place to touch on the wonders of swing-wings. Swing-wings give a very efficient cruising speed which extends the range of the aircraft greatly. The trouble is that it is a very slow cruise by comparison with traditional fighters. No swing-wing aircraft will enter an area where enemy fighters may be encountered with its wings extended. They will be swept back for faster cruise. Then, once in contact with the enemy, the swing-wing fighter is penalised by having to haul tons of pivot around the sky. The computerised wing-spread mechanism of the F-14 Tomcat may partly offset this

passes close inboard of the A-4 with wings fully swept back preparatory to accelerating out and repositioning. The angle of wing sweep can indicate energy status of the Tomcat.

disadvantage but carries a built-in penalty of its own. An opponent in close combat with a Tomcat will be able to see its approximate energy status at a glance by looking at the degree of wing sweep, and the extra weight is undesirable once combat is joined.

However, to return to the main point, if a fighter can maintain a higher cruising speed in the combat area than his opponent, his chances of achieving surprise are considerably increased and his chances of avoiding surprise are reduced.

Finally, to avoid being surprised, a good view from the cockpit, particularly to the rear, is essential. World War II saw the emergence of "teardrop" canopies which gave excellent rearward vision. Then with the accent on attaining enormous maximum speeds, canopies began to be faired into the fuselage. The view to the rear deteriorated and many pilots of many nations died in combat as result of not seeing an attacker closing from astern. Reason has since prevailed and the latest Western fighters have excellent all-round visibility.

EFFECTIVE FORCE SIZE

This is the next priority on our list. It is essential to possess numerical strength sufficient to meet the enemy in *adequate* strength every time he comes up. To do this it is not necessary or even particularly desirable to outnumber the enemy on the ground, as this only provides targets. The term "adequate strength" needs clarification. If a fighter can take off

Pilot's Visibility From Cockpit

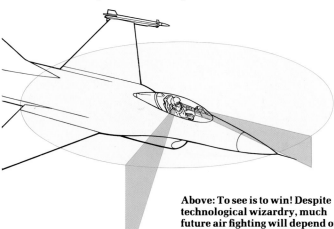

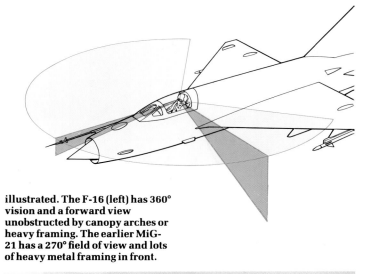

Above: To see is to win! Despite technological wizardry, much future air fighting will depend on the human eyeball. The range of vision from the cockpits of two generations of fighters are illustrated. **The F-16 (left) has 360° vision and a forward view unobstructed by canopy arches or heavy framing. The earlier MiG-21 has a 270° field of view and lots of heavy metal framing in front.**

carrying four "beyond visual distance" missiles and achieve a 50 per cent kill rate with them every time; all other things being equal, that type of fighter can afford to be outnumbered three to one in the air because the odds reduce to evens before the close fighting starts. Furthermore, in such a contest an adversary's morale would suffer from consistently losing aircraft to an unseen assailant. The opposing pilots would feel threatened directly they approached the combat zone, whether or not there was a real threat present.

It is often overlooked that success in an air engagement can be gained without the destruction of the enemy. A strike force on its way to attack a surface target can be foiled by the menace of an attack. Loaded down with munitions the aircraft are sitting ducks. If they can be forced to jettison their warloads to survive, the interception has succeeded. If they are more determined, the attack forces them to light 'burner and expend precious fuel and time in evasive manoeuvring. This may equally ruin their attack. Fuel state has become a major factor in air combat. But to achieve results the interception must be made every time and sufficient numerical strength must be available to do it.

But maintaining that strength can be difficult. Modern fighters are very costly and budgets are limited. The United States made a clear attempt to break away from the treadmill of rising costs and produced the F-16 Fighting Falcon by cutting out many of the "nice to have" gadgets and reverting to a more austere approach. One of the "nice to have" gadgets was an engine! Twin-engined fighters are good in peacetime; if one engine fails the aircraft can often be recovered on the other. The same comment obviously applies in war, but to a lesser degree. Battle damage is potentially far more lethal than most forms of engine failure. Yet even in times of peace, it has never been established to the writer's knowledge that the attrition rate due to engine failure

Right: One engine or two? The Netherlands operates the F-104, F-5, and F-16. In peacetime, twin-engined safety is the cry. Yet the latest F-5 variant has a single.

on single-engined fighters is double that of twins.

Omitting an engine has several advantages. Initial cost is one; plus the extra cost of servicing and replacement. The size (and visible area) of the fighter is reduced, as is all the extra structural weight needed to mount two engines. Finally the fuel bill is almost halved. One could even cynically say that omitting an engine halves the likelihood of engine failure.

Nevertheless the Fighting Falcon is the best close-combat fighter in the world today, although its cost has increased as all the "nice to have" gadgets have been tacked back on, to give it real mission capability.

To return to the question of effective force size, it seems clear that the costly but very capable fighter is an essential. It is equally clear that once the confusion factor arises, it can be swamped by sheer numbers. The American Aggressor Squadrons, practising dissimilar air combat in their inexpensive F-5Es have consistently demonstrated this against the mighty F-15s. What appears to be needed is a mix of deadly stand-off interceptors such as Tornado

backed by twice or three times as many austere, dedicated dog-fighters. The total quantity will be determined by a combination of budgetary considerations and available high quality pilots. It is useless to achieve a large force at the expense of pilot quality; it merely produces a "target-rich environment" for the enemy.

The final quality needed is the ability to operate from a damaged airfield. For this, good short-field performance is required. Having lots of aeroplanes is useless if they are grounded by runway damage.

OUTMANOEUVRING AN OPPONENT

This is fourth in our list of priorities; fourth place out of five may not seem very important but it

should be remembered that our criteria are judged from the lessons of the past, and some of the past lessons are very recent. The ability to outmanoeuvre an opponent *is* important and will remain so until missiles reach the stage of development which has been so often promised but never fulfilled: able to track a target unerringly, following its every attempt at evasion, and knock it down every time. The lesson of history is that for every technological breakthrough a countermeasure is found. The commonsense approach to guided missiles is that history is sure to repeat itself and, while it does, manoeuvring combat is here to stay.

The manoeuvre phase of combat is the most spectacular part of air warfare and thus attracts the most interest. What qualities does a fighter need most in a dogfight? First, it needs a good rate of turn. Examination of the tables in the section on aerodynamics reveals that, as speed increases, the radius of turn becomes enormous. But turn radius is not so important, because the attacking fighter may be 2,000 to 3,000ft (600 to 900m) astern of its victim. Therefore it can continue to track its target as it closes even though incapable of matching the target aeroplane's radius of turn. The diagram shows

Left: Name of the game is dissimilar air combat. An Aggressor Squadron F-5E keeps station on an F-16 on their way to the exercise area.

Rate of Turn versus Radius of Turn

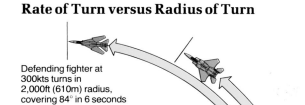

Defending fighter at 300kts turns in 2,000ft (610m) radius, covering 84° in 6 seconds

Right: More important than radius of turn is rate of turn. The faster fighter (500kts) turns through a wider radius than his slower (300kts) opponent, yet covers 90° in six seconds against his foe's 84°.

the target aeroplane at 300 knots is turning as tightly as possible at 4g with a radius of turn of just over 2,000ft (600m). The attacker, driving in at 500 knots, can manage a turn radius of only 3,200ft (975m), but is hauling his nose around the horizon at 15 degrees per second by comparison with the target's 14 degrees per second. The attacker in this situation has a slight but distinct manoeuvring advantage. This is why rate of turn is usually more important than radius of turn.

Returning to the rate of turn table, it can be seen that at the best manoeuvre combat speeds of today – which are at or just above the corner velocity – even an exceptional fighter would be hard-pressed to complete a full circle in less than 20 seconds, and 20 seconds in combat is an eternity. At high altitudes, where aerodynamic rather than structural considerations limit turning ability, horizontal turns take much, much longer.

Attacking fighter at 500kts turns on much wider radius (3,200ft/975m) and covers 90° in 6 seconds

G-FORCE "BLACKOUT"

Low altitudes, where the wings can grip the denser air, is the domain of heavy manoeuvring. Here, though, the fighting limitation becomes that of the pilot rather than the machine. The phenomenon of "blackout" has been known for many decades. The cause of "blackout", or more correctly "grey-out", is the g forces draining the blood away from the pilot's brain. As the g increases, so the pilot loses his colour perception and his vision takes on the appearance of a monochrome movie. This is followed by loss of peripheral vision, the tunnel vision effect, followed by complete loss of sight.

The degree to which this affects the pilot depends on his physical well-being. "Grey-out" can start at as low as 4g or as high as 7g for the same man on different days. From this we can deduce that the sustained 9g turn of the Fighting Falcon is purely defensive; to press home a successful attack the pilot must be in reasonable control of his

Above: The F-16 Fighting Falcon is probably the best fighter in the world at knife range. Contrails stream from the wingtips as the example illustrated pulls g.

fighter with the lowest wing-loading can turn the tightest, speed for speed. Wing loading notwithstanding, above corner velocity it is usually the slowest moving aeroplane that has the advantage in the turn.

The second quality a fighter needs is good acceleration, especially from low speeds where the 'burner is inefficient. As stated in the aerodynamics section, a fighter needs extra lift in a turning fight; it gains this by increasing its angle of attack, which creates extra drag which in turn bleeds off energy in the form of speed. This energy needs to be regained as rapidly as possible, which can be done through acceleration.

Advantage of Specific Excess Power

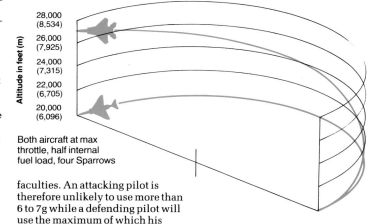

Altitude in feet (m)

28,000 (8,534)
26,000 (7,925)
24,000 (7,315)
22,000 (6,705)
20,000 (6,096)

Both aircraft at max throttle, half internal fuel load, four Sparrows

faculties. An attacking pilot is therefore unlikely to use more than 6 to 7g while a defending pilot will use the maximum of which his aeroplane is capable.

How does one achieve a good rate of turn? It is directly proportional to the amount of lift that the fighter can generate, and can be roughly measured in inverse proportion to the wing loading. The coefficient of lift of the wing plays a part; this depends on the aerofoil section; on the wing shape, and on high-lift devices, but basically it is true to say that the

Above: A high thrust/weight ratio is a tremendous asset to a modern fighter. At 20,000ft (6,096m) and Mach 0.9 a Phantom (with thrust/weight ratio approximately 0.84) turns at 4g without speed or height loss. By contrast, the F-15 Eagle, with a thrust/weight ratio exceeding unity, can gain no less than 7,100ft (2,164m) of height while matching the Phantom for speed and turn radius.

Acceleration figures are rarely published, simply because too many variable factors are involved. On the other hand it is reasonable to assume that acceleration is linked to the stated initial climb rate, and that the fighter with the highest initial climb rate has the best acceleration. This is, however, a rule of thumb only.

In manoeuvring combat, as so far stated, we need an aeroplane with an excellent rate of turn and sparkling acceleration. These two qualities oppose each other. To achieve good turning qualities an aeroplane needs a low wing loading – lots of wing to carry little weight. Acceleration demands a high thrust/weight ratio, the smallest possible aeroplane wrapped around the biggest possible engine, a small and thin inefficient wing with little drag and high wing loading. Any fighter is therefore a compromise.

OUTLASTING THE OPPONENT

The final manoeuvring quality is combat persistence. The lesson of history is that, as speeds have increased, time spent in manoeuvring combat has reduced. The use of afterburner is essential in a dogfight and a considerable amount of fuel needs to be preserved for the "bug out" (disengagement).

A pilot maintaining a 6g turn at 500 knots takes over a half a minute to turn through a full circle. At high altitude he may take over a minute. From this it can be deduced that the number of manoeuvres he can make during a fight – whether turns, climbs, or accelerations – is very limited. It is important to try to outlast an opponent in the fight; to make him break off first, because this is where he becomes very vulnerable.

The obvious way to achieve high combat persistence would be to pack the greatest possible amount of fuel into the fighter. But this makes for greater bulk and therefore more drag; and greater weight, not only of the fuel itself, but of the extra structure necessary to carry it. Not only does performance suffer but fuel is used at a greater rate in pushing all this extra drag and weight around the sky.

The answer which has emerged in recent years is "fuel fraction". This is the weight of internal fuel carried, expressed as a percentage of the clean take-off weight with the guns loaded. The optimum fuel fraction appears to be above 30 per cent. Twenty-six per cent produces a fighter that lacks combat persistence, while 34 per cent gives persistence for the penalty of lost performance.

KILLS FROM FLEETING OPPORTUNITIES

This is the final requirement of an outstanding fighter. History shows that scoring even one hit on a moving target is an exercise fraught with difficulty. Therefore each hit should be potentially lethal. Again the designers have been forced to compromise. World War I saw flimsy, canvas-covered biplanes using machine guns to shoot at each other, frequently without success. The rifle-calibre bullet could do little harm unless they struck somewhere vital and the vital spots were mainly limited to the engine, the pilot, and the highly explosive fuel tank.

World War II opened with the Royal Air Force using eight-gun fighters. The initial reasoning was to spray a lot of lead through a large area of sky to increase the probability of scoring a few hits,

with the hope that at least some bullets would strike somewhere vital. This was quickly amended to align all the guns on one spot, so that if the aim was true, a lot of hits would be scored. Satisfactory results were not always forthcoming; armour plate and self-sealing fuel tanks made aircraft less vulnerable to small calibre projectiles. Something larger and more deadly was needed.

By the end of the war, fighters of all the major combatant nations were using cannon, although the preferred American weapon was the 0.50 calibre heavy machine gun. Against fighters these weapons were all sufficiently effective. The Germans used very large 30mm, 50mm and 75mm cannon, but these were mainly to destroy heavy bombers. Two or three hits from 20mm shells were generally enough to sink a fighter.

The problem was the same in both World Wars; how to mount really deadly firepower in a fighter without appreciably penalising its fighting ability. This dilemma was thrown into clear relief in the Korean War, where large-scale air battles took place between F-86 Sabres and MiG-15s.

The Sabre was armed with six 0.50 calibre heavy machine guns delivering 110 rounds per second. The 0.50 projectile had excellent ballistic qualities; coupled with the high muzzle velocity of the gun, hits were often scored on MiG-15s at ranges of 400 to 500 yards (365m to 457m).

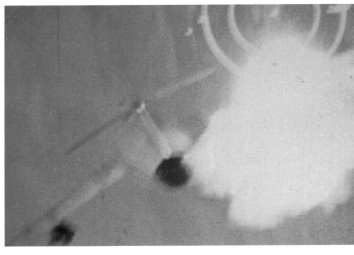

Above: A MiG-15 goes down under the guns of an F-86 Sabre over Korea. Despite the success of the American fighter, it's armament of six 0.5 machine guns was replaced by cannon.

Unfortunately for United Nations forces the MiG-15 was a tough aeroplane and often survived.

The armament of the Soviet-designed MiG was one 37mm and one or two 23mm cannon. The Russian guns had a relatively low muzzle velocity and a slow rate of fire. The time of flight of the shells was comparatively long; this made scoring hits on an evading target difficult.

The differing characteristics of the two types of cannon caused aiming problems. On the other

hand, just one or two hits on a Sabre usually inflicted mortal damage. The choice is clear: lots of small hits or one big one!

The advent of guided missiles in the 1950s promised to change things. They were expected to eliminate manoeuvring combat. They were to be able to follow an evading target and hit it at long range. They carried a warhead large enough to inflict lethal damage.

Unfortunately for the experts it didn't work out like that, for two reasons. First, the wonder weapons failed to perform as advertised. Second, countermeasures of varying effectiveness were devised. Two very unexpected effects emerged. The heat-homing missile, far from

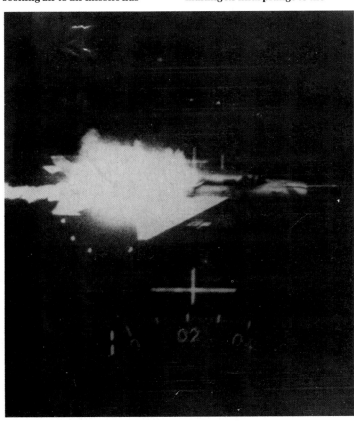

Below: The last moments of an Egyptian MiG-21 are captured by the gun camera of an Israeli Phantom. A direct hit from a heat-seeking air to air missile has caused catastrophic damage and an uncontrollable fire. Below right: the MiG, trailing smoke and flame, turns on its back before making its final plunge to the

ground. Every possible space in a modern fighter is packed with equipment, fuel and hydraulics, so that every hit is likely to damage something important. But flight stresses have caused them to be built strongly indeed, so the added vulnerability is to a degree offset by strength. Missiles need to be very destructive.

eliminating manoeuvring combat, actually increased the need to turn hard. Back in the old-fashioned gunfighting days, a widely used defensive ploy had been to open the throttle and dive away out of range. To do this against a heat missile merely presented a beautiful infra-red target. The defending pilot now had to turn as hard as possible to keep his hot exhaust away from the missile's seeker head.

Also, missiles had rather long minimum firing distances, at less than which they were unable to start homing. Consequently, gunless fighters sometimes found themselves embroiled in dogfights at ranges too close to launch.

It should not be forgotten that guns and missiles do not exist in isolation but – with the aeroplane, the pilot, the black boxes and the fighter control system – are merely the cutting edge of an integrated weapons system.

A look at the requirements met by the Tornado F.2 gives some idea of potential.
1. To counter mass-raid tactics employed to saturate the defences, the interceptor is required to carry as many air-to-air missiles as possible and its fire control system must have the ability to engage multiple targets in rapid succession.
2. The interceptor's weapon system must be highly resistant to jamming and must be able to operate with the minimum assistance from good early warning and control systems which may themselves be degraded by jamming.

The main weapon carried by Tornado is the Sky Flash semi-active radar homer. This "shoot-them-in-the-face" from beyond

Above: Guns in the sky! The 20mm M61A-1 cannon protruding from under the nose of this Phantom contrasts with the twin 23mm cannons in the tail turret of the TU-95.

visual distance missile has the drawback that it has to be illuminated all the way to the target. Ideally it should be a "fire-and-forget" missile, but while the fight remains at medium range (not long with closing speeds greater than 20 miles/32km per minute) it is likely to be very effective. Heat seekers close the gap between the medium range weapon and the gun. They are essentially visual-distance weapons, and have always given better results in combat than radar homers. But when the enemy is very close only the gun remains.

The gun as an air-to-air weapon remains a compromise. Most cannon are now based on the revolver principle developed by

Germany in the closing years of World War II. But, whereas in those days a fighter carried four cannon, the other weaponry of the current fighter reduces the available space down to two or even one. Aircraft are tougher than ever. The same problem holds: one large and very destructive hit, or several smaller ones?

Also, as fighting speeds have increased, so have shooting distances. In 1917, many victories were scored from less than 30 yards (30m). In 1945, 150 yards (140m) was considered close. Nowadays less than 300 yards (275m) is considered almost suicidal. To knock lumps off an adversary at close range is to build an FOD (foreign object damage) trap. The jet engine of the attacker

Below: Seen during a test firing from Tornado F-2, Skyflash is the most advanced semi-active radar-homing missile in the world, with snap up and snap down capability.

will ingest debris which will do it no good at all.

Modern fighters are unlikely to be knocked down by a single hit. Yet a fleeting chance gives little opportunity for many hits to be scored. The gun needs the highest possible rate of fire in order to put the greatest number of shells through the smallest possible space. Provided the aim is true, this gives the best chances of scoring multiple hits. Given that no more than two or three hits are likely to be scored on an evading or rapidly crossing target, the shell needs to be as lethal as possible, and that means large. Finally, in order to be effective at ranges out to 500 yards (450m), the shell needs the highest possible muzzle velocity and the best possible ballistic qualities.

These attributes fight each other and compromises are, as in most areas of air combat, necessary. Guns have a secondary role for ground strafing; this also cannot be ignored. The problems inherent in air-to-air gunnery will be discussed later.

DESIRABLE QUALITIES OF A GOOD FIGHTER

To summarise, the qualities of an outstanding fighter are as follows. It needs the cleverest possible electronics for long distance detection coupled with lots of "fire-and-forget" long range "shoot-them-in-the-face" type missiles. it needs good ECM and a secure communications system. It needs every possible device to warn the pilot of impending attack, including the elementary one of an all-round good view from the cockpit. Having all these things "built in", it still needs to be kept as small as possible.

It should have a high combat cruising speed – or good fuel economy at full military power would do at a pinch. It needs just the right fuel fraction to balance structural weight and combat persistence. It should be cheap, both to buy and to fly, and be very reliable. It should have excellent short-field capability. These qualities give numerical strength coupled with a high sortie rate.

It should have good manoeuvre capability, rate of climb and acceleration. A high maximum speed is not so important. It should carry as many short-range dogfight missiles as possible, plus a gun (or two) with the highest possible instantaneous rate of fire, coupled with the greatest possible muzzle velocity. Unfortunately for fighter designers, all these factors contradict each other.

Aircraft not engaged in defensive fighter operations might have to fight their way to and from the target. To this end aircraft fly in tactical formations which are a compromise between manoeuvrability, look-out for other fighters and vulnerability. They must have a defensive capability between aircraft and elements (see diagrams).

Air Combat – The Methods

The five distinct phases of air combat are not inevitable; combats have occurred – and will do so in the future – which have omitted certain phases when circumstances have rendered them unnecessary. The most extreme case of this would be an F-14 Tomcat detecting a single "bandit" at long range and in a favourable position for a Phoenix missile shot. The sequence would then reduce to detection-attack, omitting the closing phase. If the attack proved successful, manoeuvre and disengagement would have become redundant. At the other extreme, if two fighters in a confused melée became aware of each other simultaneously in a situation where neither had an advantge, detection would be followed immediately by manoeuvre.

DETECTION

A saying exists in the fighter fraternity, "The first to spot the enemy wins!" While this is an exaggeration, the ability to detect and identify a target before one is oneself detected and identified confers the initiative. But more is involved than air-to-air detection by the radar of individual fighters. The fighter controller, whether on the ground or airborne in an AWACS, has an important role to play.

Soviet Colonel Dubrove summed up the lessons of Vietnam and the Middle Eastern air wars in *Aviatsiya i Kosmonautika*, March 1978, in the following words:

"... responsibility for the outcome of combat was now evenly divided between the pilot and ground control facility, since airborne search equipment and the ground identification and guidance system possessed differing capabilities to detect a target and establish its identity. Smooth co-ordination and clear-cut distribution of duties betwen them predetermined the success of combat at the first stage.

"... Modes of conduct of search began to be more sharply divided into search over friendly territory and search in enemy airspace. In the first instance fighters ... were being monitored by friendly radar. The flyers were a component of the overall search system, and received up to the moment information when a hostile aircraft was detected. The pilot had time to analyse the situation and to make a considered decision.

"The situation became much more complex when the mission involved penetrating enemy airspace.... The initiative ... was on the side of the defenders if intensive jamming was not employed."

While many Western observers may feel that Colonel Dubrov is overstating the importance of the fighter controller, it should not be overlooked that the control system's picture of the situation is much wider than that of the individual pilot. The benefits are twofold. The controller can place his fighters in the best possible positions from which to start their own search. The fighter can therefore leave his radar on "standby" until the time comes to use it, rather than electronically reveal his presence by protracted use of the "search" mode. This should lead to rapid detection of the hostile force and immediate initiation of the closing/attack phases.

Also, the pilot of a single-seat fighter has two conflicting tasks. One is to monitor his own detection system. The other is to keep a sharp visual lookout for a bandit who may have evaded the detection net. Being led into position by the fighter controller eases his workload considerably. When the range closes to visual distance, on-board detection systems tell the pilot exactly where to look, which increases the possibility of early visual detection.

The probability of intense ECM has been stressed earlier. The possibility of airborne jamming giving away the approximate position of the jamming aircraft should not be entirely overlooked, however. Historically this has always been the case. Airborne ECM takes two forms: active and passive. Active ECM is an emission, the source of which can sometimes be approximately located. Passive ECM is, for instance, "chaff", tiny pieces of aluminium foil sized to enemy wavelengths which act as radar reflectors. As far back as 1943, German night fighters, operating in an intense ECM environment, adopted the ploy of flying to where the chaff clouds were densest, then searching visually.

The reverse of detection is avoidance of detection. How is this

Below: Despite the latest advances in detection equipment, searching visually remains very important. Here an F-15 pilot checks the blind spots astern and below his wingman. Mutual cross-cover is essential.

Direction of Responsibility for Search and Reporting

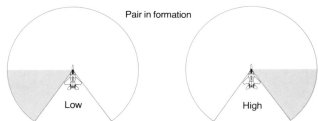

Pilots spend ¾ of their time searching their primary direction (unshaded), and ¼ searching secondary direction (shaded). All sightings are reported

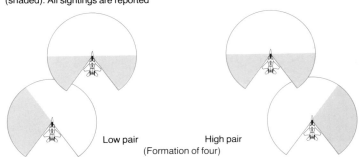

Above: Like everything else in air combat, visual search is a matter of teamwork. Each pilot's area of vision is divided into primary and secondary sectors. These areas vary according to the formation flown.

Above is shown the primary and secondary areas for a pair (top), and a four. Each pilot must search both far and near, and high and low. Rarely do threats appear at the same level, but up to 10,000ft (3,048m) high or low.

best achieved? Electronic detection systems can be foiled by countermeasures, but there is no guarantee that this will succeed. Electronic Intelligence (ELINT) aircraft will monitor enemy emissions and establish whether there are any gaps in the coverage which may be exploited. Radar signals travel pretty much in a straight line and have no over-the-horizon capability. A range of hills could create a blind spot in the radar coverage, the height of which would depend on the height of the hills and the distance between them and the radar station.

Very low flying is an excellent way of avoiding radar detection, although it has two inherent disadvantages. It exposes the fighter to ground defences, including small-arms fire, which even today cannot be discounted. Second, much of the pilot's attention is given to flying the aeroplane. Attack aircraft often have terrain-following radar, but fighters do not. Thus much of the pilot's attention is distracted from his primary task of seeking out the enemy. Airborne pusle-doppler radar has a look-down capability. The computer automatically screens out echoes that are moving in conformity with the flight path – houses, ground features – and shows only moving objects.

Below: An FB-111 streaks low over the wilderness. Terrain-following radar enables low-level strikes at night or in bad weather to be made. This capability sets the defences one of their more difficult problems.

Pulse-doppler radars "sort" received signals and eliminate non-targets, but some suffer from over-sensitivity. If a low-flying aircraft's passive detector picks up a pulse-doppler signal it informs the pilot that he has been detected. Fuel status and task priorities permitting, he can turn 90 degrees angle-off to the offending radar so that he is travelling in conformity with the flight path. The radar computer then hopefully removes him from the screen.

All the old rules of concealment dating from 1916 still apply. Do not silhouette the aircraft against cloud; attack if possible from the

Advantages/Disadvantages of Pulse-doppler Radar

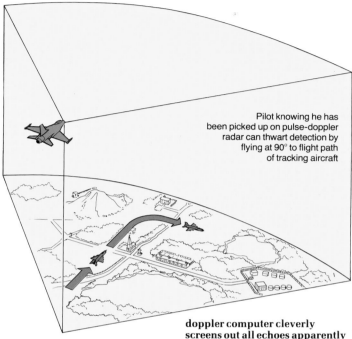

Pilot knowing he has been picked up on pulse-doppler radar can thwart detection by flying at 90° to flight path of tracking aircraft

Above: Pulse-doppler radar helps counter the low-level intruder. Ordinary radar directed downwards picks up a myriad echoes from the ground. Pulse-doppler computer cleverly screens out all echoes apparently moving in conformity with the flight path, and shows the rest, which are moving objects. But an object moving at 90° to the flight path is usually screened out also.

Sun; attack from astern. (It is ironic that the armament in a fighter invariably points forward but a high proportion of successful attacks come from astern. But see suggestions in our Technology section.) In these days of long-range missiles, it is also unhealthy to fly in the contrail belt, which makes one visible for miles, as the water vapour released by the burnt fuel forms a trail of ice crystals at high altitudes.

Fighters should initially operate in pairs, well spread out. In this way each pilot is responsible for covering his partner's vulnerable blind spot, astern and below.

Finally, air-to-air and air-to-ground radio transmissions should be kept to an absolute minimum. Radio chatter gives enemy ground stations time to fix a position, establish identity without question and give away intentions. Communications-out is the way to go.

CLOSING

When a formation is detected, whether unidentified or definitely hostile, the decision whether to attack must be made. Ideally the decision should be taken by a fighter controller, who should have a picture of the overall situation. Situations will, however, always arise in which the man in the cockpit must decide.

The controller should have at his fingertips details of any gaps or shadows in the enemy radar coverage which may be utilised by his fighters to close the range undetected and achieve a favourable firing position. Ideally

he will know where the opposing SAM belts are sited. He is not going to vector his fighters over the ground defences of either side if it can be avoided. In theory, positions of other hostile formations should be known, and provision made for dealing with them. The fighter controller, armed with this information, can hopefully direct the best-placed of his fighters on a course which gives the best chance of a successful interception. With their radars on standby, they are not emitting, which reduces the likelihood of their being detected.

For the man in the cockpit, the decision is not so clear cut. If ground or airborne control is available, he will use it. If not, he has to answer some questions very quickly. Does the contact pose an immediate threat? Is his priority fighters or strike aircraft? Which of these is the contact? What are the relative positions, altitudes, headings, and speeds? What are his weaponry capabilities against those probably carried by the adversary? Which will give the best chance of a successful engagement? How many hostiles are there? What support is available? Very important, is there enough fuel to intercept, possibly conduct a manoeuvre combat, then disengage?

The decision is made to attack. Regardless of what form of attack is to be used, a favourable position must first be achieved. To do this,

the pilot must close with the enemy.

The two essentials of closing are speed and concealment. Speed aids concealment as it reduces the time available for the attacker's approach to be detected. Rapid acceleration is vital to the closing process as it not only means that an attacking position will be reached as swiftly as possible, but it increases the energy available to the fighter for manoeuvre combat or disengagement should either become necessary. Early detection followed by swift acceleration vastly increases the probability of a successful attack.

Concealment is very difficult to achieve in the sense of remaining undetected by the enemy. ECM may be used, but the pilot has no way of knowing how effective it is. Flying close to the ground can be a shield against enemy radar, but as we have seen, maximum speeds are at their lowest at that level. If the contact is travelling at Mach 1.6 at 20,000ft (6,100m) can it be caught by a low-flying fighter, or must the fighter pull away from the shelter of the ground in order to effect the interception?

It is impossible to guarantee that the fighter will remain undetected. However, deception remains a possibility. Some progress was made along these lines in the Arab/Israeli wars. In the clear blue skies and predominantly flat terrain of the Middle East, concealment proved almost

impossible. Attempts were therefore made, not to achieve physical concealment, but to conceal intentions for as long as possible. This was done by concentrating formations on the approach so that they appeared as a single blip on the ground radar screens. Only at the last possible moment did the approaching formation break up into its component parts and reveal its plan of attack to the enemy. In small wars, this probably retains some relevance, but is of dubious value in a large-scale conflict.

Russian commentators occasionally refer to feints, such as sending a small force across the track of an incoming raid as a diversion, while other fighters slip in around the rear. This also appears to be of dubious value. A modern fighter is very expensive bait. It seems reasonable to suppose that in a war where large numbers of aircraft are used by both sides, closing will be most successfully achieved by a rapid and direct run-in under cover of both ECM and general confusion.

At current cruising speeds, a bandit detected at 50 miles (80km) range on an opposite heading will become a threat in a very few minutes. If identification at beyond visual distance proves impossible, the closing phase will extend down to the range at which positive visual identification can be made.

As has been noted, closing runs

on into the attack phase and the type of attack decided before closing is initiated. A certain amount of jockeying for position is inevitable during the run-in, especially if positive identification has not been made. Although this appears to be part of the closing phase, it is more directly related to the type of attack and is therefore considered under the attack heading.

ATTACK

This is the phase which the historical record tells us has accounted for about four out of every five aerial victories. It is thus potentially by far the most decisive phase of air combat. Two factors affect the nature of the attack; the tactical situation and the available weaponry. The attack must be launched from the position which gives the best chance of success. Surprise is vital and electronic countermeasures permitting, the beyond visual distance missile is the weapon to use.

All air-to-air missiles have one factor in common. Their motor accelerates the weapon to its maximum speed very quickly, then burns out. From this point, the projectile is coasting, slowly losing speed. Any manoeuvres it makes while homing onto its target also serve to decay the speed. Consequently the effective range varies tremendously with the aspect and speed of the target. This

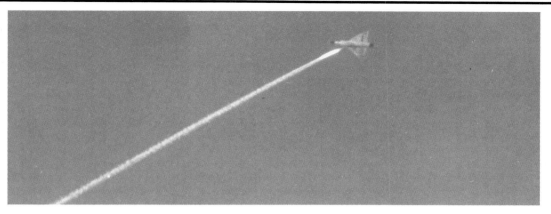

Left: An AIM-7 Sparrow fired from an F-15 Eagle homes on a fast and high target drone, apparently at a steep crossing angle. The drone's contrail makes it very easy to see. Pilots would try to avoid this.

Above: The all-angle Sidewinder. The AIM-9L lives up to the claims made for it as it homes onto a PQM 102 (Phantom) drone from the front quarter during early tests at Holloman AFB, New Mexico.

Below: A direct hit sends the drone down blazing uncontrollably. Added sensitivity in the seeker allows the AIM-9L to detect a warm aircraft against a cold sky from any angle.

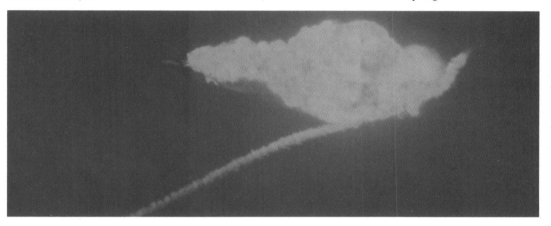

Comparative Ranges for Head-on and Astern SARH Missile Attacks

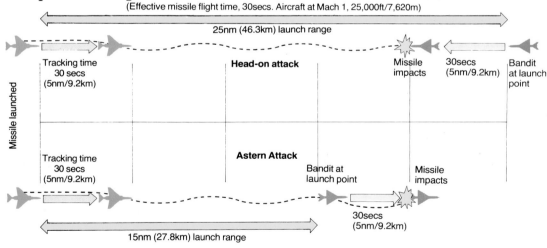

(Effective missile flight time, 30secs. Aircraft at Mach 1, 25,000ft/7,620m)

25nm (46.3km) launch range

Missile launched

Tracking time 30 secs (5nm/9.2km)

Head-on attack

Missile impacts

30secs (5nm/9.2km)

Bandit at launch point

Tracking time 30 secs (5nm/9.2km)

Astern Attack

Bandit at launch point

Missile impacts

30secs (5nm/9.2km)

15nm (27.8km) launch range

Above: Comparative missile ranges for head-on and astern attacks, for a fictitious SARH missile with an effective flight

is one reason why the head-on attack is favoured by some authorities. From the head-on aspect, the target is closing rapidly; therefore the effective range of the missile is at its maximum.

As an example, the AIM-7F Sparrow, an SARH missile, has a maximum speed of about Mach 4, with a range given as just over 60 miles (96km). It is reasonable to assume, then, that its time of flight is something exceeding a minute and a half. An on-coming target at

time of 30 seconds. In the head-on attack, the launch range is 25nm. In the astern attack, the launch range is only 15nm. Yet in each

Mach 1 and medium altitude is closing the range at about 10 miles (16km) per minute. Assuming that Sparrow's performance optimises at about 30 miles (48km); the missile could be launched at a range of 40 miles (64km) with a good chance of scoring. On the other hand, the launching fighter is committed to a fairly predictable flight path for about one minute as it illuminates the target. In the combat zone this is far too long, and makes the launching fighter

case, the missile flies 20nm in 30 seconds. Thus target speed and heading vary the launch envelope considerably.

vulnerable. Yet to shorten the time of flight in order to reduce the vulnerability period also has its drawbacks. The range must be closed considerably which increases the probability of detection. If the target aircraft carries a "fire-and-forget" missile, it may visually acquire the attacker in the last few seconds and launch its weapon. The destruction of the target is thus quickly followed by the destruction of the attacking fighter. The head-on attack has its

drawbacks with SARH weapons.

What of other angles? It is possible to fire Sparrow at a target with a 90 degree crossing angle. Missiles, like people, perform simple tasks best. The more a missile has to do to follow its target, the greater the chance of a miss. This leaves the traditional attack from astern. Unless the initial positions and headings at the detection stage are particularly favourable, the closing phase will take longer, as the attacking fighter has further to travel. The effective range is much shorter as the missile has to overhaul the target. Effective launch range against the same target as before would therefore be about 15 miles (24km) rather than 40 miles (64km), the time of flight remaining the same. Reducing the time of flight (and therefore tracking) by any appreciable amount would entail approaching almost into visual distance. The probability of the attacker being detected would increase considerably. However, the approach from astern is safer.

The conclusions to be drawn about the SARH missile are threefold. First, it is a very valuable weapon while detection and ECM technology are more advanced than those of the enemy. If the technological lead is lost it becomes a potential liability. Second, its greatest weakness lies in the target having to be continuously illuminated by radar. If the radar could be trained to look sideways, or even backwards, the launching fighter would become much less vulnerable during the tracking period. Third, the SARH is a potential (if very expensive) source of confusion to a large incoming strike. Even if no hits are scored, a couple of Sparrows flashing past might well break up the cohesion of the formation.

The other type of air-to-air missile in widespread use is the infra-red homer, which guides on to heat emissions. The Sidewinder is the best known of the IRH family. IR homers are generally slower but more accurate than SARH. They are also smaller, simpler, and cheaper. In combat they are essentially a visual distance weapon and have the tremendous advantage that they are a "fire-and-forget" weapon. Once the IRH is launched it needs no further assistance from the parent fighter, which is free to manoeuvre as necessary. The latest of the Sidewinder family, the AIM-9L, is one-sixth of the weight of a Sparrow, has a range of 11 miles (18km) and a speed of about Mach 3. It can be launched from a fighter manoeuvring at 6g and has a minimum release distance of about 1,000ft (300m).

The AIM-9L has a much vaunted "all-angle" capability, and can be launched at head-on targets. This notwithstanding, it still performs best when launched from astern at a glowing afterburner.

Finally, the gun: the age-old, instantly available, very reliable, close-range fighter weapon. The gun is often considered a defensive weapon only, and one that, in the missile age, would only be used in the dogfight.

Many fighters (but few types) today carry only two missiles. In a big fight, they will soon be expended. Should any further attack opportunities arise, the gun will be the only weapon available. The traditional gun attack is from astern with an overtake speed of between 50 and 150 knots. The historical record shows that the aces of past generations took far more head-on shots than is generally realised.

It may be assumed that the high speeds of modern fighters invalidate the head-on gun attack, but, rather surprisingly perhaps, they can still be made even at supersonic speeds. The technique is to open fire at a range of two miles, pulling the sighting pipper up through the target. This hangs a curtain of shells in the air in front of the oncoming fighter, although it is more a question of the target flying into the shells than the shells hitting the target. This form of attack is unlikely to achieve good results consistently, but it would certainly tend to put the other guy off his stroke, which is always valuable.

HOW TO USE THE WEAPONS

These then are the weapons. The aircraft carrying them are described in the relevant section. How best to use them determines the mode of the attack phase. Concentration of force is a widely accepted principle of warfare, but it is difficult to apply in the fluid, fast-moving air arena. Returning to the historical record, four out of every five air victories are scored in the attack phase.

From this it is reasonable to deduce that in any engagement the advantage lies with the aircraft that open fire first, with the obvious proviso that they are within effective range. If the attackers can also launch missiles from an angle at which they are immune to counterfire, such as astern, they really have a tremendous advantage. The system of weapons employment should therefore be longest-ranged missiles first, then closing to visual range for heat homers and guns.

Not all fighter pilots will agree with this, but it should be remembered that there are no hard and fast rules. The counter-argument is that fighters should position themselves for a gun attack and fire missiles only when opportunity offers, the case for this view being that a proficient and determined pilot attacking with guns is more difficult to defend against than a missile which is making a kamikaze attack. The flaw in this argument seems to be that a missile fired from beyond visual distance is much more difficult to spot than a fighter closing to gun range.

This digression notwith-standing, the beyond-visual-distance attack delivered from astern seems the way to go. Even if the missile attack is a complete failure, the enemy formation is in no position to deliver an immediate counter-attack. It is unlikely that the initial attack will be a complete success, even delivered by aircraft such as the Tornado F.2 with its ability to strike at six different targets simultaneously. The attack from the rear, if delivered at a high overtaking speed, will enable the attacking fighter to close the range to visual distance and follow up with heat missiles or even guns. While this can also be done from head-on, astern still presents the best aspect for an IR missile to home on the hot exhaust gases of an enemy, while retaining the advantage of denying the target a return shot.

One further principle of war also applies to the attack phase. History shows many examples in all branches of warfare where a force with considerable numerical superiority has been decisively defeated. Examination of these examples reveals that almost without exception, the result has been due to what British historian Basil Liddel-Hart called "the indirect approach". US General George S. Patton summed it up pithily as, "Hold them by the nose and kick them in the pants!"

Is there any way in which a fighter formation can be "held by the nose"? The short answer to the question is yes. It has been noted earlier that feints are wasteful of expensive aeroplanes. A genuine threat can, however, be used as a distraction. In its simplest form, one flight of fighters shapes up for a head-on run in full view of enemy radar surveillance while a second flight works around the beam at high speed and low level. The first, diversionary flight, carries out a head-on attack but breaking away before visual distance is reached while the attack flight closes, ready to take advantage of the confusion caused.

Alternatively roles can be reversed, with the second flight visible to enemy radar, which the enemy fighter controller would direct his aircraft to intercept, while the first flight approaches from head-on at low level, ready to pull up and spring the trap. In either case the diversionary force stands by to join the scrum if needed.

One essential in any attack is positively to identify the opposing formation. If one machine is approaching fast at 10,000ft (3,000m), where is his wingman? Which side is he? Is he high or low? Or – a favourite Russian ploy – is he in trail, two or three miles back, just waiting for some enthusiastic

young fighter jockey to jump in behind his leader?

A classic example of this type took place during a "Red Flag" RAF/USAF air combat exercise a few years ago. A pair of F-15 Eagles spotted a pair of RAF Jaguars hurtling along on a low-level strike. The leader swung down to attack, leaving his wingman high to cover him, only to run straight in front of the guns of a second pair of Jaguars previously undetected. The pilot of the second F-15 looked carefully around, then dropped in behind the second pair of Jaguars. After all, everyone knows that modern aircraft fly in pairs or fours. The only snag was that in this instance there were six Jaguars, the third pair of which gratefully accepted the F-15 which dropped neatly down in front of their gun cameras.

The moral of this story is, never take anything for granted. Flying in V-formation of three aircraft was outdated in 1940. But if one of a formation of four aircraft sprang a leak after takeoff and aborted, it is conceivable that a threesome, probably consisting of a leader with a combat spread pair trailing him, could be encountered.

If there is more in this section about tactical considerations in the attack phase than there is about method, it is for two reasons. First, the number of tactical situations is

Head-on Gun Attack at Supersonic Speed

Attacking fighter hangs a curtain of shells in front of oncoming enemy fighter

2 miles (3.2km)

Above: The head-on gun attack has been very successful in past wars. With present-day closing speeds of the order of 500 to 1,000 yards per sec (457-914m/sec), it now appears a doubtful proposi-tion, with effective gun range of about 500yd (457m). Yet the head-on gun pass is still valid. The technique is to sight at about 2 miles (3.2km) range, then pull the nose up, producing a curtain of shells through which the target must fly. **Below: A pair of Royal Air Force Jaguars low flying. These strike fighters caused an upset during a Red Flag exercise when they gunned down a pair of mighty F-15s. It was the old story: the surprise factor.**

Using Threat of Attack as Distraction

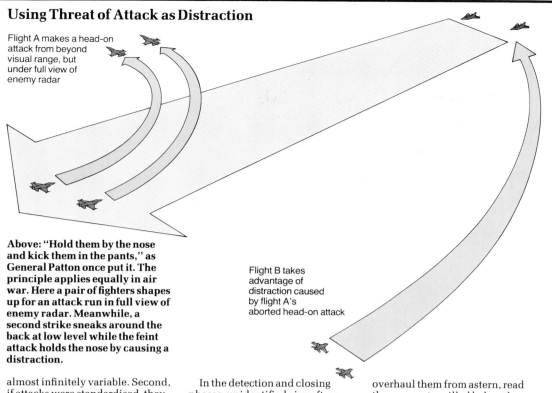

Flight A makes a head-on attack from beyond visual range, but under full view of enemy radar

Flight B takes advantage of distraction caused by flight A's aborted head-on attack

Above: "Hold them by the nose and kick them in the pants," as General Patton once put it. The principle applies equally in air war. Here a pair of fighters shapes up for an attack run in full view of enemy radar. Meanwhile, a second strike sneaks around the back at low level while the feint attack holds the nose by causing a distraction.

almost infinitely variable. Second, if attacks were standardised, they would become predictable, with fatal consequences for the users. Air combat is the art of the stab in the back. Unpredictability is one of the prime attributes.

In the detection and closing phases, unidentified aircraft, or bogeys, were frequently mentioned, as was the confusion factor. It will often become necessary to identify bogeys visually. The obvious method is to

overhaul them from astern, read the names stencilled below the canopy, then clobber them if they sound foreign. But it may be impossible to sneak behind.

One basic method, on which there are many variations, is to turn

away at about a 30 degree angle. When the intercepting pair have reached a position between 5 and 10 miles (8 and 16km) offset to the bogeys' flight path, they turn back onto a lead collision course. The best formation to use is combat spread, with the leader as "eyeball" and his wingman as "shooter". The shooter should preferably be 1½ miles (2.4km) out and low. If the bogeys notice nothing, but maintain their heading, the formations will close to visual distance. Meanwhile the shooter obtains a radar lock on the far bogey. Due to the initial offset, the eyeball will visually acquire the bogeys from the beam, while presenting his smallest, i.e. head-on, aspect to them. As soon as the bogeys are positively identified as hostile, he can radio his wingman to launch a missile. During this time the eyeball will have approached too close for SARH employment. Neither will he have a "heart of the envelope" Sidewinder shot. But if the shooter's missile is on target, the ensuing fight will be two versus one, while if it misses, the chances are that only the leader has been detected. Consequently the fight will be two versus two, but with the wingman way out and low ready to introduce the element of surprise into the subsequent manoeuvring combat.

"Eyeball"/Shooter Method of Visual Identification/Attack

Right: Confused situations may well require visual identification. Here two fighters pick up bogeys on their radar. Distance permitting, they offset their flight path by several miles before closing. As they close, the wingman prepares to fire a SARH missile against the far bogey as soon as his leader visually identifies the bogeys as bandits. Hopefully this turns a 2-versus-2 fight into a 2-vs-1 at the outset.

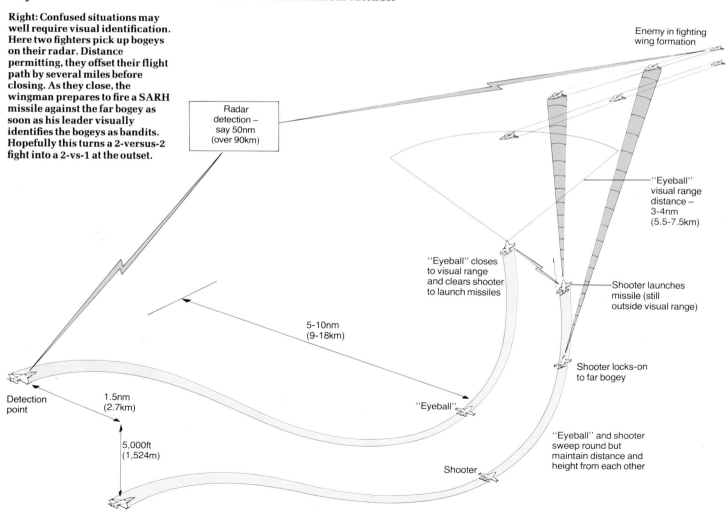

Enemy in fighting wing formation

Radar detection – say 50nm (over 90km)

"Eyeball" visual range distance – 3-4nm (5.5-7.5km)

"Eyeball" closes to visual range and clears shooter to launch missiles

Shooter launches missile (still outside visual range)

5-10nm (9-18km)

Shooter locks-on to far bogey

Detection point

1.5nm (2.7km)

"Eyeball"

5,000ft (1,524m)

"Eyeball" and shooter sweep round but maintain distance and height from each other

Shooter

Manoeuvres

Because air combat involves dynamic movement in three dimensions, one could conclude that it is an infinitely variable manoeuvre/counter-manoeuvre process. But such is not the case. A fighter pilot has only a limited number of options with which to meet a given situation. Which one he uses will be dictated more by the relative positions and energy states of himself and his opponent than by any potential technical advantages that his aircraft may possess. He will strive to deny his adversary the initiative, knowing that air combats are *lost* more often than they are won.

The pilot who holds the initiative can push his opponent around the sky, keeping him under constant pressure. The longer the pressure continues, the greater the stress on the defending pilot becomes as his life is threatened. Stress breeds mistakes and the first error may well prove fatal. Even if the defending pilot makes no errors he is likely to be forced into a series of energy-dissipating manoeuvres that deplete his very manoeuvre capability and render him ever less capable of defending himself.

The manoeuvre phase proper generally begins when a pilot realises that he is about to come, or already is, under attack. His first priority is survival; turning the tables is secondary at this stage. The opening moves are thus defensive with the attacker conforming predictably to the defender's movements. Each manoeuvre has its counter. However, it is the precision and timing of a manoeuvre which is important; the ability to out-fly an opponent. The most technically advanced fighter in the world is only as good as its pilot.

If, however, the defending aircraft can achieve an early sighting the pilot should be able to manoeuvre using normal turns to prevent the attacker from

The Break

Right: The break is a life-saving manoeuvre. It is used against an attacker who is about to achieve a firing position (or already has). It consists of a hard turn into the direction of attack, to generate angle-off as rapidly as possible to present the most difficult target.

Attacker about to achieve firing position

positioning in the lethal or vulnerability cones. Having negated the attack, the defender should either disengage (for instance, on an attack sortie the primary aim must be to complete the bombing mission) or alternatively continue manoeuvring into an attacking position.

The aspiring fighter pilot is taught basic air combat manoeuvres, some defensive, others offensive. They are: the Break, the Scissors, the High-G Barrel Roll, Jinking, the Spiral Dive, the Vertical Rolling Scissors, the Split S, the High Speed Yoyo, the Vector Roll or Rollaway, the Lag Pursuit, the Low Speed Yoyo, the Barrel Roll Attack, the Vertical Reverse, the Immelmann and various versions of and counters to these.

Defender turns sharply into direction of attack

THE BREAK

This is used when an attacker is first seen approaching or is already in the cone of vulnerability. Its purpose is twofold: to spoil the attacker's aim and to force him to overshoot. The break is always made towards the direction of attack. This generates "angle-off" as quickly as possible which makes

the defender a difficult target. The attacker may be able to cut inside the turn but he is forced to pull lead. To do this he must tighten his turn, which increases his angle of attack. It is difficult for him to pull his nose around at high angles of attack to achieve a firing solution. The defender should also alter his plane of flight to make himself a more difficult target.

Two forms of break are possible, depending on the circumstances of the attack. The defender can use a maximum-rate sustained turn in which he does not lose speed, or the hardest possible turn in which he almost certainly does. The speed loss attendant on the hard turn aids his chances of forcing the attacker to overshoot, as does the smaller radius of turn, but oft-quoted maxims such as "speed is life" act as an inhibitor. If the break succeeds in forcing the attacker to overshoot, the next manoeuvre is the Scissors.

THE SCISSORS

This is a series of turn reversals performed with the object of forcing the overshooting attacker out in front to a position of disadvantage. The initial turn is reversed when the attacker has definitely overshot *and* has drifted sufficiently wide as to prevent him from pulling back into the cone of vulnerability when the defender reverses. Timing the reversals is absolutely critical. The basic rule is that if the attacker is

Avoiding Multiple Gunshot Hits

Above: Opportunities must be taken regardless of difficulty. Here is a worst case gun shot; a high speed target at 90° deflection. If

the gun is aimed directly along the line of flight, three hits are possible, compared with one if the firing aircraft is out of plane.

Cone of Vulnerability

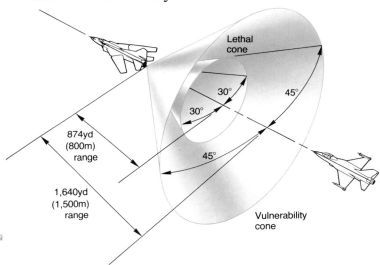

Lethal cone

30° 30°
30°
45°
45°

874yd (800m) range

1,640yd (1,500m) range

Vulnerability cone

Above: Most successful gun attacks are made from astern at 30° angle-off or less, the lethal cone. Vulnerability cone is 45° angle-off and 1,640yd (1,500m) range.

Right: An F-15 Eagle poses for the gun camera. The computerised radar ranging gunsight automatically sets up the correct lead as the pursuing fighter tracks his prey.

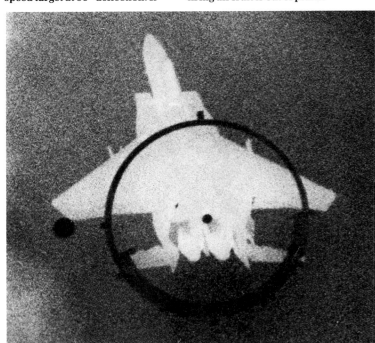

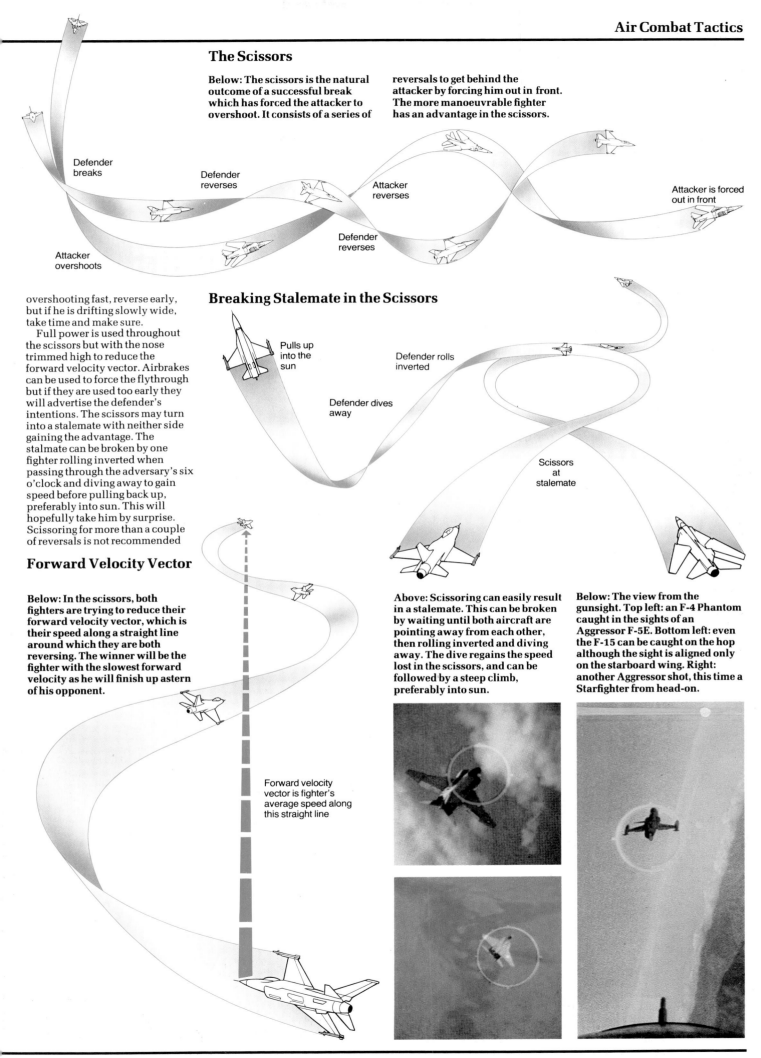

The Scissors

Below: The scissors is the natural outcome of a successful break which has forced the attacker to overshoot. It consists of a series of reversals to get behind the attacker by forcing him out in front. The more manoeuvrable fighter has an advantage in the scissors.

Defender breaks

Defender reverses

Attacker reverses

Defender reverses

Attacker overshoots

Attacker is forced out in front

Breaking Stalemate in the Scissors

Pulls up into the sun

Defender dives away

Defender rolls inverted

Scissors at stalemate

overshooting fast, reverse early, but if he is drifting slowly wide, take time and make sure.

Full power is used throughout the scissors but with the nose trimmed high to reduce the forward velocity vector. Airbrakes can be used to force the flythrough but if they are used too early they will advertise the defender's intentions. The scissors may turn into a stalemate with neither side gaining the advantage. The stalmate can be broken by one fighter rolling inverted when passing through the adversary's six o'clock and diving away to gain speed before pulling back up, preferably into sun. This will hopefully take him by surprise. Scissoring for more than a couple of reversals is not recommended

Forward Velocity Vector

Below: In the scissors, both fighters are trying to reduce their forward velocity vector, which is their speed along a straight line around which they are both reversing. The winner will be the fighter with the slowest forward velocity as he will finish up astern of his opponent.

Forward velocity vector is fighter's average speed along this straight line

Above: Scissoring can easily result in a stalemate. This can be broken by waiting until both aircraft are pointing away from each other, then rolling inverted and diving away. The dive regains the speed lost in the scissors, and can be followed by a steep climb, preferably into sun.

Below: The view from the gunsight. Top left: an F-4 Phantom caught in the sights of an Aggressor F-5E. Bottom left: even the F-15 can be caught on the hop although the sight is aligned only on the starboard wing. Right: another Aggressor shot, this time a Starfighter from head-on.

against an opponent who is able to turn faster and/or tighter, and it should not be attempted if there is more than one attacker, either. Fighter pilots recommend that unless the advantage is gained after three reversals, the pilot should, aiming to pass head-on to the attacker, since this would put him at a disadvantage in having to turn back toward the defender as he runs out.

HIGH G BARREL ROLL

This manoeuvre is used against an attacker closing fast from astern. It starts with a break, then a roll in the opposite direction to the break. The fact that it is a high g manoeuvre means that quite a lot of speed is lost, up to 100 knots in some cases, particularly if performed "over the top".

If the attacker is closing fast and is caught by surprise he may easily fly through and end up in front, the positions reversed. If he attempts to follow the barrel roll, he will probably end up high and wide of the defender who can then turn in towards him, forcing him down and in front. But woe betide the defender who attempts a barrel roll in front of a slowly closing attacker who will follow him through the manoeuvre, ending on his tail in easy gun range. His only recourse in this event is to jink.

The High G Barrel Roll is a difficult manoeuvre to execute successfully, and is in fact easy for the attacker to counter. It will only work if the attacker has been led into, or is in, a high angle-off, high overtake situation.

Attacker Overshoots in Spiral Dive

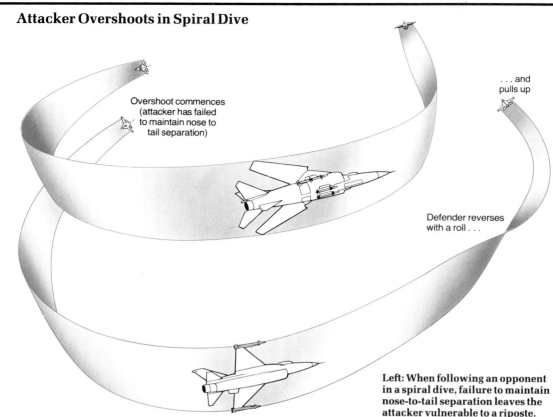

Overshoot commences (attacker has failed to maintain nose to tail separation)

. . . and pulls up

Defender reverses with a roll . . .

Left: When following an opponent in a spiral dive, failure to maintain nose-to-tail separation leaves the attacker vulnerable to a riposte.

JINKING

This is a defensive ploy against an attacker who is sitting on the defender's tail within gun range with little or no overtaking speed. It is a series of random turns, skids, pitch-ups and yaws to spoil the attacker's aim. While the attacker is able to retain the advantage, the longer he is forced to concentrate on attaining a shooting position, the more nervous he is likley to become about what is going on behind him.

Obviously, at this point the defender is in a desperate situation, about to be shot down, following a break with rapidly decaying airspeed. What is called for is application of full reheat, max plus g in one plane for about 3 to 4 seconds, followed by max minus g in *another* plane held for 3 to 4 seconds. Speed should have increased by this time. Hopefully now out of gun range, the defender can now start jinking, separating them by 30° to 60° to avoid the missile envelope – or he can turn back in for a front missile attack (if he has missiles), followed by escape.

High G Barrel Roll

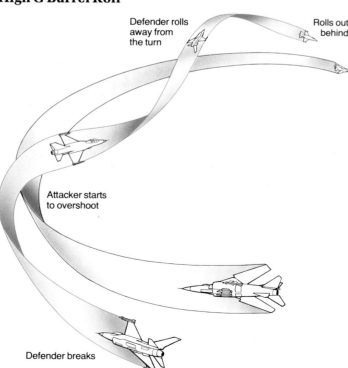

Defender rolls away from the turn

Rolls out behind

Attacker starts to overshoot

Defender breaks

Above: The High G Barrel Roll can be very effective against an attacker closing fast from astern. Commencing with a break turn to put the attacker in a high angle-off position, the roll is then carried out in the opposite direction to the turn.

Above: An F-4 Phantom trailing the thick black smoke common to so many Western fighters, neatly trapped by his opponent at 6 o'clock The poor rearward visibility from the Phantom is clearly shown. Burners unlit, the Phantom seems unaware of his peril.

SPIRAL DIVE

When all other manoeuvres fail, the spiral dive is a last-ditch attempt to shake off a resolute pursuer. This involves maintaining the highest possible rate of turn in a dive steep enough to retain manoeuvring airpeed. If the attacker follows the spiral the defender should throttle back. This tends to flatten out the spiral and reduces the rate at which height is lost. The defender will slowly lose speed. As it is extremely difficult for the attacker to notice early enough that his opponent has reduced power he may start to overshoot at this point. If he does, a hard rolling reversal and pull-up by the defender will force the attacker out in front.

VERTICAL ROLLING SCISSORS

This is similar to the scissors described earlier but is carried out in either a steep climb or dive and the reversals are often carried out by executing a complete barrel roll. The ascending vertical rolling scissors places the fighter with the better zoom climb (or the higher initial energy state) at a disadvantage at first. Otherwise the fighter with the best sustained rate of climb will have the advantage. If in a descending vertical rolling scissors the defender finds himself forced below his adversary he should attempt to place himself directly beneath his opponent and manoeuvre in phase with him. In this position he cannot be seen and can pick his moment to disengage with a split S.

The Split S

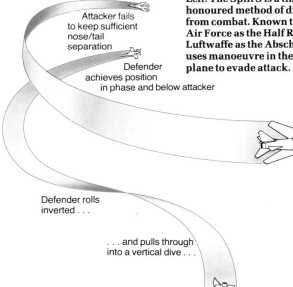

Attacker fails to keep sufficient nose/tail separation

Defender achieves position in phase and below attacker

Defender rolls inverted . . .

. . . and pulls through into a vertical dive . . .

. . . aileron turns . . .

. . . and pulls out in opposite direction

Vertical Rolling Scissors

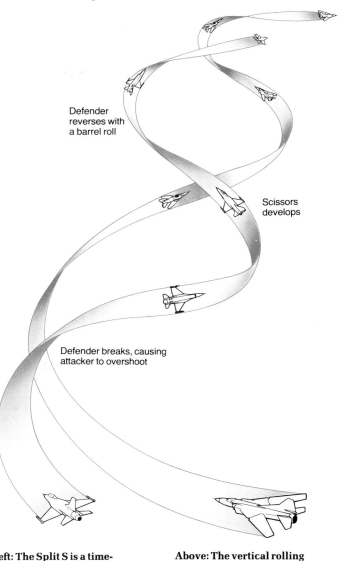

Defender reverses with a barrel roll

Scissors develops

Defender breaks, causing attacker to overshoot

Left: The Split S is a time-honoured method of disengaging from combat. Known to the Royal Air Force as the Half Roll and the Luftwaffe as the Abschwung, it uses manoeuvre in the vertical plane to evade attack.

Above: The vertical rolling scissors works on the same principles as the scissors previously described, but with the difference that reversals are more often made by executing a complete barrel roll.

Below: The off-set head-on pass may be used by the pilot of an extremely manoeuvrable fighter. Faced with a head-on attack, he can offset to one side to give himself space in which to use his superior turning ability.

Offset Head-on Pass

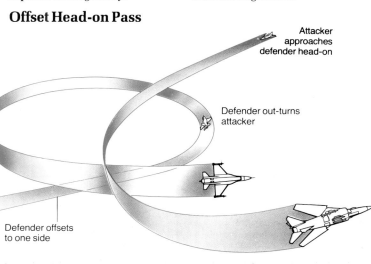

Attacker approaches defender head-on

Defender out-turns attacker

Defender offsets to one side

SPLIT S

In this the defender rolls inverted and dives away vertically, pulling out in a direction opposite to that of his opponent.

Most defensive manoeuvres are designed to counter an attack coming from astern, mainly by forcing an attacker to overshoot. What are the attacker's needs? Much depends on whether he is planning a missile or gun attack. As we saw in the attack phase, a missile attack should be fast, deadly, and conclusive. But, as World War I German Chief of Staff von Moltke observed many years ago: plans rarely survive contact with the enemy. The fighter pilot should be prepared for his attack to fail and know precisely what he will do next, either disengage or enter into manoeuvring combat.

If his attack is from head-on, much will depend on the manoeuvre potential of the two opponents. The more manoeuvrable fighter will have the edge in a turning fight. (The more manoeuvrable fighter at this stage is frequently the one travelling slowest rather than the most aerodynamically capable.) If this is the attacker he should endeavour to pass wide of his opponent to give himself turning room. If there is any doubt about relative manoeuvre potential he should pass close to deny his adversary turning room, then pull high in the turn. In either case he should pass down-Sun so that his next change of direction forces his opponent to look into the dazzle. If after a head-on pass both aircraft pull high a vertical ascending scissors may result.

A missile attack from astern is normally made at a high closing speed. If the attack fails the attacker must zoom climb to dissipate his excess speed if he wishes to continue the fight, although it is easier and probably safer to disengage at this point. A gun attack should be made with an overtake speed of about 50 knots (just under 90 feet, 27m) per second). This gives time to track the target in the sight, minimises the risk of overshooting and retains an energy advantage for manoeuvring combat.

High Speed YoYo

Defender rolls
inverted . . .

Defender
pulls up

. . . and pulls down
behind attacker

Attacker
breaks hard

The Clock Code

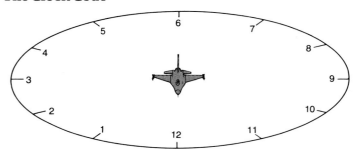

Left: The slower, better-turning enemy has always been a problem in combat. The attacker overtaking fast from astern is faced with overshooting. The remedy is to switch the attack into the vertical plane with a high speed yoyo, in which the attacker pulls high and rolls inverted before pulling down astern of his opponent.

Above: The clock code is used for indicating relative direction. The pilot imagines himself sitting in the centre of a gigantic clock face, with the nose of his fighter pointed at 12 o'clock. Threats are directionally related to the clock. Unidentified aircraft to the pilot's left would be called as "bogies 9 o'clock high" (low, or level), stating the range.

Right: Dissimilar air combat is a training success. A USN Phantom turns in to deny the Top Gun Skyhawk lateral turning room. The Phantom is passing down-sun (see shadows) which means that the Phantom's next move is to pull high into the sun to make the Skyhawk pilot lose visual contact.

The defensive manoeuvres described earlier place much stress on forcing an attacker to overshoot. It is obviously important to avoid overshooting, so how is it done?

An overshoot is caused by one of two factors. The first is an excessively large angle subtended between the fuselages of the respective aircraft. The second is excessive closing speed. This is difficult for the attacker to spot until he is fairly close in. Either way the attacker is faced with

overshooting. His first remedy is the high-speed yoyo.

HIGH-SPEED YOYO

When the attacker realises that he is unable to stay on the inside of the defender's turn, he relaxes his angle of bank a little, then pulls high. As he comes over the top he is inverted, looking down at his opponent through the top of his canopy. His speed falls due to the climb, and this diminishes his

radius of turn. The 1g of gravity is utilised by turning in the vertical plane, which reduces the radius of turn still further. The attacker should then be well placed to slide down into a firing position .

The high-speed yoyo is a very difficult manoeuvre to perform well, and demands perfect timing and precise execution. If it is commenced too early, the defender can counter by pulling up into the attack. If started too late, the attacker is forced to pull up at an

excessively steep angle to avoid overshooting. This allows the defender to disengage by diving away. A common fault in executing the high-speed yoyo is not pulling the nose high enough. This can result in the attacker ending directly above the defender. Some pilots find that they obtain better results from a series of small yoyos than one large one. A variant on this manoeuvre, used to prevent overshooting or to reduce the angle-off, is the rollaway.

The Rollaway

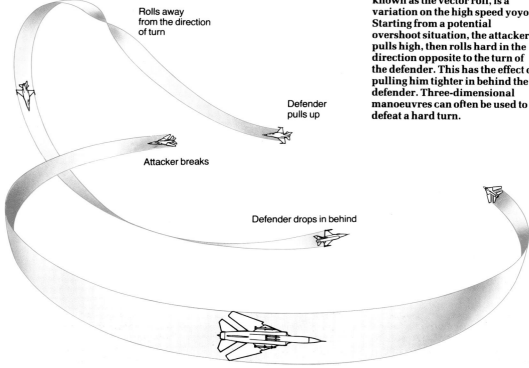

Rolls away
from the direction
of turn

Defender
pulls up

Attacker breaks

Defender drops in behind

Below: The rollaway, sometimes known as the vector roll, is a variation on the high speed yoyo. Starting from a potential overshoot situation, the attacker pulls high, then rolls hard in the direction opposite to the turn of the defender. This has the effect of pulling him tighter in behind the defender. Three-dimensional manoeuvres can often be used to defeat a hard turn.

ROLLAWAY

As the attacker reaches the top of the yoyo, he rolls rapidly in the *opposite* direction to the defender's turn. This has the effect of pulling him tighter in behind the defender.

A perfectly executed high-speed yoyo is very difficult to counter. However, there are a few tricks that the defending pilot can try. If his energy state is high enough, he can pull up into the attack, but would risk depleting his energy reserves to the point where he can no longer effectively defend himself. Alternatively, as the attacker pulls up his nose, the defender can relax his turn and spiral wide at full throttle. This would hopefully increase his speed and widen the distance. Then when the attacker comes down, the defender breaks and the situation returns to square one. However, if the attacker has misjudged his manoeuvre and rolls out close astern but high, the defender relaxes his turn to maintain speed; then, when the attacker drops his nose and dives, the defender is able to reverse hard up into him.

The second answer to overshooting is lag pursuit.

LAG PURSUIT

This can be used when the primary cause of overshooting is excess speed. Basically it consists of maintaining position astern but outside the turn radius of the defending fighter. In this manner both speed advantage and initiative are retained, the attacker matching the defender's rate of turn in degrees per second while remaining concealed in the blind spot beneath the defender's tail. Lag pursuit is best countered by tightening the turn into a spiral dive. The temptation is to reverse and commence scissoring, but this is a good way to die if the attacker is on the ball.

LAG PURSUIT ROLL

This is used when at close range with a high overtake, high speed and high angle-off. The defender gets the nose high and rolls to the outside of the turn. He uses maximum g to pull the nose up and towards the target. This puts him in a ±30° angle-off missile envelope.

LOW-SPEED YOYO

Another combat situation which can arise is a stalemate in either a tail chase or a turning match. To break the stalemate, a low-speed yoyo is used. This is based on the age-old concept of trading height for speed. If a pursuer finds that he is unable to close to within shooting range in straight flight, he can gain extra speed in a shallow dive. This will allow him to close the horizontal distance and takes him into his opponent's blind spot at six o'clock low. When a suitable position and overtaking speed have been attained, the pursuer can pull up and attack. The counter? Keep a good lookout behind!

The Lag Pursuit

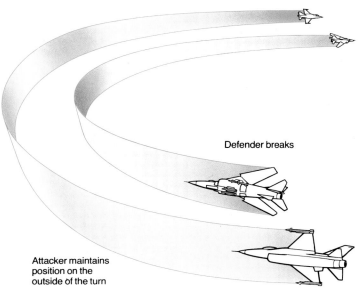

Defender breaks

Attacker maintains position on the outside of the turn

The Low Speed Yoyo (Straight Pursuit)

Defender unable to see attacker, which is now in his blind spot

Attacker pulls up within firing range

Unable to close range in level flight, attacker gains speed in shallow dive

Above: When overshooting is mainly the result of excess speed, position can be maintained outside the radius of the defender's turn by matching his rate of turn, thus maintaining both speed and initiative. The pursuer is hidden beneath the defender's tail, which could cause him to make an error. This is called lag pursuit.

Above: Two versions of the low speed yoyo exist. The first, illustrated here, is based on trading height for speed. It is used to break a stalemate in a tail chase where the attacker is unable to close to within range. He unloads in a shallow dive, gaining speed. When the distance has been closed, he pulls up into the attack.

The Low Speed Yoyo

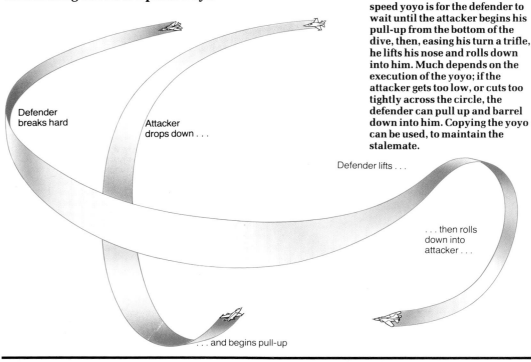

Defender breaks hard

Attacker drops down to inside of turn . . .

. . . and pulls in behind defender

Attacker can repeat manoeuvre until firing position is reached

Countering the Low Speed Yoyo

Defender breaks hard

Attacker drops down . . .

Defender lifts . . .

. . . then rolls down into attacker . . .

. . . and begins pull-up

Top row: During training an F-4 at high altitude is easily held by the A-4 as it pulls over the top. Consideration for the camera ship constrains it from leaving the Skyhawk in the dive.

Left: The most widely used variant of the low speed yoyo is used in a turning fight to break a stalemate caused by lack of overtake. Dropping his nose to the inside of the turn, the pursuer can cut across the circle.

Left: The main counter to the low speed yoyo is for the defender to wait until the attacker begins his pull-up from the bottom of the dive, then, easing his turn a trifle, he lifts his nose and rolls down into him. Much depends on the execution of the yoyo; if the attacker gets too low, or cuts too tightly across the circle, the defender can pull up and barrel down to him. Copying the yoyo can be used, to maintain the stalemate.

More often, the low-speed yoyo is used to break a stalemate in a turning fight. The attacker drops his nose to the inside of the turn, then cuts low across the circle before pulling up towards his opponent's six o'clock. The gain is often marginal, but repeating the process nibbles off a few degrees of angle each time, due to manoeuvring in the vertical plane. The pull-up should be started when a position of about 30 degrees angle-off is reached. It is important that the angle of cut-off is correct or the attacker will arrive in a fly-through situation with too much angle-off as he approaches the target. If this happens then he must endeavour to pull up into a high-speed yoyo.

Defence against the low-speed yoyo takes two forms. The first is to copy the manoeuvre while remaining in phase with the attacker. This maintains the stalemate. The second counter is more positive. The defender holds the turn until the attacker starts his pull-up. He then eases his turn a trifle, lifts his nose, and makes a rolling descending turn into his opponent.

If the attacking pilot has tried to lead the defender by too much or dived too low by being greedy, the defender can also pull up and barrel down onto the attacker.

THE BARREL ROLL ATTACK

This manoeuvre differs from the defensive high-g barrel roll in that a great loss of speed to force an attacking fighter to overshoot is not necessary. The g forces can therefore often be quite small. Closely resembling the rollaway, the barrel roll attack is used to alter the angle of approach to the defender *without* losing a lot of speed. It is used when the attacker becomes aware that he is going to overshoot a turning target. He rolls the wings level, pulls the nose hard up, then rolls *away* from the direction of turn. This three-dimensional manoeuvre is completed by sliding in astern of the target.

The counter to a well executed

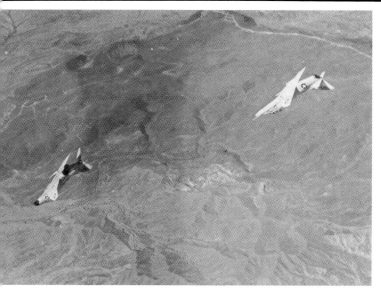

The Barrel Roll Attack

Instead of overshooting, attacker executes a three-dimensional manoeuvre to defeat a two-dimensional turn by defender

Defender turns to force overshoot but still comes under attack

Left: The barrell roll attack is used to alter the angle of approach to the victim without losing much speed.

The Vertical Reverse

Very tight radius or turn due to low speed

This is the modern equivalent of the stall turn. Few modern fighters can execute it without risking loss of control

Above: The vertical reverse is only for the fighter with exceptional low speed handling. It is used at the end of a vertical climb when all flying speed is lost, the aircraft being ruddered around sharply into a dive.

barrel roll attack is for the defender to dive away and increase speed. While doing this he must keep a sharp lookout for a missile attack and be ready to evade it. If he reverses his turn, he will probably set himself up for a gun attack.

THE VERTICAL REVERSE AND THE IMMELMANN

Two further manoeuvres are commonly used which are neither essentially offensive or defensive, but are mainly used for repositioning. They are the vertical reverse and the Immelmann.

The vertical reverse can be used when an attack or manoeuvre is completed with a vertical climb. The aircraft continues straight up until it loses flying speed. It is then ruddered around very sharply into a steep dive, gaining speed as it goes. This manoeuvre can be used at the top of a vertical ascending scissors either to disengage or to offer a pursuer a little head-on discouragement, but is mostly used to reposition for a further attack. Very few modern fighters

are controllable at such low speeds; only those that are – notably the Harrier, F-16 Fighting Falcon and F-5 Tiger II – can carry out this manoeuvre.

Back in 1916 the original Immelmann turn was more akin to the vertical reverse than its present-day counterpart. The modern version of the Immelmann is a vertical climb or half loop, possibly aileron-turning during the climb, then rolling out into level flight at the top. Its main

value lies in using the vertical plane to change the direction of flight in the smallest possible horizontal space. Horizontal turns at normal fighting speeds take up a lot of room laterally. Using the vertical plane enables the fighter to turn square corners in relation to its position above the ground. This manoeuvre makes repositioning for a further attack, or to meet a threat, much easier than would be the case using horizontal manoeuvre only.

The Immelmann

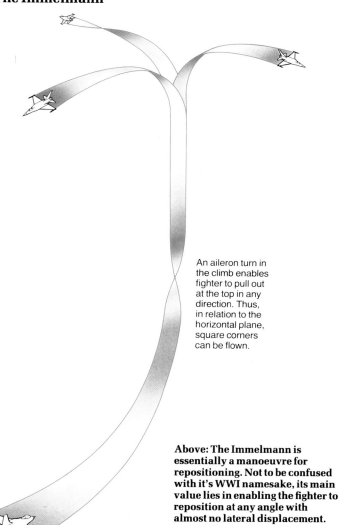

An aileron turn in the climb enables fighter to pull out at the top in any direction. Thus, in relation to the horizontal plane, square corners can be flown.

Above: The Immelmann is essentially a manoeuvre for repositioning. Not to be confused with it's WWI namesake, its main value lies in enabling the fighter to reposition at any angle with almost no lateral displacement.

Manoeuvres

OTHER SKILLS NEEDED

The foregoing are the basics of air combat manoeuvring. Many variations on the described manoeuvres exist, but they are precisely that: variations. No air-display-type aerobatics have been included, because they are irrelevant to air combat. But, however skilful a pilot may be at air combat manoeuvring, his ability must be backed up by knowledge and awareness of other factors affecting the contest.

The first essential is to know the strengths and weaknesses of his own machine and be able to compare them against the fighting qualities of his opponent's aircraft. For example, it would be foolish for a Phantom to engage in a prolonged turning contest with a MiG-21 at about equal airspeed as the MiG has by far the better turning capability.

To repeat an earlier statement, one of the most important things a pilot must remember is that air combats are lost rather than won. Air combat manoeuvring is not a

series of magic formulae, one of which can be plucked from a hat to meet a given situation and guarantee a successful engagement. It is important to avoid making mistakes, and equally – if not more – important to force the opponent into making mistakes by keeping him under pressure. If the opponent can be forced into a series of energy-dissipating hard turns, he will become increasingly unable to defend himself effectively. Pressure is kept on by positive and decisive manoeuvring.

The term aggressive has been deliberately avoided, as aggression is a double-edged sword. Too much aggression can lead to mental tunnel vision: total preoccupation with obtaining the kill. If other hostile fighters are near, this can easily prove disastrous

Probably the most common fault of a novice fighter pilot is depleting his energy state to a level where his ability to manoeuvre has all but vanished. He should endeavour to keep his speed up near the corner

velocity for his aeroplane if at all possible. The old saying, "out of altitude, airspeed, and ideas" is very true; every fighter pilot has at one time or another been faced with a situation where he has run out of ideas. In this situation, his only recourse is to attempt to point his nose at the enemy.

Also, trite though it may sound, he should never give up. This is not as peculiar as it at first seems; the records of air warfare give many examples of flyers who did give up and presented their victor with an easy target. The extreme emotional, physical, and psychological stress of air combat accounts for this phenomenon. With a bandit neatly trapped at six o'clock, the position may appear hopeless, but he has not lost yet. The attacker has still to solve the problems of closure rate, range and deflection, missile firing limitations, and even setting the correct switches. If the defender can keep the attacker busy by just staying in a favourable position, the defender's chances of survival increase considerably.

SUSTAINED VERSUS TRANSIENT MANOEUVRING

A concept which has recently been proposed regarding fighter design is that of sustained manoeuvre capability. The idea stems from the "speed is life" maxim, the point being that it should be possible to make and hold hard manoeuvres without the fighter losing speed. According to the concept, it could be achieved by building a fighter with a thrust/weight ratio exceeding unity, which also possesses a fairly high aspect ratio wing with good lifting qualities and a moderate wing loading. The F-16 Fighting Falcon, with its much publicised ability to sustain 9g turns, epitomises the sustained manoeuvre concept, but how valid is it?

As we saw earlier, the visual acuity of the pilot is impaired by accelerations of 7g and over, and weapons become unusable at high g forces. Therefore this impressive sustained turning performance is

essentially defensive in character.

The attack will generally materialise from somewhere astern. To defeat it, fighters need to break into it as hard as possible. Fighter aircraft can generally exceed their design loadings by a considerable margin without pulling their wings off and, initial velocity permitting, can exceed 9g for a brief period (mere seconds), albeit with a serious loss of speed.

Many of the defensive air combat manoeuvres described earlier are designed to force an attacker to overshoot. More often than not the attacker will be travelling faster than his intended victim; this, allied to the speed loss normally attendant on a hard break, should assist the chance of an overshoot, particularly as the defender's turn will tighten as speed is lost down to corner velocity. Once the attacker is definitely overshooting, the defender's next move is to reverse his turn and either commence scissoring, or take a heat missile shot at the attacker's departing tailpipe. The requirement therefore seems to be

the fastest possible break into the attack, followed by the fastest possible reverse to turn the tables. This is achieved by having a fast rate of roll or, less often, a high rate of pitch. This is transient performance; the ability to change flight mode rapidly.

On the other hand, what does the attacker need? The attacker also needs a rapid rate of roll, to match his target's moves; he also needs to be able to "dump" speed so as to avoid overshooting. Both attacker and defender then need excellent acceleration to regain the lost energy as quickly as possible. Sustained performance thus appears to be a middle ground, which fighters only touch briefly as they pass through it on their way from one end of the flight performance envelope to the other.

It can always be argued that the pilot of the fighter designed for sustained manoeuvring has the best of both worlds, since by throttling back he can fight a transient performance combat if he wishes. However, there are snags to this. The first is that engines also

have their transient performance. Instant acceleration is just not available on demand; the engine takes several seconds to wind itself up when the throttle is opened. Therefore no pilot is likely to throttle back in combat, except under very unusual circumstances. Secondly, the fighter designed for sustained performance pays a penalty in transient performance. The type of wing fitted to fighters like this tends to reduce the rate of roll, and the extra drag caused by its excellent lifting qualities retards acceleration. Both penalties may appear marginal, but they nevertheless exist.

The reduced rate of roll is very noticeable in training films showing F-5 Tiger IIs versus F-15 Eagles. The tiny F-5 is outclassed by the big superfighter in all modes except one: rate of roll. In close manoeuvre combat, this makes life very difficult for Eagle pilots.

Close to the ultimate in transient performance is the Harrier, which can alter the angle of its jet thrust in flight – usually referred to as

vectoring in forward flight, or VIFF. This can be used to force an overshoot by using full reverse nozzle, causing a dramatic drop in speed. Returning the nozzles to the normal position gives instant acceleration because the engine is still running at full throttle. No fighter in existence can stay behind a Harrier if its pilot does not want him there.

VIFF can also be employed in other ways. In a turning contest it can be used to tighten up the turn and spit the pursuer out to one side, while in pursuit it can be used to nibble off a few degrees of angle to achieve a firing position. In addition, the Harrier remains controllable at speeds down to 60 knots, whereas most orthodox fighters are capable only of dipping their noses and staggering away, virtually devoid of any manoeuvre capability, at twice that speed.

The problem of using excess VIFF is that so much conventional performance is lost: it may be better to use this only as a last ditch manoeuvre to force the flythrough if conventional tactics have failed.

PAIRS MANOEUVRES

A single aircraft in a hostile environment is extremely vulnerable. Therefore fighters usually fly in elements of two. Although larger formations are often used for specific tasks, the pair is the basic element. Combat spread, also known as wide battle, is the most commonly used formation. Combat spread is a widely spaced formation, 5,000 to 9,000ft (roughly 1,520 to 2,740m) laterally, with between 3,000 and 5000ft (900 and 1,520m) of altitude separation, exact distances depending on the visibility conditions prevailing at the time. The high man is always the pilot flying furthest from the angle of the sun.

Left: In the US Navy's "Top Gun" fighter training programme adversary aircraft selected for their performance similarities to Soviet machines are used. The A-4 simulates the MiG-17, and the F-5E (seen here engaging a Phantom) the Mig-21. "Aggressor" squadrons of the USAF soon followed.

Below: Two Mirage F1s of the Armée de l'Air equipped for the air superiority role, with R-550 Magic missiles on the wingtips; and the leader also sports two Super 530s. Two 30mm cannon make up the weaponry. The formation shown here is welded wing. Useful in the days when the gun was the only air to air weapon, it is not used in combat.

Combat Spread Formation

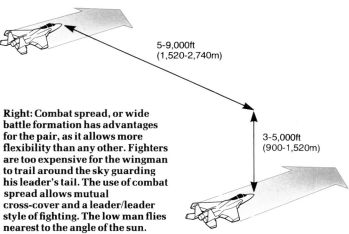

5-9,000ft
(1,520-2,740m)

3-5,000ft
(900-1,520m)

Right: Combat spread, or wide battle formation has advantages for the pair, as it allows more flexibility than any other. Fighters are too expensive for the wingman to trail around the sky guarding his leader's tail. The use of combat spread allows mutual cross-cover and a leader/leader style of fighting. The low man flies nearest to the angle of the sun.

Manoeuvres

A pair working as a team is much more effective than two fighters working individually. They guard each other's visual blind spots and, as illustrated in the Attack Section, hunt as a co-ordinated unit. The wide spacing is dictated by two factors: the long reach of contemporary weaponry, and the large amounts of sky needed for manoeuvre at high subsonic or transonic speeds. There are few set manoeuvres for the pair; just a few general tricks to meet certain situations, as follows.

THE CROSS-TURN

This is a method of reversing course without causing undue horizontal displacement of the formation. It can be used to meet a threat developing from astern, or to turn in pursuit after a head-on engagement. Each fighter breaks hard inward, the high man going low and the low man high or, where the tightest possible turn is needed, both men pulling high. In either case the high man at the end of the turn will be furthest from the Sun. The cross-turn, or inward turnabout as it is sometimes known, has the advantage that the pilots can clear each other's blind spots as they pass. The disadvantage is that they may briefly lose visual contact with each other.

THE SANDWICH

For a pair, the "sandwich" is the oldest trick in the book. A fighter attacked from the rear quarter outside the formation breaks into the attack. If he is followed by an enemy, his wingman slots neatly into place behind the bandit for a rear quarter shot, taking great care, of course, not to fire a heat missile until his comrade has cleared the danger area.

The Cross-turn or Inward Turnabout

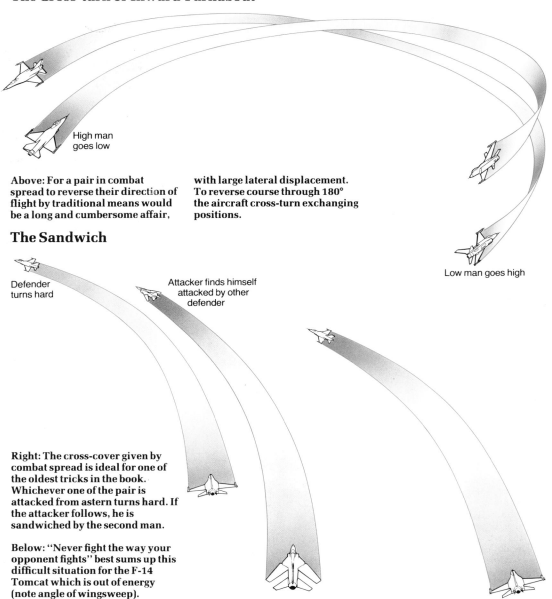

High man goes low

Low man goes high

Above: For a pair in combat spread to reverse their direction of flight by traditional means would be a long and cumbersome affair, with large lateral displacement. To reverse course through 180° the aircraft cross-turn exchanging positions.

The Sandwich

Defender turns hard

Attacker finds himself attacked by other defender

Right: The cross-cover given by combat spread is ideal for one of the oldest tricks in the book. Whichever one of the pair is attacked from astern turns hard. If the attacker follows, he is sandwiched by the second man.

Below: "Never fight the way your opponent fights" best sums up this difficult situation for the F-14 Tomcat which is out of energy (note angle of wingsweep).

The Offensive Split (One Version)

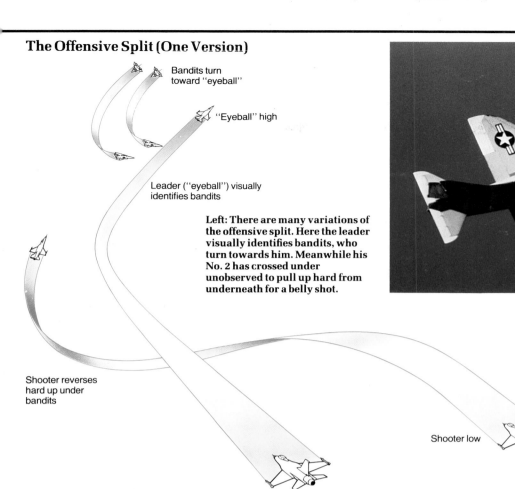

Bandits turn toward "eyeball"

"Eyeball" high

Leader ("eyeball") visually identifies bandits

Left: There are many variations of the offensive split. Here the leader visually identifies bandits, who turn towards him. Meanwhile his No. 2 has crossed under unobserved to pull up hard from underneath for a belly shot.

Shooter reverses hard up under bandits

Shooter low

Above: A beautiful high altitude shot of a Tomcat storming in on a Skyhawk like an avenging fury. The Skyhawk, with the sun at about seven o'clock, sets up a full deflection shot for the Tomcat, whose wings are extended, possibly indicating that his energy state is not all it might be. While dissimilar air combat practice is good fun, it is not the way the Tomcat should be used against a subsonic lightweight. Rather, the speed should be kept high and slashing attacks made, using its weaponry advantages.

THE OFFENSIVE SPLIT

A pair of fighters can carry out the "offensive split" manoeuvre in a variety of ways. In one version the nearest man is in combat spread, drawing the attention of the bandits, while his partner (hopefully unobserved) sneaks around the back either high or low, depending on relative altitudes at the start of the encounter. For example, referring back to the eyeball/shooter attack, when the lookout gains visual contact and clears the shooter to fire at the far bogey. The lookout will be visible to the enemy at much the same time, and the bandit will almost certainly react by turning towards him. The shooter, still low, still hopefully undetected, can swing across behind his leader, then reverse into a hard climbing turn which should bring him out into a good attacking position.

THE DEFENSIVE SPLIT

In the defensive split, the attackers have to choose between two targets. When they choose one they leave the other free as a potential threat to sandwich them. The defensive split is executed by a two-aircraft element in both horizontal and vertical planes. From the attacker's point of view it is preferable to follow the high man. The fighter that has split upwards will lose energy faster than the low man. Provided that the attackers entered the fight with

The Defensive Split

Below: The defensive split is used by a pair to divide the attention of the attackers. The split is made in both the vertical and horizontal planes. Whichever one the attackers choose to follow leaves them liable to counterattack by the other.

Attackers' dilemma: which to attack, high or low?

If attacked high man must try to bring fight down, and so gain support from his low man

If low man is not menaced, he must be ready to pitch up

a surplus of energy, the high man represents their best chance of a kill. Furthermore it will take the low man longer to get back into a fight high above him than it will for the high man to drop down. Also, the low man has more difficulty in spotting a fight above him than does the high man looking down. From the defender's point of view, the low man must be ready to pitch

up into the fight as soon as it becomes clear that he is not menaced, while the high man must attempt to bring the fight down as quickly as possible to enable the low man to support him. Of course, it is possible that an attacker, faced with a defensive split, will break off and look for an easier victim, in which case the split has succeeded.

MULTI-BOGEY CONSIDERATIONS

The air combat manoeuvres described earlier are essential skills in numerically small engagements which may sometimes occur in a shooting war, but untidy multi-participant actions are much more likely. The result is that fastening onto one opponent and following him through a series of set-piece manoeuvres makes the attacker predictable, and therefore vulnerable. The priorities in a multi-bogey engagement have to be established.

A combat mission starts with preparation on the ground. The mission briefing outlines the basic task and the way in which it is to be carried out. Then it is up to the pilots. Everything depends on teamwork, and the "what if" factors should be ironed out before the turbines start to spin. If AWACS and ground control are performing as they should, the mission might just go like clockwork. Against a background of intense ECM there is no such hope, and a series of "worst cases" must be catered for. The answers to

the following questions must be formulated before takeoff; there will be no time later.

How do flight members communicate if the radio is unusable? Must they guard against being pulled out of position? What happens if two flight members simultaneously acquire targets? Who decides who will attack? If the bandits are coming in waves, do the defenders hit the first wave, or evade and then intercept the rearmost enemies? Under what circumstances does a flight member take the lead? If the radar is jammed solid, do the pilots go high/low and search visually? Will 'burner be used for the first engagement, will pilots be selective? Do pilots try to manoeuvre into an astern position, or fearlessly charge straight into battle? Will the "eyeball search" be positioned high or low? Will defending aircraft reposition after an attack?

The questions to be answered are many, but the decisions must be made before the pilots engage the enemy. The line between teamwork and chaos is a very thin one. As US Navy Vietnam War ace Randy Cunningham has stated, "Have a plan. Have an alternate plan. Be prepared for the plan not to work." While at first glance this sounds like a staff instruction, it is a reminder to stay flexible.

Flexibility is the keynote in multi-bogey combats. Pilots should expect the unexpected, because it will happen. In peacetime training it is generally known how many aircraft will be involved. In wartime, extra bandits can be anticipated at any time,

literally out of the blue. All thoughts of outmanoeuvring an adversary can be abandoned. There is simply no time to cycle through complicated manoeuvre patterns: the process degenerates into look-shoot-break, or often just look-break. The best way to fight and survive is to keep energy levels high and fly in a series of short hard turns (hooks), interspersed with brief straight-line accelerations, taking shots of opportunity rather than creating them by sustained manoeuvre. Target fixation is a

problem, but more than a few seconds concentration on one bandit may well prove fatal.

Teamwork often breaks down in the confusion of a large-scale air battle, but, while the probability of the minority surviving a two-versus-six encounter is not good, the survival chance in a six-versus-eighteen combat (same mathematical odds) is much better, due to the amount of coincidental support available. The fight is multi-bogey on both sides.

It has even been argued that it is

Above: Mirage F1.Cs of l'Armée de l'Air patrol in fluid four formation, with the lower pair stepped down towards the sun. They are flying in the contrail belt, which they would not do in wartime.

Below: Lt. Randy Cunningham and Lt.(jg) William Driscoll of the USN board their F-4J Phantom. On May 10 1972, they shot down three MiG-17s in one engagement to become the first American aces in Vietnam. Their third victim was the ranking NVN ace.

an advantage to be outnumbered in a visual-distance turning fight, the reasoning being that a pair (for example) could take snap shots without having to worry overmuch about identification, while the numerically superior force would be inhibited by having to keep track of who was who. The exchange ratio of the outnumbered force would therefore be better; in theory, all the battles would be lost but the war would be won! The theory appears to overlook totally the survival instinct which would negate such an approach. As a Royal Flying Corps scout pilot commented in 1917, "Most crack fighters did not get their victims in dogfights. They preferred safer means."

DISENGAGEMENT

The final stage in air combat is disengagement. Colonel Dubrov's comments on the subject are revealing: "It is never given adequate attention and the inexperienced pilot frequently believes that, following an attack pass, particularly a successful one, the engagement is over and he can relax". Diminished vigilance at this stage is therefore a potential cause of loss. The question is thus posed, what is the best way out?

The ideal way to disengage is to destroy the enemy, but this is rarely achieved. Yet the rate at which modern fighters burn fuel has made disengagement more important than ever. Pre-flight preparation helps by identifying the approximate point(s) at which fuel shortage will become critical, bearing in mind that an economical cruise home is a peacetime luxury. Furthermore, the "home" base may not be available if it has been the target of enemy attack. Disengagement must therefore be made with sufficient fuel both to fight on the

way back if necessary, and to handle a diversion to an alternative airfield.

The method of disengagement should be considered before commencing the attack. A high-speed strike followed by a high-speed angle-off exit is the simplest method. Getting free from a dogfight is much more difficult. The timing must be immaculate. The time to break off manoeuvre combat is when the situation is neutral, with neither aircraft having an advantage.

Above: The MiG-21 has been updated over the years, but remains basically an air superiority fighter. One great advantage is its small size: from head-on it is nearly invisible at two miles range.

Below: Contrasts in fighter design. A two-seat, twin-engined F-4 Phantom is flanked by two single-seat, single-engined F-104 Starfighters, while two single-seat, twin-engined F-15 Eagles bring up the rear. Compare relative sizes for ease of spotting.

If a pilot comes under attack, and recovers to a neutral position, then disengages without damage, he has won the fight. However, if he is the assailant, and his opponent outmanoeuvres him and attains a neutral position, it is then time to depart and look for easier prey. If he waits until he becomes disadvantaged, disengagement becomes fraught with peril.

SPLIT S DISENGAGEMENT

Among manoeuvres which can be used to disengage, the Split S has some merit. Ground returns can be used to provide a certain amount of masking against radar and heat detection. There is also a marked reluctance on the part of fighter pilots to follow anyone down while more bandits remain above. If sufficient energy is available, a zoom climb into the Sun might cause a pursuer to lose visual contact. Alternatively a head-on pass followed by a dive for separation may be used, as many miles can be gained before the opponent can get turned around. The prime requirement of disengagement is therefore a good head of steam. Energy dissipated in manoeuvre combat is no longer available – which is an argument for entering manoeuvre combat only when forced; that is, defensively. A fight in which a pilot keeps his energy state high, and restricts himself to slashing attacks, is easier to disengage from.

Disengagement is one of the most difficult and most important areas of air combat. This is why combat persistence is rated so highly as a prime quality of a fighter aeroplane. The combatant who is forced to break off the fight through fuel shortage is at a disadvantage. If the effect of low fuel state can be minimised, it reduces the risk considerably.

To the individual pilot, survival is very important. He can always come back tomorrow or the next day to achieve a kill. To be able to do that, he must survive today. Most importantly, he must be cautious enough to realise when he is in over his head, and he must remain vigilant at all times.

In summary, the pilot should remember the following once he is engaged in any form of air combat that will put himself into a firing position, or alternatively one that makes him vulnerable to enemy fire: he must, once close combat has begun, maintain visual contact with the enemy, and in a turning contest if he does lose sight of him he must not stop turning. The pilot should always turn towards the enemy to counter his attack, trying to meet him with the maximum angle off. As he does this he must decide whether to stay and fight or disengage. He should never reverse a turn unless he is sure he has forced the enemy to fly through.

The pilot should make the best use of his aircraft's performance, and use the vertical. If he is losing out in combat, he must disengage at his earliest opportunity.

Training

The modern fighter pilot is a highly skilled technician trained to get the utmost out of his machine, his weapons, and also the tactical position in which he finds himself. In order to do this he must constantly seek to expand his own limits, both physically and psychologically. Psychological preparation is perhaps the most important factor of all.

His first task is to master his aeroplane; to fly it to the limits of its performance envelope without straying over the boundary into the region of lost control. This must be practised until it becomes totally automatic. His aim is to be able to give all his attention to using his machine to fight. There will be precious little concentration to spare for flying in the heat of battle. He must also be able to cope with aircraft malfunctions and remain in control of the situation.

The limits of the flight performance envelope are explored partly in a simulator on the ground and partly in the air. Confidence must be gained in pure flying.

Training to cope with equipment malfunctions is essential. Modern fighters are extremely costly, as are pilots, and every effort must be made to preserve them when something goes wrong. This aspect is the responsibility of the simulator team. All sorts of difficult situations can be created on the simulator and the pilot can learn the correct reactions without hazarding both himself and an expensive aeroplane. The pilot should now be able to handle his fighter well and safely; not that training and practice ever ceases throughout his entire flying life.

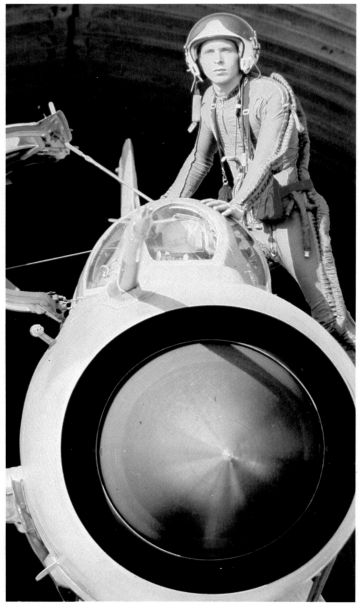

Above: Thoughts of Mother Russia are apparent in this idealised pose of a young Soviet pilot about to board his trusty MiG-21. According to Soviet propaganda, his motivation is mainly political. In practice it is likely to be country rather than creed.

Right: Despite the red star on the bone-dome, thoughts of Mother Russia are not in evidence as Captain Eric Coloney of the 527th TFT (Aggressor) Squadron prepares for takeoff. His F-5E has a performance comparable to the MiG-21, which it simulates.

His next task is to learn to fight.

Detection systems and weapon capabilities must next be mastered, his own and also those of any opponent he may have to face. He cannot know too much about the capabilities of a potential enemy, flight performance, weapons, detection equipment potential etc. He must know the areas and circumstances where his equipment has the edge, or where he may be disadvantaged. Tactics enters at this stage. Knowing the right trick to pull out of the bag in any given situation is the name of the game. But unfortunately there is no universal key. It is impossible to take a set of circumstances and say "this is the way to do it." Air combat is far too complex for that. Even though Russian commentators have a penchant for chess similies, air combat cannot be reduced to set-piece moves. All the pilot can do is to play the percentage moves which experience has taught him work more often than not. Following the high man in countering the defensive split is a good example of a percentage move. But what really determines the tactics used is respective initial positions and weaponry.

Air combat manoeuvring is an essential part of training. It has become fairly refined, with basic moves and standard counters. Much combat practice is perforce against fellow squadron members. With both participants flying similar aircraft, the contest becomes one of flying skill, and is of little value when compared with combat practice against an opponent flying a fighter with a totally different set of

Top: Typical scene in a crew locker room as pilots of the Aeronautica Militare Italiano check their radio and oxygen equipment at the Godfrey Test Cabinet. Kitting up to fly a modern fighter is a tedious process.

Above: Debriefing is very important. With the help of taped transmissions and gun camera film, the mission is reconstructed and the actions of the participants analysed. An Aggressor debrief is conducted by Capt. Coloney.

Above: ". . . and as he overshot . . ." Major Nikolai Skorofod relishes an event of the past mission. This picture, from an airfield in the soviet Red Banner Bakinsky District, typifies the fighter fraternity worldwide.

Below: Laden down with parachute and survival gear, Captain Coloney boards his F-5E. Preparation for the flight began about two hours earlier. Everything has been double checked. Now it is time to go.

The Well-dressed Fighter Pilot

1. Helmet, individually form fitted, worn over skull cap.
2. Visor control lowers visor from inside front of helmet. This is single visor type; double visor helmet worn by low-flyers to guard against birdstrikes.
3. Moleskin paper strip protects canopy from scratches during violent manoeuvres.
4. Parachute harness.
5. Oxygen connector.
6. Underarm life preserver.
7. Parachute leg fastener.
8. G suit bladder.
9. Velcro kneeboard patch.
10. G suit, over overalls.
11. Knee cut-outs in G suit.
12. Survival knife.
13. G suit hose.
14. Leather lined Nomex fire-proof gloves.
15. Parachute delay timer.
16. Parachute D handle.
17. Oxygen hose and micro-phone lead.
18. Oxygen mask with integral microphone.

A Typical Fighter Pilot

Born at Gloversville, N.Y. in 1951, Eric Coloney has an Air Force background. His father flew Mustangs in WW II and, remaining in the service after the war, attained the rank of Lt. Col. Eric decided at an early age that he wanted to be a fighter pilot. On leaving college, he entered Norwich University, Vermont, where he learned to fly. Graduating in 1974 with a B.Sc. in Business Administration, he was immediately commissioned into the USAF. Graduate Pilot Training occupied the next year, followed by the Fighter Lead-in Course. On completion, he was posted to the 311th Tactical Fighter Training Squadron at Luke AFB. His first operational posting was to Hahn, West Germany, in January 1977, and he spent the next three years flying F-4E Phantoms. Next came Aggressor training at Nellis, then a posting to the 527th Aggressor Sqn at Alconbury in the United Kingdom. Described by a former commander as "The very finest type of young man America produces", his manner is modest and laid back. This, coupled with a wry sense of humour, masks an iron will and a determination to excell. As he himself admits, a fighter pilot with a small ego just does not exist.

characteristics. Yet however dissimilar the aeroplanes, one versus one is a peacetime practice; good fun, but hardly likely to arise in wartime. Even should it occur in wartime, only a very complacent pilot would treat it as such; another bandit or three is likely to join the party unexpectedly.

The fighter pilot is part of a highly trained and co-ordinated team. He fights as part of a team in which mutual support is essential to survival. After one versus one, two versus two and even larger combats are used in training. Sometimes "cut-throat", or everybody against everybody fights are organised. This gives the pilot experience in the co-incidental support which occurs in large multi-bogey fights. It also teaches him not to fasten onto one opponent for more than a few seconds.

The greatest difficulty that training seeks to overcome is the confusion factor. The pilot who handles his fighter to its limits

Above: Alpha Jets of l'Armée de l'Air practising formation flying. For the advanced training role fairly good performance is needed, otherwise the object of the exercise cannot be fulfilled. It provides a valuable stepping stone between basic training and the front line fighter. The Alpha Jet also has a secondary function as a light strike/reconnaissance fighter.

Below: Chinese Nancheng Q-5s form an impressive lineup. Some sort of "Dismounted Flight Training" is in progress, as everybody is walking around holding a model aeroplane.

using conditioned reflexes and automatic responses to manoeuvre requirements has more time consciously to weigh up potential threats and opportunities, and to make decisions based on his own personal experience. He must be able to develop a three-dimensional awareness, summing up the situation in terms of time, distance, and relative movement.

Randy Cunningham has no doubts about the value of air combat training. Two further sound pieces of advice are attributed to him: "There are no points for second place", and "You fight like you train". Making the correct decisions in combat is directly related to the experience levels built up in training, which in turn is directly related to the effort expended. World War II American ace Walker Mahurin attributed part of his success to the fact that long before he ever met a German in the air, he spent hours "sitting in the sack", figuring out possible moves to counter certain situations. On more than one occasion a similar situation did arise. Mahurin, having mentally been there before, was able to exploit it to advantage.

Analysed data from both world wars – defining "decisive combats" as those in which a pilot was either shot down or shoots down his opponent – has concluded that only one pilot in every fifteen had a better than even chance of surviving his first "decisive combat". Yet after surviving five "decisive combats", his chance of surviving his sixth had increased by a factor of twenty. Flying ability was hardly likely to have improved sufficiently to account for the difference; enhanced experience level would be the dominant factor. From this, it is not difficult to conclude that rigorous training standards can pay very high dividends.

DISSIMILAR AIR COMBAT TRAINING

At this point, mention must be made of the USAF "Aggressor" and USN "Top Gun" fighter training units. In both, highly skilled pilots fly aircraft which perform similarly to those of possible opponents, their function being to expose squadron pilots to the nearest possible simulation to actual warfare. In other words, they take fighter pilots through a close approximation of the early "decisive combats" in which experience levels grow rapidly. The "Top Gun" programme was initiated in time for USN fliers to benefit towards the end of the war in Vietnam and was vindicated by a greatly improved kill ratio.

Training can, however, have a certain negative value. Like most things, training has two sides. The good side we have just examined; the negative side is obvious when the matter is considered. Only rarely is anyone killed, and then by accident, not design. This produces a sterile environment. At

Top: A Hawk trainer of the Royal Air Force, the best subsonic jet trainer in the world. In time of war it would carry two Sidewinders and make a useful supplement to the local air defences.

Above: A tight formation of USAF T-38 advanced trainers. With their exemplary handling qualities, these supersonic trainers have helped over 50,000 pilots gain their wings.

Below: The ultimate in training is provided by the USAF's Aggressor (shown here) and USN's Top Gun squadrons, with their facilities for successful dissimilar air combat instruction.

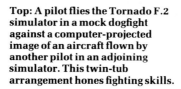

Top: A pilot flies the Tornado F.2 simulator in a mock dogfight against a computer-projected image of an aircraft flown by another pilot in an adjoining simulator. This twin-tub arrangement hones fighting skills.

Above left: Royal Air Force pilots watch a re-run of a simulator combat in the computer room at BAe Warton. The central display shows relative positions of the combatants together with readouts of speed, height, etc.

Above and below: Some idea of the realism attainable by simulator displays is given in these shots of F-16s as seen in the CT-5 system developed by Rediffusion Simulation. The distance perspective in the top picture is

excellent and the detail in the background of the lower shot is outstanding. The CT-5 system can simulate day, dusk, or night, and has various modes—weapon delivery, carrier operations, and air combat.

the end of the day, the participants head home for a cold beer, TV and an armchair. But first, they need a "kill" to report at debriefing, both to prove that they haven't been wasting their time, also to prop up their ego. To obtain a kill, they will often take chances that they would not take in wartime. When live missiles are flying, few pilots are prepared to be fancy. Also militating against training effectiveness are the safety regulations. Whilst necessary in peacetime, they detract from realism.

But training in the air is a very expensive occupation, particularly in fuel. A fairly recent development, is the "twin-tub" air combat simulator. Two identical pressurised domes, each containing a simulator, enable pilots to fly against each other. An ingenious system of models and mirrors, linked by computer, projects an image of the opponent as he manoeuvres in mock combat. While the twin-tub is limited (at present) to one versus one combats, there is no limitation on the type of fighter that may be flown provided that a computer programme exists for it. One early lesson learned in a simulator is that putting the gunsight on the target too early is a mistake; as the range closes, a "square corner" develops which it is impossible to "brute force" through. The result is either an overshoot, or a series of roller-coaster type gyrations in an attempt to stay in an attacking position. The principle of lead pursuit was quickly learned.

The Russians have an even cheaper method of simulation, suitable for multi-aircraft combats.

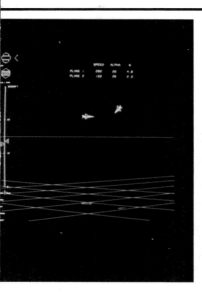

Above left: Close-up of a debriefing terminal in the BAe computer room at Warton. At the debrief pilots can see the entire combat replayed and learn from where they went wrong.

Above right: Morale is an important factor in warfare, and leadership boosts morale. Soviet Maj. Gen. Alexei Prokhorov talks to students at the M. V. Frunze Military Academy.

Below: Come in No. 3, your time is up! Air Combat Manoeuvring Instrumentation of the USAF records a head-on AIM-7F "kill" on aircraft No. 3, now enclosed in a symbolic coffin.

It is called dismounted flight training, and consists of "walking through" combat situations holding a model aeroplane. The purpose is to instil a sense of time/spatial relationship.

The value of careful and rigorous training cannot be denied. It does, however, pose the question, are aces born or can they be made?

What does the historical record show? What qualities do the great aces, of whatever nationality, have in common? Above-average flying ability is one, marksmanship another, determination a third. Yet these qualities are possessed by many pilots, while the great aces are a mere handful, barely one in every hundred. The main quality that they shared was the ability to survive while those around them fell. We have already established that the dominant factor in air fighting is surprise. It is therefore reasonable to conclude that the great aces were masters of the surprise attack, and were equally difficult to take by surprise, whether in the bounce, or in the whirling shambles of the dogfight. By implication, they therefore possessed the quality of alertness and situational awareness to an exceptional degree. They also possessed another, indefinable quality: luck. This is not to denigrate their achievements in any way, but with few exceptions they were all shot down, many of them more than once, or brought home badly damaged aircraft. Another inch to the right . . .! We should also consider the environment in which they fought. The massive expansion of air forces in both world wars inevitably led to a lowering of standards, both in recruitment and in training. Consequently, the ratio of aces to "average" pilots was low, and the success of the aces was in a large part at the expense of the others. Very few conclusive combats took place between aces. The preponderance of those with less ability notwithstanding, the aces had to survive some very messy multi-aircraft engagements. Survive is the operative word. If survival can be taught, then aces can be made.

Glossary

A

A/A Air-to-air
AAA Anti-aircraft artillery
AAM Air-to-air missile
AAR Air-to-air refuelling
AR Airbase
active Emitting EM radiation
ADC Air-data computer
ADF Automatic direction finding
ADI Attitude/director indicator
AFB Air Force Base (US)
A/G Air-to-ground
AGL Above ground level
AI Airborne interception

ANG US Air National guard
AOA Angle of attack, angle at which wing meets oncoming air
AR Air refuelling
ARBS Angle-rate bombing system
aspect ratio Slenderness of wing in plan-form, numerically span²/area
ASPJ Advanced self-protection jammer
ASW Anti-submarine warfare
ATC Air traffic control
ATO Assisted takeoff
Awacs Airborne warning and control system
azimuth Angular measure in the horizontal plane, or direction

B

BG USAF Bomb Group
BIT(E) Built-in test (equipment)
B-type scan Horizontal axis is bearing, vertical axis is range
BW USAF Bomb Wing
bypass ratio Turbofan ratio of bypass cold airflow to hot flow through central core of engine

C

camber Curvature of a surface in an airflow

CAP Combat air patrol
CAS Close air support
CBLS Container, bomb, light store
CBU Cluster bomb unit
CC Central computer
CCV Control-configured vehicle
CFAR Constant false-alarm rate
CG Centre of gravity
CNI Communications, navigation, identification
Comed Combined map and electronic display
conformal Shaped to fit closely against aircraft exterior
CRT Cathode-ray tube

McDonnell-Douglas F/A-18A Hornet

1. Radome
2. Flight refuelling probe, extended
3. M61-A1 Vulcan, 20-mm rotary cannon
4. Ammunition magazine
5. Hinged Windscreen (access to instruments)
6. Instrument panel and cockpit displays
7. Head-up display
8. Canopy
9. Martin-Baker Mk10L "zero-zero" ejection seat
10. Avionics equipment bay
11. Structural space provision for second seat (TF-18 trainer variant)
12. Leading edge root extension
13. Position light
14. Fuselage bag-type fuel tanks
15. Leading edge flap, down
16. Starboard wing integral fuel tank
17. AIM-9L Sidewinder air-to-air missile
18. Missile launch rail
19. Wing tip navigation light
20. Wing fold hinge joint
21. Starboard wing folded position
22. Drooping aileron
23. Flap vane
24. Single slotted flap
25. Flap hydraulic jack
26. Hydraulic reservoirs
27. Fuel vent
28. Strobe light

29. Rudder hydraulic actuator
30. Tail navigation light
31. Radar warning aerial
32. Fuel jettison
33. Starboard all-moving tailplane
34. Airbrake, open
35. ECM aerial
36. Radar warning aerial
37. Airbrake hydraulic jack
38. Formation lighting strip
39. Afterburner nozzles
40. Afterburner nozzle actuators
41. Port all-moving tailplane
42. Tailplane spigot mounting
43. Arrestor hook, lowered
44. Tailplane hydraulic actuator
45. General Electric F404 Afterburning turbofan engine
46. Formation lighting strip
47. Aileron hydraulic actuator
48. Wing fold rotary actuator and gearbox
49. AIM-9L Sidewinder, air-to-air missile
50. Leading edge flap rotary actuator
51. Port wing integral fuel tank
52. Outboard stores pylon mounting
53. Leading edge flap drive shaft
54. Engine shaft driven accessory equipment gearbox
55. Auxiliary power turbine
56. Aft retracting main undercarriage
57. Inboard stores pylon mounting
58. AIM-7 Sparrow, air-to-air missile

59. Leading edge flap drive motor and gearbox
60. Main undercarriage retraction jack
61. Air conditioning equipment bay
62. Cockpit pressurisation and air conditioning ram air intake
63. Nose undercarriage hydraulic jack
64. Liquid oxygen converter
65. Boarding ladder, extended
66. Forward retracting nose undercarriage
67. Catapult launch strop
68. Control column
69. Rudder pedals
70. Ammunition feed chute
71. Angle of attack transmitter
72. Pitot head
73. Formation lighting strip
74. Radar equipment bay
75. Forward ECM aerial
76. Radar scanner gimballing mechanism
77. Radar scanner (flat plate)

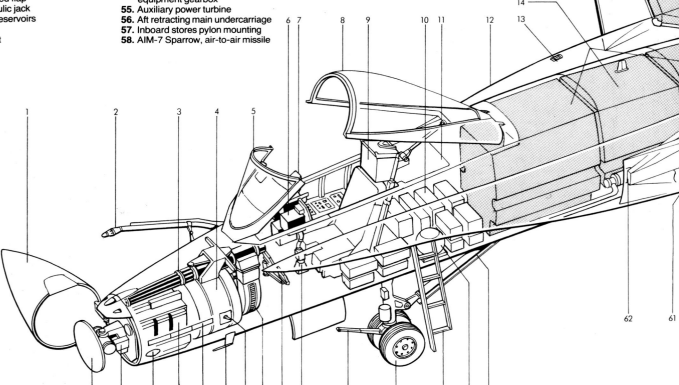

CW Continuous-wave EM radiation

D

DBS Doppler beam sharpening
DECM DEception (or defensive) ECM
dedicated Used for that particular purpose only
DF Direction finding
digital Calculating by numbers or other discrete bits of information which are counted, not measured
DLI Deck-launched intercept
DME Distance-measuring equipment
DoD US Department of Defense

dogtooth Sharp kink in leading edge of wing or tailplane to generate a strong vortex
doppler Radar making use of shift in frequency of signals reflected from Earth ahead of or behind aircraft (to give measure of true groundspeed) or of signals received from fixed (Earth) and moving targets, to give MTI

E

ECCM Electronic counter-countermesures
ECM Electronic countermeasures

EHF Extra high frequency
EM Electromagnetic (radiation includes radio, radar, light and heat)
EO Electro-optical
ESM Electronic support (or surveillance) measures
EW Electronic warfare

F

FA Soviet Frontal Aviation
FAC Forward air control(ler)
Fast Fuel and sensor, tactical
FBW Fly by wire, ie electrical signalling
FLIR Forward-looking IR

FMICW Frequency-modulatd interrupted (or intermittent) CW
FOV Field of view
Fowler Type of flap which rolls out on tracks from beneath the rear of the fixed wing, thus increasing wing area
FR Flight refuelling

G

g Acceleration due to Standard Gravity, 9.8m/s^2, unit of linear acceleration
G-band EM radiation of 4 to 6GHz
GCI Ground-controlled interception
GHz Gigahertz, thousands of millions of

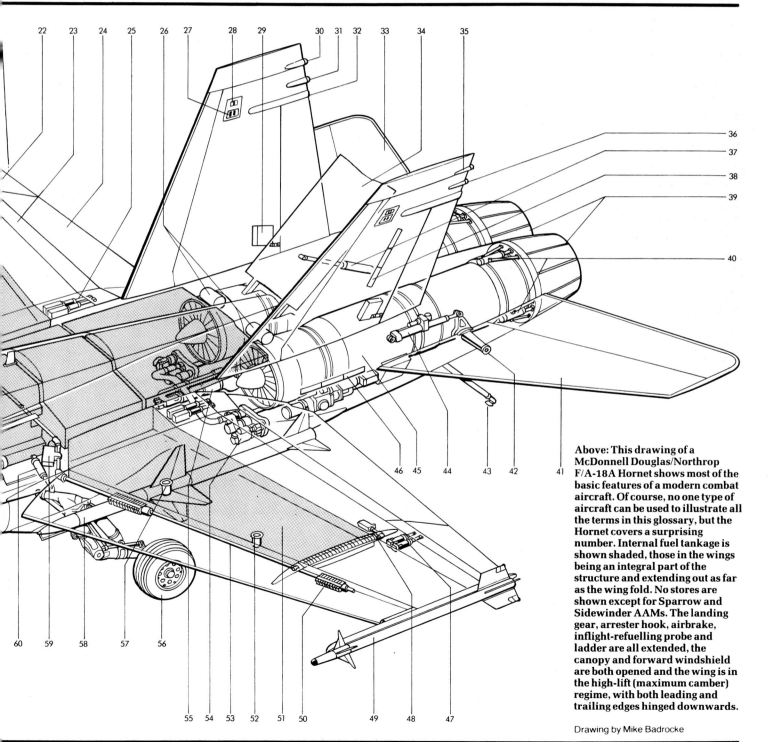

Above: This drawing of a McDonnell Douglas/Northrop F/A-18A Hornet shows most of the basic features of a modern combat aircraft. Of course, no one type of aircraft can be used to illustrate all the terms in this glossary, but the Hornet covers a surprising number. Internal fuel tankage is shown shaded, those in the wings being an integral part of the structure and extending out as far as the wing fold. No stores are shown except for Sparrow and Sidewinder AAMs. The landing gear, arrester hook, airbrake, inflight-refuelling probe and ladder are all extended, the canopy and forward windshield are both opened and the wing is in the high-lift (maximum camber) regime, with both leading and trailing edges hinged downwards.

Drawing by Mike Badrocke

cycles per second
GP General-purpose (bomb)
GPNS Global positioning navigation system

H

H-band EM radiation 6 to 8GHz
hardpoint Local region of structure strengthened and adapted to carry a pylon or other external load
HAS Hardened aircraft shelter, offering some protection against non-nuclear attack
HDD Head-down display, ie inside cockpit
HE High-explosive
HF High-frequency
hi High altitude, typically over 30,000ft, 9km
Hotas Hands on throttle and stick
HP High pressure
HSD Horizontal situation display
HSI Horizontal situation indicator

HUD Head-up display
Hudwas HUD weapon-aiming sight

I

IA-PVO Manned interceptor forces of Soviet air-defence forces
I-band EM radiation 8 to 10 GHZ
IFF Identification friend or foe
IIR Imaging IR
ILS Instrument landing system
INAS Inertial nav/attack system
INS Inertial navigation system
IR Infra-red, EM radiation longer than deepest red light but sensed as heat
IRCM IR countermeasures
IRWR IR warning receiver

J

J-band EM radiation 10 to 20GHz
jammer ECM emitter designed to smother hostile emissions
JTIDS Joint tactical information distribution system

K

kHz Kilohertz, thousands of cycles per second
Kruger Flap unfolded from below wing leading edge to give bluff high-lift entry to a thin high-speed wing
kT Kilotonnes yield of nuclear device
kVA Kilovolt-amperes, unit of electric power
kW Kilowatts, unit of DC electric power

L

LABS Low-altitude bombing system
LAD Low-altitude dispenser
Lantirn Low-altitude navigation and targeting IR for (or at) night
LE Leading edge
Lerx LE root extension
LGB Laser guided bomb
LL(L)TV Low light (level) TV
lo Low altitude, as low as safe to fly, typically 200 to 1,000ft, 90-300m

Lox Liquid oxygen
LRMTS Laser ranger and marked-target seeker
LST Laser spot tracker

M

m Metres
MCAS Marine Corps air station
MDC Miniature detonating cord
MFD Multifunction display
MHz Megahertz, millions of cycles per second
MRM Medium-range missile
MTI Moving-target indication, radar can eliminate returns from all except moving targets
MTO Maximum takeoff (weight)

N

NACA US National Advisory Committee for Aeronautics
NAS Naval air station
nav/attack Used for navigation and to aim weapons against surface target

Index

Page numbers in bold type refer to subjects of captions or charts, etc.

A

A-4 Skyhawk, **118-9, 189, 204, 206, 211**
A-5 Nanzhang Q-5, Type 5 Qianjiji, **138-9**
A-7 Corsair II, **166-7**
A-10 Thunderbolt II, **37, 102-3, 176, 182**
AA-5 Ash missile, **41**
AAM carriage, **29**
ACA, **15, 17**
AIM-7 Sparrow, **46, 47, 197**
AIM-9 Sidewinder, **38, 39, 43, 86-7; 94-5, 197**
AIM-54 Phoenix, **44-5, 76-7, 187, 188**
AIM-120 Amraam, **45**
AM-X EMBRAER, **80-1**
AV-8B Harrier II, **120-1**
Acceleration, **176-7, 191**
  G forces, **179**
Aeritalia/Aermacchi/EMBRAER AM-X, **80-1**
Aerodynamics, **18-25, 177-81**
Afterburners, **176-7**
Agile Combat Aircraft, **15, 17**
Airfield strikes, **183-4**
Alpha Jet, **93-3**
Alpha Jet wings, **18, 25**
Amraam (AIM-120), **45**
Angle of attack (OAO), **178-9**
Armament, **36-47**
  see also under specific aircraft
Arnold Engineering Development Center, **10-11**
Ash (AA-5) missile, **41**
Atmospheres, **176**
Attack methods, **175, 196-9**
Avenger gun (GAA-8/A), **36, 37**
AWACS (E-3A), **186**

B

Barrel roll attack, **206-7**
Battlefield interdiction, **183**
Blended roots, **29**
Boeing E-3A AWACS, **186**
Bombing, **183, 185**
Break maneuver, **200**
British Aerospace
  Agile Combat Aircraft, **15, 17**
  Buccaneer and Mk. 50, **82-3**
    with ECM pod, **64**
  Harrier, **84-5, 185**
    RWR in, **51**
  Hawk, **86-7**
  Lightning, **88-9**
  Sea Harrier FRS.1, **79, 90-1**
BAe/McDonnell Douglas AV-8B harrier II, **120-1**

Brewer, **168-9**
Buccaneer and Mk. 50, **82-3**
  with ECM pod, **64**

C

CCV, **23-4, 55-6**
CNIAR/Soko IAR-93 Orao, **152-3**
Canard foreplanes, **22-4, 28**
Chaff, **56-7**
Closing, combat methods, **175, 195-6**
Cockpit displays, **66-75**
Combat manoevures, **175, 200-13**
Combat methods, **194-9**
Combat/payload radius, **27**
Combat, phases of, **175, 194-213**
Combat spread formation, **209**
Composite materials, **26, 27, 28, 29**
Cone of vulnerability, **200**
Conformal pallets, **62**
Control-configures vehicle, **23-4, 55-6**
Coot-A (Il-18) EW aircraft, **61**
Corsair II (A-7), **166-7**
Costs, **15-17**
Cross-turn, **210**

D

Dassault-Breguet
  Alpha Jet, **92-3**
  Mirage III and 5, **22, 94-5**
  Mirage F-1, **19, 96-7, 182, 209, 212**
  Mirge 2000, **14, 41, 98-9**
  Super Etendard, **100-1**
Deception ECM (DECM), **55-6**
Defensive split, **211**
Design, **14-18**
Detection, and its avoidance, **175, 194-5**
Direct lift control (DLC), **24**
Direct side force control (DSFC), **25**
Disengagement manoeuvres, **175, 213**
Dispensers, ECM, **57, 78**
Displays, **66-75**
Distraction, combat methods, **199**
Dornier/Dassault Breguet Alpha Jet, **92-3**
Drag, **176, 177**
Draken, **146-7**
Dress, pilots, **215**

E

E-3A AWACS, **186**
EA-6B Prowler EW aircraft, **68-60, 65**
ECM, **53-65**
  deception ECM (DECM), **55-6**
  pods, **55-6, 59, 62-5, 78, 122-3**
EF-111A Electric Fox, **58-61**
EW see Electronic warfare
Eagle (F-15), **124-5, 185-6, 197, 200-1, 213**
  cockpit, **70-2**
  radar, **48, 49, 53**

Electric Fox (EF-111A), **58-61**
Electronic warfare, **48-65**
  aircraft, **58-65**
    internal vs. external installations, 61-5
    Russian, **60-1, 61**
  see also specific aircraft, eg Electric Fox
EMBRAER AM-X, **80-1**
Energy state, **178**
Engines, **30-5**
  see also under specific aircraft
"Eyeball"/shooter method, **199, 211**

F

F-1 Mirage, **19, 96-7, 182, 209, 212**
F-1 (Mitsubishi), **136-7**
F.2 Tornado, **16, 17, 18, 22, 47, 56, 142-3, 187, 193**
F-4 Phantom II, **16-17, 47, 122-3, 174, 177, 181, 184, 192, 193, 202, 204, 206, 208, 212, 213**
  radar, **48-9**
  with Pave Tack, **63**
F-5, **140-1, 190, 208**
  cockpit, **68**
F-14 Tomcat, **18, 21, 44-5, 76-7, 112-13, 187, 188, 189, 210, 211**
  cockpit, **69**
F-15 Eagle, **124-5, 185-6, 197, 200-1, 213**
  cockpit, **70-2**
  radar, **48, 49, 53**
F-16 Fighting Falcon, **15, 20, 23, 29, 43, 46, 62-3, 106-7, 178, 187, 190, 191**
  cockpit, **66, 69, 71-4**
  AFTI, **25**
F-104 Starfighter, **14, 116-17, 213**
F-111, **19, 79, 108-9**
  antennae, **52-3**
  cockpit, **67**
F/A-18 Hornet, **65, 72, 126-7**
FBW (Fly-by-wire), **24, 25**
FRS.1 Sea Harrier, **79, 90-1**
Fairchild Republic A-10 Thunderbolt II, **37, 102-3, 176, 182**
Fencer (Su-24), **162-3, 184**
Fighter engine development, **32-3**
Fighting effectiveness, **186-93**
  requirements met by Tornado F.2, **193**
Fighting Falcon (F-16), **15, 20, 23, 29, 43, 62-3, 106-7, 178, 187, 190, 191**
  cockpit, **66, 69, 71-4**
  AFTI, **25**
Fire power, **192-3**
Fishbed see MiG-21
Fitter see Sukhoi Su-17
Flagon see sukhoi Su-15
Flight performance envelopes, **26, 27, 180-1**
Flogger see MiG-23, MiG-27

Fluid four formation, **212**
Fly-by-wire (FBW), **24, 25**
Forward-swept wings (FSW), **26, 27**
Forward velocity vector, **201**
Foxbat see MiG-25
Freedom Fighter (F-5A), **140-1**

G

G forces, **179**
Gear, pilots, **215**
General Dynamics
  EF-111A Electric Fox, **58-61**
  F-16 Fighting Falcon, **15, 20, 23, 29, 43, 46, 62-3, 10607, 178, 187, 190, 191**
    cockpit, **66, 67, 71-4**
    AFTI, **25**
  F-111, **19, 69, 108-9**
    antennae, **52-3**
    cockpit, **67**
  YF-16 prototype, **24**
General Electric engines
  F101, **33**
  F404, **31**
  J79, **33**
General Electric guns
  GAU-13, **38**
  Avenger (GAU-8/A), **36, 37**
  Vulcan (M61), **37, 38**
Grippen (JAS-39) cockpit, **74**
Grumman
  A-6 Intruder, **110-11**
    cockpit, **67**
  EA-6B Prowler EW aircraft, **58-60, 65**
  F-14 Tomcat, **18, 21, 44-5, 76-7, 112-13, 187, 188, 189, 210, 211**
    cockpit, **69**
  X-29A prototype, **27**
Guidance, missiles, **38-47, 188**
Gun attack, **198, 200**
  avoiding multiple hits, **200**
Guns, **36-8, 192-3**
  helmet pointing gun system, **75**
Gust response, **20-1**

H

HUD, **42, 71-75**
  see also Cockpit displays
Half roll, **203**
  disengagement, **213**
Hands on throttle & stick (Hotas), **73-4**
Harrier, **84-5, 185**
  RWR, **51**
  Harrier II (AV-8B), **120-1**
  Sea Harrier FRS.1, **79, 90-1**
Hawk, **86-7**
Head-on gun attack, **198**
Head-on visibility, **189**
Head-up displays, **42, 71-5**
  see also Cockpit displays

NIS NATO identification system
nm Nautical mile, 6,080ft. 1.853km

O

OKB Soviet experimental construction (ie design) bureau

P

pallet Platform upon which one or more mission equipments is mounted for installation in or beneath aircraft
passive Non-emitting
PD Pulse-doppler radar
pod Streamlined container for equipment carried outside aircraft
PPI Plan-poistion indication
PRF Pulse-repetition frequency
PVO See IA-PVO

R

R&D Research and development
raster Picture generated by large number of close parallel lines, as in domestic TV

RBC Rapid-bloom chaff
RCJ Reaction control jet
RCS Radar cross-section, apparent size of target to radar
RDT&E Research, development, test and evaluation
RHAWS Radar homing and warning system
RHWR Radar homing and warning receiver
RMTS See LRMTS
RPV Remotely piloted vehicle
RWR Radar warning receiver

S

SAC USAF Strategic Air Command
SAM Surface-to-air missile
SAR Synthetic-aperture radar
SARH Semi-active radar homing
semi-active Not itself emitting but homing on radar or other signals reflected from a target
SIF Selective interrogation facility
signature Characteristic 'fingerprint' of

every emitted waveform or EM signal
SLAR Sideways-looking airborne radar
slick Low-drag streamlined bomb
smart Self-guided, especially homing on target illuminated by laser
SOJ Stand-off jammer
SRM Short-range missile
STO(VL) Short takeoff (and vertical landing), hence STOL

T

TAC USAF Tactical Air Command
Tacan Tactical air navigation
taileron Tailplane (horizontal stabilizer) in left/right halves able to function as both elevators and ailerons
Tarps Tactical aircraft reconnaissance pod system
TCS Television camera set
TED Threat evaluation display
TFR Terrain-following radar; hence TF flight, TF mode
TRAM Target-recognition attack

multisensor
TsAGI Soviet central aero and hydrodynamics institute
TWS Track while scan
TWT Travelling-wave tube

U

UHF Ultra-high frequency, 300MHz to 3GHZ

V

VAS Visual augmentation system
VDI Vertical display indicator
UFD Up-front display
VG Variable geometry, especially pivoted swing-wing
VHF Very high frequency, 30 to 300MHz
VOR VHF omnidirectional range
VSD Vertical situation display
V/STOL Vertical or short takeoff and landing, hence VTO(L)

Z

zero/zero Usable at rest at ground level

Helmet pointing gun system, **75**
High G barrel roll, **202**
HiMAT, **17, 28-9**
High speed yoyo, **204**
Homing see guidance
Hornet (F/A-18), 126-7
Hornet EW aircraft (F/A-18A), **65**
  cockpit, **72**
Hotas, **73-4**

I

IAR-93 Orao, **153-3**
IR (Infra-red)
  homing missiles, 38-9
  IRCM 57
  warning receivers, 52, **53**
IFF, 43-4
Ilyushin Il-18 Coot-A EW aircraft, **61**
Immelman manoeuvre, **207**
Indication of microwave propagation (IMP), 52
Infra-red see IR
Inlets, **30-5**
Intruder (A-6), **110-11**
  cockpit, **67**
Inward turnabout, **210**
Israeli Aircraft Industries (IAI) Kfir, **114-5**
  cockpit, **68**

J

JA-37 Viggen, **15, 22-3, 78, 148-9, 184**
  displays, **68**
  ECM systems, **56**
  RWR pod, **51**
JAS-39 Grippen cockpit, **74**
Jaguar, **150-1, 184, 198**
  cockpit, **68**
Jamming, **53-65**
  EW aircraft, **58-65**
Jinking, 202
Johnson, Kelly, 14

K

KCA guns, **37**
KMU-35 bomb, **183**
Kfir, **114-5**
  cockpit, **68**
Kills from fleeting opportunities, 193-3
Kindelberger, Dutch, 14
Kit, pilots, **15**

L

Lag pursuit, **205**
Lift, 178
Lightning, **88-9**
Load factor, sustained, 26
Lockheed F-104 Starfighter, **14, 116-17, 213**
Low speed yoyo, **205-6**

M

M53 engine, 30
MiG-15, **192**
MiG-21, **128-9, 189, 190, 192, 213**
MiG-23, **130-1**
  cockpit, **66**
  RWR pods, **51**
MiG, **15, 30, 132-3**
MiG-27, **134-5**
  cockpit, **66**
McDonnell Douglas
  A-4 Skyhawk, **118-19, 189, 204, 206, 211**
  F-4 Phantom II, **16-17, 47, 122-3, 174, 177, 181, 184, 192, 193, 202, 204, 206, 208, 212, 213**
    radar, **48-9**
    with Pave Tack, **63**
  F-15 Eagle, **124-5, 185-6, 197, 200-1, 213**
    cockpit, *70-2*
    radar, **48, 49, 53**
McDonnell Douglas/BAe AV-8B Harrier II, **120-1**
McDonnell Douglas/ Northrop
  F/A-18 Hornet, **126-7**
  F/A-18A Hornet EW aircraft, **65, 72**
Mach number, 176
Magic (R.550), **40, 43, 148-9, 209**
Manoeuvrability, 14-15, 190-2
  sustained manoeuvre capability, 208-9
Manoeuvre envelopes, 180-1
Manoeuvres, 175, 200-13
Marine patrolling, **183**, 185
Materials, 26, 27, 28, 29
Matra missiles
  R.530, **94-5**
  R.550 magic, **40, 43, 148-9, 209**
  Super 530, **43, 209**
Methods of combat, 194-9
Mikoyan, Artem, 14
Mikoyan-Gurevich aircraft see MiG
Minimum flying speeds at altitude, 178-9
Mirage
  III and 5, **22, 94-5**
  F-1, **19, 96-7, 182, 209, 212**
  2000, **14, 41, 43, 98-9**
Missiles, **38-47**
  attack rnges, 197
Mitsubishi F-1, **136-7**
Multi-bogey combats, 211-13

N

NKC-135, **58**
Nanzhang Q-5, Type 5 Qianjiji, **138-9**
Nesher see Kfir
North American Aviation see Rockwell

Northrop
  F-5A Freedom Fighter, **140-1**
  F-5E Tiger II, **140-1, 190, 209**
Northrop/McDonnell Douglas
  F/A-18 Hornet, **126-7**
  F/A-18A Hornet EW aircraft, **65, 72**
nozzles, **30-5**
  two-dimensional, **35**
Nudelmann-Richter NR-30 gun, **36**

O

Oerlikon KCA gun, **37**
Offensive split, **211**
Operational requirements (ORs), 15
Orao (IAR-93), **152-3**

P

Pairs manoeuvres, 208-13
Panavia
  Tornado F.2, **16, 17, 18, 22, 47, 56, 142-3, 187, 193**
  GR.1, **78**
  IDS, **66, 144-5**
Pave Tack laser designator pod, **63**
Paveway, **108-9, 183**
Payload/combat radius, 27
Phantom II (F-4), **16-17, 47, 122-3, 174, 177, 181, 184, 192, 202, 204, 206, 208, 212, 213**
  radar, **48-9**
  with Pave Tack, **63**
Phoenix (AIM-54), **44-5, 76-7, 187, 188**
Pilot, typical, *214-5*
Plenum-chamber burning (PCB), 32, **22**
Pratt & Whitney engines
  F100, **31**
  TF30-414A, **35**
Propulsion, **30-5**
Prowler (RA-6B), **58-60**
Pucarà, **104-5**
Pulse-doppler radar, **195**

Q

Q-5 Qianjiji, **138-9**

R

R.530, **94-5**
R.550 Magic, **40, 43, 148-9, 209**
RAF, and EW aircraft, **61, 64**
Radar, **48-53**
  cross section (RCS), **53**
  guidance, missiles, 39,47, 186, 188
  jamming, 53-65
    EW aircraft, **58-65**
  rearward-facing, 47
  under the radar attacking, **52**
  warning receiver (RWR), **50-3**
Ranges
  radar, 45

SARH missiles, 45, 197
Rapid-bloom chaff, 56
Rearward-facing radar, 47
Reconnaissance task, 182, **183**
Relaxed static stability (CCV), **23-4, 55-6**
Requirements for fighting effectiveness, 186-93
  met by Tornado F.2, 193
Retarded bombs, **79, 166-7**
Roads, as airfields, **184**
Rockwell
  HiMAT, **17, 28-9**
  XFV-12A, 17
Rollaway, **204**
Rolls-Royce Pegasus jet-lift engine, **32, 33**

S

SNEB rockets, **84**
Saab
  Draken, **146-7**
  Viggen (JA-37), **15, 22-3, 78, 148-9, 184**
    displays, **68**
    ECM systems, **56**
    RWR pod, **51**
Sandwich, *210*
Scissors, **200-2**
Sea Harrier FRS.1, **79, 90-1**
Search methods, 94-5
Seating arrangemengs, 66-9
Semi-active radar guidance, 41
SEPECAT Jaguar, **150-1, 184, 198**
  cockpit, **68**
Sidewinder (AIM-9L), **38, 39, 43, 86-7, 94-5, 197**
Simulators, **218**
Skyhawk (A-4), **118-19, 189, 204, 211**
Skyflash, **47, 187, 193**
Slender wings, 19
Snakeye bombs, **166-7**
Soko/CNIAR IAR-93, Orao, **152-3**
Sparrow (AIM-7), **46, 47, 197**
Speed, 14-15, 177
  minimum flying speeds at altitude, 178-9
Speed of sound, 176
Spiral dive, **202, 203**
Splits, offensive nd defensive, **211**
Split S, **203**
  disengagement, 213
Starfighter (F-104), **14, 116-17, 213**
Strength, air force, 189-90
Strike tasks, **183-4**
Structures, 26-9
Sukhoi
  Su-7, **154-5**
  Su-9, Su-11, **156-7**
  Su-15, **43, 158-9**
  Su-17/22, **160-1**

Su-24 Fencer, **162-3**, 184
Super 530, **41**, **209**
Super Etendard, **100-1**
Supercritical wings, **19**
Supply-carrying, **183**, 185
Supply-route interdiction, 182, **183**
Support tasks, 182-5
Surprise, 188-9
Swing wings, **19**, **21**

T

Tu-95, **193**
Tu-128, **41**, **164-5**
Tail geometries, **22**
Tasks of air forces, 182-5
Terrain-following, 67
radar, 60
Thunderbolt II (A-10), **37**, **102-3**, **176**, 182

Tiger II (F-5E), **140**, **190**, **209**
Tomcat (F-14), 18, 21, 44-5, 76-7, 112-
13, 187, 188, 189, 210, 211
cockpit, **69**
Tornado (F.2), 16, 17, 18, 22, 47, 56,
142-3, 187, 193
Training, 214-19
aircraft, 216-7
simulators. 218
Troop carrying tasks, **183**, 185
Tumansky engines, 30
Tupolev
Tu-95, **193**
Tu-128, **41**, **164-5**
Turbofan and turbojet engines, **30-5**
Turbo-Union RB199 engine, **30**, 32
Turns, 26, 29, 179-80, **191**

V

Variable geometry (VG) Swing wings,
19, **21**
Vector roll, **204**
Vertical reverse, **207**
Vertical rolling scissors, **203**
Victor (K.2), 16
Viggen (JA-37), **15**, **22-3**, **78**, **148-9**,
184
displays, **68**
ECM systems, **56**
RWR pod, **51**
Visibility, **189-90**
Vought A-7 Corsair II, **166-7**
Vulcan gun (M61, T-171), 37, **38**, 72
Vulnerability cone, 200

W

Wartime tasks, 182-5
Weapons, 36-47
see also under specific aircraft
Wings, 18-35
parasol, **10-11**

X

X-29A, **27**
XFV-12A, 17

Y

Yakovlev
Yak-28, **168-9**
Yak-36MP, **170-1**
Yoyo, **204**, **205**

Picture Credits

The publishers wish to thank all the organisations and individuals who have
provided photographs for this book; they are listed by page number below.

Back cover: Top left, McDonnell Douglas; Top right, Saab-Scania; centre left, USAF;
centre right, McDonnell Douglas; bottom left, Charles Colmer/Salamander; bottom
right, McDonnell Douglas. **Endpapers:** McDonnell Douglas. **Page 1:** Saab-Scania.
Pages 2-3: Charles Colmer/Salamander. **4-5:** Turbo-Union. **6-7:** McDonnell Douglas.
8-9: Top left, Panavia; bottom left, McDonnell Douglas; centre, US Department of
Defense (DoD); right, Robert L. Lawson. **10-11:** USAF. **12-13:** Top left, British
Aerospace; remainder, McDonnell Douglas. **14-15:** Top left, Lockheed; centre left,
Dassault Breguet; bottom left, Saab-Scania; top right, General Dynamics; centre right,
Salamander; bottom right, British Aerospace. **16-17:** Top left, British Ministry of
Defence (MoD); bottom left, British Aerospace; remainder, Rockwell. **18-19:** Top left,
US Navy; bottom left, British Aerospace; centre, Dassault Breguet; right, Royal
Australian Air Force (RAAF). **20-21:** Top left, General Dynamics; top right, USN.
22-23: Top left, Turbo-Union; bottom left, US DoD; centre left, Dassault Breguet;
centre right, General Dynamics; right, Saab-Scania. **24-25:** Top left, General
Dynamics; top right, MBB; centre and bottom right, General Dynamics. **26-27:** Top
left, MBB; bottom left and top right, General Dynamics; bottom right, Grumman.
28-29: Both left, Rockwell; centre, Saab-Scania; right, General Dynamics. **30-31:** Top
left: US DoD; bottom left, Turbo-Union; top right, McDonnell Douglas; centre and
bottom right, Pratt & Whitney. **32-33:** Top left, British Aerospace; bottom left,
Rolls-Royce; top right, Rolls-Royce; centre and bottom, Pratt & Whitney. **34-35:** Left,
McDonnell Douglas; top right, Pratt & Whitney; centre and bottom, General
Dynamics. **36-37:** Top left, Salamander; centre left, US DoD; bottom left, General
Electric; top right and centre right, US DoD; bottom right (both), Oerlikon. **38-39:** Top
left and centre left, General Electric; bottom left, Bofors; centre, British Aerospace;
right, General Dynamics. **40-41:** Left, all Matra; top right, Matra; centre, Salamander;
bottom, Hughes. **42-43:** Top left: McDonnell Douglas, bottom, Ferranti; top right, US
DoD; centre left, Dassault Breguet; centre right, General Dynamics; bottom right, US
DoD. **44-45:** All Hughes. **46-47:** Left, all Raytheon; top right, all Hughes; bottom right,
British Aerospace. **48-49:** Top left, Westinghouse; bottom left and centre, Hughes;
bottom right, Westinghouse. **50-51:** Top left, Panavia; bottom left, Hughes; centre,
MoD; top right, TASS; bottom right, Saab-Scania. **54-55:** Left,
Northrop; centre top, Thomson-CSF; top right, Selenia SpA; bottom right,
Westinghouse. **56-57:** Left, all Philips; top right, Goodyear Aerospace; centre and
bottom, Alkan. **58-59:** Left, both US DoD; right, both Grumman. **60-61:** Top left:
Grumman; top right, MoD; bottom right, British Aerospace. **62-63:** Westinghouse;
top right, ford Aeroneutronics; bottom right, US DoD. **64-65:** Left, all Westinghouse;
top right, Grumman; bottom right, Ford Aeroneutronics. **66-67:** Top left, via Bill
Gunston; centre left, General Dynamics; bottom left, Panavia; centre right, General

Dynamics; top right, J. Rotramel; bottom right, Grumman. **68-69:** Top left, Charles
Colmer/Salamander; bottom left, General Dynamics; top centre, Saab-Scania; below
centre, Robin Adshead/British Aerospace; top right, General Dynamics; bottom
right, Grumman. **70-71:** Left and both top right, McDonnell Douglas; bottom right,
both General Dynamics. **72-73:** Top left, both General Dynamics; bottom left and
right, all McDonnell Douglas. **74-75:** Top left, General Dynamics; bottom left, Saab-
Scania; top right, Marconi; bottom right, Marconi. **76-77:** Hughes. **78-79:** Top left,
MBB; bottom left, Saab-Scania; centre, Dassault Breguet; top right, US DoD; bottom
right, British Aerospace. **80-81:** Aeritalia. **82-83:** British Aerospace. **84-85:** Left,
British Aerospace; right, MoD. **86-87:** British Aerospace. **88-89:** Left, British
Aerospace; right, MoD. **90:** British Aerospace. **92:** Dassault Breguet. **94:** Left, Dassault
Breguet; right, Dornier. **96:** Dassault Breguet. **98:** Dassault Breguet. **100:** Dassault
Breguet. **102:** Fairchild Republic. **104:** FMA. **106:** US DoD. **108:** Ford
Aeroneutronics. **110:** US Navy. **112:** US Navy. **114:** Israel Aircraft Industries. **116:**
Italian Air Force. **118:** Left, Israeli Air Force; right, US Navy. **120:** McDonnell
Douglas. **122:** US Air Force. **124:** McDonnell Douglas. **126:** Northrop. **128:**
Salamander. **130:** Top, US DoD; bottom, P. Steinemann. **132:** US DoD. **134:** TASS.
136: Mitsubishi. **138:** Salamander. **140:** Charles Colmer/Salamander. **142:** British
Aerospace. **144:** British Aerospace. **146:** Saab-Scania. **148:** Saab-Scania. **150:** Matra.
152: via J. W. R. Taylor. **154:** US DoD. **156:** Salamander. **158:** Top, US DoD; bottom,
via Michael Gething. **160:** Top, Salamander; bottom, US DoD. **162:** US DoD. **164:**
Salamander. **166:** US DoD. **168:** Tass. **170:** Tass. **172-173:** US DoD. **174-175:** Left, US
AF; right, MoD. **176-177:** Fairchild; right, US DoD. **178-179:** General Dynamics.
180-181: McDonnell Douglas. **182-183:** Top left: Dassault Breguet; bottom left,
Fairchild; top right, Texas Instruments. **184-185:** Top left, British Aerospace; far left,
US DoD; centre left, Saab Scania; top right, McDonnell Douglas; bottom right, British
Aerospace. **186-187:** Left, both US DoD; top right, British Aerospace; centre right,
Grumman; bottom right, General Dynamics. **188-189:** Left, Hughes; right, both
Robert L. Lawson. **190-191:** Top left, General Dynamics; bottom left, US DoD; right,
General Dynamics. **192-193:** Top, US DoD; bottom left, Salamander; bottom right,
British Aerospace. **194-195:** US DoD. **196-197:** Left, McDonnell Douglas; right,
Raytheon. **198-199:** British Aerospace. **200-201:** Photo-Sonics; **202-203:** Robert L.
Lawson. **204-205:** Robert L. Lawson. **206-207:** Robert L. Lawson. **208-209:** Left,
Robert L. Lawson; right, Dassault Breguet. **210-211:** Robert L. Lawson. **212-213:** Top
left, Dassault Breguet; bottom left, US Navy; top right, MoD; bottom, US DoD.
214-215: Left, Tass; centre, Charles Colmer, Salamander; top right, Italian Air Force;
right cente and bottom right, Charles Colmer/Salamander; far right, Tass. **216-217:**
Top left, Dassault Breguet; bottom left, Hsinhua; top right, British Aerospace; right
centre and bottom, USAF. **218-219:** Top left and left, British Aerospace; left centre
and bottom, Rediffusion; centre top, British Aerospace; top right, Salamander;
bottom right, Rediffusion.

PRINTED IN BELGIUM BY

INTERNATIONAL BOOK PRODUCTION

Even in an F-15 you dare not stop eyeballing the sky around you.